the **Best** of the **Best**

MUTUAL FUNDS & BLUE-CHIP STOCKS for CANADIANS

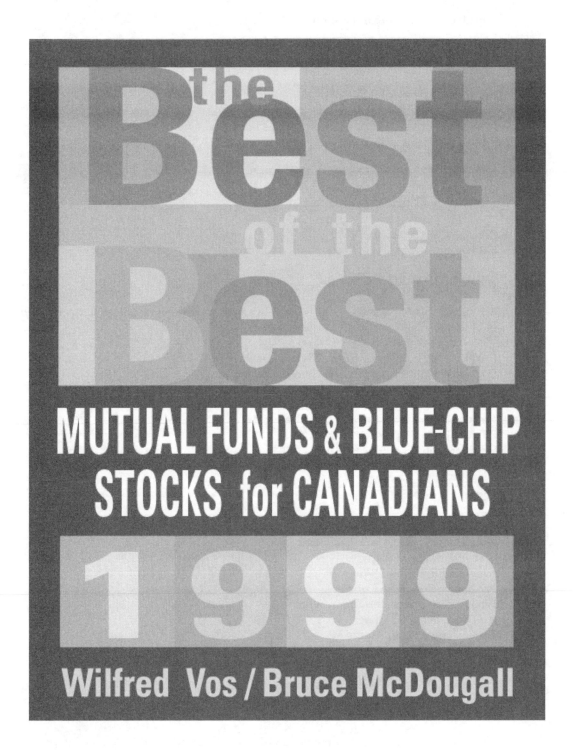

the Best of the Best

MUTUAL FUNDS & BLUE-CHIP STOCKS for CANADIANS

1999

Wilfred Vos / Bruce McDougall

Prentice Hall Canada Inc.
Scarborough, Ontario

Canadian Cataloguing in Publication Data

Vos, Wilfred, 1972–
   The best of the best : mutual funds and blue-chip stocks for Canadians

ISBN 0-13-083888-8

1. Mutual funds—Canada.   2. Stocks—Canada.   3. Investments—Canada.
I. McDougall, Bruce, 1950–   .   II. Title.

HG5154.5.V67 1999   332.63'27   C99-933025-7

Prentice-Hall Canada Inc.
Scarborough, Ontario

Prentice-Hall, Inc., Upper Saddle River, New Jersey
Prentice-Hall International (UK) Limited, London
Prentice-Hall of Australia, Pty. Limited, Sydney
Prentice-Hall Hispanoamericana, S.A., Mexico City
Prentice-Hall of India Private Limited, New Delhi
Prentice-Hall of Japan, Inc., Tokyo
Simon & Schuster Southeast Asia Private Limited, Singapore
Editora Prentice-Hall do Brasil, Ltda., Rio de Janeiro

ISBN 0-13-083888-8

Director, Trade Group: Robert Harris
Acquisitions Editor: Dean Hannaford
Copy Editor: Carol Fordyce
Assistant Editor: Joan Whitman
Production Editor: Lu Cormier
Production Coordinator: Shannon Potts
Art Direction: Mary Opper
Cover Design: Sarah Battersby
Page Layout: B.J. Weckerle

1 2 3 4 5   W   03 02 01 00 99

Printed and bound in Canada

This publication contains the opinions and ideas of its authors and is designed to provide useful advice in regard to the subject matter covered. The authors and publisher are not engaged in rendering legal, accounting, or other professional services in this publication. This publication is not intended to provide a basis for action in particular circumstances without consideration by a competent professional. The authors, data providers, authors' employers, and publisher expressly disclaim any responsibility for any liability, loss, or risk, personal or otherwise, which is incurred as a consequence, directly or indirectly, of the use and application of any of the contents of this book.

Visit the Prentice Hall Canada Web site! Send us your comments, browse our catalogues, and more. **www.phcanada.com**

To my wife, Jenny Lynn, and our newborn (October 1, 1998)
baby girl, Taylor Nicole.

Thank you.

Wilfred

Table of Contents

Part B: Stocks

Foreword

Choosing the best mutual funds and stocks is a difficult and sometimes daunting task. I know that from long experience. No one expects to get it right all the time. But anyone who can't consistently pick more winners than losers had better look for another line of work.

What makes it so difficult? Basically, the number of variables. There is no single indicator of a security's failure or success. It's a matter of weighing many elements, including past performance, risk, management style, economic prospects, and momentum.

No matter how much care and skill go into the process, there are always surprises. That's why, when mutual fund companies caution that past returns are no guarantee of future results, they aren't kidding. History has shown us that often last year's hero is this year's goat.

That's why people who do this for a living, including myself, are always seeking to improve the odds. We're constantly on the lookout for new insights and new methodologies that will enable us to better understand where we have been and where we are going from the perspective of investment success.

A few years ago, I came across a new approach to reporting historical fund data that impressed me greatly. It was the All Times Periods (ATP) system that had been developed by Wilfred Vos while he was in university. At the time I first learned about it, Wilfred was doing fund analysis for Altamira.

I felt that ATP provided some unique insights into a mutual fund's track record. Most historical fund data is presented to investors as a snapshot in time. If you bought a fund five years ago, on the first day of the month, here's how your returns would have looked. If you bought 10 years ago, again on the first of the month, you can refer to another column to see how you did over that time.

But what do those numbers really mean to people? Unfortunately, not very much. They don't tell us anything about how the fund came to its current position, how much volatility it showed along the way, or how it performed against its peers in good markets and in bad ones.

Wilfred Vos found a way to improve the presentation of the data. The ATP method highlights the best and the worst periods of a fund's performance, and tells us the historical probability that a fund will achieve a specific range of profit or loss within any given time frame. This information is incredibly useful. For example, as I write this I am looking at the profile of a balanced fund to the end of May 1998 that shows it achieved an average annual compounded rate of return of better than 10 per cent more than 80 per cent of the time in any given 10-year period since it was launched. The same profile also tells me that the chance of a loss over any 10-year period was zero. Even more impressive, it was also zero over any five-year period and only 1 per cent over any three-year period.

This gives the investor a much better sense of how a fund has performed over time than the snapshot method, which can be highly misleading and can sometimes show big variations from month to month.

Altamira has been gracious enough to allow me to have access to Wilfred's research to help in the preparation of the reviews and ratings for my annual *Buyer's Guide to Mutual*

Funds. But I have always regretted that space limitations did not allow us to reproduce some of his impressive charts and tables, which contain a wealth of valuable information.

With *The Best of the Best,* that has now been remedied. In the pages that follow, you'll find a detailed explanation of how the ATP system works, and you'll see how the authors have used it to identify the top mutual funds and stocks. It perhaps will not come as any surprise that almost all of their fund picks also receive high marks in my own *Buyer's Guide.*

You'll also see for the first time in print the extraordinary detail that is contained in Wilfred's tables and charts. If you are the type of person who wants to know all the background and history before putting down your money on a mutual fund or stock, you will find this book to be an exceptional resource.

You'll also find some investing ideas that have an excellent chance of making a profit, while keeping your risk to a minimum. That's what we're all looking for these days, isn't it?

Gordon Pape
Toronto, Ontario

Preface

With a multitude of different investments available, many investors are intimidated by the number of choices accessible to them. Furthermore, many investors have a difficult time understanding the underlying characteristics of their investments.

For these reasons, we decided to produce an easy-to-read but comprehensive guide to investing in Canada. We appropriately called it *The Best of the Best: Mutual Funds and Blue-Chip Stocks for Canadians*, and we believe that this book is truly unique and that it will enable investors to make better and more informed investment decisions.

Acknowledgements

I would especially like to thank Bruce McDougall, without whose co-authorship this project would never have been completed.

I would also like to take this opportunity to thank the many people who have helped bring this book to fruition. There were my colleagues at Altamira who encouraged, helped, and supported me as I worked on the project: Lori, Darren, Gordon, Dogal, Paul, Chris, Francis, Brian, and Philip. Appreciation goes also to John Lane at FP DataGroup and Tim McGowan at Datastream for providing data, and to all the unnamed individuals at all the mutual fund companies and Canadian corporations who helped me gather data on the underlying funds and their respective company histories. Thanks are due also to Gordon Pape for allowing me to assist with his annual buyer's guide for the past three years.

Thank you to the people at Prentice Hall, especially Dean Hannaford, and to Carol Fordyce of Fordyce Publishing Services who polished the work to make it ready for publication.

To my family and friends, thank you for your patience and understanding. And I thank God for giving me the ability and skill to complete this project.

Wilfred Vos

Introduction

The 1990s will be remembered as the decade when large numbers of investors first became involved with mutual funds. In 1988, investments in mutual funds in Canada amounted to only $28 billion. Since then, this amount has increased to more than $350 billion. These funds range from money market funds to aggressive specialty funds.

With over 1,936 mutual funds available in Canada, many investors are asking the question: Which fund is right for me? Although we cannot answer that question for you, we are able to reduce the list from 1,936 to 50, a more manageable number. We acknowledge that there are other good funds that investors could consider, but we felt that drawing a line at 50 leaves investors with a reasonable number of funds to choose from.

Our research shows that mutual funds are a value-added investment for investors; that is, they allow investors to earn a higher rate of return than traditional investments, at a given level of risk. However, investors are still having some difficulty in selecting the investments which are right for them. Historically, sophisticated investors have relied on such statistical tools as time-weighted rates of return (the returns investors see in newspapers), standard deviation (a risk measure), Beta, Sharpe ratio, coefficient variation, variance, and Alpha (to name just a few) to measure how good an investment is. Our research shows that some of these measures are actually misleading and may not be appropriate for investors trying to select a good mutual fund. In addition, our research shows that many investors still invest using a "flavour of the month" approach. If we track the sales data for different mutual funds and compare sales with performance, we see that funds which have performed well recently have generated more sales, on average, than funds that have not performed as well.

On the other hand, if we calculate the weighted-average rate of return for the basket of mutual funds within our study, we can conclude that investors still have the potential to do better than they could using the traditional tools. In short, investors still need help with their mutual fund investments. In addition, a quantitative analysis of investor behaviour that was conducted by DALBAR Financial Services in 1997 concluded that most mutual fund investors who do not invest for the long term do not fully benefit from the upside potential of mutual funds. In this book, we clearly identify investments with long-term growth potential and show how investors can utilize these investments for their own financial gain.

Investors will also notice that the information that is provided in *The Best of the Best* on a particular investment is both easy to read and very thorough. All mutual funds included have been analyzed using the All Time Periods Methodology. Each fund receives a Vos Value Rating and a WilStar Rating, comprehensive ratings that take into consideration 12 different factors—seven related to reward and five related to risk—when rating a fund in comparison with similar funds. Each mutual fund has a summary which includes a fund profile and sections on performance and risk. In addition, we include some information on a mutual fund's future prospects. There is information on the historical performance of the fund laid out in an easy-to-read format, referred to as the All Time Periods (ATP) chart.

The ATP chart gives many pertinent details for a fund. For investors seeking more diversification by investing internationally, the chart indicates how much of the fund is invested outside Canada. The ATP chart provides investors with the best, average, and worst rates of return for the fund, ending in August 1998. Investors will be able to update this information themselves and quickly assess the upside and downside potential for each fund over different time frames. Investors will be able to see how often the fund made or lost money, and to assess the fund's downside risk. The relative performance graph (Quartile Ranking) will allow investors to assess how well the fund performed relative to similar funds over any 12-month period. The Rolling 12-Month Period graph will allow investors to assess the performance of a mutual fund from one year to the next. Some mutual funds perform well consistently; others perfrom well sporadically. The ATP chart will highlight the performance of a fund in an easy-to-read format for quick reference.

Investors will benefit also from the chapter on portfolio building as we introduce Relative Portfolio Theory (RPT) and illustrate its use by building three sample portfolios.

We have added a new element to a buyer's guide: We have included information on stocks. Many investors can increase their investment knowledge and, in turn, their investment returns if they have a better understanding of their investments. To help investors better understand their investments, we decided to include a section on the stocks included in the TSE 35, an index that measures the stock appreciation for large Canadian corporations from a variety of sectors. Information is provided on each company's background, and the company's financial data and historical stock performance data are also included. Investors will learn about the companies that currently shape and change the country we live in. The companies covered include retailing giant Canadian Tire, entertainer and distiller Seagram, and Canada's largest chartered bank, the Royal Bank.

We believe that investors will acquire a new and better understanding of their investments by relying on the information provided in this book. Investing wisely is never easy; it requires judgement, discipline, and commitment. However, the single best thing you can do for your own investment portfolio is start early. If you invested $1,000 for 10 years at 10 per cent, your investment would grow to $2,594, but if you invested for 20 years your investment would increase to $6,728. Set a goal, establish a plan, and commit yourself to achieving your goal. In business, nobody ever plans to fail—people fail to plan. The same principle applies for your financial goals—a little planning can pay a big dividend.

We hope that you will enjoy this book, and we encourage readers to write to us with their comments. May every investment be a successful investment!

Part A

Mutual Funds

Introduction to Mutual Funds

The mutual fund industry has expanded steadily as we've proceeded through the economic growth of the 1990s. Interest rates have fallen, and governments have wrestled inflation into submission, at least for the present time. The interest earned on investments such as guaranteed investment certificates (GICs), bonds, and term deposits is adequate but low; the only investments that promise higher returns are equities. But all equities are not created equal, and the average investor isn't always prepared or equipped to distinguish one stock from another. Leaving the selection of stocks and other investments to professional money managers, but seeking the higher returns promised by treasury bills, bonds, and stocks, investors have turned to mutual funds.

In addition to higher returns, mutual funds offer a number of potential advantages over other types of investment:

- They are run by professional investment managers, who charge a reasonable price for their services.
- Mutual funds reduce volatility and temper risk by spreading investments over a diversified portfolio.
- The average investor, making even a small contribution, gains direct access to a broad range of investments.
- An investor can also choose from a multitude of funds to meet a specific investment objective.
- Mutual funds can be easily bought and sold.

On the other side of the coin, mutual funds bring a few disadvantages as well:

- The fees charged by fund managers reduce a fund's total return, although they are usually reasonable.
- The individual investor has no influence on the specific investments selected by a fund manager.
- One investment held in a fund may perform well, but another may perform poorly, so the investor never enjoys the full benefit of a good investment. (Of course, the mutual-fund investor never suffers the full impact of a single bad investment, either.)
- Mutual funds are not guaranteed, and investors can lose money if they buy when the fund price is high and sell when it is low.

Probably the most attractive aspect of a mutual fund is the opportunity it affords the average investor to diversify his or her investment portfolio. As individuals, few people can afford to buy even one share of each of 100 companies. As investors in a mutual fund, however, people can reap the benefits of diversification while sharing the costs. The mutual fund pools an individual's money together with money from many other investors. With a pool of money at hand, the mutual fund manager can invest in a broad range of stocks, bonds, or other instruments.

In fact, diversification is one of the cardinal investment strategies for limiting stock-market risk. If you buy just one stock, such as IBM, and it goes down—or away down, as in IBM's case in the early 1990s—you will lose money. If you buy shares in 100 companies, there's a good chance that some of the stocks in the portfolio will lose money, while the others will make money. At the end of the day, week, month, quarter, or year, a single stock may have gone up or down. But the diversified portfolio of a well-managed mutual fund will usually make a profit. That's the power of diversification. And that's what you get with a mutual fund.

In the 1990s, mutual funds have offered investors a chance to reap some of the benefits of an expanding economy without incurring excessive risk. In fact, mutual funds have historically been low-risk investments, although some are extremely volatile. Even if a mutual fund invests in risky securities—gold-mining shares, for example, whose value may rise and fall considerably—the fund itself remains stable. In fact, since the first open-end mutual fund was introduced in Canada in 1932, no one has ever lost money as a result of a fund company's going out of business.

Canadians have now invested more than $350 billion in mutual funds, and there are more than 1,936 funds currently operating in Canada. Not only are there more people than ever investing in mutual funds, but there are also more mutual-fund products and investment alternatives than ever to choose from.

Despite the proliferation of funds, only a relative handful of them have attracted most of the money. Of the total amount invested in Canadian mutual funds, approximately half has been placed with just 80 funds. The rest is divided among the remaining 1,856.

There are a number of reasons why investors are attracted to the largest funds. Even seasoned investors are cautious. Understandably, they don't want to put their money into a risky investment. They assume that other investors know at least as much as they do, and they don't feel confident enough to defy conventional wisdom. If one mutual fund attracts the lion's share of investments, then it must be doing something right, and that's the fund that most conventional investors will choose.

In addition, investors base their decisions on a variety of factors, from catchy marketing to the recommendations of their next-door neighbours and associates at work. Their decisions are not necessarily wrong, but they could make better and more-informed decisions. Our research shows that most Canadians could benefit from applying more rigorous criteria to their investment decisions. That's why we have developed the **All Time Periods (ATP)** methodology. The ATP methodology is explained in the second chapter in this book.

Buying and selling mutual funds

This book will help you to identify some of the better-performing funds available in Canada. Once you have identified them, you should then determine your investment objectives and tolerance for risk. Selecting the funds that correspond to your objective and risk factors, you should then gather as much information about these funds as you can.

You can find a lot of information in daily newspapers, magazines, and business journals. You can find more information using the World Wide Web. Finally, you should obtain prospectuses for funds of interest to you.

The prospectus describes a mutual fund's investment objectives, the fees that it charges, and the risks associated with purchasing the mutual fund. The prospectus also includes the fund's most recent financial statements. You can order a copy of a fund's prospectus directly from the mutual fund company. You may also get a copy from a financial advisor.

Although many investors decide to develop their own investment strategies and execute their own buying and selling decisions, a good advisor can provide support and guidance to investors who need such reassurance. Your friends who have made sound investments can likely provide you with the names of some good advisors. Your accountant or tax preparer can also help. They see their own clients' income statements, and they know which advisors make money for clients. Your local newspaper advertises investment seminars and workshops from time to time. If you attend a few of these, you'll meet advisors affiliated with the companies that sponsor these events.

The people who sell, advise on, and manage mutual funds must be registered with their provincial securities commission. Before they can register, they must meet specific training and education requirements. The advisor should also be registered with one of the following:

- The Canadian Association of Financial Planners   (416-593-6592)
- The Investment Dealers Association of Canada   (416-364-6133)

Open-end and closed-end funds

Most mutual funds currently traded in Canada are open-end. If a fund is open-end, there is not a limit on the number of shares which can be issued. The mutual fund company will always be able to sell you more shares, at the current net asset value, or to buy back the shares which you hold. The most popular mutual funds today that are listed in the mutual-fund section of your daily newspaper are open-end, such as Altamira, AGF, Trimark, Royal Trust, and so forth.

Although we don't deal with them in this book, there are a few closed-end mutual funds in Canada as well. These funds issue a limited number of shares when they are first set up. Once they sell all the shares and there are none left to sell, the fund is closed. At that point, no new shares are issued, and the fund company will no longer redeem your shares. You can still buy and sell shares in a closed-end fund on the stock exchange. The price will fluctuate up and down, just like shares in other companies. Sometimes the price per share will be higher than the NAV—selling at a premium. Sometimes it will be less—selling at a discount

Investing in a mutual fund

Mutual funds are bought and sold through a number of channels, including:

- **Financial planners:** Investors should realize that all financial planners cannot sell all mutual funds. Although selling a variety of mutual funds, a planner may work for just one particular fund company and restrict recommendations to that company's funds. You should ask a financial planner at the outset what limitations there are on his or her access to funds.
- **Stock brokers:** Employed by investment dealers, stock brokers sell a wide range of mutual funds. They usually charge a commission for each transaction they conduct on your behalf. They can also provide you with a wealth of information and guidance on investing.
- **Discount brokers:** These organizations charge lower fees than conventional stock brokers, but provide little or no guidance or information about particular investments.
- **Banks, trust companies, credit unions, and caisses populaires:** Your local financial institution sells a variety of mutual funds, including its own.
- **Insurance salespersons:** Your insurance representative usually sells mutual funds on behalf of his or her employer.
- **Buying direct:** Many mutual fund companies sell directly to the public.

You can sell your mutual fund investments within two or three business days through the outlet where you purchased them. You may choose to sell your entire investment, or you can choose to sell units in smaller amounts. One popular method is to redeem your units through regular withdrawal plans that allow weekly, monthly, or quarterly withdrawals.

Of course, nothing is free in the world of investing. Mutual funds make money on your investment, in at least one of several ways. First, many mutual fund companies charge a sales commission, either when investors purchase shares or when investors sell shares in the fund. These are called *load funds*. A mutual fund manager also receives a fee for managing the fund and for supervising its day-to-day administration and operations. This is called a management fee, which is deducted from the fund's total income. The management fee can range from 0.2 per cent to 3 per cent of the fund's income. These fees are explained in the fund's annual report.

Load, no-load, and so on

Fund companies commonly charge a commission on the shares they sell. This commission is also called a load. This commission compensates the fund company, financial planner, or stockbroker for providing you with a service.

Today, more than ever, competition among mutual funds is fierce. Every fund company wants you to invest your money with it. And fund companies have come up with innovative products to get you started at the least possible cost, such as:

- **Front-end-load fund:** If you choose a front-end-load fund, you pay a commission ranging from 2 per cent to 9 per cent every time you buy shares.

- **Back-end-load fund:** With a back-end-load fund, your entire initial investment goes into the mutual fund. You pay no direct sales commission up-front. But you have to leave your money in the fund for a minimum period; otherwise you have to pay a commission when you remove it, called a back-end load. The typical back-end-load fund charges a 6 per cent commission in the first year, based on the value of your portfolio when you sell your shares, 5 per cent in the second year, 4 per cent after three years, and so on. Long-term investors usually keep their money in a fund for at least five years.

- **No-load fund:** With no-load funds, you don't have to pay a commission to buy or sell your shares. However, all mutual funds, including no-loads, pay their investment advisory team an annual management fee of between 0.2 per cent and 2 per cent of the fund's assets. This compensates them for making all the fund's investment decisions. Mutual funds also have to pay operating expenses. These additional charges are deducted from the assets in the fund's portfolio and explained in the fund's prospectus.

Fund categories

All mutual-fund families offer investors a number of different types of mutual funds from which to choose. These include:

- Domestic equity funds
- International equity funds
- Fixed income funds
- Balanced funds
- Money market funds

Domestic equity funds

Equity funds invest in common stocks. They can be specialty funds that invest in Canada's resource sector, or they can be dividend funds that invest in large dividend-paying Canadian corporations. These funds aim for long-term capital appreciation. That means that the mutual fund will increase in value over the long term, but may experience some short-term setbacks.

Specialty funds are equity funds which invest in only one sector, such as gold funds, resource funds, or energy funds. Because sectors perform on a cyclical basis, last year's hot specialty funds can be next year's big losers.

If you are trying to double your money by the next year, equity funds will not usually do the trick. If you are saving for retirement or other long-term goals, then equity funds are a good bet. Investors who can wait patiently for five years or more for their money to grow could put 60 to 70 per cent of their investments in equity funds. Over the long term, equity funds have outperformed all other investment vehicles, although with more risk. If they did not outperform other investments, nobody would invest in them because of the risk.

All equity funds invest in common stocks, but the similarities end there. Some funds invest for value. They look for stocks that are priced cheaply relative to assets or earnings. Others invest for growth. They look not for stocks that are priced cheaply but for stocks that are issued by companies that are growing. Other funds invest in a combination of the two. To complicate matters further, some equity funds invest strictly in smaller companies and are called small cap funds. Others stick with bigger blue-chip companies.

International equity funds

Canada has the sixth-largest stock market in the world, but all the money that's invested on Canadian stock markets adds up to only 3 per cent of the total amount available to companies throughout the world. This means that, if you limit your equity investments to Canada, you miss about 97 per cent of the opportunities available.

With this in mind, some mutual funds invest in stocks in other countries such as Japan, Britain, Germany, France, Italy, Mexico, and the Far East. (Some of these funds are specialty funds.) The economies of these countries and regions often grow more quickly than Canada's. When they do, companies in these areas reap higher profits. With higher profits come higher stock prices. In addition, investors are able to reduce the volatility in their portfolios by investing internationally.

Fixed income funds

Fixed income funds aim to produce income, not capital gains. That means they are not expecting their investments to increase substantially in value. They just want the investments to generate money in predictable amounts. A large percentage of the money in such a fund is always invested in government bonds, corporate bonds, and strip-coupon bonds of issuers in Canada and around the world. Mortgage funds are also fixed income funds.

Like individual bonds, bond mutual funds respond to interest rates. When interest rates rise, bond mutual funds fall in value. When interest rates fall, bond mutual funds rise in value. The price fluctuation (volatility) of a particular bond fund is related to two characteristics of the fund: (1) the average time to maturity (and thus repayment of the principal) of the bonds in the fund's portfolio, and (2) the timing and frequency of interest payments for all the bonds in the fund. The longer it takes, on average, for the bond fund's holdings to receive their interest payments and to mature, the more sensitive the fund will be to changes in interest rates. In general, funds that invest primarily in long-term bonds (maturing in 20 to 25 years) will be more volatile than funds that invest primarily in intermediate-term bonds (maturing in 5 to 10 years). A short-term bond fund that invests primarily in bonds maturing in one to three years will be the least volatile.

As with equities, investors should look beyond Canada in selecting a bond fund. The Canadian bond market represents only 4 per cent of the world's government bond market, so if you're limiting your bond investments solely to Canada, you may be missing out. Consider these examples:

- 1986: Japanese bonds earned 37 per cent; Canadian bonds earned 13 per cent.
- 1987: United Kingdom bonds earned 35 per cent; Canadian bonds, 3 per cent.
- 1988: Australian bonds earned 18 per cent; Canadian bonds, 9 per cent.
- 1989: Canadian bonds were the top performers, earning around 13 per cent.
- 1990: United Kingdom bonds earned 23 per cent; Canadian bonds, 20 per cent.
- 1991: Australian bonds earned 23 per cent; Canadian bonds, 20 per cent.

Before you can purchase another country's bonds, you must convert your money into that country's currency. For instance, if you want to purchase German bonds, you must first convert your Canadian dollars into German marks. Buying the German bonds doesn't guarantee a profit, even if you are right in your timing and German bonds appreciate in value. The deutsche mark could fall in value faster than the Canadian dollar, so when you sell your German bonds for marks, then use the marks to buy Canadian dollars, you will end up with fewer dollars than you started with. This is called currency risk.

To counter currency risk, some global funds hedge their bets by buying less volatile currencies. A fund manager purchasing German bonds, for example, would sell marks on the foreign exchange market and buy a currency that will not fall so much in value, such as the US dollar. The result is a currency-hedged German bond position. This type of fund is much less volatile than a non-hedged bond fund. However, because of the hedging, the potential profits are lower than for non-hedged funds.

These funds are appropriate for investors who want income but very little risk, such as individuals collecting pensions.

Balanced funds

Using a balanced investment approach, these funds invest in some stocks, some bonds, some gold, and some real estate. The fund manager determines and maintains the balance. Over the long term, these funds usually generate lower returns than most equity funds, but investors also incur less risk. In addition, investors can invest in domestic balanced funds within their RRSPs and in international balanced funds outside their RRSPs.

Money market funds

Money market funds invest primarily in treasury bills. Treasury bills are very short-term bonds. They mature in three months, six months, or one year. In essence, they are IOUs backed by the Canadian government. They are among the safest investments in the world. And there's a huge market for them, which makes them very easy to buy and sell. (Britain and the United States also issue treasury bills.)

Money market funds almost always pay a higher rate of interest than a bank savings account, and all the interest earned will be converted into additional shares in your account.

As with all other mutual funds, your money is highly liquid. If you want to take your money back, you can usually have a cheque in your hands within 24 to 48 hours. These funds offer an excellent place to store your money while you decide what to do with it over the long term.

Evaluating your portfolio

Fund companies issues shares in return for your investment. The price of a mutual fund's shares varies from day to day. Some days it's a little higher; other days it's a little lower. Over the long term, however, the share price usually goes up. Some go up more than others.

You can determine the value of your mutual-fund holdings by examining the net asset value (NAV) of each fund in your portfolio. The NAV is calculated by dividing the mutual fund's total net assets by the total number of shares outstanding. (This information is included in the daily investment tables published in newspapers.) The resulting figure is the price that you have to pay for one share in the mutual fund. The NAV fluctuates daily. Some days it may be up 5 cents; other days it may be down 10 cents. That's called volatility.

The share price for an individual company fluctuates in relation to the company's future prospects. When prospects are good, there are more buyers than sellers and the share price rises. When prospects are bad, there are more sellers than buyers and the share price falls. When the stocks that make up the mutual fund rise in price, so too will the mutual fund's share price. When the stock prices fall, so will the fund's share price.

Getting the data

You can keep track of the performance of mutual funds over the Internet. At *www.globefund.com*, for example, and at *www.quicken.ca*, you can find charts, graphs and information about fund characteristics and performance. Other good sources of information include:

Investorama	www.investorama.com
Thomson information	www.marketedge.com
US information	www.wallstreetcity.com
Stock information	www.sedar.com

The ATP Methodology

Using the All Time Periods (ATP) methodology, investors can make decisions based on something more substantial than a whim, a hunch, marketing hype, or misleading data. In preparing this book, for example, we've used the ATP methodology to select 50 of the best-performing funds in Canada. They are not the only funds available, and they may not perform better than all the others at all times. But we know from our research that investors can invest in these funds with confidence that their wealth will grow over time at a faster rate than it would if they had selected a fixed-income investment such as a GIC. Unfortunately, we rate only funds that have a three-year track record. We are therefore unable to rate funds offered by Scudder Funds of Canada, Clarington Capital Management Inc., Stone & Company Ltd., et cetera, because these funds have established operations within the last three years.

Wilfred Vos developed the All Time Periods methodology while he was still at university. In 1995, as an intern with Bick Financial Security Corporation in Ancaster, a financial planning company, Vos was asked to devise a graphical depiction of risk that would help the average investor understand how mutual funds perform. Unlike other methods of evaluating performance, the ATP methodology which he had already developed would be transparent and readily accessible. The investor would not have to conduct any complex calculations, apply obscure formulae, or take a fund's marketing campaign at face value to reach a conclusion about the fund. All the investor had to do was look at a graph that presented the fund's performance over the course of its entire existence and interpret its message. With some refinements, Vos made it even easier for an investor to distinguish one fund's performance from another's, to evaluate the risks involved in a particular fund, and to make an investment decision based on a fund's long-term potential performance.

Wilfred Vos continued refining the ATP methodology to provide even more benefits to investors. For the last three years, he has applied it to selecting and evaluating funds for Gordon Pape, whose annual *Buyer's Guide to Mutual Funds* relies on the ATP methodology for its recommendations. *The Best of the Best* takes the methodology one step further, enabling investors to see for themselves some of the underlying data without overwhelming the reader with background information and calculations. Although readers see only the conclusions drawn from the methodology, they can feel confident that ATP is a unique and proven approach to selecting the best-performing mutual funds on the market. Investors can use the information in this book to confirm or adjust their own evaluations, confident that it is based on all the available data about a particular mutual fund.

In the course of his research, Vos proved categorically that diversification and time are an investor's two most powerful allies. Both work to reduce risk. Diversification works as a benefit by spreading an investor's money over a number of investments whose performance is affected by different factors at different times. Time works to an investor's benefit, because the longer an investor leaves his or her money in a particular fund and the more regularly an investment is made the better are the chances of harvesting a superior return.

To reap the benefits of time in their portfolios, investors do not have to time the market or apply any other theory to their investment approach. All they have to do is invest regularly in good mutual funds such as the ones we have selected in this book.

Time: The investor's ally

Once an investor has decided to invest $1,000 per calendar year, there are three options:

1. Invest at the yearly high.

2. Invest at the yearly low.

3. Invest 12 times a year (monthly).

If an investor is a perfect market timer, he or she will invest the yearly contribution at the yearly low; if an investor is the worst market timer, annual contributions will be made at the yearly high. Assume that in January 1962, instead of timing the market perfectly, an investor initiated a systematic plan by investing $83.33 per month in the stock market through a pension plan, group RRSP, RRSP, or other investment plan.

The graph below illustrates the growth of a portfolio invested in the TSE 300 from January 1962 to February 1998. Investors who made their annual contributions at the market low had a portfolio valued at $511,910, while investors who contributed at the market high had a portfolio value of $433,254. An investor who decided to invest monthly would have had a portfolio valued at $469,317. Finally, investors who put all their money in treasury bills (T-bills) would have generated a portfolio valued at $221,155, significantly less than the portfolio of a poor market timer. Thus, even an investor who has poor market-timing skills can improve performance by investing systematically in equities and holding for the long term. Systematic investing in equities over time brings superior results to any fixed-income investment held over the same period.

MARKET TIMING STRATEGIES COMPARED	
Strategy	**Return**
T-bills	211,155
Market high	433,254
Monthly plan	469, 317
Market low	511,910

Investors who consider risk an enemy should find an ally in time. Increase your time horizon, invest systematically, don't worry about timing stock markets, and you should outperform T-bills. Develop a plan, implement it, and let the benefits of investing in mutual funds come to fruition.

An investor will certainly benefit from choosing the best-performing funds, but such choices are not necessary to obtaining superior performance. An investor can obtain superior returns simply by getting onto a plan, diversifying his or her investments over a range of funds, and sticking to the plan over a long period.

Evaluating a mutual fund

Mutual fund investors tend to evaluate the performances of their investments by looking in the newspaper once a week or once a month to see how their selections have performed over a particular period. Based on a fund's performance over the previous month, year, or three-year period, the investor makes a decision. Usually, if the fund has performed well over the particular period, the investor will leave his or her money where it is or even invest more in the fund.

This is a good start to disciplined investing. In the process, an investor can see how funds perform and gain a better appreciation of volatility and fluctuations in performance. But the statistics published in Canadian newspapers show only a mutual fund's historical performance ending at one particular point. So a fund's performance becomes end-date sensitive. For example, a fund may show no growth at all over an 11-month period; in the twelfth month, it may suddenly gain 20 per cent in value. Based on this performance, at the end of the twelfth month the fund would show a one-month return of 20 per cent; it would also show a 20 per cent return over the previous year. The data would not necessarily indicate the inconsistency of the fund's performance. It is very difficult to evaluate the consistent performance of a mutual fund by looking at only one time period. Applying the ATP methodology, however, inconsistency and its implications become readily apparent. With the ATP methodology, an investor can distinguish the consistently good performers from the funds that perform well only sporadically.

The following table illustrates the performance of one fund, Fund A, as analyzed in each of two consecutive months. For each month, the return and quartile rating are given for the month for which the analysis is being done, for the three-month period ending with that month, and for the one-year, three-year, and five-year periods ending with that month. The quartile rating shows in which group of 25 comparable funds—the first or top 25 per cent, or the second, third, or fourth 25 per cent—this fund is placed. As the table indicates, the performance shown for the two months is drastically different.

FUND A ANALYZED IN TWO CONSECUTIVE MONTHS

Time period	1 month	3 months	1 year	3 years	5 years
Fund A return, month 1	3.1%	6.7%	23.0%	13.7%	24.1%
Fund A quartile, month 1	1	2	1	1	1
Fund A return, month 2	−5.9%	−0.5%	14.0%	8.8%	22.9%
Fund A quartile, month 2	4	4	2	3	1

Unlike other methods that assess a fund's performance over an established and arbitrary period, the ATP methodology is based on a fund's performance over a variety of periods, with lengths from one month to 15 years. Using the ATP methodology, we review a fund's history, gather all the figures ever printed about its performance, and summarize them.

As the ATP methodology gains in popularity, many fund companies have adopted it with changes to suit their own purposes, for instance, disclosing only calendar-year returns as opposed to all 12 one-month periods. But this does not eliminate end-date sensitivity. Over a particular quarter, a fund's performance may place it within the first quartile of funds in the same category, but, measured over a longer period, the fund may rank only in the second or third quartile.

The funds we have selected for this book have recorded superior performance over time. We have included funds from all categories, including equity funds, sector funds, and regional funds. As you will see from the data that accompany each fund, none performs well in every quarter or even in every year. However, the funds we've selected have performed over time better than comparable funds in the same category. If a fund has a bad period, investors can feel quite confident that, over time, this fund will turn its performance around.

Measuring risk

In developing our system of measuring risk and reward, Wilfred Vos evaluated all the current methodologies used by financial analysts. The following discussion is somewhat technical, but it provides some detailed background to the development of the Vos Value Ratings and the WilStar Ratings used in this book.

Risk analysis has been an intrinsic element of investing since the 1950s, when Harry Markowitz showed mathematically exactly how diversification reduced volatility. Risk is important. *How* we measure risk affects every investment decision, from evaluating a mutual fund to selecting the assets and investments for building a portfolio. Measuring risk correctly can lead to making the best investment decisions.

All measures of risk attempt to show how the risk of a particular choice compares with risk levels associated with other options—in other words, how the uncertainty of returns from a particular fund compares with the uncertainty of returns from other funds. The uncertainty of returns is calculated by measuring the degree to which an investment can either outperform or underperform its average rate of return. A risky investment has a higher chance of earning a return either below or above its average rate of return; hence, investors are uncertain about future performance. All single-number risk measures such as standard deviation, value at risk (VAR), mean absolute deviation (MAD), downside risk, and shortfall probability attempt to summarize the historical returns and distinguish between more risky and less risky investments. "Hence all the definitions of risk will attempt to capture in a single number the essentials of risk more fully described in the complete distribution," observes Ronald N. Kahn in an article on mutual fund risk in *BARRA Research Insights*. "Each definition of risk will have at least some shortcomings, due to this simplification." Of these measures, standard deviation has reigned for almost four decades as the measurement of choice to measure risk.

Standard deviation is one measure of the risk level of a fund. It measures a fund's historical risk by indicating the volatility of the fund's historical monthly performance. The standard deviation of a fund is based on an analysis of the deviations of the fund's monthly returns from its average monthly return (over a specified period of time). The greater the monthly deviations are, either above or below the average, the higher will be the standard deviation of the fund, and the higher the fund's standard deviation the higher will be the risk that the fund will not earn the average rate of return.

The standard deviation of a fund is compared with the standard deviations of other funds to determine which fund is riskiest. However, standard deviation assumes that returns are symmetric; that is, that historically there have been as many monthly returns above as below the average monthly rate of return. In statistical terminology, the assumption is that historical returns are accurately represented by the normal distribution, also known as the bell curve. In addition, the fact that standard deviation treats upside surprises as equivalent to downside surprises of similar magnitude is a serious flaw. Risk-averse investors appreciate that the utility from gains and losses of similar size is not equivalent. The erratic gains that are so critical to investing (especially in equities) become warning flags to potential investors when variance-based risk measures are used.

Recent work by Brian Rom introduced an excellent concept called **downside risk**, which recognizes that investors have diminishing marginal utility curves. Brian Rom argues that investors are concerned about losing money; they are not concerned about risk when their investments are increasing in value. Thus, having an accurate measure of downside risk is very important. Brian Rom argues that standard deviation relies on three assumptions:

1. Risk must be measured only in relation to the average return.

2. Above-average and below-average returns are equally likely to occur.

3. Returns closer to the average are more likely than extreme returns.

Unfortunately, these assumptions are not applicable to mutual fund investments, and an alternative risk measurement system has to be utilized.

Time-weighting problems

The Association for Investment Management and Research (AIMR) requires money managers to disclose the time-weighted rates of return (average annual compounded rates of return) of their portfolios. However, the fatal flaw in time-weighted rates of return is that they are end-date sensitive. A particular fund could go from the first quartile over three years down to the third quartile over three years by moving the valuation period up by one month. The beauty of time-weighted rates of return is simplicity, but what it gains in simplicity it loses in accuracy. The one-, three-, five-, and ten-year rates of return distributed by newspapers and mutual fund companies alike are all tied to one single ending date. We should not reward funds that earn erratic gains just prior to the evaluation date, so we must measure the performance of a mutual fund by another method to supplement existing data.

The ATP Methodology: A new approach

Given that asymmetry in investment returns is present and that it can affect investment decisions and conclusions, we need to find the best way to measure investment risk.

The All Time Periods Methodology is a new way to evaluate and select investment options. Its two components, which allow investors to identify quickly which funds have the most favourable performance, are:

1. **The Vos Value Rating (VVR)**, which compares a fund with others in the same narrowly defined category

2. **The WilStar Rating,** which compares a fund with other funds in a similar broad category.

Investors who have identified funds with high VVR and WilStar Ratings can then examine the historical performance of a particular fund by reading its All Time Periods (ATP) chart in the next chapter of this book. The whole procedure of evaluating funds and reviewing their ATP charts is referred to as the ATP Methodology. The ratings identify favourable funds and the charts disclose the actual historical performance.

The Vos Value Rating (VVR)

The Vos Value Rating (VVR) is broken down into three different modules. They include the VVR reward module (VVR P), which measures the performance of the mutual fund; the VVR risk module (VVR R), which measures the underlying risk of the mutual fund; and the VVR best balance between risk and reward module (VVR B), which identifies the funds that score highest on a combination of the VVR reward and the VVR risk modules (that is, deliver the best trade-off between risk and reward). The funds included in this book that score the highest receive a five-star (★★★★★) rating, and the funds that score the lowest receive a one-star (★) rating. The top 20 per cent of all similar funds within the VVR category receive a five-star rating; the next 20 per cent receive a four-star rating; the middle 20 per cent receive a three-star rating; the next 20 per cent receive a two-star rating; and the bottom 20 per cent receive a one-star rating.

Reward module

The VVR reward module considers seven variables that measure the historical performance of a particular fund relative to the mutual fund's peers:

1. **Maximum** is the best one-month rate of return posted by the fund.

2. **First quartile** is the one-month rate of return that is lower than 25 per cent of all this fund's other monthly rates of return but higher than 75 per cent of all this fund's other monthly rates of return.

3. **Median** is the monthly rate of return that is lower than 50 per cent of all this fund's other monthly rates of return but higher than 50 per cent of all this fund's other monthly rates of return.

4. **Third quartile** is the one-month rate of return that is lower than 75 per cent of all this fund's other monthly rates of return but higher than 25 per cent of all this fund's other monthly rates of return.

5. **Average** is the average monthly rate of return posted by the fund.

6. **Average percentile rank (APR)** is the average of the fund's monthly percentile ranks when compared with other funds. For example, if the fund posted the fifteenth highest rate of return out of 30 funds, the fund would have an APR of 0.5 or the fiftieth percentile for that particular month. After calculating each month's percentile rank, the module takes their average. Therefore, if the fund placed consistently in the first quartile month after month it would have a very high APR. The higher the APR, the more often the fund does well from month to month when compared with other funds within the mutual fund's peer group.

7. **Sum of all gains** is simply the addition of all the positive monthly rates of return. The cardinal rating increases with the number and size of positive rates of return.

After determining each variable's cardinal rating, we give the fund an ordinal position within its peer group. The fund with the highest average ordinal position of all seven variables is the best performer. This fund would receive a five-star rating since it would be in the top 20 per cent of the funds being compared. This measure is more complex than time-weighted rate of return, but it takes into consideration several measures of dispersion that influence upside potential and consistency.

Risk module

The VVR risk module considers five variables when measuring the historical risk of a particular fund relative to its peers. It attempts to enhance the current information available and aid in the initial screening of the fund. The best screening is still to look at the underlying portfolio, but preferably after an initial screening to reduce the work load.

The five variables are:

1. **Frequency up** is the historical probability that the fund will earn a positive rate of return after one month.

2. **Minimum** is the worst one-month rate of return historically posted by the fund.

3. **Expected loss** is the fund's probability of loss multiplied by its worst one-month rate of return.

4. **Sum of all losses** is the addition of all this fund's negative monthly rates of return. The sum of all losses increases with the number and size of the negative rates of return.

5. **Volatility of average percentile rank** is calculated by first determining the average percentile rank (APR) of each of the monthly rates of return. For example, if a fund placed fifteenth out of 30 funds, it would have an APR of 0.5 or be positioned at the fiftieth

percentile for that one month. Then you calculate the standard deviation of each month's percentile rank. If the fund ranked consistently in the first quartile month after month, it would have a very low standard deviation of its monthly percentile ranks. The lower the standard deviation of the monthly percentile rank, the more consistent the fund is from month to month.

After the cardinal (numeric) rating for each variable has been determined, the fund is given an ordinal—assigned a position within its peer group. The fund with the highest average ordinal position of all five variables is the least risky. This measure is more complex than standard deviation, but it considers several measures of dispersion that influence upside potential and downside risk. Thus the fund that scores highest on the VVR risk measure will be less risky than others, because the value of the fund declines less often and with less severity. In addition, the fund would also be more consistent from month to month. Therefore, this fund would not likely appear at the bottom of its peer group. This fund would receive a five-star rating since it would be in the top 20 per cent of the funds being compared.

Best balance between risk and reward module

The fund with the highest average of the performance and risk components cardinal scores receives the highest rating (five-star) on the VVR best balance between risk and reward module. A fund that scores high on the VVR best balance module must score high on all the variables, not just variables that measure either reward or risk.

The VVR summarized

What does this do? The VVR is designed to summarize historical performance and is not designed to predict the future. This reinforces the warning made by Amy C. Arnott: "Many commentators insist on treating the star rating as a predictive measure of a short-term trading signal. The rating, which is clearly labelled as a historical profile, does neither. The rating does not reflect Morningstar's opinion of a fund's future potential; it is simply a first-stage screen that summarizes how well each fund has historically balanced risk and return."

The VVR illuminates and eliminates weaknesses displayed by existing tools that are used to measure performance. It also provides more information to investors, which will aid them in making their investment decisions. Considering different risk variables can and will lead to different allocations of assets when creating portfolios. The result is that an investor can use this information to construct a better portfolio.

The **Vos Value Rating** assesses the performance of a fund measured against other funds in the same category. It is based on the fund's monthly performance during the previous three years. To determine a fund's VVR, Wilfred Vos has assessed the performance of all the funds in this book in every single month for three years. A fund will receive a high VVR if it historically adds value within the scope of its investment objectives compared with other funds in its category. The VVR compares funds in more than 20 narrowly defined categories, including among others dividend funds, precious metal funds, Japanese funds, and European funds.

The WilStar Rating: Categorical performance

The **WilStar Rating** is a second rating that compares a fund's performance relative to a larger peer group. It is designed to identify the right fund within a broad category or asset class. Thus the VVR will tell investors which funds have done well relative to other funds in one of 20 asset classes, and the WilStar will evaluate funds within a more broadly defined asset class. The WilStar Rating uses the same methodology as the VVR, but evaluates funds for the previous five years, categorized into five peer groups:

1. Domestic equity funds
2. International equity funds
3. Fixed income funds
4. Balanced funds
5. Money market funds

As with the VVR, the funds included in this book that score the highest in their WilStar peer group receive a five-star (★★★★★) rating, and the funds that score the lowest receive a one-star (★) rating. The top 20 per cent of all similar funds within the WilStar category receive a five-star rating; the next 20 per cent receive a four-star rating; the middle 20 per cent receive a three-star rating; the next 20 per cent receive a two-star rating; and the bottom 20 per cent receive a one-star rating.

In summary

Investors can select an above-average fund that has outperformed funds in its own narrowly defined VVR asset class by identifying a fund which has a high Vos Value Rating. The entire universe of mutual funds in Canada is broken down into 20 peer groups or asset classes for VVR analysis. Each peer group tends to perform differently under different economic conditions. In order to identify a peer group that has performed well, investors then refer to the selected fund's WilStar Rating, where it is compared with funds in a much broader peer group—the entire universe of mutual funds in Canada is grouped into only five asset classes. If a fund scored very well in its VVR category but poorly in its broader WilStar class, then its whole VVR category has underperformed other funds within the WilStar category. Thus, the WilStar Ratings indicate which VVR asset classes are performing well.

For example, Latin American funds have recently performed poorly as a VVR category, and all funds in this peer group receive a relatively low WilStar Rating. However, within the VVR category some funds will receive high ratings, indicating that they are good choices *within this narrowly defined category*. Thus, an investor could invest in the right mutual fund in its VVR category, but in the wrong WilStar asset class. On the other hand, an investor could have invested in the wrong fund in a VVR category but still enjoy excellent performance because the investment was in the right WilStar asset class.

Appendix on asymmetric returns

This appendix is provided for those who wish to delve more deeply into the technical statistical study of risk management.

Statisticians who believe returns are asymmetric have used the standard measures of skewness and kurtosis to measure non-normality in historical rates of return.

Skewness characterizes the degree of asymmetry of a distribution around its mean. Positive skewness indicates a distribution with an asymmetric tail extending towards more positive values (value is greater than zero). Negative skewness indicates a distribution with an asymmetric tail extending towards more negative values. Theoretically, positive skewness would indicate that a mutual fund actually incurred less risk than indicated by standard deviation. Therefore, investors who rely on standard deviation as a risk measure when returns are skewed could make erroneous investment decisions or misleading conclusions about a manager's historical performance.

Kurtosis characterizes the relative peakedness or flatness of a distribution compared with the normal distribution. Positive kurtosis indicates a relatively peaked distribution. Negative kurtosis indicates a relatively flat distribution.

It is important to understand how non-normality is prevalent and what effect it might have on investment decisions. The results of an analysis of the 15-year track records of mutual funds indicates that standard deviation, if used as a sole risk measure, can be dangerous and misleading (see the table below). In addition, skewness and kurtosis do not consistently rectify some of the deficiencies found in standard deviation.

WHICH FUND WOULD YOU CHOOSE?

	(1) Average between first and third quartile	(2) Average	(3) Median	(4) Standard deviation of columns (1) to (3)	(5) Standard deviation	(6) Kurtosis	(7) Skewness	(8) Percentage of returns within 1 standard deviation
Average	1.04	1.03	1.04	0.09	3.13	4.16	(0.40)	74
Median	1.02	1.03	1.02	0.07	3.59	3.45	(0.48)	74
Maximum	1.69	1.62	1.96	0.39	7.36	25.80	3.06	90
Minimum	0.42	0.41	0.13	0.00	0.21	(0.68)	(1.75)	59

Of the 194 mutual funds surveyed, only 16 per cent had a variance of less than nine basis points when comparing the monthly average return, monthly median return, and average between the first- and third-quartile monthly returns. If the historical rates of return were normally distributed, the variance among these three variables should have been zero. Therefore, these statistical tests confirm that asymmetry is present, but do not show to what extent.

Skewness and kurtosis would measure the extent of non-normality. A kurtosis greater than 1 could indicate that a fund had a high number of monthly returns around the mean (average). An analysis of a large sample of mutual funds showed that, on average, 74 per cent of the observations of monthly returns fell within one standard deviation of the mean, suggesting that returns of most mutual funds fall around the mean more often than is indicated when using standard deviation as a measure. Standard deviation would assume that 68 per cent of observations would fall within one standard deviation of the mean. However, the correlation between kurtosis and the percentage of observations found within one standard deviation of the mean was only 0.64. This means that investors who rely on kurtosis to measure the asymmetric rates of return do not arrive at the same conclusion as investors who count the number of observations around the mean.

Measures of skewness generated similar results. The average fund had a negative skewness of 40 basis points. The negative skewness was not generated by the frequency of observations in the left tail of the distributuion but by the severity of one or two observations on the left side of the distribution that were not offset by large observations in the right tail of the distribution.

Brian Rom suggests that Post Modern Portfolio Theory (PMPT) will eliminate the deficiencies in standard deviation. "PMPT, which is gaining acceptance with institutional investors worldwide, replaces standard deviation with downside risk, which differentiates between upside and downside variability," write Rom and co-author Kathleen Ferguson in *Pensions & Investments*. "In so doing, it treats as risky only those returns that have fallen below some target or benchmark return." Jessica Keyes, writing in *Pension Management*, adds, "One of the reasons downside risk is an increasingly popular measure is that it can capture risk for assets with skewed return distributions more accurately." Authors differ in defining downside risk. Some calculate the standard deviation of all observations below a target or benchmark, while others calculate the standard deviation of all observations below zero.

Intuitively, **shortfall probability** is perhaps most closely related to the mutual fund investor's concept of risk. In this context, the probability of making a gain in any standard time period is most relevant. Ignoring (for now) the magnitude of any gains, the idea is to measure in black and white terms the odds of making or losing money in any month or year. In this way, the investor gains insight into the distribution of the returns within the overall variance.

Selected Funds

Each fund included in this book has been analyzed using the ATP Methodology and has shown itself to be a worthwhile investment. The two-page spread for each fund provides general information about the fund and its performance, and includes an evaluation chart which gives Vos Value and WilStar Ratings for reward, risk, and best balance between risk and reward. The ratings are explained in detail in the chapter entitled The ATP Methodology, on pages 14 to 17. If a fund does not have WilStar ratings, this means that it has not been in existence for five years. Each right-hand page is an ATP chart, mentioned on page 14 and explained below.

How to read an All Time Periods (ATP) chart

The All Time Periods (ATP) chart presents a combination of tables that illustrate the historical performance of a mutual fund. There is an ATP chart for each mutual fund analyzed in this book. The six tables included in a one-page ATP chart are illustrated and explained below.

FUND DETAILS

Fund name	**Altamira Bond**	Start date for data shown	Dec 1987
Fund family	Altamira Investment Services Inc.	Fund size (in $ millions)	$427
Mutual fund classification	Canadian bond	Percentage in foreign holdings	14.60
RRSP eligible	Yes	Dividend frequency	Quarterly
		Sales charge	No
VVR peer group	Canadian bond	Redemption charge	No
Number of mutual funds in VVR category	178	Management fee	1.00
WilStar peer group	Fixed income	Management expense ratio	1.30

Fund name: This line discloses the name of the fund being analyzed.

Fund family: This discloses the name of the mutual fund company that sells the fund.

Mutual fund classification: This line indicates the investment objective of the mutual fund. In this example, the mutual fund classification is Canadian bond. Therefore, this mutual fund invests in Canadian bonds, and the fund is compared with other mutual funds that also invest in Canadian bonds.

RRSP eligible: If the mutual fund is RRSP-eligible, it can be held in an RRSP without affecting the foreign content limit. (Canadians are allowed to hold up to 20 per cent of their RRSP investments in foreign securities.) If the fund's RRSP eligibility is designated as foreign, then if it is held within an RRSP it will count as foreign content.

VVR (Vos Value Rating) peer group: This is the peer group or category that the mutual fund is compared with for the VVR reward, risk, and best balance between risk and reward ratings. These 20 peer groups are subgroups of the broad categories described on pages 7 and 8.

Number of mutual funds in VVR category: This shows the number of mutual funds that are included in the peer group analysis.

WilStar peer group: This is the peer group or category that the mutual fund is compared with for the WilStar reward, risk, and best balance between risk and reward ratings. The WilStar peer groups are the five broad categories listed and described on pages 7 and 8: money market, fixed income, balanced, domestic equity, and international equity.

Start date for data shown: This is the date at which the analysis for the fund began. This date is usually the inception date, but there are some exceptions.

Fund size: This is the total amount of money currently invested in the mutual fund.

Percentage in foreign holdings: This shows the portion of the assets held in the mutual fund that are invested outside Canada.

Dividend frequency: This discloses the timing of the dividends that the mutual fund pays out. The frequency may be monthly, quarterly (every three months), or annually.

Sales charge: This line indicates whether or not investors in this mutual fund are charged a fee for buying shares in the fund.

Redemption charge: This indicates whether investors in this mutual fund are charged a fee for cashing in their investment.

Management fee: This discloses the size of the fee charged to the fund annually by the mutual fund company to cover its administrative and other costs and to compensate its fund managers.

Management expense ratio: This measures the total expenses charged to the mutual fund against the fund's assets. The fee includes the management fee in addition to fees for accounting and legal and trading costs associated with the operation of the fund.

FUND PERFORMANCE

	1 month	1 year	3 years	5 years	10 years	15 years
Returns ending Aug 1998	−0.5%	16.6%	15.0%	11.0%	12.7%	
Best historical return	7.5%	28.5%	19.4%	14.4%	12.7%	
Average historical return	1.0%	12.8%	12.3%	12.2%	12.5%	
Worst historical return	−6.0%	−10.3%	6.8%	9.0%	12.3%	

Returns ending August 1998: These are the returns earned by the fund for the periods ending August 1998. For example, the one-month rate of return for the Altamira Bond fund was a decline of −0.5 per cent. The one-year rate of return from September 1, 1997, to August 31, 1998, was 16.6 per cent; the three-year rate of return for the fund from September 1, 1995, to August 31, 1998, was 15.0 per cent annualized. In short, the fund's average rate of return for the period September 1, 1995, to August 31, 1998, was 15 per cent per year for three years. The five-year rate of return from September 1, 1993, to August 31, 1998, was 11.9 per cent annualized, and the ten-year rate of return for the fund from September 1, 1988, to August 31, 1998, was 12.7 per cent annualized. This format is the same format as investors receive from their mutual fund companies or major newspapers in their monthly mutual fund reviews.

The rest of this table summarizes the information you would accumulate if you gathered every single mutual fund review published by *The Globe and Mail, The Toronto Star,* or *The Financial Post* and looked at the historical performance of each fund. It discloses a range of results based on analysis of all this data.

Best historical return: The best historical return discloses the very best performance that the fund has ever achieved. The best one-month return for the Altamira Bond Fund was a gain of 7.5 per cent. An investor who invested in this bond fund prior to its best one-month period would gain 7.5 per cent. The best one-year rate of return was a gain of 28.5 per cent. An investor who invested in this fund and held the investment over the course of its best year would have gained 28.5 per cent. The best three-year rate of return was a gain of 19.4 per cent annualized. The best five-year rate of return was a gain of 14.4 per cent annualized, and the best ten-year rate of return for the fund was a gain of 12.7 per cent. Here investors can determine whether recent performance—the performance of the mutual fund ending August 1998—is the fund's best performance, or its performance falls short of its best performance. Investors can update this information by following the fund's current performance. *Note:* All numbers are calculated using average annual compounded rates of return.

Average historical return: The average historical rate of return shows how well the mutual fund has performed historically on average. Investors who invested in the Altamira Bond Fund, on average, earned 1 per cent per month. After one year, investors, on average, earned 12.8 per cent; the average three-year rate of return for the fund was 12.3 per cent; the average five-year rate of return for the fund was 12.2 per cent, and the average ten-year rate of return was 12.5 per cent.

Worst historical return: The worst historical return indicates the downside risk associated with a particular fund, that is, how an investor would fare if he or she invested in a fund at the worst possible time, and the fund subsequently declined in value. The worst historical return indicates the losses posted by the fund over different periods. Investors in the Altamira Bond Fund who invested prior to the fund's worst one-month loss would have seen their investment decline in value by 6 per cent in one month. The worst loss posted by the fund after 12 months was a decline of 10.3 per cent. The worst rate of return posted by the fund after three years was a gain of 6.8 per cent annualized. Thus, investors who invested in this fund for a minimum of three years have never lost money historically. The worst five-year rate of return for the fund was a gain of 9 per cent, and the worst ten-year rate of return was a gain of 12.3 per cent. In turn, investors who invested for the long term always made money, and investors never lost more than 10.3 per cent in any given year. If risk is your enemy, time is your ally.

RETURNS GREATER THAN						
	1 month	1 year	3 years	5 years	10 years	15 years
10 per cent	0%	65%	72%	90%	100%	
Zero	69%	93%	100%	100%	100%	
Percentage of time fund lost $	31%	7%	0%	0%	0%	
Number of periods evaluated	129	118	94	70	10	

This table illustrates the frequency with which a particular mutual fund achieves or fails to meet an investor's goals. The table discloses how often a fund achieved the most common objectives:

1. The frequency with which the fund achieved a return greater than 10 per cent over different periods
2. The frequency with which the fund achieved a return greater than zero
3. The frequency with which the fund achieved a return of less than zero (or lost money)

In this example, the Altamira Bond Fund achieved a return greater than zero after one month 69 per cent of the time; the fund achieved a return greater than zero after one year 93 per cent of the time. When a fund achieves a return greater than zero 93 per cent of the time after one year, it means the investor who invested in this fund for a period of one year made money 93 per cent of the time. Mutual funds go up and down in value over time; this fund went up in value after one year 93 per cent of the time. It achieved a return greater than 10 per cent after one year 65 per cent of the time. After three, five, and ten years, the fund has always posted a return greater than zero. The last line in the table—Number of periods evaluated—indicates that the ATP chart looked at 129 one-month returns to calculate the best, average, and worst returns and their frequency. The more periods evaluated, the longer the fund has been available to investors and the more information is available to investors for making a decision. For the Altamira Bond Fund, there were 118 one-year periods evaluated. When a fund has posted a one-month return, the ATP chart will evaluate one month of performance; if a fund has posted two monthly rates of return, the ATP chart will evaluate two months of performance; when a fund has posted twelve months of monthly returns, the ATP chart will evaluate twelve monthly returns and one one-year rate of return. When a fund has posted thirteen months of monthly returns the ATP chart will evaluate thirteen monthly returns and two one-year rates of returns (the first twelve months equals one year and the second month plus the remaining eleven months provides another one-year rate of return).

DOWNSIDE RISK

	Worst setback since start date	In bear 1987	In bear 1990	In bear 1994	In bear 1998
Setback for mutual fund	−17.3%		−4.2%	−17.3%	−1.0%
Setback for peer group	−10.8%		−4.6%	−10.8%	−1.7%
Setback ended in	June 1994		April 1990	June 1994	Aug 1998
Months to recover from loss	11		2	11	−

A change in economic conditions is characterized by changes in the growth of the economy, changes in interest rates, and changes in investors' outlook on the future. The downside risk table evaluates the performance of the mutual fund during different periods when capital markets have displayed significant declines in value as the result of changing economic conditions. Periods when capital markets decline are referred to as *bear markets*. A bear market is characterized as a period when investments decline in value. During such periods, different investments will react differently to changing economic conditions.

It is useful for investors to evaluate the performance of their investments during more difficult economic times. Some investments will decline significantly during a bear market; others will not. Investors can read the downside risk table and get a good idea of how a fund has reacted during such difficult times.

This table provides data on the fund's worst setback since it was established and on its performance during four bear-market periods (1987, 1990, 1994, and 1998). The **Worst setback** column measures the worst decline an investor could have experienced since the start date of the fund. The figure indicates the worst setback experienced by an investor who invested in a fund at the top of the market before the fund declined to its lowest value. In other words, it discloses the largest drop from high to low the fund has ever posted. The Altamira Bond Fund declined in value by 17.3 per cent over a period ending in June 1994. During the same period the fund's peer group (similar funds) declined in value by 10.8 per cent. However, after incurring this loss, the Altamira Bond Fund regained its value within 11 months. Investors should note that this column discloses the worst setback for the fund since its start date.

The columns that indicate the fund's performance during the four bear markets evaluate the performance of the fund only during those particular periods. The worst setback since the start date may be different from a fund's loss during a bear market. The columns headed **In Bear 1987, 1990, 1994**, and **1998** highlight the downside risk displayed by the fund during those particular periods, respectively.

QUARTILE RANKING OF MUTUAL FUND PERFOMANCE AFTER 12 MONTHS OVER TIME

Canadian bond

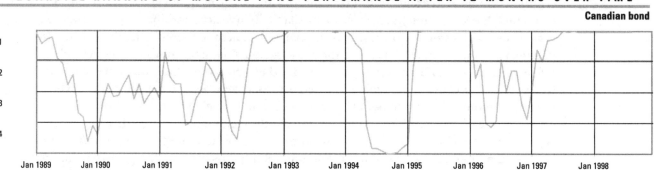

1 is first quartile; 2 is second quartile; 3 is third quartile; 4 is fourth quartile. First quartile means that the fund outperformed 75 per cent of other similar funds after 12 months.

This table is a relative performance graph that shows how the fund's total return for a twelve-month period (one year) compares with the returns for all the other funds with similar investment objectives. These are the same funds used to calculate the Vos Value Rating. The range of relative performance is expressed from the top of the graph to the bottom. The graph is also broken down into quartiles. The first quartile is represented by 1, the second quartile by 2, the third by 3, and the fourth by 4. The fund's relative performance is plotted within the range over time. If the fund is continuously number 1 within its peer group, it will, of course, always be in the first quartile and its relative performance line will be plotted at the top of the graph at all times.

Funds in quartile 1 performed best; funds in quartile 4 performed worst. If a fund's returns lie in the first quartile—quartile 1—its return was within the top 25 per cent of all the funds in its category, and the fund performed better than at least 75 per cent of all the other funds with similar investment objectives. While many mutual funds try to achieve first quartile performance consistently, very few can actually achieve this objective. Most mutual funds aim to be in the first or second quartile at all times. If there are ten mutual funds in a category, and one fund outperforms eight others after twelve months (one year) but underperforms one fund, then it would be in the first quartile. If a mutual fund underperformed eight funds and outperformed one fund, it would be a fourth quartile performer.

For example, the Altamira Bond Fund for the period February 1, 1988, to January 31, 1989, posted a return that placed it in the first quartile, indicating that the fund did better than the majority of other Canadian bond funds. Rolling ahead by one month, the investor can determine the relative performance of the Altamira Bond Fund for the period March 1, 1988, to February 28, 1989. Here the fund lost some ground against other Canadian bond mutual funds. For the 12-month period ending January 1989, the fund had fallen to the fourth quartile. As investors read the graph from left to right, they can appreciate the fund's relative performance from 1989 to the present. A fund that is consistently first quartile is more desirable than other funds.

ROLLING 12-MONTH TOTAL RATE OF RETURN FOR THE MUTUAL FUND OVER TIME

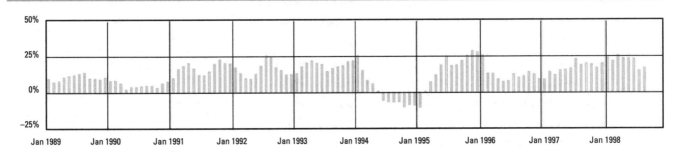

The ATP chart will evaluate all twelve-month (one-year) rates of return posted by the fund. If a fund posts a one-year rate of return from July 1, 1996, to June 30, 1997, the ATP chart evaluates this return as a one-year return, and the ATP chart will evaluate the one-year return from August 1, 1996, to July 31, 1997, that is, the one-year rate of return posted by the fund the following month. The ATP chart will keep rolling forward one month at a time until all the combinations of returns that have been posted by the fund are evaluated, hence the term *rolling period returns*. The one-year return from July 1, 1996, to June 30, 1997, was the return for the fund ending June 1997. Roll forward one month, and we get the fund's one-year return ending July 1997, which evaluates the fund's one-year performance for the period August 1, 1996, to July 31, 1997.

The rolling 12-month total rate of return table illustrates the fund's 12-month performance over time. The left side of the fund table illustrates the fund's performance for the period February 1, 1988, to January 31, 1989. The next bar illustrates the performance for the period March 1, 1988, to February 28, 1989. Moving progressively to the right, the bars illustrate the performance of the fund as it approaches the current date. Thus, the return for the Altamira Bond Fund for the one-year period ending August 31, 1998, is 16.6 per cent, and the bar at the far right illustrates this performance. Investors should note that some investments experience large swings in performance from one period to the next.

Selected funds

The following is a comprehensive list of mutual funds that were selected as excellent, based on their performance during the previous three to five years. (Funds must have a three-year track record to be eligible.) When two mutual funds exhibited similar risk and return patterns, the fund that is more widely available for investors was selected. The selection criteria include the Vos Value Rating, the WilStar Rating, the All Time Periods (ATP) chart, diversifiable risk, and a qualitative assessment of the mutual fund and mutual fund company. These 50 funds have displayed superior performance relative to similar mutual funds. However, with over 1,936 mutual funds to select from, more than 50 mutual funds deserve recognition. Unfortunately, we had to draw the line at 50. The funds selected are listed and described in an order which proceeds from the least risky peer group to the most risky peer group (adjusted for RRSP eligibility).

Investors who want to invest in more than one mutual fund should read the portfolio building chapter of this book, beginning on page 128. Portfolio building will help investors select a combination of mutual funds to achieve a superior risk and return profile.

TOP FUNDS 1999

Fund name	Fund objective	Page number
Bissett Money Market	Canadian money market	28
Phillips, Hager & North $US Money Market	International money market	30
London Life Mortgage	Mortgage	32
Altamira Bond	Canadian bond	34
CI Canadian Bond	Canadian bond	36
Phillips, Hager & North Bond	Canadian bond	38
Guardian Foreign Income A	International bond	40
Universal World Income RRSP (Mackenzie)	International bond	42
Asset Builder Series II (Primerica)	Balanced	44
Atlas Canadian Balanced	Balanced	46
Bissett Retirement	Balanced	48
Fidelity Canadian Asset Allocation	Balanced	50
Global Strategy Income Plus	Balanced	52
Ivy Growth and Income (Mackenzie)	Balanced	54
AGF American Tactical Asset Allocation	International balanced	56
AIM GT Global Growth and Income	International balanced	58
CI International Balanced	International balanced	60
Bissett Dividend Income	Dividend	62
BPI Dividend Income	Dividend	64
Phillips, Hager & North Dividend Income	Dividend	66
AIC Diversified Canada	Canadian equity	68
Atlas Canadian Large Cap Growth	Canadian equity	70
Bissett Canadian Equity	Canadian equity	72
Ethical Growth	Canadian equity	74
Investors Summa	Canadian equity	76
Ivy Canadian (Mackenzie)	Canadian equity	78
Spectrum United Canadian Investment	Canadian equity	80
Standard Life Equity	Canadian equity	82
Bissett Small Cap	Canadian small cap	84
Fidelity Canadian Growth Company	Canadian small cap	86
GBC Canadian Growth	Canadian small cap	88
Millennium Next Generation	Canadian small cap	90
Bissett Multinational Growth	International equity	92

Fund name	Fund objective	Page number
BPI Global Equity Value	International equity	94
Fidelity International Portfolio	International equity	96
Greystone Managed Global	International equity	98
AIC Value	US equity	100
Investors US Growth	US equity	102
Optima Strategy US Equity	US equity	104
Atlas European Value	European equity	106
Universal European Opportunities (Mackenzie)	European equity	108
Dynamic Far East	Asia and Pacific Rim	110
Navigator Asia Pacific	Asia and Pacific Rim	112
Scotia Excelsior Pacific Rim	Asia and Pacific Rim	114
AGF International—Japan Class	Japanese equity	116
Scotia Excelsior Latin American	Latin America and emerging markets	118
AIM Global Health Sciences	Special equity	120
Dynamic Real Estate Equity	Special equity	122
Royal Precious Metals	Precious metals	124
Royal Energy	Resource	126

BISSETT MONEY MARKET FUND

Vos value rating			WilStar rating		
Reward	**Risk**	**Best balance**	**Reward**	**Risk**	**Best balance**
★★★★★	★★★★★	★★★★★	★★★★★	★★★★★	★★★★★

Fund profile

The Bissett Money Market Fund is managed by Michael Quinn, the lead fixed-income manager of Bissett and Associates Investment Management. The investment objective of the fund is to achieve maximum income with no volatility through short-term high-quality money market securities with a maximum maturity of one year. All the investments within the fund must receive a credit rating of R1 middle or higher by the Dominion Bond Rating Services.

Investors should not expect to earn any real money on a money market fund after taking into consideration inflation and taxes. With yields on fixed income investments at historic lows, achieving a return greater than 4 per cent will be impressive. In fact, investors seeking the highest yield on their cash investments could invest in almost any money market mutual fund. The difference in performance among the funds is not immense. In addition, companies like ING Direct and Altamira offer deposit accounts that pay 4.25 per cent and 4.5 per cent respectively, and they do not require a large minimum investment.

Investments made by the Bissett Money Market Fund include debt obligations issued by the Government of Canada (treasury bills), the provinces of Canada, and Canadian chartered banks.

Fund performance

The Bissett Money Market Fund has consistently been first quartile since its inception. The outperformance can be attributed to a rock bottom management expense ratio (MER) and the manager's ability to react to short-term government fiscal and monetary policies. The fund attained the highest ratings for each of the reward, risk, and best balance between risk and reward categories based on both the Vos Value and WilStar Ratings. However, the upside is limited, because investors do not incur risk. The best 12-month period was a positive return of 7.2 per cent, and this return is likely not going to occur again within this economic environment.

Fund risks

This fund has never lost money. Therefore, there's not much risk here. The worst one-month rate of return was 0.2 per cent and the worst 12-month rate of return was 3.2 per cent. Thus, from a financial perspective, there is no risk. However, investors who earn such low rates of return risk the possibility of not having enough capital at retirement. Therefore, investors will have to make additional contributions to achieve their financial goals.

Future prospects

The return on money market mutual funds depends highly on the Bank of Canada's monetary, fiscal, and political policies. In addition, the strength of the Canadian dollar and any open-market activities by the government will affect the yields on money market instruments. The primary objective of this fund is capital preservation. Without a global financial crisis, your money should be safe. Investors who need a temporary parking spot for their cash will find that any money market fund will meet their needs. Investors should be aware, though, of any redemption charges if they do invest in money market funds for the short term.

FUND DETAILS

Fund name	**Bissett Money Market**	Start date for data shown	Sept 1991
Fund family	Bissett and Associates Investment Management Ltd.	Fund size (in $ millions)	$73
Mutual fund classification	Canadian money market	Percentage in foreign holdings	0.00
RRSP eligible	Yes	Dividend frequency	Monthly
		Sales charge	No
VVR peer group	Canadian money market	Redemption charge	No
Number of mutual funds in VVR category	146	Management fee	0.50
WilStar peer group	Money market	Management expense ratio	0.50

FUND PERFORMANCE

	1 month	1 year	3 years	5 years	10 years	15 years
Returns ending Aug 1998	0.4%	3.8%	4.4%	4.9%		
Best historical return	0.7%	7.2%	5.8%	5.9%		
Average historical return	0.4%	5.2%	5.4%	5.3%		
Worst historical return	0.2%	3.2%	4.4%	4.9%		

RETURNS GREATER THAN

	1 month	1 year	3 years	5 years	10 years	15 years
10 per cent	0%	0%	0%	0%		
Zero	100%	100%	100%	100%		
Percentage of time fund lost $	0%	0%	0%	0%		
Number of periods evaluated	84	73	49	25		

DOWNSIDE RISK

	Worst setback since start date	In bear 1987	In bear 1990	In bear 1994	In bear 1998
Setback for mutual fund	n/a			n/a	n/a
Setback for peer group	n/a			n/a	n/a
Setback ended in	n/a				n/a
Months to recover from loss	?				n/a

QUARTILE RANKING OF MUTUAL FUND PERFOMANCE AFTER 12 MONTHS OVER TIME

Canadian money market

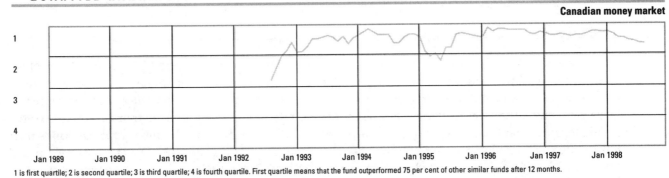

1 is first quartile; 2 is second quartile; 3 is third quartile; 4 is fourth quartile. First quartile means that the fund outperformed 75 per cent of other similar funds after 12 months.

ROLLING 12-MONTH TOTAL RATE OF RETURN FOR THE MUTUAL FUND OVER TIME

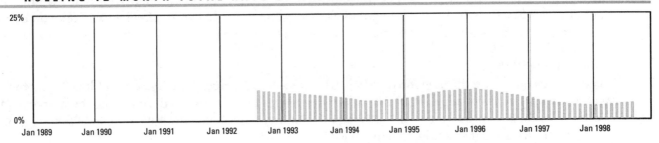

PHILLIPS, HAGER & NORTH $US MONEY MARKET FUND

Vos value rating			WilStar rating		
Reward	**Risk**	**Best balance**	**Reward**	**Risk**	**Best balance**
★★★★★	★★★★★	★★★★★	★★★★	★★★★	★★★★

Fund profile

The Phillips, Hager & North US Money Market Fund is managed by Lynn Delahey of Phillips, Hager & North Investment Management. The fund's investment objective is to achieve a high level of current income while preserving capital. The fund invests in government T-bills and corporate short-term notes that are denominated in US dollars. (*Note:* This fund is valued in US dollars.)

Hurrah for the falling Canadian dollar! Investors have picked up some additional return by investing in US-denominated money market funds. With the loonie hurting from the Asian flu, investors who put their investments in US dollars have a lot to be thankful for. International money market funds protect investors against a falling Canadian dollar. But in turn a rising Canadian dollar would decrease the value of investors' holdings in this fund. Money market mutual funds closely resemble GICs, except that money market mutual funds do not guarantee a return and are completely liquid. In addition, money market funds add stability to a well diversified portfolio.

The Phillips, Hager & North US Money Market Fund invests in short-term discount notes offered by provincial governments. In addition, the fund invests in short-term discount notes offered by Ford Credit Canada, Chevron Corporation, Northern Telecom, and Bank of Montreal.

Fund performance

This fund's performance has been slow and steady with low rates of return. The biggest benefit of investing in money market funds is that investors incur virtually no risk. Investors can expect to earn approximately 4 per cent to 5 per cent in the future, representing the yield on short-term notes.

Fund risks

Since the fund's start date in December 1990, it has never lost money. The worst 12-month rate of return was a positive 2.6 per cent (in US dollars). The relative performance of international money market funds is extremely uniform, and investors can choose among them with relative indifference. Investors must be aware, however, that after inflation and taxes the real rate of return could be extremely low. Investors saving for retirement may need a higher rate of return than those provided by money market funds over the long term. An investment of $1,000 at 5 per cent for 10 years will grow to $1,628; at 10 per cent, it will grow to $2,593. Thus, investors who do not want to risk outliving their investments during retirement should try to achieve a higher rate of return. Investing in money market mutual funds can be a prudent investment decision during economic downturns, but it is not a sound long-term policy for your entire portfolio. Investors with short-term goals like buying a house or a boat or taking a vacation would find money market mutual funds appropriate for their investment needs.

Future prospects

The future is more predictable for money market investors, because they know what they are going to get. Investors wanting some assurance about investment performance will find a money market fund suitable for their investment needs. Note that the minimum investment for this fund and Phillips, Hager & North funds is $25,000, and $5,000 for an RRSP.

FUND DETAILS

Fund name	**PH & N $US Money Market**	Start date for data shown	Dec 1990
Fund family	Phillips, Hager & North Ltd.	Fund size (in $ millions)	$76
Mutual fund classification	International money market	Percentage in foreign holdings	0.0
RRSP eligible	Yes	Dividend frequency	Monthly
		Sales charge	No
VVR peer group	International money market	Redemption charge	No
Number of mutual funds in VVR category	19	Management fee	0.50
WilStar peer group	Money market	Management expense ratio	0.52

FUND PERFORMANCE

	1 month	1 year	3 years	5 years	10 years	15 years
Returns ending Aug 1998	0.4%	5.1%	5.1%	4.7%		
Best historical return	0.6%	6.0%	5.2%	4.7%		
Average historical return	0.4%	4.4%	4.3%	4.3%		
Worst historical return	0.2%	2.6%	3.3%	4.1%		

RETURNS GREATER THAN

	1 month	1 year	3 years	5 years	10 years	15 years
10 per cent	0%	0%	0%	0%		
Zero	100%	100%	100%	100%		
Percentage of time fund lost $	0%	0%	0%	0%		
Number of periods evaluated	93	82	58	34		

DOWNSIDE RISK

	Worst setback since start date	In bear 1987	In bear 1990	In bear 1994	In bear 1998
Setback for mutual fund	n/a			n/a	n/a
Setback for peer group	n/a			n/a	n/a
Setback ended in	n/a				n/a
Months to recover from loss	?				n/a

QUARTILE RANKING OF MUTUAL FUND PERFOMANCE AFTER 12 MONTHS OVER TIME

International money market

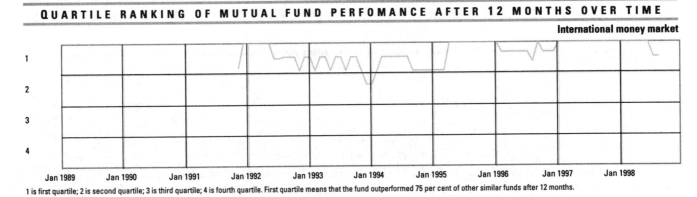

1 is first quartile; 2 is second quartile; 3 is third quartile; 4 is fourth quartile. First quartile means that the fund outperformed 75 per cent of other similar funds after 12 months.

ROLLING 12-MONTH TOTAL RATE OF RETURN FOR THE MUTUAL FUND OVER TIME

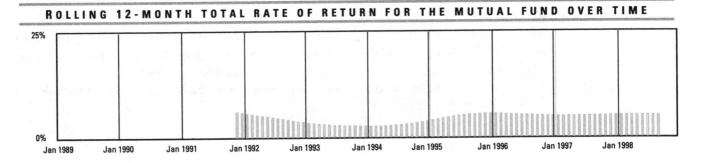

LONDON LIFE MORTGAGE FUND

Vos value rating			WilStar rating		
Reward	**Risk**	**Best balance**	**Reward**	**Risk**	**Best balance**
★★★★	★★★★★	★★★★★	★★	★★★★★	★★★★

Fund profile

The London Life Mortgage Fund is managed by Grant McIntosh of London Life Investment Management. The fund invests in mortgages of prime residential, industrial, and commercial properties located within major cities across Canada. In addition, some of the investments are made in single-family homes and apartment buildings guaranteed under the National Housing Act, administered by CHMC.

Mortgage funds are considered boring by many investors, but they are also safe, secure, and consistent. In today's low-interest-rate environment, investors do not earn or lose a lot of money in mortgage funds. Investors who are worried about current stock market conditions and dissatisfied with current yields on money market funds might consider a good mortgage fund like this one. Investors could systematically invest the earnings from their mortgage fund into a more aggressive mutual fund to increase their portfolio's returns while keeping risk low.

The fund invests in short-term cash investments and Canadian mortgages.

Fund performance

Initially, investing in mortgage funds may seem boring, but investors have earned a respectable rate of return without any of the major setbacks incurred by most equity, balanced, and bond funds. This fund has frequently been first or fourth quartile after 12 months relative to other mortgage funds during the last 10 years. However, during the last three years relative performance has improved, and the fund achieved a five-star Vos Value Rating for risk and also for best balance between risk and reward and a four-star rating for reward. This indicates that during the last year the fund has done well compared with other mortgage funds but could improve its performance. The London Life Mortgage Fund achieved a WilStar four-star rating for best balance between risk and reward. Thus, mortgage funds deliver an adequate rate of return for the given level of risk compared with other fixed-income funds.

Fund risks

Mortgage funds are less risky than bond funds and are not as susceptible to interest-rate fluctuations. This fund has posted positive rates of return after 12 months 97 per cent of the time, and the worst 12-month period for the fund was a loss of 10.9 per cent. The London Life Mortgage Fund has less downside risk than other mortgage funds. During bear markets the fund has outperformed other mortgage funds. Relative to other mortgage funds, it has fluctuated between first and fourth quartile after 12 months frequently over the last 10 years, primarily because of the small variance of absolute performance among mortgage funds.

Future prospects

Conservative investors who are worried about an increase in interest rates may find a mortgage fund a prudent investment. The London Life Mortgage Fund has had three years of good performance, and in turn scored well on the Vos Value Ratings for reward, risk, and best balance between risk and reward. However, the door is open for another mortgage fund to outperform this one in the future. Still, investors should not be disappointed with this conservative fund.

FUND DETAILS

Fund name	**London Life Mortgage**	Start date for data shown	July 1980
Fund family	London Life Insurance Compay	Fund size (in $ millions)	$467
Mutual fund classification	Mortgage	Percentage in foreign holdings	0.00
RRSP eligible	Yes	Dividend frequency	
		Sales charge	No
VVR peer group	Mortgage	Redemption charge	Deferred
Number of mutual funds in VVR category	33	Management fee	2.00
WilStar peer group	Fixed income	Management expense ratio	2.00

FUND PERFORMANCE

	1 month	1 year	3 years	5 years	10 years	15 years
Returns ending Aug 1998	−1.1%	5.1%	6.7%	6.3%	8.7%	9.9%
Best historical return	11.0%	47.2%	24.3%	20.6%	15.2%	12.9%
Average historical return	0.8%	11.5%	11.6%	11.3%	11.1%	11.5%
Worst historical return	−5.9%	−10.9%	6.3%	6.3%	8.7%	9.9%

RETURNS GREATER THAN

	1 month	1 year	3 years	5 years	10 years	15 years
10 per cent	0%	49%	58%	62%	58%	85%
Zero	85%	97%	100%	100%	100%	100%
Percentage of time fund lost $	15%	3%	0%	0%	0%	0%
Number of periods evaluated	218	207	183	159	99	39

DOWNSIDE RISK

	Worst setback since start date	In bear 1987	In bear 1990	In bear 1994	In bear 1998
Setback for mutual fund	−13.7%	−0.8%	−0.7%	−4.7%	−1.1%
Setback for peer group	−3.6%	−1.0%	−0.9%	−5.2%	−1.0%
Setback ended in	Aug 1981	May 1987	May 1990	June 1994	Aug 1998
Months to recover from loss	8	7	2	8	?

QUARTILE RANKING OF MUTUAL FUND PERFOMANCE AFTER 12 MONTHS OVER TIME

Mortgage

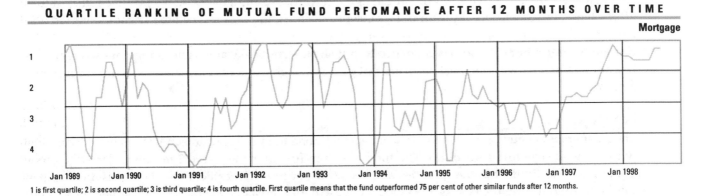

1 is first quartile; 2 is second quartile; 3 is third quartile; 4 is fourth quartile. First quartile means that the fund outperformed 75 per cent of other similar funds after 12 months.

ROLLING 12-MONTH TOTAL RATE OF RETURN FOR THE MUTUAL FUND OVER TIME

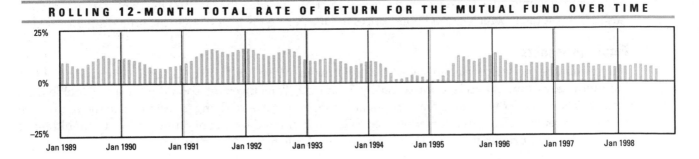

ALTAMIRA BOND FUND

Vos value rating			WilStar rating		
Reward	**Risk**	**Best balance**	**Reward**	**Risk**	**Best balance**
★★★★★	★	★★★	★★★★★	★	★★★★

Fund profile

The Altamira Bond Fund is managed by Robert Marcus of Altamira Management Ltd. The fund's investment objective is to provide investors with superior investment returns over the long term with regard to the safety of investor capital, while limiting the downside risk of the fund, by investing in Canadian government and provincial bonds.

Investors in the Altamira Bond Fund have not been disappointed! Federal government and provincial bonds provided the fund with both income and capital gains. Canadian interest rates declined, providing capital gains to bond investors. The decline in interest rates has reduced the yields on government bonds to record levels. However, bond investors should not expect double-digit returns going forward, if interest rates remain unchanged. Historically, this fund has exhibited characteristics associated with a top-performing Canadian balanced fund.

The Altamira Bond Fund invests in government bonds with a maturity in 2027 and 2029; these are called long bonds. Long bonds do not have to pay back their principal for 30 years or more. The manager takes an active role and buys and sells various bonds frequently.

Fund performance

Long-term bonds were the place to be in recent years. Interest rates and yields on bonds declined, and bond investors increased their returns. The performance of this fund over the last 10 years has been sensational. No other bond fund has produced similar returns. The fund scored a five-star Vos Value Rating for reward and a five-star WilStar Rating for reward. The fund has posted a positive rate of return after 12 months 93 per cent of the time since inception. The fund's best return for a 12-month period was a positive 28.5 per cent, and the fund has averaged a 12.8 per cent return over 12 months since inception.

The Altamira Bond Fund has managed to put short-term peaks and valleys together to create the highest mountain. Investors must be aware that going through valleys is normal in the course of climbing a mountain.

Fund risks

The Altamira Bond Fund is more risky than the average bond fund, but investors can diversify this risk away within a well structured portfolio. The fund has been first quartile after 12 months relative to other Canadian bond funds, but the fund has also been third or fourth quartile after 12 months. Investors in this bond fund during the bear of 1994 would have experienced a decline in their investment of 17.3 per cent, but they would have broken even again within 11 months after that. In 1994 the Canadian central bank raised interest rates, which caused bond prices to fall. During the bear of 1998 the fund outperformed.

Future prospects

If interest rates and yields remain stable, the performance of the fund will be equal to the current yield on long-term government bonds, approximately 5 per cent. Thus investors should not expect double-digit returns. The manager will make the appropriate changes to the underlying investments in the fund when economic events dictate. Investors who hold a Government of Canada bond until maturity should make money, since the principal and coupon payments are made by the Canadian government.

FUND DETAILS

Fund name	**Altamira Bond**	Start date for data shown	Dec 1987
Fund family	Altamira Investment Services Inc.	Fund size (in $ millions)	$427
Mutual fund classification	Canadian bond	Percentage in foreign holdings	14.60
RRSP eligible	Yes	Dividend frequency	Quarterly
		Sales charge	No
VVR peer group	Canadian bond	Redemption charge	No
Number of mutual funds in VVR category	178	Management fee	1.00
WilStar peer group	Fixed income	Management expense ratio	1.30

FUND PERFORMANCE

	1 month	1 year	3 years	5 years	10 years	15 years
Returns ending Aug 1998	−0.5%	16.6%	15.0%	11.0%	12.7%	
Best historical return	−7.5%	28.5%	19.4%	14.4%	12.7%	
Average historical return	1.0%	12.8%	12.3%	12.2%	12.5%	
Worst historical return	−6.0%	−10.3%	6.8%	9.0%	12.3%	

RETURNS GREATER THAN

	1 month	1 year	3 years	5 years	10 years	15 years
10 per cent	0%	65%	72%	90%	100%	
Zero	69%	93%	100%	100%	100%	
Percentage of time fund lost $	31%	7%	0%	0%	0%	
Number of periods evaluated	129	118	94	70	10	

DOWNSIDE RISK

	Worst setback since start date	In bear 1987	In bear 1990	In bear 1994	In bear 1998
Setback for mutual fund	−17.3%		−4.2%	−17.3%	−1.0%
Setback for peer group	−10.8%		−4.6%	−10.8%	−1.7%
Setback ended in	June 1994		April 1990	June 1994	Aug 1998
Months to recover from loss	11		2	11	?

QUARTILE RANKING OF MUTUAL FUND PERFOMANCE AFTER 12 MONTHS OVER TIME

Canadian bond

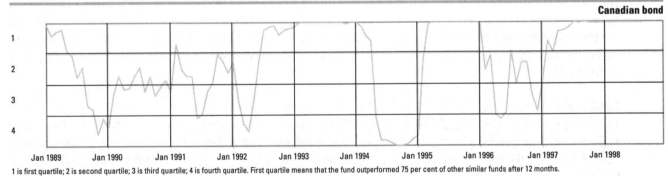

1 is first quartile; 2 is second quartile; 3 is third quartile; 4 is fourth quartile. First quartile means that the fund outperformed 75 per cent of other similar funds after 12 months.

ROLLING 12-MONTH TOTAL RATE OF RETURN FOR THE MUTUAL FUND OVER TIME

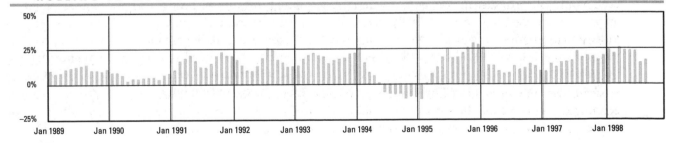

CI CANADIAN BOND FUND

Vos value rating			WilStar rating		
Reward	**Risk**	**Best balance**	**Reward**	**Risk**	**Best balance**
★★★★★	★★★★	★★★★★	★★★★★	★★★★	★★★★★

Fund profile

The CI Canadian Bond Fund is managed by John Zechner of J. Zechner and Associates. The investment objective of the fund is to invest in high-quality fixed income securities of Canadian issuers. The fund will invest in government, provincial, and corporate bonds.

Investors have been rewarded for holding bonds over the last three years as interest rates have declined and, in turn, bonds have increased in value. The yield of long-term Government of Canada bonds is currently around 5 per cent. Since these yields are at historic lows it is difficult for investors to continue to earn rates of return around 10 per cent on bonds without capital gains. In addition, a significant increase in interest rates could generate capital losses for bond funds in the short term.

In addition to long-term (federal) government and provincial bonds, the fund invests approximately 16 per cent of its portfolio in corporate bonds, including those issued by Clearnet Communications, Trizec Hahn, and Canadian Tire.

Fund performance

This fund has been able to outperform other bond funds by strategically investing in some corporate bonds. This was a prudent strategy in the past and, if credit spreads remain stable, future investors will be rewarded. The fund has outperformed the average bond fund by 2.1 per cent after 12 months since the inception of the fund. It has consistently been first quartile after 12 months over the last three years. The fund experienced some difficulty in 1994 and 1995 when interest rates increased. The fund's best 12-month period was 20.2 per cent, and the average 12-month return was 9.8 per cent. The fund has posted a positive rate of return 86 per cent of the time after 12 months. It generated a five-star Vos Value Rating for reward. Over the longer term, the fund generated a five-star WilStar Rating for reward and also for best balance between risk and reward.

Fund risks

Corporate bonds are inherently more risky than government bonds. However, corporate bonds do offer diversification, can be less volatile, and can trade like equities. The CI Canadian Bond Fund scored a four-star Vos Value Rating for risk and a five-star rating for best balance between risk and return. The worst 12-month return was a loss of 4.9 per cent. During the bear of 1998, the fund declined 1.8 per cent. Thus, this fund's real strength is performance and its secondary strength is capital preservation.

Future prospects

The fund will provide income as the federal government, provinces, and corporations make coupon payments. Interest rates are not likely to decline significantly and thus the likelihood of capital gains is minimal. Investors can benefit from the corporate bond exposure if credit spreads remain stable. Investors should expect to receive a lower rate of return than in the past. This yield will approximate the yield on government bonds, which is currently above 5 per cent. Conservative investors who require income on a regular basis could consider this fund for a portion of their bond investments.

FUND DETAILS

Fund name	**CI Canadian Bond**	Start date for data shown	Feb 1993
Fund family	CI Mutual Funds Inc.	Fund size (in $ millions)	$170
Mutual fund classification	Canadian bond	Percentage in foreign holdings	0.00
RRSP eligible	Yes	Dividend frequency	Monthly
		Sales charge	Optional
VVR peer group	Canadian bond	Redemption charge	Optional
Number of mutual funds in VVR category	178	Management fee	1.40
WilStar peer group	Fixed income	Management expense ratio	1.65

FUND PERFORMANCE

	1 month	1 year	3 years	5 years	10 years	15 years
Returns ending Aug 1998	−1.8%	5.5%	11.0%	8.4%		
Best historical return	4.2%	20.2%	14.5%	10.1%		
Average historical return	0.7%	9.8%	10.9%	9.7%		
Worst historical return	−3.4%	−4.9%	7.0%	8.4%		

RETURNS GREATER THAN

	1 month	1 year	3 years	5 years	10 years	15 years
10 per cent	0%	66%	56%	13%		
Zero	75%	86%	100%	100%		
Percentage of time fund lost $	25%	14%	0%	0%		
Number of periods evaluated	67	56	32	8		

DOWNSIDE RISK

	Worst setback since start date	In bear 1987	In bear 1990	In bear 1994	In bear 1998
Setback for mutual fund	−9.2%			−9.2%	−1.8%
Setback for peer group	−10.8%			−10.8%	−1.7%
Setback ended in	June 1994			June 1994	Aug 1998
Months to recover from loss	10			10	?

QUARTILE RANKING OF MUTUAL FUND PERFOMANCE AFTER 12 MONTHS OVER TIME

Canadian bond

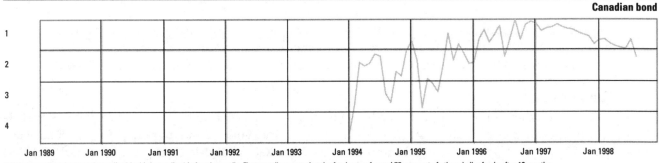

1 is first quartile; 2 is second quartile; 3 is third quartile; 4 is fourth quartile. First quartile means that the fund outperformed 75 per cent of other similar funds after 12 months.

ROLLING 12-MONTH TOTAL RATE OF RETURN FOR THE MUTUAL FUND OVER TIME

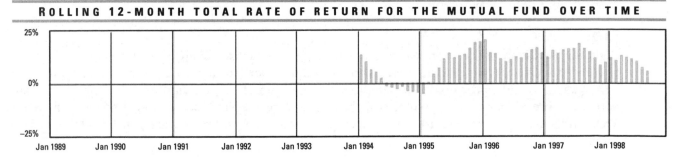

PHILLIPS, HAGER & NORTH BOND FUND

Vos value rating			WilStar rating		
Reward	**Risk**	**Best balance**	**Reward**	**Risk**	**Best balance**
★★★★★	★★★★	★★★★★	★★★★★	★★★★	★★★★★

Fund profile

The Phillips Hager & North Bond Fund is managed by Scott Lamont of Phillips Hager & North Investment Management. The investment objective of the fund is to pursue high returns through a combination of interest income and capital growth. The fund invests in high-quality fixed income government and corporate bonds.

Investors in the Phillips Hager & North Bond Fund have enjoyed consistent returns for the life of the fund, and the past 12 months have been no exception. The environment has been favourable to bond investors. The current yield on long-term Government of Canada bonds is approximately 5 per cent, and investors should not expect much higher rates of return from bonds over the long term. The Phillips Hager & North Bond Fund has an advantage over other bond funds with its rock bottom management fee. Investors seeking income with some conservative growth won't be disappointed with this fund.

The fund invests in federal, provincial, and corporate bonds including Government of Canada, Ontario provincial, and Ontario Hydro corporate bonds.

Fund performance

The fund's performance, short-term and long-term, has been magnificent! The fund scored a five-star WilStar Rating for reward and for best balance between risk and reward. The fund also achieved five-star Vos Value Ratings for reward and for best balance between risk and reward.

Thus, the PH & N Bond fund delivered an adequate rate of return given the level of risk incurred by investors, and achieved superior performance relative to other bond funds during the last three and five years. The best 12-month rate of return for the fund was 45.3 per cent, and the average rate of return after 12 months has been 13.2 per cent since the start date in May 1980. The fund has been consistently first quartile after 12 months for the last 10 years relative to other Canadian bond funds. The fund has outperformed the average Canadian bond fund 86 per cent of the time after 12 months. In addition, the fund has outperformed the average Canadian bond fund by an average of 1.6 per cent after 12 months.

Fund risks

Relative to other bond funds, this one has been first quartile consistently. Therefore, the risk that the relative performance for this fund will decline is low. The worst 12-month period for this fund was a loss of 12 per cent. The fund scored a four-star Vos Value Rating for risk. During the bear market of 1994, the fund declined by 11.2 per cent and took 10 months to recover. Investors should remember that bond funds decline in value when interest rates increase.

Future prospects

Bond funds offer income for conservative investors. If interest rates remain stable, investors could expect to earn 5 per cent to 6 per cent. Investors who are cautious about stock-market conditions could invest in bonds and invest the proceeds of the coupon payments into equity mutual funds. Investors who want bond exposure will not be disappointed with the Phillips, Hager & North Bond Fund. A bonus for investors: This fund's management fee is rock bottom, but the minimum investment is steep at $25,000, and $5,000 for an RRSP.

FUND DETAILS

Fund name	PH & N Bond	Start date for data shown	July 1980
Fund family	Phillips, Hager & North Ltd.	Fund size (in $ millions)	$2,000
Mutual fund classification	Canadian bond	Percentage in foreign holdings	0.00
RRSP eligible	Yes	Dividend frequency	Quarterly
		Sales charge	No
VVR peer group	Canadian bond	Redemption charge	No
Number of mutual funds in VVR category	178	Management fee	0.50
WilStar peer group	Fixed income	Management expense ratio	0.57

FUND PERFORMANCE

	1 month	1 year	3 years	5 years	10 years	15 years
Returns ending Aug 1998	−1.3%	5.7%	10.1%	8.4%	11.2%	12.0%
Best historical return	11.0%	45.3%	23.6%	22.4%	16.7%	14.8%
Average historical return	1.0%	13.2%	13.2%	13.0%	12.8%	13.1%
Worst historical return	−8.2%	−12.0%	6.6%	8.4%	10.6%	11.7%

RETURNS GREATER THAN

	1 month	1 year	3 years	5 years	10 years	15 years
10 per cent	1%	65%	78%	96%	100%	100%
Zero	68%	92%	100%	100%	100%	100%
Percentage of time fund lost $	32%	8%	0%	0%	0%	0%
Number of periods evaluated	218	207	183	159	99	39

DOWNSIDE RISK

	Worst setback since start date	In bear 1987	In bear 1990	In bear 1994	In bear 1998
Setback for mutual fund	−17.4%	−4.1%	−5.4%	−11.2%	−1.5%
Setback for peer group	−7.6%	−4.9%	−4.6%	−10.8%	−1.7%
Setback ended in	Sept 1981	Sept 1987	April 1990	June 1994	Aug 1998
Months to recover from loss	2	3	3	10	?

QUARTILE RANKING OF MUTUAL FUND PERFOMANCE AFTER 12 MONTHS OVER TIME

Canadian bond

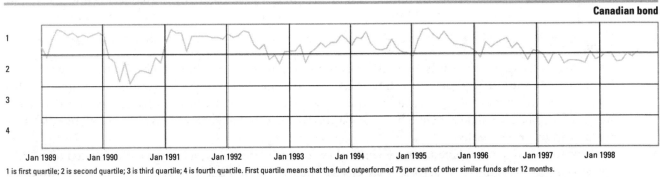

1 is first quartile; 2 is second quartile; 3 is third quartile; 4 is fourth quartile. First quartile means that the fund outperformed 75 per cent of other similar funds after 12 months.

ROLLING 12-MONTH TOTAL RATE OF RETURN FOR THE MUTUAL FUND OVER TIME

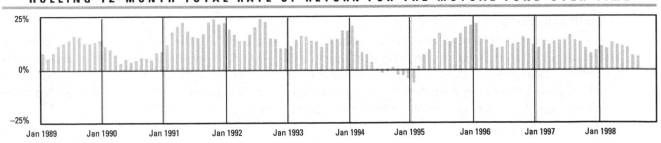

GUARDIAN FOREIGN INCOME FUND A

Vos value rating			WilStar rating		
Reward	**Risk**	**Best balance**	**Reward**	**Risk**	**Best balance**
★★★★★	★★★★	★★★★★			

Fund profile

The Guardian Foreign Income Fund is managed by Laurence Linklater of Kleinwort Guardian Overseas Ltd. The investment objective of the fund is to provide a high level of income and capital appreciation in bonds denominated in currencies other than the Canadian dollar, issued by Canadian corporations, or guaranteed by the Government of Canada.

Let the Canadian dollar fall! Investors in the Guardian Foreign Income Fund have benefitted from the decline in the Canadian dollar as their investments have increased in value. The additional benefit is that the fund is RRSP-eligible. With no signs of inflation, the likelihood of a large interest-rate increase remains slim. Thus, the outlook for bonds remains positive, although investors should have realistic expectations about performance in the future.

The fund invests in foreign-pay bonds (bonds that pay interest in a currency other than the Canadian dollar) such as Seagram short-term notes. The fund also invests in US-pay Canadian bonds.

Fund performance

Fund performance has been lifted by a decline in the Canadian dollar. The fund's performance relative to other international bond funds has also improved. The fund scored five-star Vos Value Ratings for reward and for the best balance between risk and reward. It provided an adequate level of return based on the level of risk incurred by investors. The fund has posted a positive rate of return 100 per cent of the time since its start in August 1994. The best 12-month period was a positive rate of return of 24.3 per cent, and the fund's average 12-month period was a return of 11.5 per cent. The fund has recently been first quartile after 12 months relative to other international bond funds, but it was occasionally third quartile after 12 months during 1995. The fund has a great three-year track record, and being RRSP-eligible is a really nice bonus.

Fund risks

Investing in bonds is inherently less risky than investing in equities, although investing in international bonds can be more risky than investing in a Canadian bond fund. International bond funds can also increase and decline in value because of currency fluctuations. Recently this has been a benefit to investors, but it can also become a detriment. This fund has the flexibility to hedge its currency exposure, but the hedge is not always implemented.

This fund has not displayed any downside risk currently. However, it has underperformed on a short-term basis occasionally, although this underperformance has not been severe enough to keep investors awake at night.

Future prospects

If the Canadian dollar remains stable or continues to decline the Guardian Foreign Income Fund should continue to do well. Investors holding bonds in their RRSPs should consider investing a portion of their holdings in an international bond fund. Investors have the opportunity for capital appreciation, yield pick-up, and a declining currency. In addition, international bond funds historically have added value to a portfolio by reducing the risk without sacrificing return.

FUND DETAILS

Fund name	**Guardian Foreign Income A**	Start date for data shown	Aug 1994
Fund family	Guardian Group of Funds Limited	Fund size (in $ millions)	$15
Mutual fund classification	International bond	Percentage in foreign holdings	18.81
RRSP eligible	Yes	Dividend frequency	Quarterly
		Sales charge	Yes
VVR peer group	International bond	Redemption charge	No
Number of mutual funds in VVR category	70	Management fee	1.10
WilStar peer group	Fixed income	Management expense ratio	1.68

FUND PERFORMANCE

	1 month	1 year	3 years	5 years	10 years	15 years
Returns ending Aug 1998	5.8%	24.3%	14.7%			
Best historical return	5.8%	24.3%	14.7%			
Average historical return	1.0%	11.5%	11.3%			
Worst historical return	−2.2%	3.8%	9.7%			

RETURNS GREATER THAN

	1 month	1 year	3 years	5 years	10 years	15 years
10 per cent	0%	61%	86%			
Zero	71%	100%	100%			
Percentage of time fund lost $	29%	0%	0%			
Number of periods evaluated	49	38	14			

DOWNSIDE RISK

	Worst setback since start date	In bear 1987	In bear 1990	In bear 1994	In bear 1998
Setback for mutual fund	−2.6%			−1.2%	−2.1%
Setback for peer group	−2.1%			−1.8%	−1.5%
Setback ended in	Mar 1998			Sept 1994	Mar 1998
Months to recover from loss	4			2	2

QUARTILE RANKING OF MUTUAL FUND PERFOMANCE AFTER 12 MONTHS OVER TIME

International bond

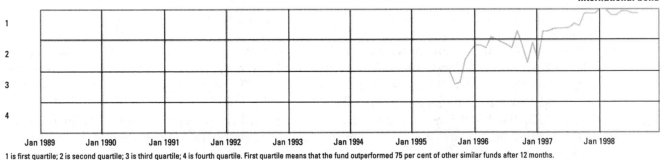

1 is first quartile; 2 is second quartile; 3 is third quartile; 4 is fourth quartile. First quartile means that the fund outperformed 75 per cent of other similar funds after 12 months.

ROLLING 12-MONTH TOTAL RATE OF RETURN FOR THE MUTUAL FUND OVER TIME

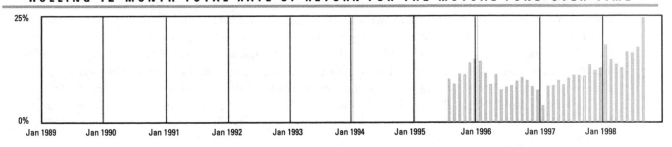

UNIVERSAL WORLD INCOME RRSP FUND (MACKENZIE)

Vos value rating			WilStar rating		
Reward	**Risk**	**Best balance**	**Reward**	**Risk**	**Best balance**
★★★★★	★★★★★	★★★★★			

Fund profile

The Mackenzie Universal World Income RRSP Fund is managed by Leslie Ferris of Mackenzie Investment Management Inc., Florida. The investment objective of the fund is to duplicate the investment returns of a diversified international bond fund while remaining 100 per cent RRSP-eligible. The fund will also invest in more risky emerging-country and corporate bonds. For tax reasons, this fund is suitable only for investors who want international bond exposure within an RRSP.

International bond markets have been favourable to investors. With a declining Canadian dollar and lower interest rates, investors have incurred capital gains on bond and currency fluctuations. Inflation has remained in check, and global growth has been sustainable. The yield on most long-term government bonds is currently 5 per cent to 6 per cent and is expected to decline.

The fund has exposure to bonds issued by Canada, France, Germany, Italy, Spain, the United Kingdom, and the United States.

Fund performance

For an international bond fund that is still RRSP-eligible, the fund's performance has been sensational. The fund scored a triple five-star Vos Value Rating for reward, risk, and best balance between risk and reward. This high triple five-star rating indicates that the fund has outperformed other international bond funds during the previous three years. The fund's best 12-month rate of return was a gain of 16.5 per cent, and its average 12-month rate of return has been 11.4 per cent since its start in October 1994. The fund has been consistently first quartile after 12 months relative to other international bond funds.

Fund risks

This fund has not displayed any downside risk. The fund's worst 12-month period was a positive rate of return of 5.1 per cent. The fund's worst one-month rate of return was a loss of 2.3 per cent, and it posted a positive rate of return after 12 months 100 per cent of the time. The worst setback was a loss of 2.7 per cent, and the fund took three months to regain the loss.

Unlike Canadian bond funds, international bonds come with currency risk. However, international bond funds can diversify across several countries. In turn, investors have the benefit of diversification and the potential for higher rates of return.

Future prospects

With management which is consistently adding value, the Mackenzie Universal World Income RRSP Fund is a natural choice for investors seeking international bond exposure. Investors seeking conservative foreign income within an RRSP should also consider an international bond fund. Investors who want to add a mutual fund to a portfolio will find international bonds an excellent choice to reduce risk while preserving returns. The fund uses derivative investments to gain exposure to international bond markets in order to remain RRSP-eligible, so investors who will be taxed on their mutual fund holdings should not invest in this fund.

FUND DETAILS

Fund name	**Universal World Income RRSP**	Start date for data shown	Oct 1994
Fund family	Mackenzie Financial Corporation	Fund size (in $ millions)	$632
Mutual fund classification	International bond	Percentage in foreign holdings	18.47
RRSP eligible	Yes	Dividend frequency	Annual
		Sales charge	Optional
VVR peer group	International bond	Redemption charge	Optional
Number of mutual funds in VVR category	70	Management fee	1.75
WilStar peer group	Fixed income	Management expense ratio	2.15

FUND PERFORMANCE

	1 month	1 year	3 years	5 years	10 years	15 years
Returns ending Aug 1998	1.4%	15.2%	11.9%			
Best historical return	4.7%	16.5%	12.2%			
Average historical return	0.9%	11.4%	11.4%			
Worst historical return	−2.3%	5.1%	10.2%			

RETURNS GREATER THAN

	1 month	1 year	3 years	5 years	10 years	15 years
10 per cent	0%	69%	100%			
Zero	74%	100%	100%			
Percentage of time fund lost $	26%	0%	0%			
Number of periods evaluated	47	36	12			

DOWNSIDE RISK

	Worst setback since start date	In bear 1987	In bear 1990	In bear 1994	In bear 1998
Setback for mutual fund	−2.7%			−1.5%	−1.2%
Setback for peer group	−2.1%				−1.5%
Setback ended in	Mar 1996				Feb 1998
Months to recover from loss	4				3

QUARTILE RANKING OF MUTUAL FUND PERFOMANCE AFTER 12 MONTHS OVER TIME

International bond

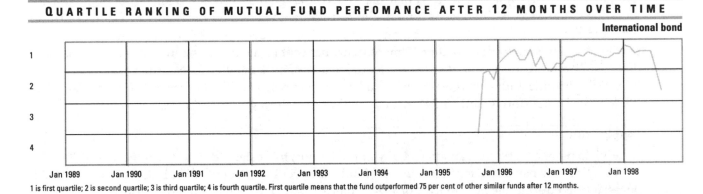

1 is first quartile; 2 is second quartile; 3 is third quartile; 4 is fourth quartile. First quartile means that the fund outperformed 75 per cent of other similar funds after 12 months.

ROLLING 12-MONTH TOTAL RATE OF RETURN FOR THE MUTUAL FUND OVER TIME

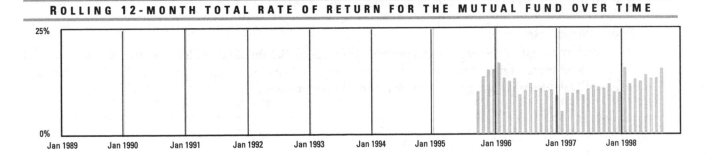

ASSET BUILDER SERIES II FUND (PRIMERICA)

Vos value rating			WilStar rating		
Reward	**Risk**	**Best balance**	**Reward**	**Risk**	**Best balance**
★★★★★	★★★★★	★★★★★			

Fund profile

The Asset Builder Series of five balanced funds is offered by Primerica Life Insurance Company of Canada. The Asset Builder funds are life cycle funds in which the asset mix changes as the fund gets older and you get closer to your retirement. Current performance of the various funds in the series has been similar, but this summary will highlight only the performance of the Series II Fund. More aggressive investors should consider the Series IV or Series V Fund, and more conservative investors should consider the Series I or Series III Fund. The Asset Builder funds have been managed by Jerry Javasky of Mackenzie Financial Corporation since July 1997. The investment objective of the fund is to achieve a high level of long-term growth while maintaining a diversified portfolio of investments to preserve capital and reduce risk. The fund will change its asset mix among stocks, bonds, and cash when economic conditions change.

Slow and steady wins the race! Investors in a balanced fund certainly have had a lot to talk about as conservative investors have recently enjoyed the upside potential of equity funds. This upside potential came to fruition because of the great bull market and an interest-rate environment that was favourable to bonds. Investors incurred a setback in performance during August 1998, but investors in the Asset Builder funds still made money year after year.

Asset Builder II has invested in Suncor Energy and Shell Canada, two of Canada's largest oil and gas companies.

Fund performance

Even with increased volatility in the capital markets, conservative investors were not disappointed when investing in the Asset Builder Series II fund. The best 12-month period for the fund was a gain of 40.5 per cent, and the average 12-month rate of return was a gain of 18.6 per cent. 1997 was a great year. The fund posted a positive rate of return after 12 months 100 per cent of the time. The fund has frequently been first quartile after 12 months, although it was fourth quartile after 12 months in 1996. The fund scored a triple five-star Vos Value Rating on reward, risk, and best balance between risk and reward. This indicates that the fund has outperformed other Canadian balanced funds during the previous three years.

Stock risks

Relative to more aggressive Canadian equity mutual funds, this balanced fund has done an excellent job of managing downside risk for investors. The fund has never lost money after a 12-month period, and it outperformed during the bear market of 1994. Unfortunately, the fund did not outperform by as large a margin during the bear market of 1998, declining in value by 11.6 per cent.

Future prospects

Conservative investors looking for income and growth potential should consider an excellent balanced fund for their retirement saving. Balanced funds are not immune to economic downturns, but they have provided a reasonable rate of return given the risk incurred by investors.

FUND DETAILS

Fund name	**Asset Builder Series II**	Start date for data shown	Feb 1994
Fund family	Primerica Life Insurance Co. of Canada	Fund size (in $ millions)	$79
Mutual fund classification	Canadian balanced	Percentage in foreign holdings	14.19
RRSP eligible	Yes	Dividend frequency	Annual
		Sales charge	No
VVR peer group	Canadian balanced	Redemption charge	Deferred
Number of mutual funds in VVR category	268	Management fee	2.10
WilStar peer group	Balanced	Management expense ratio	2.26

FUND PERFORMANCE

	1 month	1 year	3 years	5 years	10 years	15 years
Returns ending Aug 1998	−9.7%	4.7%	16.1%			
Best historical return	6.5%	40.5%	21.8%			
Average historical return	1.0%	18.6%	18.7%			
Worst historical return	−9.7%	2.1%	13.1%			

RETURNS GREATER THAN

	1 month	1 year	3 years	5 years	10 years	15 years
10 per cent	0%	80%	100%			
Zero	67%	100%	100%			
Percentage of time fund lost $	33%	0%	0%			
Number of periods evaluated	55	44	20			

DOWNSIDE RISK

	Worst setback since start date	In bear 1987	In bear 1990	In bear 1994	In bear 1998
Setback for mutual fund	−11.6%			−2.9%	−11.6%
Setback for peer group	−13.0%			−8.9%	−13.0%
Setback ended in	Aug 1998			June 1994	Aug 1998
Months to recover from loss	?			2	?

QUARTILE RANKING OF MUTUAL FUND PERFOMANCE AFTER 12 MONTHS OVER TIME

Canadian balanced

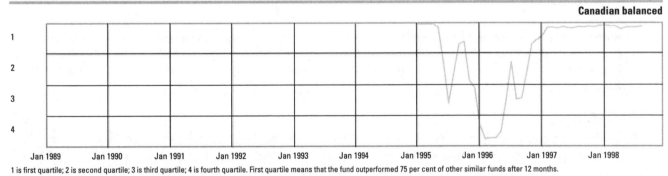

1 is first quartile; 2 is second quartile; 3 is third quartile; 4 is fourth quartile. First quartile means that the fund outperformed 75 per cent of other similar funds after 12 months.

ROLLING 12-MONTH TOTAL RATE OF RETURN FOR THE MUTUAL FUND OVER TIME

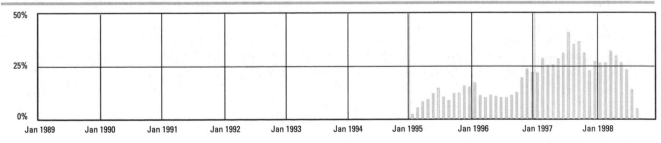

ATLAS CANADIAN BALANCED FUND

Vos value rating			WilStar rating		
Reward	**Risk**	**Best balance**	**Reward**	**Risk**	**Best balance**
★★★★★	★★★★★	★★★★★	★★★★★	★★★★★	★★★★★

Fund profile

This fund is managed by Len Racioppo of Jarislowsky Fraser and Company. This investment-management firm was formed over 40 years ago. Emphasizing risk control, the firm relies on fundamental analysis—the careful examination of a company's balance sheets to invest in high-quality stocks for the long term. The investment objective is to generate a high level of total returns through investment in fixed income and equity securities. The fund invests primarily in high-quality short- and long-term government and corporate debt obligations and high-quality stocks of Canadian companies. The fund also invests in foreign securities when it is appropriate.

Investing in a combination of investments, the fund generates a consistent, predictable rate of return over the longer term. With a decline in interest rates and an increase in corporate profits, investors in the Atlas Canadian Balanced Fund have participated in the growth of the Canadian economy.

This mutual fund holds investments in Canadian banks such as CIBC, Royal Bank, and TD, which have recently announced merger plans and are increasingly trying to expand their international presence. In addition, the fund holds investments in stable companies such as Imasco Ltd., as well as federal, provincial, and corporate bonds.

Fund performance

This fund has recently been able to reinvent itself, as Jarislowsky Fraser turned performance around from deep fourth quartile after 12 months in the early 1990s to first quartile today. The fund has improved its track record and received an outstanding triple five-star Vos Value Rating for reward, risk, and the best balance between risk and reward. In addition, the fund received a triple five-star WilStar Rating for reward, risk, and the best balance between risk and reward. The fund has managed to post positive rates of return after 12 months more than 90 per cent of the time. The best 12-month period was a positive return of 29 per cent, and the average 12-month return currently is 10.8 per cent. However, performance has not always been this rosy. The fund experienced severe underperformance relative to other balanced funds in the early 1990s.

Fund risks

Taking a balanced approach to investing usually does not fail. This mutual fund is less risky than holding 100 per cent of your investments in equity mutual funds. With this increased safety, the fund also has limited upside potential, although downside risk is also reduced. The fund's worst 12-month period was a loss of 6.5 per cent. In addition, the fund experienced a setback of 8.3 per cent during the bear market of 1998.

Future prospects

If Jarislowsky Fraser continues with the magic touch, this fund should continue to reward investors in the future. However, this fund has underperformed before, so monitor it closely.

FUND DETAILS

Fund name	**Atlas Canadian Balanced**	Start date for data shown	Sept 1989
Fund family	Atlas Asset Management Inc.	Fund size (in $ millions)	$330
Mutual fund classification	Canadian balanced	Percentage in foreign holdings	19.99%
RRSP eligible	Yes	Dividend frequency	Quarterly
		Sales charge	Optional
VVR peer group	Canadian balanced	Redemption charge	Optional
Number of mutual funds in VVR category	268	Management fee	1.00
WilStar peer group	Balanced	Management expense ratio	2.21

FUND PERFORMANCE

	1 month	1 year	3 years	5 years	10 years	15 years
Returns ending Aug 1998	−7.2%	4.8%	13.5%	10.5%		
Best historical return	5.0%	29.3%	18.2%	13.8%		
Average historical return	0.7%	10.8%	10.3%	9.9%		
Worst historical return	−7.2%	−6.5%	4.9%	5.4%		

RETURNS GREATER THAN

	1 month	1 year	3 years	5 years	10 years	15 years
10 per cent	0%	55%	44%	45%		
Zero	68%	92%	100%	100%		
Percentage of time fund lost $	32%	8%	0%	0%		
Number of periods evaluated	108	97	73	49		

DOWNSIDE RISK

	Worst setback since start date	In bear 1987	In bear 1990	In bear 1994	In bear 1998
Setback for mutual fund	−8.5%		−6.9%	−8.5%	−8.3%
Setback for peer group	−8.9%		−7.2%	−8.9%	−13.0%
Setback ended in	June 1994		Sept 1990	June 1994	Aug 1998
Months to recover from loss	9		5	9	?

QUARTILE RANKING OF MUTUAL FUND PERFOMANCE AFTER 12 MONTHS OVER TIME

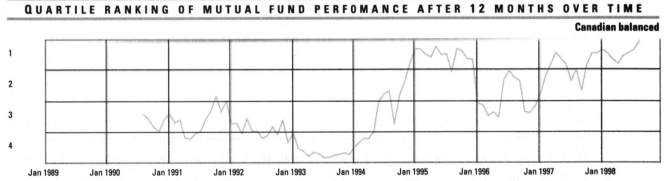

Canadian balanced

1 is first quartile; 2 is second quartile; 3 is third quartile; 4 is fourth quartile. First quartile means that the fund outperformed 75 per cent of other similar funds after 12 months.

ROLLING 12-MONTH TOTAL RATE OF RETURN FOR THE MUTUAL FUND OVER TIME

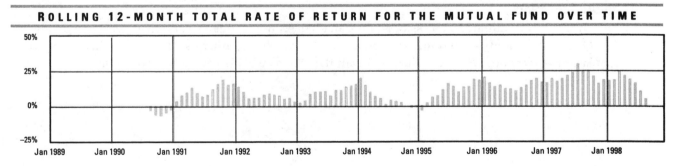

BISSETT RETIREMENT FUND

Vos value rating			WilStar rating		
Reward	Risk	Best balance	Reward	Risk	Best balance
★★★★★	★★★★★	★★★★★	★★★★★	★★★★★	★★★★★

Fund profile

The Bissett Retirement Fund is a fund of funds. It buys units of other Bissett funds to achieve its investment objective, which is to balance fixed income and equity investments to combine capital stability and income with superior returns over time.

The managers have done a great job of adjusting the mix of investments in the fund from time to time to react to economic conditions. Performance will be stable over time since the fund is well diversified, holding a variety of investments. The performance of a balanced fund like this one is not linked to any specific asset class or segment of the economy but to the performance of several asset classes in aggregate. Therefore, not all asset classes have to do well at the same time for investors to earn money. Occasionally, however, all asset classes do poorly and, in turn, balanced funds do poorly too. This scenario occurred in 1994, when many balanced funds had a difficult time breaking even.

This fund's underlying investments include Government of Canada, provincial, and corporate bonds, and stocks such as Royal Bank, Fairfax Financial, and Geac Computers.

Fund performance

This fund has consistently been first quartile after 12 months during the last three years, relative to other balanced funds. In the mid-1990s the fund was second quartile after 12 months relative to other balanced funds. The Bissett Retirement fund's best 12-month period produced a gain of 34.7 per cent, and the fund posted positive rates of return after 12 months 93 per cent of the time. The best three-year return was 21.6 per cent compounded annually, and the best five-year rate of return was 17.0 per cent compounded annually. The average three-year and five-year rates of return were 14.2 per cent and 14.7 per cent compounded annually. This fund scored a triple five-star Vos Value Rating for reward, risk, and best balance between risk and reward. The fund has outperformed other balanced funds 100 per cent of the time after three years since its start date in August 1991.

Fund risks

This fund is less risky than most balanced funds. The worst 12-month loss was 5.3 per cent, and the worst one-month loss was 9.5 per cent in August 1998. The worst setback was a loss of 12.1 per cent during the bear of 1998. Thus, balanced funds are not immune to losing money; they just lose less than more aggressive equity funds.

Future prospects

This fund is not immune to a recession in the Canadian economy, but conservative investors who dislike severe market volatility should find it more suitable than a pure equity fund. This fund will be more risky than a GIC or a money market mutual fund, but the returns will also be higher over time.

FUND DETAILS

Fund name	**Bissett Retirement**	Start date for data shown	Aug 1991
Fund family	Bissett & Associates Investment Management Ltd.	Fund size (in $ millions)	$191
Mutual fund classification	Canadian balanced	Percentage in foreign holdings	0.00
RRSP eligible	Yes	Dividend frequency	Annual
		Sales charge	No
VVR peer group	Canadian balanced	Redemption charge	No
Number of mutual funds in VVR category	268	Management fee	0.00
WilStar peer group	Balanced	Management expense ratio	0.44

FUND PERFORMANCE

	1 month	1 year	3 years	5 years	10 years	15 years
Returns ending Aug 1998	−9.5%	−0.7%	14.0%	11.1%		
Best historical return	5.9%	34.7%	21.6%	17.0%		
Average historical return	1.0%	15.2%	14.2%	14.7%		
Worst historical return	−9.5%	−5.3%	7.9%	11.1%		

RETURNS GREATER THAN

	1 month	1 year	3 years	5 years	10 years	15 years
10 per cent	0%	70%	88%	100%		
Zero	68%	93%	100%	100%		
Percentage of time fund lost $	32%	7%	0%	0%		
Number of periods evaluated	85	74	50	26		

DOWNSIDE RISK

	Worst setback since start date	In bear 1987	In bear 1990	In bear 1994	In bear 1998
Setback for mutual fund	−12.1%			−7.9%	−12.1%
Setback for peer group	−13.0%			−8.9%	−13.0%
Setback ended in	Aug 1998			June 1994	Aug 1998
Months to recover from loss	?			10	?

QUARTILE RANKING OF MUTUAL FUND PERFOMANCE AFTER 12 MONTHS OVER TIME

Canadian balanced

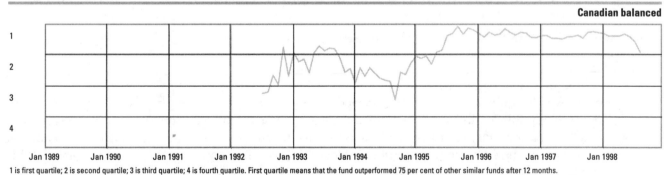

1 is first quartile; 2 is second quartile; 3 is third quartile; 4 is fourth quartile. First quartile means that the fund outperformed 75 per cent of other similar funds after 12 months.

ROLLING 12-MONTH TOTAL RATE OF RETURN FOR THE MUTUAL FUND OVER TIME

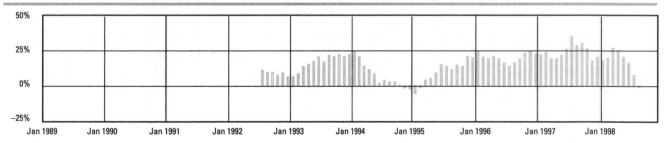

FIDELITY CANADIAN ASSET ALLOCATION FUND

Vos value rating			WilStar rating		
Reward	**Risk**	**Best balance**	**Reward**	**Risk**	**Best balance**
★★★★★	★★★	★★★★★			

Fund profile

The Fidelity Canadian Asset Allocation Fund is managed by the team of Dick Habermann, Alan Radlo, and Ford O'Neil. The investment objective of the fund is to achieve high rates of return for investors by allocating funds among Canadian stocks, bonds, and cash.

Investors have benefitted from the strategic asset mix decisions in this fund over the last three years. In these volatile market conditions, the Fidelity Canadian Asset Allocation Fund seemed to do all things right. The managers of the fund consider a broad range of variables in selecting and changing the asset mix of the fund. The individual securities are selected by researching each company thoroughly. Investors looking for growth with less volatility will benefit from the conservative nature of balanced funds. However, balanced funds are not immune to economic conditions, and favourable economic conditions must persist for balanced funds to continue posting double-digit returns.

The Fidelity Canadian Asset Allocation Fund has made investments in such companies as Power Corporation of Canada and Great West Life Insurance Company, and in utility companies such as Teleglobe and BCE.

Fund performance

This fund shows outstanding performance. The risk in this fund is a little higher than in other balanced funds, in the short term, but investors are rewarded through higher returns. The fund has consistently been first quartile after 12 months since its inception in January 1995. The best 12-month period for the fund was a positive return of 41.6 per cent, and the average 12-month period was 23.7 per cent. The fund scored a five-star Vos Value Rating for reward. In addition, the fund scored a five-star Vos Value Rating for best balance between risk and reward. This rating indicates that the fund achieved a superior return given the level of risk incurred by the fund.

Fund risks

This fund may take wide swings in its asset mix. When the managers of a fund can either over-weight or under-weight equities in the fund, performance can vary widely, which can be good or bad for investors, who are susceptible to more downside risk if the managers make an inappropriate asset-mix decision.

The fund scored a three-star Vos Value Rating for risk, because relative to other Canadian balanced funds this one has displayed more short-term risk. However, over the long term, the fund has managed this risk well. Its worst 12-month rate of return was a gain of 3.6 per cent.

Future prospects

Adding value over the long term is what Fidelity does best. This fund is not immune to unfavourable economic conditions such as a global recession. However, over the long term, conservative investors looking for income and growth are likely not going to be disappointed by the Fidelity Canadian Asset Allocation Fund.

FUND DETAILS

Fund name	**Fidelity Canadian Asset Allocation**	Start date for data shown	Jan 1995
Fund family	Fidelity Investments Canada Limited	Fund size (in $ millions)	$2,997
Mutual fund classification	Canadian balanced	Percentage in foreign holdings	13.52
RRSP eligible	Yes	Dividend frequency	Quarterly
		Sales charge	Optional
VVR peer group	Canadian balanced	Redemption charge	Optional
Number of mutual funds in VVR category	268	Management fee	2.00
WilStar peer group	Balanced	Management expense ratio	2.48

FUND PERFORMANCE

	1 month	1 year	3 years	5 years	10 years	15 years
Returns ending Aug 1998	–9.8%	3.6%	16.7%			
Best historical return	6.3%	41.6%	23.9%			
Average historical return	1.4%	22.7%	22.1%			
Worst historical return	–9.8%	3.6%	16.7%			

RETURNS GREATER THAN

	1 month	1 year	3 years	5 years	10 years	15 years
10 per cent	0%	97%	100%			
Zero	68%	100%	100%			
Percentage of time fund lost $	32%	0%	0%			
Number of periods evaluated	44	33	9			

DOWNSIDE RISK

	Worst setback since start date	In bear 1987	In bear 1990	In bear 1994	In bear 1998
Setback for mutual fund	–11.8%			–1.1%	–11.8%
Setback for peer group	–13.0%			–1.5%	–13.0%
Setback ended in	Aug 1998			Jan 1995	Aug 1998
Months to recover from loss	?			1	?

QUARTILE RANKING OF MUTUAL FUND PERFOMANCE AFTER 12 MONTHS OVER TIME

Canadian balanced

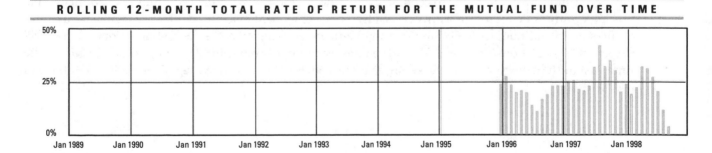

1 is first quartile; 2 is second quartile; 3 is third quartile; 4 is fourth quartile. First quartile means that the fund outperformed 75 per cent of other similar funds after 12 months.

ROLLING 12-MONTH TOTAL RATE OF RETURN FOR THE MUTUAL FUND OVER TIME

GLOBAL STRATEGY INCOME PLUS FUND

Vos value rating			WilStar rating		
Reward	Risk	Best balance	Reward	Risk	Best balance
★★★★★	★★★★	★★★★★	★★★★★	★★★★	★★★★★

Fund profile

The Global Strategy Income Plus Fund is managed by Tony Massie of Global Strategy Financial Inc. The fund aims for high returns from a diversified portfolio of secure income-producing investments including stocks, bonds, and cash. The manager uses a conservative bottom-up approach, investing in companies with solid balance sheets and growth potential.

Conservative investors seeking long-term growth and income have not been disappointed by the performance of this fund. It provides an excellent balance between growth and income with superior downside protection and upside potential. The fund is not immune to a slowdown in the Canadian economy, and the stocks of Canadian corporations will have to continue to appreciate for investors to continue to earn double-digit returns.

The fund has made strategic investments in major Canadian chartered banks such as CIBC, Bank of Nova Scotia, Royal Bank, and TD Bank. In addition, the fund has invested in Noranda and Shell Canada.

Fund performance

This fund has improved its performance and earned five-star Vos Value Ratings for reward and for best balance between risk and reward. Over the longer term the fund earned five-star WilStar Ratings based on reward and on best balance between risk and reward. The fund's best 12-month period was a return of 32.8 per cent, and the fund's average 12-month return was 16.1 per cent since the start date in May 1992. The fund has recently been consistently first quartile after 12 months. However, in the mid 1990s, the fund was third to fourth quartile after 12 months. The fund adds value for investors during bull markets and remains at par during bear markets.

Fund risks

Over the longer term, investors should expect short periods of underperformance. The fund has done an exceptional job of managing the downside risk; the worst 12-month rate of return was a loss of 4.9 per cent. The fund posted a positive rate of return after 12 months 91 per cent of the time. It scored a four-star WilStar risk rating, indicating that this balanced fund is slightly more risky than other conservative balanced funds. During the bear of 1998 the fund declined by 14 per cent, and during the bear of 1994 it declined by 8.4 per cent and took 11 months to regain its losses.

Future prospects

Balanced funds are not immune to economic downturns. During 1994, balanced funds had a difficult time posting positive rates of return. However, with a bond component in the fund, investors will have a source of income. In addition, with a bottom-up and value investment style, the fund should continue to meet investors' expectations. Investors should remember top-performing funds are not first quartile all the time, just most of the time. Find a good investment—such as the Global Strategy Income Plus Fund—and stay with it.

FUND DETAILS

Fund name	**Global Strategy Income Plus**	Start date for data shown	May 1992
Fund family	Global Strategy Financial Inc.	Fund size (in $ millions)	$1,974
Mutual fund classification	Canadian balanced	Percentage in foreign holdings	0.00%
RRSP eligible	Yes	Dividend frequency	Quarterly
		Sales charge	Optional
VVR peer group	Canadian balanced	Redemption charge	Optional
Number of mutual funds in VVR category	268	Management fee	1.75
WilStar peer group	Balanced	Management expense ratio	2.40

FUND PERFORMANCE

	1 month	1 year	3 years	5 years	10 years	15 years
Returns ending Aug 1998	−10.1%	−1.2%	14.0%	11.0%		
Best historical return	6.1%	32.8%	22.1%	16.9%		
Average historical return	1.0%	16.1%	14.5%	15.4%		
Worst historical return	−10.1%	−4.9%	9.8%	11.0%		

RETURNS GREATER THAN

	1 month	1 year	3 years	5 years	10 years	15 years
10 per cent	0%	74%	95%	100%		
Zero	70%	91%	100%	100%		
Percentage of time fund lost $	30%	9%	0%	0%		
Number of periods evaluated	76	65	41	17		

DOWNSIDE RISK

	Worst setback since start date	In bear 1987	In bear 1990	In bear 1994	In bear 1998
Setback for mutual fund	−14.0%			−8.4%	−14.0%
Setback for peer group	−13.0%			−8.9%	−13.0%
Setback ended in	Aug 1998			June 1994	Aug 1998
Months to recover from loss	?			11	?

QUARTILE RANKING OF MUTUAL FUND PERFOMANCE AFTER 12 MONTHS OVER TIME

Canadian balanced

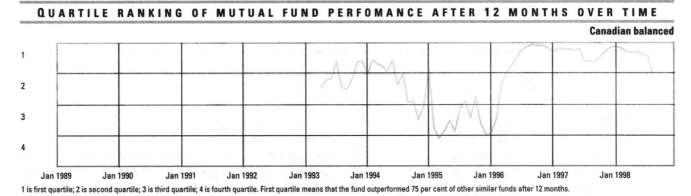

1 is first quartile; 2 is second quartile; 3 is third quartile; 4 is fourth quartile. First quartile means that the fund outperformed 75 per cent of other similar funds after 12 months.

ROLLING 12-MONTH TOTAL RATE OF RETURN FOR THE MUTUAL FUND OVER TIME

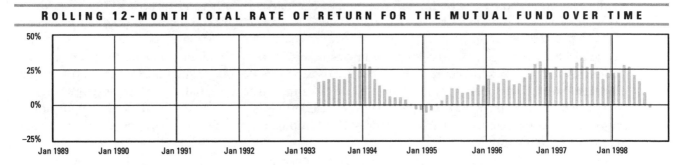

IVY GROWTH AND INCOME FUND (MACKENZIE)

Vos value rating			WilStar rating		
Reward	**Risk**	**Best balance**	**Reward**	**Risk**	**Best balance**
★★★★★	★★★★★	★★★★★	★★★★★	★★★★★	★★★★★

Fund profile

The Mackenzie Ivy Growth and Income Fund has been managed by Jerry Javasky of Mackenzie Financial Corporation since July 1997, when Gerald Coleman left to start the Harbour Funds at CI Mutual Funds. The investment objective of the fund is to provide the potential for capital appreciation in conjunction with a prudent fixed-income strategy. The fund will change its asset mix of stocks, bonds, and cash when economic conditions change.

Slow and steady wins the race! Investors in a balanced fund certainly have had a lot to talk about, as conservative investors have enjoyed the upside potential of equity funds recently. This upside potential came to fruition because of the great bull market and an interest rate environment that was favourable to bonds. Investors should have realistic expectations about the future performance of balanced funds. Balanced funds provide a conservative level of income and capital appreciation. Average returns of 10 per cent seem more realistic than 20 per cent.

This fund's asset mix is approximately 50 per cent bonds and 50 per cent equities. The fund owns shares in Viceroy Homes, a North American leader in the the design, manufacture, and distribution of high quality pre-engineered custom homes.

Fund performance

This fund's investment performance has been superior. The fund has frequently been first quartile after 12 months, and outperformed the average balanced fund after 12 months 79 per cent of the time since its start date in November 1992. The fund scored a triple five-star Vos Value Rating for reward, risk, and best balance between risk and reward. In addition, the fund scored a triple five-star WilStar rating for reward, risk, and best balance between risk and reward. This is an indication that the fund did extremely well compared with other balanced funds during the last three and five years. The best 12-month rate of return was a positive 27.9 per cent (comparable with Ivy Canadian Fund), and the average rate of return was 13.7 per cent.

Fund risks

Balanced funds are inherently less risky than equity funds and provide an excellent alternative to low GIC rates. However, unlike GICs, balanced funds are not guaranteed and may decline in value over the short term. The worst 12-month rate of return for this fund was a loss of 1.6 per cent, and the worst one-month loss was 7.5 per cent in August 1998. The fund has earned a positive rate of return after 12 months 92 per cent of the time and has outperformed during the bear markets of 1994 and 1998.

Future prospects

Balanced funds are conservative, long-term investments for people looking for stability, income, and the potential for capital appreciation. Balanced funds are more volatile than bond funds but offer higher rates of return. Going forward, investors should have realistic expectations about performance. If stock markets do correct, the benefit of investing in balanced funds is that managers will use the opportunity to purchase shares in companies at lower prices. In addition, investors will still earn income from the bond component in the fund.

FUND DETAILS

Fund name	**Ivy Growth and Income**	Start date for data shown	Nov 1992
Fund family	Mackenzie Financial Corporation	Fund size (in $ millions)	$2,410
Mutual fund classification	Canadian balanced	Percentage in foreign holdings	7.16
RRSP eligible	Yes	Dividend frequency	Annual
		Sales charge	Optional
VVR peer group	Canadian balanced	Redemption charge	Optional
Number of mutual funds in VVR category	268	Management fee	1.75
WilStar peer group	Balanced	Management expense ratio	2.12

FUND PERFORMANCE

	1 month	1 year	3 years	5 years	10 years	15 years
Returns ending Aug 1998	−7.5%	4.6%	15.5%	11.5%		
Best historical return	5.2%	27.9%	20.4%	14.4%		
Average historical return	0.9%	13.7%	14.8%	13.3%		
Worst historical return	−7.5%	−1.6%	6.8%	11.5%		

RETURNS GREATER THAN

	1 month	1 year	3 years	5 years	10 years	15 years
10 per cent	0%	66%	80%	100%		
Zero	73%	92%	100%	100%		
Percentage of time fund lost $	27%	8%	0%	0%		
Number of periods evaluated	70	59	35	11		

DOWNSIDE RISK

	Worst setback since start date	In bear 1987	In bear 1990	In bear 1994	In bear 1998
Setback for mutual fund	−9.2%			−5.4%	−9.2%
Setback for peer group	−13.0%			−8.9%	−13.0%
Setback ended in	Aug 1998			June 1994	Aug 1998
Months to recover from loss	?			8	?

QUARTILE RANKING OF MUTUAL FUND PERFOMANCE AFTER 12 MONTHS OVER TIME

Canadian balanced

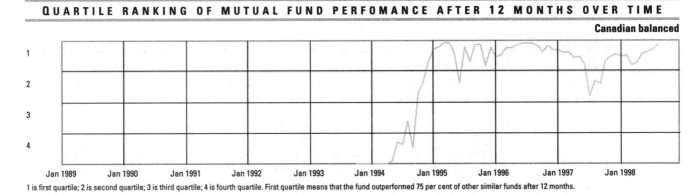

1 is first quartile; 2 is second quartile; 3 is third quartile; 4 is fourth quartile. First quartile means that the fund outperformed 75 per cent of other similar funds after 12 months.

ROLLING 12-MONTH TOTAL RATE OF RETURN FOR THE MUTUAL FUND OVER TIME

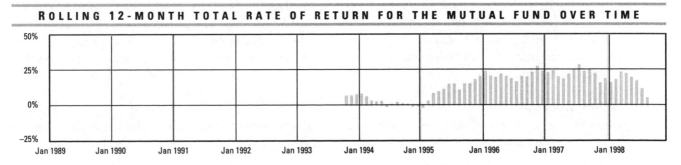

AGF AMERICAN TACTICAL ASSET ALLOCATION FUND

Vos value rating			WilStar rating		
Reward	**Risk**	**Best balance**	**Reward**	**Risk**	**Best balance**
★★★★★	★★★★	★★★★★	★★★★★	★★★★	★★★★★

Fund profile

The AGF American Tactical Allocation Fund has been managed by Kathy Taylor of Barclays Global Investors since June 1996. The fund invests in a combination of shares from the Standard and Poors (S&P) 500 index, using the firm's qualitative model. In addition, the fund invests in long-term and US Treasury bonds. Therefore, this fund aims to add value by reducing risk and providing income and growth potential. The fund has made investments in such large US companies as General Electric, Microsoft, Coca Cola, Exxon, and Merck & Company.

Many mutual funds aim to add value for their investors by selecting excellent investments that will appreciate over the long term. This fund also adds value by selecting the appropriate mix of "asset classes" considering the current economic environment. Investors who want to participate in the growth of the US stock market with less risk will find this fund suitable for their investment needs. However, because the fund focusses only on US stocks, it will not have the same degree of geographic diversification as other international balanced funds, which invest in other countries outside the United States. If the manager does a good job of continuing to make prudent asset class decisions, investors should not experience any adverse downside risk.

Fund performance

The fund has delivered an excellent rate of return given the level of risk incurred. In turn, the fund scored five-star Vos Value Ratings for reward and for best balance between risk and reward. The fund also scored five- star WilSTar Ratings for reward and for best balance between risk and reward. The best 12-month rate of return for the fund was 36.6 per cent and the average 12-month rate of return for the fund was 13.9 per cent. The fund posted a positive rate of return after 12 months 97 per cent of the time since its start date in November 1988. The fund has frequently been first quartile after 12 months relative to other international balanced funds, but it has also ranked in the third or fourth quartile.

Fund risks

The fund did not achieve top marks reducing the risk associated with investing in international balanced funds. However, investors did not experience large setbacks, so conservative investors should still be able to sleep well at night. During the bear of 1998 the fund declined by 6.2 per cent less than the average. In 1994 the fund declined by 7.3 per cent more than the average, but it took only four months to recover the loss. The worst 12-month rate of return was a loss of 5.1 per cent, and the fund posted negative rates of return after 12 months 3 per cent of the time. The fund's worst one-month loss was a decline of 6.2 per cent incurred in August 1998. Investors must be aware that this fund does experience occasional periods of underperformance.

Future prospects

Conservative investors who want exposure to the US economy and to achieve stable growth over the long term could consider this fund for a portion of their mutual fund portfolios.

FUND DETAILS

Fund name	**AGF American Tactical Asset Allocation**	Start date for data shown	Nov 1988
Fund family	AGF Funds Inc.	Fund size (in $ millions)	$423
Mutual fund classification	International balanced	Percentage in foreign holdings	0.00
RRSP eligible	Foreign	Dividend frequency	Annual
		Sales charge	Optional
VVR peer group	International balanced	Redemption charge	Optional
Number of mutual funds in VVR category	66	Management fee	2.00
WilStar peer group	Balanced	Management expense ratio	2.56

FUND PERFORMANCE

	1 month	1 year	3 years	5 years	10 years	15 years
Returns ending Aug 1998	−6.2%	24.3%	18.5%	13.5%		
Best historical return	9.4%	36.6%	20.7%	16.5%		
Average historical return	1.0%	13.9%	13.6%	13.4%		
Worst historical return	−6.2%	−5.1%	5.7%	9.9%		

RETURNS GREATER THAN

	1 month	1 year	3 years	5 years	10 years	15 years
10 per cent	0%	64%	81%	98%		
Zero	70%	97%	100%	100%		
Percentage of time fund lost $	30%	3%	0%	0%		
Number of periods evaluated	118	107	83	59		

DOWNSIDE RISK

	Worst setback since start date	In bear 1987	In bear 1990	In bear 1994	In bear 1998
Setback for mutual fund	−7.3%		−2.9%	−7.3%	−6.2%
Setback for peer group	−3.8%		−8.2%	−5.5%	−8.2%
Setback ended in	Sept 1994		Sept 1990	Sept 1994	Aug 1998
Months to recover from loss	4		2	4	?

QUARTILE RANKING OF MUTUAL FUND PERFOMANCE AFTER 12 MONTHS OVER TIME

International balanced

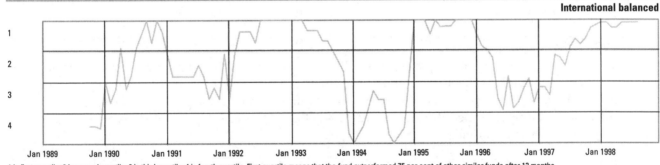

1 is first quartile; 2 is second quartile; 3 is third quartile; 4 is fourth quartile. First quartile means that the fund outperformed 75 per cent of other similar funds after 12 months.

ROLLING 12-MONTH TOTAL RATE OF RETURN FOR THE MUTUAL FUND OVER TIME

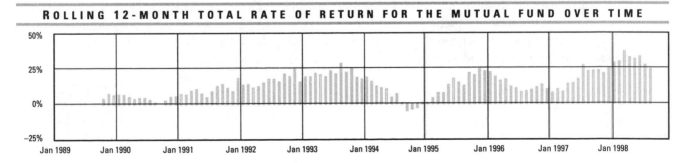

AIM GT GLOBAL GROWTH AND INCOME FUND

Vos value rating			WilStar rating		
Reward	**Risk**	**Best balance**	**Reward**	**Risk**	**Best balance**
★★★★★	★★★★★	★★★★★			

Fund profile

The AIM GT Global Growth and Income Fund is managed by Nicholas Train of LGT Asset Management, a division of AMVESCAP PLC, the parent company of AIM GT. The investment objective of this fund is to obtain long-term capital appreciation in conjunction with a current level of income. The investment objective of the fund is accomplished by employing a conservative investing strategy. Thus, the fund invests in blue-chip equity securities and high-quality government bonds of issuers throughout the world.

Investors in the AIM GT Global Growth and Income Fund were not disappointed during the last year. The Canadian dollar declined and international stock and bond markets appreciated, increasing the value of the fund. Investors holding international investments benefitted from a decline in the Canadian dollar. Most of their investments increased in value because of the change in the exchange rate.

The AIM GT Global Growth and Income Fund invests in a combination of assets, holding cash, bonds, and stocks to reduce volatility. The fund made investments in such companies as Union Bank Switzerland, Royal Dutch Petroleum, and EMI Group. In addition, the fund held bonds and treasury notes issued by the United Kingdom, the United States, and Germany.

Fund performance

The fund was first quartile for the last 12 months and has done reasonably well during the last three years. However, the fund has left the door open for other international balanced funds to outperform in the future. Its recent excellent performance has catapulted the fund into new territory. The AIM GT Global Growth and Income fund scored a triple five-star rating based on the Vos Value Rating for reward, risk, and best balance between risk and reward. On the upside, the best 12-month period for the fund was a 26.6 per cent increase, and the fund's average 12-month return was 15.6 per cent.

Fund risks

The fund has struggled in the past and could struggle again, but its long-term performance has been excellent. The fund has been third and fourth quartile after 12 months relative to other international balanced funds and has posted positive rates of return after 12 months 100 per cent of the time. In addition, the fund had outperformed during the bear market of 1998, declining in value less than the average international balanced fund.

Future prospects

The fund has a proven ability to under- and outperform other international balanced funds. Going forward, the fund is not immune to a global recession, and investors could experience new levels of downside risk. Conservative investors who seek income with some upside potential will be ideally served by an international balanced fund such as the AIM GT Global Growth and Income Fund.

FUND DETAILS

Fund name	**AIM GT: Global Growth and Income**	Start date for data shown	Nov 1994
Fund family	AIM GT Investment Management Inc.	Fund size (in $ millions)	$54
Mutual fund classification	International balanced	Percentage in foreign holdings	86.78
RRSP eligible	Foreign	Dividend frequency	Quarterly
		Sales charge	Optional
VVR peer group	International balanced	Redemption charge	Optional
Number of mutual funds in VVR category	66	Management fee	2.25
WilStar peer group	Balanced	Management expense ratio	2.87

FUND PERFORMANCE

	1 month	1 year	3 years	5 years	10 years	15 years
Returns ending Aug 1998	–3.5%	26.4%	18.0%			
Best historical return	5.2%	26.6%	18.2%			
Average historical return	1.1%	15.6%	15.4%			
Worst historical return	–3.5%	6.1%	11.7%			

RETURNS GREATER THAN

	1 month	1 year	3 years	5 years	10 years	15 years
10 per cent	0%	89%	100%			
Zero	76%	100%	100%			
Percentage of time fund lost $	24%	0%	0%			
Number of periods evaluated	46	35	11			

DOWNSIDE RISK

	Worst setback since start date	In bear 1987	In bear 1990	In bear 1994	In bear 1998
Setback for mutual fund	–3.5%			–0.4%	–3.5%
Setback for peer group	–8.2%			–1.8%	–8.2%
Setback ended in	Aug 1998			Dec 1994	Aug 1998
Months to recover from loss	?			3	?

QUARTILE RANKING OF MUTUAL FUND PERFOMANCE AFTER 12 MONTHS OVER TIME

International balanced

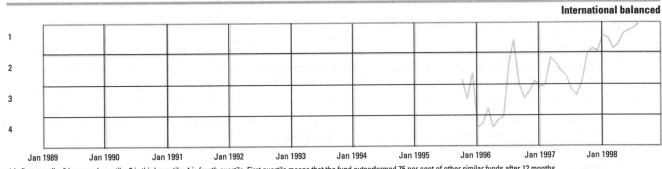

1 is first quartile; 2 is second quartile; 3 is third quartile; 4 is fourth quartile. First quartile means that the fund outperformed 75 per cent of other similar funds after 12 months.

ROLLING 12-MONTH TOTAL RATE OF RETURN FOR THE MUTUAL FUND OVER TIME

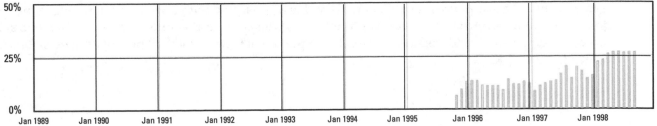

CI INTERNATIONAL BALANCED FUND

Vos value rating			WilStar rating		
Reward	**Risk**	**Best balance**	**Reward**	**Risk**	**Best balance**
★★★★★	★★★★★	★★★★★			

Fund profile

The CI International Balanced Fund is managed by William Sterling of BEA and Associates. Its investment objective is to obtain the maximum total return by investing in any combination of equity and debt securities. The manager will adjust the asset mix when economic conditions change. The fund appeals to investors seeking global exposure in their investments while reducing risk through diversification.

Investors have benefitted from the strength in international stock markets and a decline in the Canadian dollar. Investors have also benefitted from a decline in interest rates and the higher yields attainable on international bonds. The CI International Balanced Fund still invests approximately 50 per cent of its assets in equities, and a severe setback in stock markets could send the fund lower. However, the bond component of the fund reduces its volatility and provides income for investors.

The fund has made investments in companies like Home Depot, Wal-Mart Stores, Microsoft, and Hershey Foods. The fund also invests in foreign debt from countries like Germany, the United Kingdom, and Sweden.

Fund performance

The fund has been first quartile frequently during the last three years, but it has occasionally taken investors for a short wild ride. The fund scored a triple five-star Vos Value Rating for reward, risk, and the best balance between risk and reward. However, the fund left room for improvement. Its best 12-month period was a positive rate of return of 25.6 per cent and the average 12-month return was 16.6 per cent. The fund has outperformed other international balanced funds after 12 months 91 per cent of the time since its start date in November 1994.

Fund risks

This fund is not immune to an international recession or fluctuations in interest rates or currencies. However, the fund has done a good job of preserving capital. Its worst 12-month rate of return was a positive 9.6 per cent. The fund has exposure to several different asset classes to reduce the volatility of investment performance.

The worst setback the fund incurred was a decline of 5.4 per cent during the bear of 1998. The fund's major risk is underperforming other international funds.

Future prospects

Going forward, the fund will exhibit a very different risk-reward profile. However, with a combination of stock, bond, and cash investments the fund should have lower volatility than other funds while providing some income. The CI International Balanced fund is a good fund with low risk, but there is room for improvement in performance. Conservative investors who are investing outside an RRSP but who still need regular income could consider this fund for a portion of their investment portfolios or even foreign content in their RRSPs.

FUND DETAILS

Fund name	**CI International Balanced**	Start date for data shown	Nov 1994
Fund family	CI Mutual Funds Inc.	Fund size (in $ millions)	$175
Mutual fund classification	International balanced	Percentage in foreign holdings	75.60
RRSP eligible	Foreign	Dividend frequency	Annual
		Sales charge	Optional
VVR peer group	International balanced	Redemption charge	Optional
Number of mutual funds in VVR category	66	Management fee	2.00
WilStar peer group	Balanced	Management expense ratio	2.41

FUND PERFORMANCE

	1 month	1 year	3 years	5 years	10 years	15 years
Returns ending Aug 1998	−5.4%	13.0%	15.5%			
Best historical return	4.8%	25.6%	17.6%			
Average historical return	1.2%	16.5%	16.4%			
Worst historical return	−5.4%	9.6%	14.4%			

RETURNS GREATER THAN

	1 month	1 year	3 years	5 years	10 years	15 years
10 per cent	0%	97%	100%			
Zero	80%	100%	100%			
Percentage of time fund lost $	20%	0%	0%			
Number of periods evaluated	46	35	11			

DOWNSIDE RISK

	Worst setback since start date	In bear 1987	In bear 1990	In bear 1994	In bear 1998
Setback for mutual fund	−5.4%				−5.4%
Setback for peer group	−8.2%				−8.2%
Setback ended in	Aug 1998				Aug 1998
Months to recover from loss	?				?

QUARTILE RANKING OF MUTUAL FUND PERFOMANCE AFTER 12 MONTHS OVER TIME

International balanced

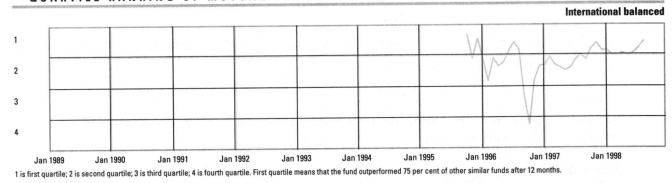

1 is first quartile; 2 is second quartile; 3 is third quartile; 4 is fourth quartile. First quartile means that the fund outperformed 75 per cent of other similar funds after 12 months.

ROLLING 12-MONTH TOTAL RATE OF RETURN FOR THE MUTUAL FUND OVER TIME

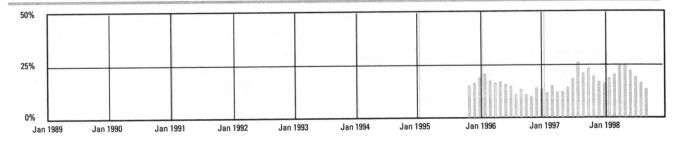

BISSETT DIVIDEND INCOME FUND

Vos value rating			WilStar rating		
Reward	**Risk**	**Best balance**	**Reward**	**Risk**	**Best balance**
★★★★★	★★★★★	★★★★★	★★★★★	★★★★★	★★★★★

Fund profile

This fund is managed by Fred Pynn of Bissett and Associates Investment Management. The fund's investment objective is to achieve a consistent after-tax return through investments in dividend-paying Canadian stocks. The fund will invest in a diversified portfolio of Canadian and US corporations that issue preferred shares. The fund will also invest in debt securities on occasion to reduce volatility.

If it's cool to invest, then dividend mutual funds must be the coolest place to be. Dividend funds appreciated in value after a decline in interest rates and increased corporate profits. In addition, many dividend funds were loaded with bank and utility stocks, which have led the bull market.

The Bissett Dividend Income Fund has made investments in companies like BCE Inc., the parent company of Bell Canada, one of Canada's largest publicly traded companies. In addition, the fund has made investments in banks such as Bank of Montreal, Laurentian Bank, National Bank, and CIBC.

Fund performance

Investors have enjoyed this ride. During the last three years this fund went up and didn't come down. The Bissett Dividend Income fund has frequently been first quartile after 12 months relative to other dividend funds, although it has slipped recently. The fund scored a triple five-star WilStar Rating for reward, risk, and the best balance between risk and reward, and a triple five-star Vos Value Rating for reward, risk, and the best balance between risk and reward.

On the upside, the fund had a gain of 39 per cent after 12 months and posted positive rates of return after 12 months 90 per cent of the time. The fund has underperformed other Canadian dividend funds after 12 months prior to 1995. (Investors should note that this fund has been RRSP-eligible only recently; this explains some of the underperformance prior to 1995.)

Fund risks

This fund is slightly more risky than a balanced fund, but less risky than a pure Canadian equity fund. The fund's worst 12-month return was a loss of 12.2 per cent, and the worst monthly loss was 11.0 per cent in August 1998. During the bear of 1998, the fund declined by 14.5 per cent, while the average dividend fund declined by 15 per cent. During the bear markets of 1990 and 1994, the fund declined by 12.8 per cent and 7.9 per cent respectively.

Future prospects

Dividend funds do provide a safe, secure alternative to balanced funds, but they are not immune to an economic downturn or recession. If interest rates, the Canadian dollar, and Canadian economic growth continue to remain stable, the fund should provide a return greater than GICs do. However, investors should note that this is not guaranteed. Investors could also consider the BPI Dividend fund as a more conservative dividend fund; Phillips, Hager & North Dividend Income fund is more aggressive. The Bissett Dividend Income Fund is a excellent balance, lying between the two.

FUND DETAILS

Fund name	**Bissett Dividend Income**	Start date for data shown	June 1988
Fund family	Bissett & Associates Investment Management Ltd.	Fund size (in $ millions)	$44
Mutual fund classification	Canadian dividend	Percentage in foreign holdings	8.89
RRSP eligible	Yes	Dividend frequency	Quarterly
		Sales charge	No
VVR peer group	Canadian dividend	Redemption charge	No
Number of mutual funds in VVR category	73	Management fee	1.00
WilStar peer group	Domestic equity	Management expense ratio	1.50

FUND PERFORMANCE

	1 month	1 year	3 years	5 years	10 years	15 years
Returns ending Aug 1998	–11.0%	–1.5%	16.6%	13.4%	10.3%	
Best historical return	6.4%	39.0%	25.7%	19.1%	12.0%	
Average historical return	0.8%	12.4%	11.6%	11.2%	11.3%	
Worst historical return	–11.0%	–12.2%	1.7%	4.7%	10.3%	

RETURNS GREATER THAN

	1 month	1 year	3 years	5 years	10 years	15 years
10 per cent	0%	56%	52%	56%	100%	
Zero	66%	89%	100%	100%	100%	
Percentage of time fund lost $	34%	11%	0%	0%	0%	
Number of periods evaluated	123	112	88	64	4	

DOWNSIDE RISK

	Worst setback since start date	In bear 1987	In bear 1990	In bear 1994	In bear 1998
Setback for mutual fund	–14.5%		–12.9%	–7.9%	–14.5%
Setback for peer group	–17.0%		–8.6%	–8.0%	–17.0%
Setback ended in	Aug 1998		Oct 1990	June 1994	Aug 1998
Months to recover from loss	?		7	9	?

QUARTILE RANKING OF MUTUAL FUND PERFOMANCE AFTER 12 MONTHS OVER TIME

Canadian dividend

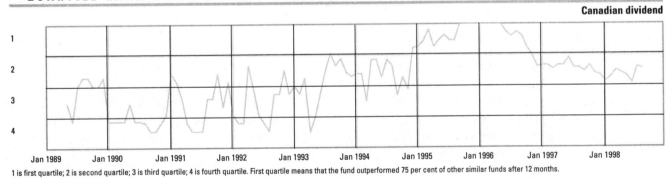

1 is first quartile; 2 is second quartile; 3 is third quartile; 4 is fourth quartile. First quartile means that the fund outperformed 75 per cent of other similar funds after 12 months.

ROLLING 12-MONTH TOTAL RATE OF RETURN FOR THE MUTUAL FUND OVER TIME

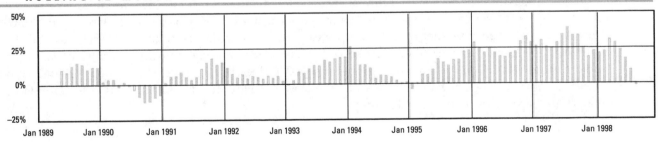

BPI DIVIDEND INCOME FUND

Vos value rating			WilStar rating		
Reward	**Risk**	**Best balance**	**Reward**	**Risk**	**Best balance**
★★★★	★★★★★	★★★★★	★★★★	★★★★★	★★★★★

Fund profile

The BPI Dividend Income Fund has been managed by Eric Bushell of BPI Mutual Funds since January 1995. The investment objective is to provide a high level of current income while preserving investor capital through the prudent use of diversification in a portfolio of high-quality preferred shares. Dividend funds have rewarded investors during the previous three to five years as corporate profits increased and interest rates declined. Conservative investors enjoyed the higher rates of return associated with dividend funds and, in turn, dividend funds grew in popularity. However, the party experienced a temporary setback in August 1998 as Canadian stock markets experienced their largest correction since 1987. Within this volatile context, the BPI Dividend Income Fund has added value while reducing risk by outperforming during bear markets.

The BPI Dividend Income Fund has made investments in the telecommunications companies Nortel Networks and Telus. In addition, the fund has invested in TransCanada PipeLines and BCE. The fund has also made investments in all of the major Canadian chartered banks.

Fund performance

The BPI Dividend Income Fund has earned big marks for reducing risk while delivering an adequate rate of return. It has not been first quartile after 12 months relative to other Canadian dividend funds, but the fund has delivered value by reducing the risk associated with investing in Canadian dividend or equity funds. The fund scored five-star Vos Value Ratings and WilStar Ratings for risk and for best balance between risk and reward ratings. This indicates that the fund has displayed less risk over the previous three and five years respectively. The fund tends to outperform during bear markets; in turn, it does not have to outperform during bull markets to achieve above-average performance over the long term.

Fund risks

If you hate risk but like mutual funds, this fund is for you! The fund scored top marks for preserving investors' capital. It declined in value during the bear market of 1998 by 11.4 per cent, while the average Canadian dividend fund declined by 17 per cent. In addition, the fund also outperformed during the bear markets of 1987, 1990, and 1994. The fund has posted negative rates of return after 12 months 10 per cent of the time since its start date in July 1980. The worst 12-month rate of return for the fund was a loss of 4.4 per cent.

Future prospects

Dividend funds do provide a safe, secure alternative to balanced funds, but they are not immune to an economic downturn or recession. This was the case during the bear of 1998. However, this fund's conservative style ensures that investors experience less downside risk than the average balanced or dividend fund. If interest rates, the Canadian dollar, and Canadian economic growth continue to remain stable, the fund should provide a return greater than a GIC does, but investors should note that there is no guarantee. This fund will never be top quartile consistently, relative to other Canadian dividend funds, but scores high marks for conservative investors.

FUND DETAILS

Fund name	**BPI Dividend Income**	Start date for data shown	July 1980
Fund family	BPI Capital Management Corporation	Fund size (in $ millions)	$573
Mutual fund classification	Canadian dividend	Percentage in foreign holdings	0.58
RRSP eligible	Yes	Dividend frequency	Monthly
		Sales charge	Optional
VVR peer group	Canadian dividend	Redemption charge	Optional
Number of mutual funds in VVR category	73	Management fee	1.00
WilStar peer group	Domestic equity	Management expense ratio	1.21

FUND PERFORMANCE

	1 month	1 year	3 years	5 years	10 years	15 years
Returns ending Aug 1998	−9.9%	1.7%	14.1%	12.0%	9.0%	8.5%
Best historical return	6.6%	32.1%	21.9%	15.8%	10.7%	10.2%
Average historical return	0.8%	10.6%	9.7%	8.7%	8.1%	9.4%
Worst historical return	−9.9%	−4.4%	3.0%	4.2%	6.0%	8.3%

RETURNS GREATER THAN

	1 month	1 year	3 years	5 years	10 years	15 years
10 per cent	0%	45%	37%	31%	15%	5%
Zero	72%	90%	100%	100%	100%	100%
Percentage of time fund lost $	28%	10%	0%	0%	0%	0%
Number of periods evaluated	218	207	183	159	99	39

DOWNSIDE RISK

	Worst setback since start date	In bear 1987	In bear 1990	In bear 1994	In bear 1998
Setback for mutual fund	−11.4%	−6.9%	−5.4%	−7.9%	−11.4%
Setback for peer group	−17.0%	−9.7%	−8.6%	−8.0%	−17.0%
Setback ended in	Aug 1998	Oct 1987	Oct 1990	June 1994	Aug 1998
Months to recover from loss	?	6	3	9	?

QUARTILE RANKING OF MUTUAL FUND PERFOMANCE AFTER 12 MONTHS OVER TIME

Canadian dividend

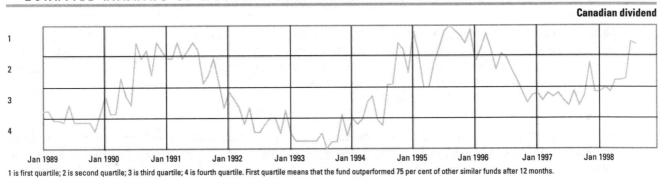

1 is first quartile; 2 is second quartile; 3 is third quartile; 4 is fourth quartile. First quartile means that the fund outperformed 75 per cent of other similar funds after 12 months.

ROLLING 12-MONTH TOTAL RATE OF RETURN FOR THE MUTUAL FUND OVER TIME

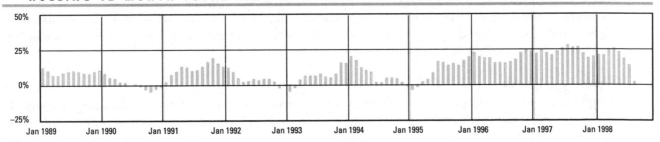

PHILLIPS, HAGER & NORTH DIVIDEND INCOME FUND

Vos value rating			WilStar rating		
Reward	**Risk**	**Best balance**	**Reward**	**Risk**	**Best balance**
★★★★★	★★	★★★★★	★★★★★	★★★★★	★★★★★

Fund profile

The Phillips, Hager & North Dividend Income Fund is managed by Bill Slatter of Phillips, Hager & North Investment Management. The investment objective of the fund is to provide long-term capital growth and income. The fund achieves this objective by investing primarily in income-producing Canadian corporations that have a relatively high level of income.

Dividend funds were the place to be in the last couple of years. As interest rates declined, corporate profits and share prices went up. Currently the stock prices of many of these companies are high, and their shares are trading at high multiples. Corporations will have to find new venues of growth to sustain such high stock prices. The Canadian dollar and interest rates should remain stable to ensure that this growth can be realized. In addition, the Asia and Pacific Rim crisis should be resolved. If these conditions do not materialize, investors can expect higher than average volatility in the future. Investors can also benefit from favourable tax treatment by investing in Canadian dividend funds, although investors who invest in a dividend fund within an RRSP will forego this favourable tax treatment.

The fund invests in all the major Canadian banks and utilities. In addition, the fund has made investments in such companies as BC Gas, IPI Energy, Suncor, and TransCanada Pipelines.

Fund performance

The fund has scored a triple five-star WilStar Rating for reward, risk, and best balance between reward and risk. This indicates that the Phillips, Hager & North Dividend Income Fund outperformed other domestic equity funds during the last five years. The fund also scored five-star Vos Value Ratings for reward and for best balance between risk and reward. The best 12-month period for the fund was a positive gain of 57.9 per cent, and the average 12-month rate of return has been a gain of 14.5 per cent since the start date in May 1980. The fund has been first quartile after 12 months relative to other dividend funds, but it was frequently fourth quartile after 12 months during the mid 1990s.

Fund risks

The manager has done an excellent job of managing the upside potential of this fund, but it has incurred more risk than the average dividend fund. During the bear market of 1994, the fund was down 10.6 per cent, while the average dividend fund was down 8 per cent. During the bear of 1998, the fund declined by 21.6 per cent, more than the average dividend fund. The fund also underperformed during the bear markets of 1987 and 1990, but in each case the fund took less than nine months to recover its losses. The fund scored a two-star Vos Value Rating for risk, indicating that the fund has more short-term risk than most dividend funds. The worst 12-month rate of return for the fund was a loss of 13.6 per cent, which is less than the average diversified Canadian equity fund.

Future prospects

High-yielding dividend-paying companies have been on a run lately, and many dividend-paying stocks have acted like growth stocks. Therefore, going forward, dividend-paying stocks could act like growth stocks on the downside. This was the case in August 1998. Investors looking for current income and long-term potential growth could consider a dividend fund.

FUND DETAILS

Fund name	**PH & N Dividend Income**	Start date for data shown	July 1980
Fund family	Phillips, Hager & North Ltd.	Fund size (in $ millions)	$540
Mutual fund classification	Canadian dividend	Percentage in foreign holdings	0.00
RRSP eligible	Yes	Dividend frequency	Quarterly
		Sales charge	No
VVR peer group	Canadian dividend	Redemption charge	No
Number of mutual funds in VVR category	73	Management fee	1.00
WilStar peer group	Domestric equity	Management expense ratio	1.21

FUND PERFORMANCE

	1 month	1 year	3 years	5 years	10 years	15 years
Returns ending Aug 1998	−16.1%	4.1%	21.9%	16.4%	13.1%	11.9%
Best historical return	9.3%	57.9%	33.0%	24.5%	16.5%	15.2%
Average historical return	1.0%	14.5%	13.0%	12.0%	11.2%	12.7%
Worst historical return	−16.1%	−13.6%	2.3%	5.7%	9.1%	10.3%

RETURNS GREATER THAN

	1 month	1 year	3 years	5 years	10 years	15 years
10 per cent	0%	58%	67%	59%	67%	100%
Zero	68%	88%	100%	100%	100%	100%
Percentage of time fund lost $	32%	12%	0%	0%	0%	0%
Number of periods evaluated	218	207	183	159	99	39

DOWNSIDE RISK

	Worst setback since start date	In bear 1987	In bear 1990	In bear 1994	In bear 1998
Setback for mutual fund	−21.6%	−15.9%	−12.1%	−10.6%	−21.6%
Setback for peer group	−17.0%	−9.7%	−8.6%	−8.0%	−17.0%
Setback ended in	Aug 1998	Oct 1987	Sept 1990	June 1994	Aug 1998
Months to recover from loss	?	12	6	10	?

QUARTILE RANKING OF MUTUAL FUND PERFOMANCE AFTER 12 MONTHS OVER TIME

Canadian dividend

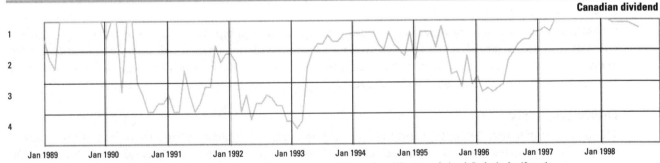

1 is first quartile; 2 is second quartile; 3 is third quartile; 4 is fourth quartile. First quartile means that the fund outperformed 75 per cent of other similar funds after 12 months.

ROLLING 12-MONTH TOTAL RATE OF RETURN FOR THE MUTUAL FUND OVER TIME

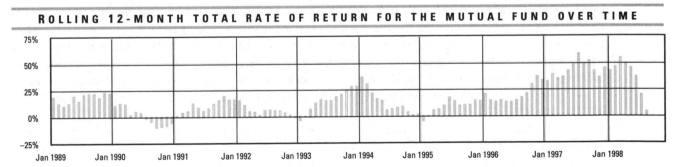

AIC DIVERSIFIED CANADA FUND

Vos value rating			WilStar rating		
Reward	Risk	Best balance	Reward	Risk	Best balance
★★★★★	★★★★★	★★★★★			

Fund profile

The AIC Diversified Fund is managed by Jonathan Wellum of AIC Limited. The fund aims to maximize returns while preserving investors' capital. It diversifies its holdings by investing primarily in stocks of Canadian companies in a variety of industries. These Canadian companies have proven results and excellent potential for sustainable growth.

Investing in this portfolio of companies has been beneficial for investors. With a relatively small number of investments in the fund, the AIC Diversified Fund has soared to new heights. However, AIC has invested as much as 10 per cent of its capital in one company and, with such large investments in several strategic companies, the fund's success obviously depends on those few companies.

The fund has made large investments in companies such as Bombardier, Newcourt Credit Group, Power Financial, Royal Bank, and Fairfax Financial Holdings.

Fund performance

This fund has posted performance results to which all other funds aspire. AIC built a reputation with investors because of the outstanding performance of the AIC Advantage series of funds. The Diversified fund underperformed the Advantage fund over the long term, but with less risk.

The Diversified fund scored a triple five-star Vos Value Rating for reward, risk, and balance between risk and reward. The fund has posted positive rates of return after 12 months 100 per cent of the time since its start date in January 1995. In short, the fund has been superior historically. Going forward, the fund's performance will be determined by the success or failure of the few underlying investments.

Fund risks

The fund is intrinsically more risky than the average Canadian equity fund, but none of that risk has come to fruition currently. The manager has done a great job of managing the downside risk, but the fund is not immune to economic downturn. In addition, the fund could experience a large setback because of its limited number of holdings. The fund declined by 19 per cent during the bear market of 1998.

Future prospects

The prospects for the Diversified fund are good. This fund is more diversified than the AIC Advantage Series. The AIC Advantage Series has a larger emphasis on investing in mutual fund companies. As AIC mutual funds acquire a larger market share in the mutual fund industry, these investments may endure some short-term underperformance. Thus, as AIC mutual funds grow, the funds' investments in other mutual fund companies become less attractive. Hence, investors may find the Diversified fund a more suitable investment in the future. However, the fund still holds a limited number of investments, and it will live or die by the performance of those investments. They have recently been on a tear, but that trend may or may not continue. Investors should have realistic expectations going forward, because duplicating this fund's historical track record will be a very difficult task, especially within volatile capital markets.

FUND DETAILS

Fund name	**AIC Diversified Canada**	Start date for data shown	Jan 1995
Fund family	AIC Limited	Fund size (in $ millions)	$1,866
Mutual fund classification	Canadian equity	Percentage in foreign holdings	14.90
RRSP eligible	Yes	Dividend frequency	Annual
		Sales charge	Optional
VVR peer group	Canadian equity	Redemption charge	Optional
Number of mutual funds in VVR category	283	Management fee	2.00
WilStar peer group	Domestic equity	Management expense ratio	2.39

FUND PERFORMANCE

	1 month	1 year	3 years	5 years	10 years	15 years
Returns ending Aug 1998	−16.8%	5.6%	33.1%			
Best historical return	9.2%	76.4%	45.9%			
Average historical return	2.4%	44.3%	42.0%			
Worst historical return	−16.8%	5.6%	33.1%			

RETURNS GREATER THAN

	1 month	1 year	3 years	5 years	10 years	15 years
10 per cent	0%	97%	100%			
Zero	75%	100%	100%			
Percentage of time fund lost $	25%	0%	0%			
Number of periods evaluated	44	33	9			

DOWNSIDE RISK

	Worst setback since start date	In bear 1987	In bear 1990	In bear 1994	In bear 1998
Setback for mutual fund	−19.0%			−1.5%	−19.0%
Setback for peer group	−24.3%			−3.5%	−24.3%
Setback ended in	Aug 1998			Jan 1995	Aug 1998
Months to recover from loss	?			2	?

QUARTILE RANKING OF MUTUAL FUND PERFOMANCE AFTER 12 MONTHS OVER TIME

Canadian equity

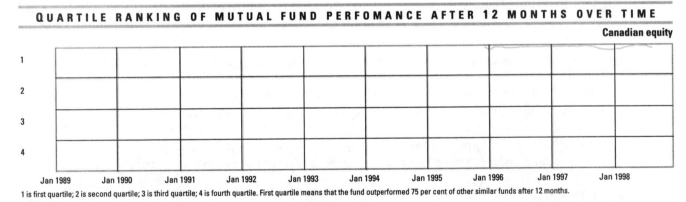

1 is first quartile; 2 is second quartile; 3 is third quartile; 4 is fourth quartile. First quartile means that the fund outperformed 75 per cent of other similar funds after 12 months.

ROLLING 12-MONTH TOTAL RATE OF RETURN FOR THE MUTUAL FUND OVER TIME

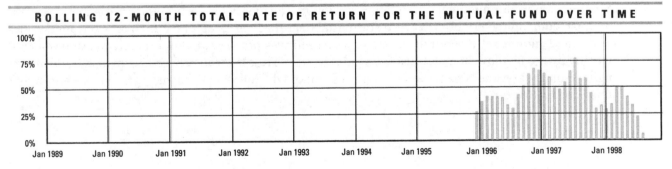

ATLAS CANADIAN LARGE CAP GROWTH FUND

Vos value rating			WilStar rating		
Reward	**Risk**	**Best balance**	**Reward**	**Risk**	**Best balance**
★★★★★	★★★★★	★★★★★	★★★★★	★★★★★	★★★★★

Fund profile

This fund has been managed by Fred Pynn of Bissett and Associates Investment Management Ltd. of Calgary since 1994. Bissett and Associates was formed in 1982 by David Bissett and now manages over $4 billion in assets on behalf of numerous clients including Atlas, Canada Trust, and other pension clients. The investment objective of this fund is to achieve superior long-term capital appreciation through investments in large Canadian corporations. This fund favours companies that have established good records of earnings, dividends, financial strength, stability, and good management.

Canadian blue-chip companies have done extremely well recently because of increased profitability from higher revenues and a reduction in costs. In addition, a low-interest-rate environment has increased stock prices of blue-chip stocks. However, these stocks are also currently trading at high valuations, so companies must generate new sources of growth to maintain these high multiples.

The fund invests in such companies as Fairfax Financial Holdings Ltd., a holding company for companies involved in the insurance industry, Magna International Inc., CIBC, and TD.

Fund performance

Like the top-rated Atlas Canadian Balanced Fund, this fund also experienced a period of underperformance during the early 1990s. However, things have improved, and investors have benefitted. The fund has appreciated in value significantly during the last three years, regularly posting returns of 30 per cent after 12 months. This phenomenon will not likely continue, but the fund did score a triple five-star Vos Value Rating for reward, risk, and best balance between risk and reward. In addition, the fund scored five stars on each of the WilStar Ratings. This is an indication that blue-chip stocks were the right place to invest in Canada. During the last three years the fund has consistently outperformed other Canadian equity funds.

Fund risks

The fund's worst 12-month loss was 15.9 per cent. It has earned positive rates of return 73 per cent of the time after 12 months since its start date in December 1985. Relative to other Canadian equity funds, this one has experienced less risk over the last three years. During the stock market crash of 1987, it declined more than 26 per cent, and it took 19 months to recover losses. Investing in Canadian equities can be more risky, but Canadian equities are still a vital component of any well-diversified portfolio.

Future prospects

This fund is not immune to an economic recession in Canada, but investing in brand name blue-chip Canadian companies should prove to be beneficial over the long term. The Canadian stock market has appreciated significantly over the last three years, so investors should now proceed with caution and diversify by holding investments outside Canada—a simple rule that can prove to be invaluable. Investors might also consider the Bissett Canadian Equity Fund, which has a lower management fee but higher minimum investment.

FUND DETAILS

Fund name	**Atlas Canadian Large Cap Growth**	Start date for data shown	Dec 1985
Fund family	Atlas Asset Management Inc.	Fund size (in $ millions)	$503
Mutual fund classification	Canadian equity	Percentage in foreign holdings	7.50
RRSP eligible	Yes	Dividend frequency	Annual
		Sales charge	Optional
VVR peer group	Canadian equity	Redemption charge	Optional
Number of mutual funds in VVR category	283	Management fee	2.00
WilStar peer group	Domestic equity	Management expense ratio	2.45

FUND PERFORMANCE

	1 month	1 year	3 years	5 years	10 years	15 years
Returns ending Aug 1998	–18.0%	–9.9%	13.3%	10.7%	8.0%	
Best historical return	8.0%	47.4%	26.3%	18.3%	11.2%	
Average historical return	0.6%	9.6%	7.8%	6.7%	7.7%	
Worst historical return	–21.5%	–15.9%	–3.2%	0.0%	5.1%	

RETURNS GREATER THAN

	1 month	1 year	3 years	5 years	10 years	15 years
10 per cent	0%	49%	27%	23%	26%	
Zero	58%	73%	91%	98%	100%	
Percentage of time fund lost $	42%	27%	9%	2%	0%	
Number of periods evaluated	153	142	118	94	34	

DOWNSIDE RISK

	Worst setback since start date	In bear 1987	In bear 1990	In bear 1994	In bear 1998
Setback for mutual fund	–26.8%	–26.8%	–18.3%	–8.3%	–23.6%
Setback for peer group	–22.7%	–22.7%	–16.0%	–9.6%	–24.3%
Setback ended in	Nov 1987	Nov 1987	Oct 1990	June 1994	Aug 1998
Months to recover from loss	20	20	31	11	?

QUARTILE RANKING OF MUTUAL FUND PERFOMANCE AFTER 12 MONTHS OVER TIME

Canadian equity

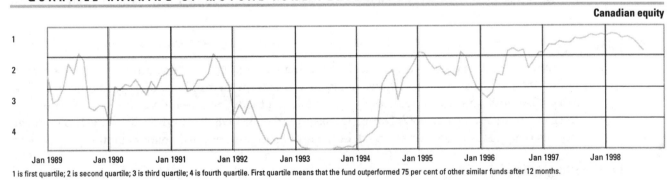

1 is first quartile; 2 is second quartile; 3 is third quartile; 4 is fourth quartile. First quartile means that the fund outperformed 75 per cent of other similar funds after 12 months.

ROLLING 12-MONTH TOTAL RATE OF RETURN FOR THE MUTUAL FUND OVER TIME

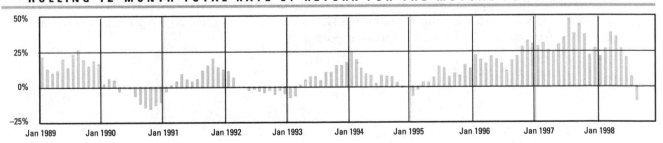

BISSETT CANADIAN EQUITY FUND

Vos value rating			WilStar rating		
Reward	**Risk**	**Best balance**	**Reward**	**Risk**	**Best balance**
★★★★★	★★★★★	★★★★★	★★★★★	★★★★★	★★★★★

Fund profile

The Bissett Canadian Equity Fund is managed by Michael Quinn and Fred Pynn of Bissett and Associates Investment Management. The fund is designed to achieve long-term capital growth while preserving capital by investing in a well-diversified portfolio of Canadian companies which, according to Bissett, will generate above-average risk-adjusted rates of return. The fund will invest in small, mid, and large cap stocks. Small and mid cap stocks provide the highest return over the long term, and large cap stocks combine adequate rates of return with security and stability. The fund invests in a variety of industries and holds investments in up to 80 companies at one time.

The Canadian economy has grown quickly over the last three years, and this Canadian equity mutual fund has participated on the upside. With a decline in interest rates and renewed growth in the economy, the fund has been able to move forward over the last three years. If the Canadian economy continues to grow and interest rates remain stable, this fund should continue to do well over the next several years.

Bissett Canadian Equity Fund invests in companies like Power Financial, Great West Life, Bombardier, Canwest Global, and Magna International.

Fund performance

If you didn't win the $22-million Super 7, this mutual fund would have been the next best thing. The fund has been first quartile after 12 months frequently during the past 10 years, dipping into third-quartile range after 12 months only once. The fund's best 12-month return was a positive 55.4 per cent, and it has posted positive rates of return after 12 months 84 per cent of the time. The fund has done extremely well during the last three years and receives a triple five-star Vos Value Rating for reward, risk, and the best balance between risk and reward.

Fund risks

Relative to other Canadian equity funds, the Bissett Canadian Equity Fund has improved its risk-return profile within the last three years. However, over the longer term the fund has displayed more risk. The fund's worst 12-month loss was a decline of 15 per cent, and the worst one-month loss was 19.6 per cent during the stock market crash of 1987. During the bear market of 1998 the fund declined by 23.6 per cent, more than the average Canadian equity fund, because of its investment in Canadian banks.

Future prospects

If the Canadian economy continues to grow and corporate profits increase while interest rates remain stable, this fund should do well. If the economic environment turns sour, this fund will not be immune to a setback, but should still hold up. The fund's performance will be dictated by the performance of Canadian chartered banks and other large Canadian corporations.

FUND DETAILS

Fund name	**Bissett Canadian Equity**	Start date for data shown	March 1983
Fund family	Bissett and Associates Investment Management Ltd.	Fund size (in $ millions)	$392
Mutual fund classification	Canadian equity	Percentage in foreign holdings	6.87
RRSP eligible	Yes	Dividend frequency	Annual
		Sales charge	No
VVR peer group	Canadian equity	Redemption charge	No
Number of mutual funds in VVR category	283	Management fee	1.00
WilStar peer group	Domestic equity	Management expense ratio	1.33

FUND PERFORMANCE

	1 month	1 year	3 years	5 years	10 years	15 years
Returns ending Aug 1998	−17.7%	−8.5%	17.2%	12.7%	12.8%	11.6%
Best historical return	9.5%	55.4%	31.4%	23.9%	16.0%	14.8%
Average historical return	1.1%	14.4%	12.7%	11.5%	11.4%	13.7%
Worst historical return	−19.6%	−15.0%	−1.0%	2.9%	9.1%	11.6%

RETURNS GREATER THAN

	1 month	1 year	3 years	5 years	10 years	15 years
10 per cent	0%	62%	58%	57%	75%	100%
Zero	63%	84%	98%	100%	100%	100%
Percentage of time fund lost $	37%	16%	2%	0%	0%	0%
Number of periods evaluated	186	175	151	127	67	7

DOWNSIDE RISK

	Worst setback since start date	In bear 1987	In bear 1990	In bear 1994	In bear 1998
Setback for mutual fund	−26.1%	−26.1%	−13.6%	−10.9%	−23.6%
Setback for peer group	−22.7%	−22.7%	−16.0%	−9.6%	−24.3%
Setback ended in	Nov 1987	Nov 1987	Oct 1990	June 1994	Aug 1998
Months to recover from loss	20	20	5	11	?

QUARTILE RANKING OF MUTUAL FUND PERFOMANCE AFTER 12 MONTHS OVER TIME

Canadian equity

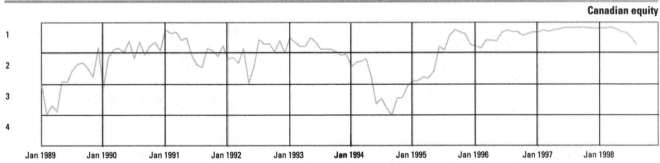

1 is first quartile; 2 is second quartile; 3 is third quartile; 4 is fourth quartile. First quartile means that the **fund** outperformed 75 per cent of other similar funds after 12 months.

ROLLING 12-MONTH TOTAL RATE OF RETURN FOR THE MUTUAL FUND OVER TIME

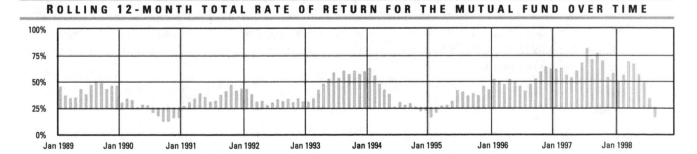

ETHICAL GROWTH FUND

Vos value rating			WilStar rating		
Reward	**Risk**	**Best balance**	**Reward**	**Risk**	**Best balance**
★★★★★	★★★★★	★★★★★	★★★★★	★★★★★	★★★★★

Fund profile

The Ethical Growth Fund has been managed by Larry Lunn of Connor Clark and Lunn Investment Management since September 1992. The fund's investment objective is to provide long-term capital appreciation by investing in a well-diversified portfolio of Canadian companies. The fund tries to invest only in companies that operate within an "ethical and moral framework."

The fund invests primarily in large Canadian companies. Fortunately, large Canadian companies were the place to invest during the last three years. During August 1998 some of these companies experienced large setbacks in the value of their stocks, but the fund still managed to outperform.

Currently, the fund has invested in large Canadian companies such as the forest company Abitibi-Consolidated, oil and gas company Suncor, and Canadian Occidental Petroleum. In addition, the fund has invested in major Canadian chartered banks such as the Royal Bank and the Bank of Montreal.

Fund performance

The Ethical Growth Fund scored a triple five-star Vos Value Rating and WilStar Rating for reward, risk and best balance between risk and reward. This indicates that the fund has generated superior performance during the previous three and five years. The Vos Value Rating indicates that the fund added more value than other Canadian equity mutual funds, and the WilStar rating indicates that the fund has been an excellent domestic equity fund. The fund has frequently been first quartile after 12 months relative to other Canadian equity mutual funds, but it experienced severe underperformance during 1992, 1993, and 1994. The fund's best 12-month rate of return was a positive gain of 47.9 per cent, and the average 12-month rate of return was a gain of 12.2 per cent.

Fund risks

The fund outperformed the average Canadian equity fund during the bear markets of 1987 and 1990 when the fund was under different management. During the bear of 1998 the fund declined in value by 21 per cent, comparable to the declines of other Canadian equity mutual funds over the same period. The worst 12-month rate of return for the fund was a loss of 11.2 per cent, which occurred after the bear of 1998. The fund posted a negative rate of return after 12 months 17 per cent of the time.

Future prospects

When stock markets are down, they provide great buying opportunities for investors. The Ethical Growth Fund invests in large Canadian corporations with great brand names and established operations. These companies will add value for investors over the long term. Investors with long-term time horizons will be rewarded for investing in blue-chip equities. A well-diversified portfolio should include some exposure to Canadian equity mutual funds. The Ethical Growth Fund provides investors with excellent exposure to these blue-chip companies.

FUND DETAILS

Fund name	Ethical Growth	Start date for data shown	March 1986
Fund family	Ethical Funds Inc.	Fund size (in $ millions)	$657
Mutual fund classification	Canadian equity	Percentage in foreign holdings	0.00
RRSP eligible	Yes	Dividend frequency	Quarterly
		Sales charge	No
VVR peer group	Canadian equity	Redemption charge	No
Number of mutual funds in VVR category	283	Management fee	1.50
WilStar peer group	Domestic equity	Management expense ratio	2.10

FUND PERFORMANCE

	1 month	1 year	3 years	5 years	10 years	15 years
Returns ending Aug 1998	−15.6%	−11.2%	12.1%	10.1%	9.8%	
Best historical return	9.1%	47.9%	23.7%	19.0%	13.3%	
Average historical return	0.8%	12.2%	11.1%	10.1%	11.2%	
Worst historical return	−15.6%	−11.2%	0.6%	5.0%	9.2%	

RETURNS GREATER THAN

	1 month	1 year	3 years	5 years	10 years	15 years
10 per cent	0%	56%	59%	34%	71%	
Zero	62%	83%	100%	100%	100%	
Percentage of time fund lost $	38%	17%	0%	0%	0%	
Number of periods evaluated	150	139	115	91	31	

DOWNSIDE RISK

	Worst setback since start date	In bear 1987	In bear 1990	In bear 1994	In bear 1998
Setback for mutual fund	−21.0%	−9.7%	−7.1%	−10.6%	−21.0%
Setback for peer group	−24.3%	−22.7%	−16.0%	−9.6%	−24.3%
Setback ended in	Aug 1998	Oct 1987	Oct 1990	June 1994	Aug 1998
Months to recover from loss	?	5	4	11	?

QUARTILE RANKING OF MUTUAL FUND PERFOMANCE AFTER 12 MONTHS OVER TIME

Canadian equity

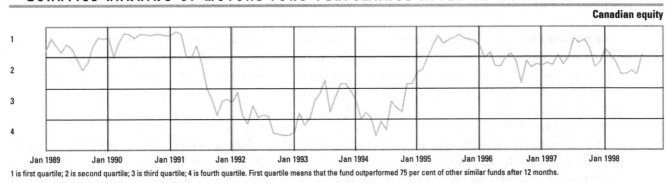

1 is first quartile; 2 is second quartile; 3 is third quartile; 4 is fourth quartile. First quartile means that the fund outperformed 75 per cent of other similar funds after 12 months.

ROLLING 12-MONTH TOTAL RATE OF RETURN FOR THE MUTUAL FUND OVER TIME

INVESTORS SUMMA FUND

Vos value rating			WilStar rating		
Reward	**Risk**	**Best balance**	**Reward**	**Risk**	**Best balance**
★★★★★	★★★★★	★★★★★	★★★★★	★★★★	★★★★★

Fund profile

The Investors Summa Fund has been managed by Allan Brown of Investors Group Inc. since January 1997. Since he began as portfolio manager, the fund's performance has significantly improved. The investment objective of the fund is to provide capital appreciation with income generation. The fund invests in common shares of socially responsible corporations that have adopted progressive standards reflecting an awareness of economic, social, and environmental issues.

If you are an Investors Group client, and you own a Canadian equity fund, you have to own this fund. It has a really cool investment objective in conjunction with excellent relative performance for a Canadian equity fund! What more could an investor want? The fund is not immune to fluctuations in the Canadian economy, and investors must be aware of the underlying risks involved when investing in equity securities.

The fund invests in such companies as Telus Corporation and Oxford Properties Group and owns shares in most of the Canadian major banks.

Fund performance

The fund's performance has improved significantly over the past three years. In turn, the fund has earned a triple five-star Vos Value Rating for reward, risk, and best balance between risk and reward. The fund's best 12-month rate of return was a gain of 46 per cent, and the average 12-month return was a gain of 11 per cent. The fund has posted a positive rate of return after 12 months 78 per cent of the time. The fund has consistently been first quartile during the last three years. However, before that its performance wasn't anything to write home about.

Fund risks

The worst 12-month period for the fund was a loss of 23.5 per cent, and the fund actually lost money after three years, a loss of 4.1 per cent compounded annually. The fund has underperformed during bear markets. Investors who came aboard during the bear of 1998 saw their investment decline by 24.1 per cent.

Future prospects

It is clear that a management change for this fund was an excellent decision. Allan Brown has turned the fund around for the benefit of investors. Going forward things will be different, and investors should note that top-performing funds occasionally underperform their respective peer groups. Investors Group clients who currently invest in Canadian equities should consider this fund as a "must hold." Management has proven they can add value, and the fund strictly avoids companies with unethical objectives—a win/win situation for any investor.

This fund's performance will be dictated by the growth in the Canadian economy. If interest rates remain low and the Canadian dollar remains stable, investors could experience double-digit gains again. However, with stock markets hitting new highs and stock multiples hitting new levels, investors should have realistic expectations about a normal rate of return. A normal rate of return for Canadian equities is approximately 3 per cent to 4 per cent above short-term interest rates. Investors can reduce the risk by investing in the fund on a regular basis.

FUND DETAILS

Fund name	**Investors Summa**	Start date for data shown	Feb 1987
Fund family	Investors Group Financial Services Inc.	Fund size (in $ millions)	$443
Mutual fund classification	Canadian equity	Percentage in foreign holdings	16.66
RRSP eligible	Yes	Dividend frequency	Annual
		Sales charge	Yes
VVR peer group	Canadian equity	Redemption charge	Deferred
Number of mutual funds in VVR category	283	Management fee	2.00
WilStar peer group	Domestic equity	Management expense ratio	2.48

FUND PERFORMANCE

	1 month	1 year	3 years	5 years	10 years	15 years
Returns ending Aug 1998	−17.8%	−8.4%	14.4%	11.0%	9.0%	
Best historical return	8.2%	46.0%	27.5%	18.4%	12.2%	
Average historical return	0.7%	11.0%	9.3%	9.1%	10.1%	
Worst historical return	−17.8%	−23.5%	−4.1%	2.4%	7.6%	

RETURNS GREATER THAN

	1 month	1 year	3 years	5 years	10 years	15 years
10 per cent	0%	55%	37%	39%	55%	
Zero	64%	77%	96%	100%	100%	
Percentage of time fund lost $	36%	23%	4%	0%	0%	
Number of periods evaluated	139	128	104	80	20	

DOWNSIDE RISK

	Worst setback since start date	In bear 1987	In bear 1990	In bear 1994	In bear 1998
Setback for mutual fund	−24.1%	−19.7%	−23.7%	−11.4%	−24.1%
Setback for peer group	−24.3%	−22.7%	−16.0%	−9.6%	−24.3%
Setback ended in	Aug 1998	Nov 1987	Oct 1990	June 1994	Aug 1998
Months to recover from loss	?	17	14	15	?

QUARTILE RANKING OF MUTUAL FUND PERFOMANCE AFTER 12 MONTHS OVER TIME

Canadian equity

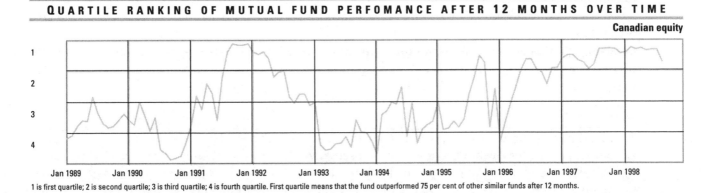

1 is first quartile; 2 is second quartile; 3 is third quartile; 4 is fourth quartile. First quartile means that the fund outperformed 75 per cent of other similar funds after 12 months.

ROLLING 12-MONTH TOTAL RATE OF RETURN FOR THE MUTUAL FUND OVER TIME

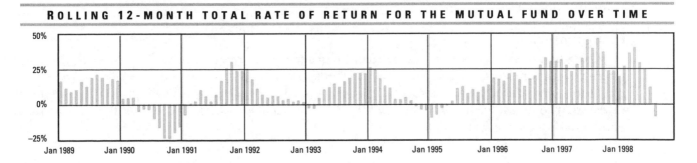

IVY CANADIAN FUND (MACKENZIE)

Vos value rating			WilStar rating		
Reward	**Risk**	**Best balance**	**Reward**	**Risk**	**Best balance**
★★★★	★★★★★	★★★★★	★★★★★	★★★★★	★★★★★

Fund profile

The Mackenzie Ivy Canadian Fund has been managed by Jerry Javasky of Mackenzie Financial since July 1997. The investment objective of the fund is to generate long-term growth while preserving investors' capital. The fund invests in high-quality large Canadian companies and a select number of international organizations.

Conservative investors who dislike downside risk and are looking for a Canadian equity fund with long-term growth potential should carefully examine the Ivy Canadian Fund. The fund regularly uses its large cash balance patiently to acquire businesses at reasonable prices. This conservative approach will lead to periods of underperformance, but inventors will also benefit from significantly less downside risk. The fund is not immune to unfavourable economic conditions, and a prolonged setback in the Canadian economy could affect future fund performance.

This fund tends to do best during bear markets largely because of its large cash position, but it also has investments in banks and utilities. The fund has investments in Loblaw Companies, which operates stores such as Loblaws, Dominion, SuperValu, No Frills, Fortinos, and others.

Fund performance

This fund adds value for inventors by reducing the downside risk. Long-term performance will be similar to that of other Canadian equity funds, because the fund has fewer losses to regain and hence has a head start into the next bull market. The fund scored a four-star Vos Value Rating for reward, indicating that, during the last three years, the fund has performed as well as other Canadian equity funds. The fund also scored a five-star rating on risk and best balance between risk and reward, indicating that it delivered a great return for the given level of risk. In addition, the fund scored a five-star WilStar Rating for reward, risk, and best balance between risk and return. The fund's best 12-month period was a positive rate of return of 31.8 per cent, and the fund has an average 12-month return of 15.1 per cent. The fund's relative performance after 12 months has been volatile.

Fund risks

This fund has shown less downside risk than any other domestic equity fund during the last five years. Conservative investors wanting to invest in a conservative Canadian equity fund have found a home in the Mackenzie Ivy Canadian Fund. The fund has posted a positive rate of return after 12 months 100 per cent of the time. During the bear of 1994 the fund declined by 3.7 per cent, and the fund regained its losses within two months.

Future prospects

The Canadian stock market has set new record highs this year. Investors who are concerned about the future downside risk in Canadian equity mutual funds (after August 1998) should experience less downside risk in this fund. Canadian equities will outperform Canadian bonds and cash over the long term. Patient investors who invest for the long term will not be disappointed with their choice of the Ivy Canadian Fund. Get on a plan and stick to it!

FUND DETAILS

Fund name	**Ivy Canadian**	Start date for data shown	Nov 1992
Fund family	Mackenzie Financial Corporation	Fund size (in $ millions)	$4,979
Mutual fund classification	Canadian equity	Percentage in foreign holdings	13.64
RRSP eligible	Yes	Dividend frequency	Annual
		Sales charge	Optional
VVR peer group	Canadian equity	Redemption charge	Optional
Number of mutual funds in VVR category	283	Management fee	2.00
WilStar peer group	Domestic equity	Management expense ratio	2.38

FUND PERFORMANCE

	1 month	1 year	3 years	5 years	10 years	15 years
Returns ending Aug 1998	–11.0%	1.0%	13.7%	11.8%		
Best historical return	5.7%	31.8%	20.3%	16.0%		
Average historical return	1.0%	15.1%	15.5%	14.8%		
Worst historical return	–11.0%	0.1%	9.7%	11.8%		

RETURNS GREATER THAN

	1 month	1 year	3 years	5 years	10 years	15 years
10 per cent	0%	78%	97%	100%		
Zero	67%	100%	100%	100%		
Percentage of time fund lost $	33%	0%	0%	0%		
Number of periods evaluated	70	59	35	11		

DOWNSIDE RISK

	Worst setback since start date	In bear 1987	In bear 1990	In bear 1994	In bear 1998
Setback for mutual fund	–13.6%			–3.7%	–13.6%
Setback for peer group	–24.3%			–9.6%	–24.3%
Setback ended in	Aug 1998			June 1994	Aug 1998
Months to recover from loss	?			2	?

QUARTILE RANKING OF MUTUAL FUND PERFOMANCE AFTER 12 MONTHS OVER TIME

Canadian equity

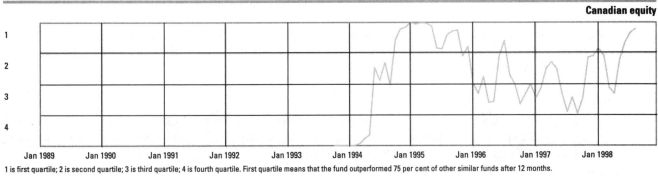

1 is first quartile; 2 is second quartile; 3 is third quartile; 4 is fourth quartile. First quartile means that the fund outperformed 75 per cent of other similar funds after 12 months.

ROLLING 12-MONTH TOTAL RATE OF RETURN FOR THE MUTUAL FUND OVER TIME

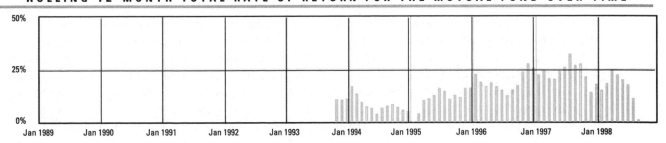

SPECTRUM UNITED CANADIAN INVESTMENT FUND

Vos value rating			WilStar rating		
Reward	**Risk**	**Best balance**	**Reward**	**Risk**	**Best balance**
★★★★★	★★★★★	★★★★★	★★★★★	★★★★★	★★★★★

Fund profile

The Spectrum United Canadian Investment Fund has been managed by Kim Shannon of AMI Partners Investment Council Inc. since 1996. The investment objective of the fund is to achieve a superior rate of return from investments that provide a blend of reliable income, safety of capital, and the potential for capital growth.

The fund's relative performance has improved significantly since new management took over the day-to-day activities of the fund. Investors in the fund have done well during the last three years, but in the future they should have realistic expectations about normal rates of return. Investors can expect increased volatility in Canadian stock markets, but prudent investors will use these opportunities patiently to acquire great investments at cheap prices. The investment style of the fund is conservative and value-oriented, and the manager selects large Canadian companies with growth potential.

The fund invests in the largest Canadian companies, including brand name companies like BCE, Royal Bank, Bank of Montreal, Imasco, Bank of Nova Scotia, Toronto Dominion Bank, National Bank, Dofasco Inc., CIBC, and TransCanada PipeLines Limited.

Fund performance

This fund has displayed less risk than the average Canadian equity fund, with reasonable upside potential. In turn the fund has scored a triple five-star Vos Value Rating for reward, risk, and best balance between risk and reward. This indicates that the fund has posted superior performance over the last three years relative to other Canadian equity mutual funds. Conservative investors who want income and stability from a Canadian equity fund would not be disappointed with the Spectrum United Canadian Investment Fund. The fund has frequently been first quartile after 12 months relative to other Canadian equity funds during the last three years. The relative performance of the fund during the mid 1990s was dismal, but with a new manager things have improved. The fund has achieved a superior rate of return, given the level of risk incurred by investors.

Fund risks

This fund has improved its risk profile during the last three years. During the bear market of 1998, the fund declined by 19 per cent, but outperformed other Canadian equity funds. During the bear of 1987, the fund declined by 24.7 per cent and took 20 months to recover.

Future prospects

The Spectrum United Canadian Investment Fund is the oldest (open-end) mutual fund in Canada. Going forward, the fund will continue to invest in the largest Canadian companies. Therefore, the performance of the fund will be similar to the TSE 100 index, an index of Canada's largest publicly traded companies. Passive investors could consider investing in HIPS or a Canadian index fund in order to reduce the management fee. Active investors who invest in the Spectrum United Canadian Investment Fund should incur less risk without sacrificing performance over the long term. These investors will have to pay a higher management fee for the additional value added by active management. In turn, conservative investors who want to invest in Canada's largest companies should not be disappointed with this fund.

FUND DETAILS

Fund name	**Spectrum United Canadian Investment**	Start date for data shown	July 1980
Fund family	Spectrum United Mutual Funds Inc.	Fund size (in $ millions)	$265
Mutual fund classification	Canadian equity	Percentage in foreign holdings	15.60
RRSP eligible	Yes	Dividend frequency	Quarterly
		Sales charge	Optional
VVR peer group	Canadian equity	Redemption charge	Optional
Number of mutual funds in VVR category	283	Management fee	1.95
WilStar peer group	Domestic equity	Management expense ratio	2.33

FUND PERFORMANCE

	1 month	1 year	3 years	5 years	10 years	15 years
Returns ending Aug 1998	−14.5%	−4.8%	14.5%	10.7%	8.1%	7.7%
Best historical return	12.5%	66.9%	26.4%	22.1%	10.6%	11.8%
Average historical return	0.8%	10.5%	9.3%	8.3%	7.2%	8.9%
Worst historical return	−21.6%	−22.6%	−3.5%	−0.8%	4.8%	6.8%

RETURNS GREATER THAN

	1 month	1 year	3 years	5 years	10 years	15 years
10 per cent	1%	51%	39%	38%	8%	26%
Zero	60%	73%	93%	98%	100%	100%
Percentage of time fund lost $	40%	27%	7%	2%	0%	0%
Number of periods evaluated	218	207	183	159	99	39

DOWNSIDE RISK

	Worst setback since start date	In bear 1987	In bear 1990	In bear 1994	In bear 1998
Setback for mutual fund	−24.7%	−24.7%	−18.7%	−9.6%	−19.0%
Setback for peer group	−22.7%	−22.7%	−16.0%	−9.6%	−24.3%
Setback ended in	Nov 1987	Nov 1987	Oct 1990	June 1994	Aug 1998
Months to recover from loss	20	20	34	11	?

QUARTILE RANKING OF MUTUAL FUND PERFOMANCE AFTER 12 MONTHS OVER TIME

Canadian equity

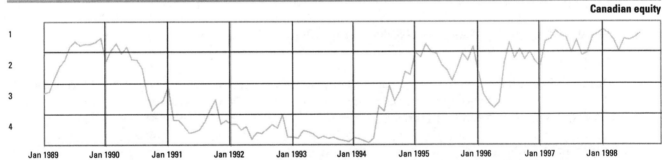

1 is first quartile; 2 is second quartile; 3 is third quartile; 4 is fourth quartile. First quartile means that the fund outperformed 75 per cent of other similar funds after 12 months.

ROLLING 12-MONTH TOTAL RATE OF RETURN FOR THE MUTUAL FUND OVER TIME

STANDARD LIFE EQUITY FUND

Vos value rating			WilStar rating		
Reward	Risk	Best balance	Reward	Risk	Best balance
★★★★★	★★★★★	★★★★★	★★★★★	★★★★★	★★★★★

Fund profile

The Standard Life Equity Fund is a Canadian equity fund managed by Peter Hill and Norman Raschkowan of Standard Life Portfolio Management Ltd. The investment objective of the fund is to provide investors with the potential for long-term capital gains while minimizing short-term volatility. The fund invests in the common shares and other securities of Canadian and some foreign companies.

Canadian stocks experienced a large setback during August 1998 after an excellent start to the year. This fund was not immune to the setback, but it did add value over the short and long terms. Because of the market correction during the bear of 1998, Canadian companies seem more attractively priced, trading at lower valuations. In addition, this fund places 19.68 per cent of its investments outside Canada, which should reduce the short-term risk of investing in stocks.

The Standard Life Equity Fund also has a tendency to invest in larger Canadian companies, such as BCE Inc., and has also invested in Canadian banks, including CIBC, Royal Bank, Bank of Nova Scotia, and Toronto Dominion Bank.

Fund performance

This little Canadian equity fund has added value over the short and long terms! In turn, this fund may not be so little in the future. The fund has posted triple five-star Vos Value and WilStar Ratings for reward, risk, and the best balance between risk and reward. The high Vos Value Rating is an indication that the fund added value relative to other Canadian equity funds during the last three years. The WilStar Rating indicates that the fund added value relative to other domestic equity funds during the past five years. In fact, large cap companies were the place to invest during the past five years. The fund's best 12-month rate of return was a gain of 41.5 per cent and the average 12-month rate of return was 16.7 per cent. The fund has frequently been first quartile relative to other Canadian equity funds after 12 months.

Fund risks

This fund has outperformed during bear markets, but the outperformance was marginal. During the bear of 1994, the fund declined by 8.0 per cent and took nine months to recover. During the more severe bear of 1998, the fund declined by 21.3 per cent.

Future prospects

Yes! Canadian equity mutual funds displayed above-average downside risk during the summer of 1998. However, stocks have still outperformed other asset classes and investments over the long term. Investors who are serious about achieving their long-term financial goals should consider investing a portion of their investments in Canadian equity mutual funds. Investors can diversify their risk by investing in other mutual funds at the same time. When Canadian equity mutual funds recover—and they will—investors can participate in the upside. Investing in stocks is risky, and the risk comes to fruition at different times. Do not become discouraged. Diversify and stick to your plan. The Standard Life Equity Fund is a great place to start.

FUND DETAILS

Fund name	**Standard Life Equity**	Start date for data shown	Nov 1992
Fund family	The Standard Life Assurance Company	Fund size (in $ millions)	$17
Mutual fund classification	Canadian equity	Percentage in foreign holdings	19.68
RRSP eligible	Yes	Dividend frequency	Quarterly
		Sales charge	No
VVR peer group	Canadian equity	Redemption charge	Deferred
Number of mutual funds in VVR category	283	Management fee	2.00
WilStar peer group	Domestic equity	Management expense ratio	2.00

FUND PERFORMANCE

	1 month	1 year	3 years	5 years	10 years	15 years
Returns ending Aug 1998	−16.7%	−7.5%	12.2%	10.5%		
Best historical return	7.3%	41.5%	23.8%	17.6%		
Average historical return	1.0%	16.7%	15.8%	16.1%		
Worst historical return	−16.7%	−7.5%	10.2%	10.5%		

RETURNS GREATER THAN

	1 month	1 year	3 years	5 years	10 years	15 years
10 per cent	0%	71%	100%	100%		
Zero	61%	95%	100%	100%		
Percentage of time fund lost $	39%	5%	0%	0%		
Number of periods evaluated	70	59	35	11		

DOWNSIDE RISK

	Worst setback since start date	In bear 1987	In bear 1990	In bear 1994	In bear 1998
Setback for mutual fund	−21.3%			−8.0%	−21.3%
Setback for peer group	−24.3%			−9.6%	−24.3%
Setback ended in	Aug 1998			June 1994	Aug 1998
Months to recover from loss	?			11	?

QUARTILE RANKING OF MUTUAL FUND PERFOMANCE AFTER 12 MONTHS OVER TIME

Canadian equity

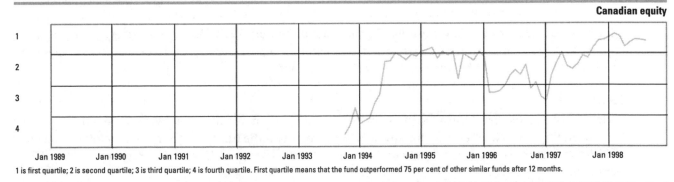

1 is first quartile; 2 is second quartile; 3 is third quartile; 4 is fourth quartile. First quartile means that the fund outperformed 75 per cent of other similar funds after 12 months.

ROLLING 12-MONTH TOTAL RATE OF RETURN FOR THE MUTUAL FUND OVER TIME

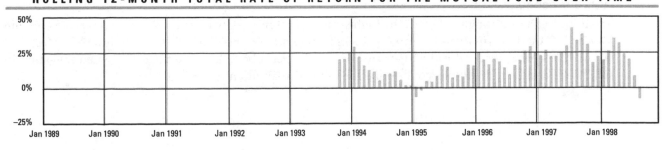

BISSETT SMALL CAP FUND

Vos value rating			WilStar rating		
Reward	Risk	Best balance	Reward	Risk	Best balance
★★★★★	★★★★★	★★★★★	★★★★★	★	★★★★

Fund profile

The Bissett Small Cap Fund is designed to give investors exposure to growing Canadian companies. The fund invests in small to medium-sized Canadian companies with a market value between $100 million and $500 million. It is fully diversified at all times to compensate for the increased volatility intrinsic in small cap investing. Since Bissett and Associates Investment Management is located in Calgary, the Bissett Small Cap Fund tends to focus on companies operating in western Canada.

Thus far, small cap stocks have had a turbulent ride in 1998 as investors sell their small cap holdings in favour of the brand names and liquidity of larger companies. Over the long run, however, small companies outperform large companies, since investors want to be compensated for the additional risk inherent in small cap investing. In addition, small companies have the ability to grow and react quickly to favourable market conditions. However, small cap investors haven't been rewarded for their additional risk since the mid 1990s. Thus, small cap investors will have to continue to be patient until investors' love affair with small cap stocks is rekindled.

The Bissett Small Cap Fund holds names such as Yogen Fruz World Wide, Shaw Industries, C-Mac Industries, Velan, Dorel Industries, and Canadian Western Bank. Most of these companies are currently not brand-name companies, but if they ever become brand names, investors will thoroughly enjoy the upside.

Fund performance

The Bissett Small Cap Fund recently experienced its worst month ever, a loss of 17.6 per cent in August 1998. Over the long term, however, the fund has been exceptional. Its best 12-month period was a gain of 116.4 per cent and the average 12-month gain was 34.2 per cent. The fund has posted positive rates of return after 12 months 86 per cent of the time since its start date of January 1992. Relative to other Canadian small cap funds, Bissett Small Cap Fund performed extremely well, scoring a triple five-star Vos Value Rating for reward, risk, and best balance between risk and reward.

Fund risks

A decline of 32.2 per cent during the bear of 1998 would leave many investors with some butterflies. The WilStar Rating for risk gives the fund one star, indicating that the fund is more risky than other domestic equity funds such as Canadian equity and dividend funds. The worst 12-month period was a loss of 25.5 per cent.

Future prospects

Small caps can be a rough ride, but the higher rates of return on occasion can be very rewarding. Going forward, Canadian small cap companies will need a stable Canadian dollar, low interest rates, and favourable economic conditions to ensure growth. Expect above-average volatility when investing in small caps and do not allocate your entire portfolio to small cap mutual funds.

FUND DETAILS

Fund name	**Bissett Small Cap**	Start date for data shown	Jan 1992
Fund family	Bissett & Associates Investment Management Ltd.	Fund size (in $ millions)	$93
Mutual fund classification	Canadian small cap	Percentage in foreign holdings	1.50
RRSP eligible	Yes	Dividend frequency	Annual
		Sales charge	No
VVR peer group	Canadian small cap	Redemption charge	No
Number of mutual funds in VVR category	98	Management fee	1.50
WilStar peer group	Domestic equity	Management expense ratio	1.90

FUND PERFORMANCE

	1 month	1 year	3 years	5 years	10 years	15 years
Returns ending Aug 1998	–17.6%	–25.5%	12.5%	9.9%		
Best historical return	16.8%	116.4%	33.1%	37.4%		
Average historical return	1.7%	34.2%	25.2%	29.0%		
Worst historical return	–17.6%	–25.5%	12.5%	9.9%		

RETURNS GREATER THAN

	1 month	1 year	3 years	5 years	10 years	15 years
10 per cent	5%	71%	100%	95%		
Zero	71%	86%	100%	100%		
Percentage of time fund lost $	29%	14%	0%	0%		
Number of periods evaluated	80	69	45	21		

DOWNSIDE RISK

	Worst setback since start date	In bear 1987	In bear 1990	In bear 1994	In bear 1998
Setback for mutual fund	–32.2%			–16.7%	–32.2%
Setback for peer group	–27.2%			–14.7%	–27.2%
Setback ended in	Aug 1998			Feb 1995	Aug 1998
Months to recover from loss	?			10	?

QUARTILE RANKING OF MUTUAL FUND PERFOMANCE AFTER 12 MONTHS OVER TIME

Canadian small cap

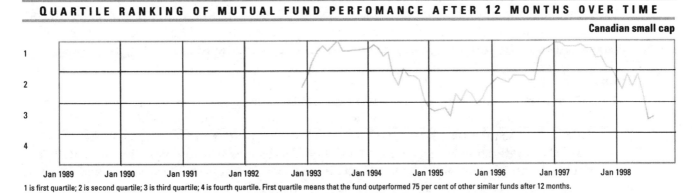

1 is first quartile; 2 is second quartile; 3 is third quartile; 4 is fourth quartile. First quartile means that the fund outperformed 75 per cent of other similar funds after 12 months.

ROLLING 12-MONTH TOTAL RATE OF RETURN FOR THE MUTUAL FUND OVER TIME

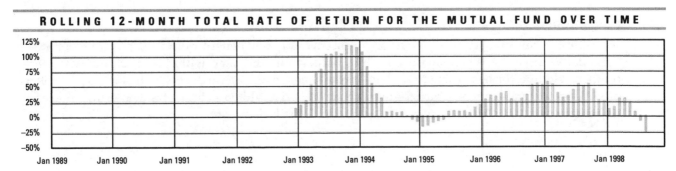

FIDELITY CANADIAN GROWTH COMPANY FUND

Vos value rating			WilStar rating		
Reward	**Risk**	**Best balance**	**Reward**	**Risk**	**Best balance**
★★★★	★★★★★	★★★★★			

Fund profile

The Fidelity Canadian Growth Company Fund has been managed by Alan Radlo from Fidelity Management and Research Co. since July 1995. The fund aims for long-term growth by investing in smaller Canadian corporations that are currently not well known.

Small Canadian corporations have not added value during the last three to five years, but this fund's unique style of investing in small, mid-sized, and larger companies, when prudent, has enabled it to outperform other small cap Canadian equity funds during volatile periods. Over the long term, small companies have outperformed larger companies, but this has not been the case recently, as investors continue to favour blue-chip companies. In the future, as the shares of larger companies become more expensive, smaller companies will become more attractive. This fund is designed to take advantage of such a future small cap rally without incurring the same degree of risk. In turn, investors should realize that this fund is not a true small cap fund, but one that has been able to add value by reducing risk.

The Fidelity Canadian Growth Company Fund has made investments in a large array of companies within Canada that vary in size. The larger companies include blue-chip Canadian corporations such as Power Corporation, Air Canada, and Chum Ltd., owner of Toronto's City TV.

Fund performance

This fund has achieved big marks for providing investors with excellent returns while taking risk into consideration. The fund scored a four-star Vos Value Rating for reward. In turn, the fund has been third or fourth quartile after 12 months relative to other small cap Canadian equity funds. However, the fund has also been first quartile after 12 months. The fund's best 12-month rate of return was a positive 41.9 per cent, and the average 12-month rate of return was 25.7 per cent. The fund has posted positive rates of return after 12 months 97 per cent of the time since its start date in August 1994.

Fund risks

This fund scores big marks for reducing the risk associated with investing in smaller companies. The fund achieved this goal by actively managing the risk and investing a portion of its assets in cash and some larger companies. The fund scored five-star Vos Value Ratings for risk and for best balance between risk and reward. The high rating reflects the fund's ability to reduce risk for investors. Unfortunately, this fund has been fourth quartile after 12 months relative to other Canadian small cap funds, and investors should expect underperformance again when small caps recover.

Future prospects

This is not a true small cap fund, but long-term investors will benefit from its exposure to a range of Canadian companies. When small companies outperform, this fund will underperform; when larger companies outperform, this fund will outperform other small cap funds. Over the long term, this will provide an adequate rate of return for the given level of risk, although investors who want a potentially higher rate of return will have to incur a higher level of risk elsewhere.

FUND DETAILS

Fund name	**Fidelity Canadian Growth Company**	Start date for data shown	Aug 1994
Fund family	Fidelity Investments Canada Limited	Fund size (in $ millions)	$1,329
Mutual fund classification	Canadian small cap	Percentage in foreign holdings	4.75
RRSP eligible	Yes	Dividend frequency	Annual
		Sales charge	Optional
VVR peer group	Canadian small cap	Redemption charge	Optional
Number of mutual funds in VVR category	98	Management fee	2.00
WilStar peer group	Domestic equity	Management expense ratio	2.47

FUND PERFORMANCE

	1 month	1 year	3 years	5 years	10 years	15 years
Returns ending Aug 1998	−15.1%	−4.6%	15.3%			
Best historical return	9.5%	41.9%	28.4%			
Average historical return	1.4%	25.7%	25.5%			
Worst historical return	−15.1%	−4.6%	15.3%			

RETURNS GREATER THAN

	1 month	1 year	3 years	5 years	10 years	15 years
10 per cent	0%	97%	100%			
Zero	76%	97%	100%			
Percentage of time fund lost $	24%	3%	0%			
Number of periods evaluated	49	38	14			

DOWNSIDE RISK

	Worst setback since start date	In bear 1987	In bear 1990	In bear 1994	In bear 1998
Setback for mutual fund	−20.9%			−3.0%	−20.9%
Setback for peer group	−27.2%			−6.7%	−27.2%
Setback ended in	Aug 1998			Nov 1994	Aug 1998
Months to recover from loss	?			1	?

QUARTILE RANKING OF MUTUAL FUND PERFOMANCE AFTER 12 MONTHS OVER TIME

Canadian small cap

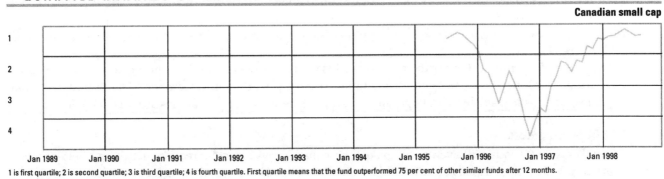

1 is first quartile; 2 is second quartile; 3 is third quartile; 4 is fourth quartile. First quartile means that the fund outperformed 75 per cent of other similar funds after 12 months.

ROLLING 12-MONTH TOTAL RATE OF RETURN FOR THE MUTUAL FUND OVER TIME

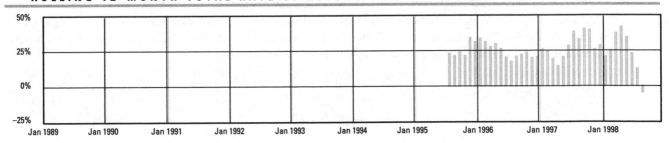

GBC CANADIAN GROWTH FUND

Vos value rating			WilStar rating		
Reward	**Risk**	**Best balance**	**Reward**	**Risk**	**Best balance**
★★★★★	★★★★★	★★★★★	★★★★★	★★	★★★★

Fund profile

The GBC Canadian Growth Fund is managed by the team of Ian Soutar, Jeffrey Tory, and Scott Taylor of Pembroke Management Ltd. The fund aims to achieve long-term capital growth through a diversified portfolio of Canadian companies that offer above-average growth potential.

Canadian small cap stocks have lagged behind their larger cap counterparts for the last three years. Fortunately for investors in the GBC Canadian Growth Fund, the managers invested a portion of the fund in larger growth companies. The fund requires a $100,000 minimum investment and is not a true small cap fund, but serious investors who desire more growth should consider it.

The fund has recently done well in a stock market in which most small cap stocks have not. This reflects the success of companies in the fund's portfolio, such as Geac Computer, Fairfax Financial Holdings, and CGI.

Fund performance

Investing in small caps is a more risky strategy than other Canadian equity mutual funds pursue, but the rewards over time balance their risk. The fund scored a five-star WilStar Rating for generating superior performance relative to other domestic equity funds over the last five years. In addition, the fund earned a triple five-star Vos Value Rating for reward, risk, and best balance between risk and reward, indicating that the fund was superior to other Canadian small cap funds. The fund's best 12-month period was a gain of 51.8 per cent, and the average 12-month gain was 20.5 per cent. The fund has frequently been first quartile after 12 months, but occasionally has been fourth quartile after 12 months. It outperforms other Canadian equity small cap funds after 12 months 75 per cent of the time and frequently outperforms during bull markets.

Fund risks

The worst 12-month period for the fund was a loss of 14.5 per cent, but the fund posted a positive rate of return after 12 months 83 per cent of the time since the start date in December 1988. Inherently, small-cap investing is more risky than large cap investing, since small cap companies are financially less flexible.

Future prospects

Small caps in Canada will eventually make their comeback as investors realize that there's better value in small caps than large caps. However, this realization will take time, and a weak Canadian economy could derail the comeback early. Over the long term, small caps have outperformed large cap stocks. Small cap stocks are more risky, though, and investors require a higher rate of return as compensation for owning more risky stocks. In order to reduce the risk of investing in small cap stocks, investors should invest in the fund on a regular basis. Investors will then be able to take advantage of the above-average volatility associated with small cap investing and reduce their average cost.

FUND DETAILS

Fund name	**GBC Canadian Growth**	Start date for data shown	Dec 1988
Fund family	GBC Asset Management Inc.	Fund size (in $ millions)	$179
Mutual fund classification	Canadian small cap	Percentage in foreign holdings	15.00
RRSP eligible	Yes	Dividend frequency	Annual
		Sales charge	No
VVR peer group	Canadian small cap	Redemption charge	No
Number of mutual funds in VVR category	98	Management fee	1.75
WilStar peer group	Domestic equity	Management expense ratio	1.90

FUND PERFORMANCE

	1 month	1 year	3 years	5 years	10 years	15 years
Returns ending Aug 1998	–18.5%	–16.5%	13.5%	9.0%		
Best historical return	9.6%	51.8%	33.5%	24.2%		
Average historical return	1.4%	20.0%	18.8%	18.2%		
Worst historical return	–18.5%	–16.5%	8.2%	9.0%		

RETURNS GREATER THAN

	1 month	1 year	3 years	5 years	10 years	15 years
10 per cent	0%	75%	96%	98%		
Zero	68%	82%	100%	100%		
Percentage of time fund lost $	32%	18%	0%	0%		
Number of periods evaluated	117	106	82	58		

DOWNSIDE RISK

	Worst setback since start date	In bear 1987	In bear 1990	In bear 1994	In bear 1998
Setback for mutual fund	–27.6%		–18.6%	–14.7%	–27.6%
Setback for peer group	–27.2%		–17.2%	–14.7%	–27.2%
Setback ended in	Aug 1998		Oct 1990	Jan 1995	Aug 1998
Months to recover from loss	?		5	6	?

QUARTILE RANKING OF MUTUAL FUND PERFOMANCE AFTER 12 MONTHS OVER TIME

Canadian small cap

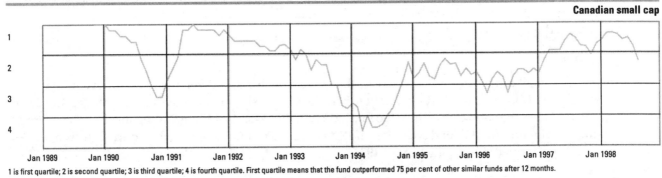

1 is first quartile; 2 is second quartile; 3 is third quartile; 4 is fourth quartile. First quartile means that the fund outperformed 75 per cent of other similar funds after 12 months.

ROLLING 12-MONTH TOTAL RATE OF RETURN FOR THE MUTUAL FUND OVER TIME

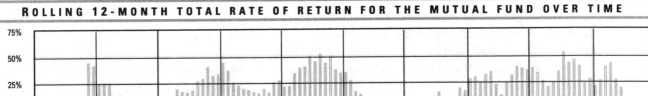

MILLENNIUM NEXT GENERATION FUND

Vos value rating			WilStar rating		
Reward	**Risk**	**Best balance**	**Reward**	**Risk**	**Best balance**
★★★★★	★★★	★★★★★			

Fund profile

The Millennium Next Generation Fund has been managed by Leslie Williams of Morrison Williams Investment Management since February 1993. The investment objective of the fund is to achieve the best rate of return through a diversified portfolio of small to mid cap Canadian companies with the potential for long-term growth.

Investors who remained loyal to small cap investing have not been rewarded for incurring more risk. Large cap Canadian equity mutual funds have enjoyed all the glory. However, it has been proven that, over the long term, small caps outperform large caps. Investors who patiently acquire a select portfolio of small cap companies should be rewarded over the long term for incurring above-average short-term risk. The current environment for Canadian small cap stocks has not been favourable as investors sell small companies to acquire larger ones. If this trend reverses, small cap investors should be rewarded as large numbers of investors chase small company stocks.

The Millennium Next Generation Fund invests in such companies as Geac Computer (which is not such a small company), which designs, sells, produces, rents, and services computer systems, hardware, and software products for financial institutions and other corporate clients.

Fund performance

This fund's performance has been sensational! The fund has frequently been first quartile after 12 months, and its best 12-month rate of return was a gain of 71.1 per cent. The fund's average 12-month rate of return since its start date on January 1994 is 27.7%, and it has posted a positive rate of return 87 per cent of the time after 12 months. The fund scored five-star Vos Value Ratings for reward and for the best balance between risk and reward. These high scores indicate that the fund has achieved excellent performance relative to other Canadian small cap funds.

Fund risks

Inherently, small cap investing is more risky than investing in a well diversified Canadian equity mutual fund, and the Millennium Next Generation Fund is more risky than the average small cap Canadian equity fund over the short term. Thus, the fund scored a three-star Vos Value Rating for risk. The worst 12-month rate of return for the fund was a loss of 17.3 per cent. The fund outperformed during the bear of 1994 and underperformed during the bear of 1998.

Future prospects

Since the variance between the performance of several small cap funds can be substantial, investors should consider holding more than one small cap fund in a large portfolio. Investors must also realize that small cap investing in Canada can be very risky. In the short term, investors can expect increased volatility as the Canadian economy enters the next millennium. Going forward, the small cap mutual funds that select the best companies will become top performers. In the past, Millennium's managers have demonstrated their ability to select great companies.

FUND DETAILS

Fund name	**Millennium Next Generation**	Start date for data shown	Jan 1994
Fund family	Morrison Williams Investment Management Ltd.	Fund size (in $ millions)	$27
Mutual fund classification	Canadian small cap	Percentage in foreign holdings	19.99
RRSP eligible	Yes	Dividend frequency	Annual
		Sales charge	Yes
VVR peer group	Canadian small cap	Redemption charge	No
Number of mutual funds in VVR category	98	Management fee	2.00
WilStar peer group	Domestic equity	Management expense ratio	2.50

FUND PERFORMANCE

	1 month	1 year	3 years	5 years	10 years	15 years
Returns ending Aug 1998	−16.9%	−17.3%	17.9%			
Best historical return	15.7%	71.1%	38.7%			
Average historical return	1.3%	27.7%	29.7%			
Worst historical return	−16.9%	−17.3%	17.9%			

RETURNS GREATER THAN

	1 month	1 year	3 years	5 years	10 years	15 years
10 per cent	5%	80%	100%			
Zero	57%	87%	100%			
Percentage of time fund lost $	43%	13%	0%			
Number of periods evaluated	56	45	21			

DOWNSIDE RISK

	Worst setback since start date	In bear 1987	In bear 1990	In bear 1994	In bear 1998
Setback for mutual fund	−27.3%			−10.1%	−27.3%
Setback for peer group	−27.2%			−14.7%	−27.2%
Setback ended in	Aug 1998			Nov 1994	Aug 1998
Months to recover from loss	?			6	?

QUARTILE RANKING OF AUTUAL FUND PERFOMANCE AFTER 12 MONTHS OVER TIME

Canadian small cap

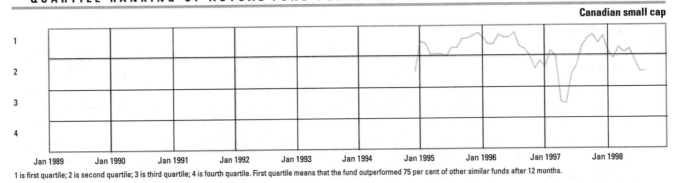

1 is first quartile; 2 is second quartile; 3 is third quartile; 4 is fourth quartile. First quartile means that the fund outperformed 75 per cent of other similar funds after 12 months.

ROLLING 12-MONTH TOTAL RATE OF RETURN FOR THE MUTUAL FUND OVER TIME

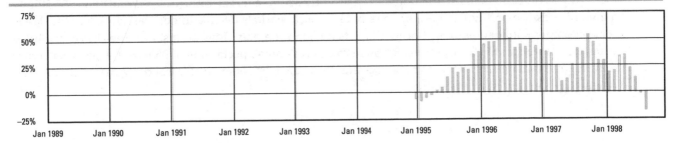

BISSETT MULTINATIONAL GROWTH FUND

Vos value rating			WilStar rating		
Reward	**Risk**	**Best balance**	**Reward**	**Risk**	**Best balance**
★★★★★	★★★★	★★★★★			

Fund profile

The Bissett Multinational Growth Fund is managed by Fred Pynn and Jeffrey Morrison of Bissett and Associates Investment Management and was originally managed by David Bissett. Its investment objective is to provide international exposure with a reasonable level of risk. The fund invests in multinational US, Canadian, and European companies that derive a substantial portion of their revenues and earnings from operations throughout the world. The companies are expected to demonstrate a dividend growth rate in excess of inflation for the foreseeable future.

European and US stock markets have rewarded investors over the past three years, and investors in the Bissett Multinational Growth Fund have participated. With the Euro dollar coming on board and US corporate profits soaring, this fund has delivered double-digit returns. However, investors cannot realistically expect this to continue. The Asian flu may cause some corporations to catch a cold, and stock prices will quickly reflect any signs of ill health.

The fund has made investments in companies such as Cadbury Schweppes, IBM, the Ford Motor Company, Mobil Corporation, and Du Pont.

Fund performance

Investors were not disappointed by this international equity fund. It scored a triple five-star Vos Value Rating for reward, risk, and best balance between risk and reward. The fund has consistently outperformed other international equity funds after 12 months. The best 12-month return was a positive 52.8 per cent, and the best three-year average annual compounded rate of return was 31 per cent. The fund does occasionally underperform for a month, but historically it has quickly rebounded.

Fund risks

The worst 12-month rate of return for the fund was a positive return of 8 per cent, and the worst one-month rate of return was a loss of 11 per cent in August 1998. Except in August 1998, the Bissett Multinational Growth Fund has historically displayed very little downside risk. The fund declined in value by 12.3 per cent during the bear of 1998, equal to the decline of the average international equity fund.

Future prospects

Going forward, the fund should continue to do well. It has exposure to more than one international market and invests in large brand-name companies. The degree to which the fund has outperformed will not likely continue, but it should still deliver consistently above-average returns. The fund is not immune to a global recession and will experience a setback if stock markets decline in general. However, the lower-than-average management fee should alleviate some of the pain. Investors should not have unrealistic expectations about this fund. It will continue to do well, but expectations of 25 per cent per year returns may be unreasonable. Investors in this fund after the bear of 1998 should enjoy above-average performance when global equity markets recover.

FUND DETAILS

Fund name	**Bissett Multinational Growth**	Start date for data shown	Aug 1994
Fund family	Bissett and Associates Investment Management Ltd.	Fund size (in $ millions)	$76
Mutual fund classification	International equity	Percentage in foreign holdings	65.87
RRSP eligible	Foreign	Dividend frequency	Annual
		Sales charge	No
VVR peer group	International equity	Redemption charge	No
Number of mutual funds in VVR category	182	Management fee	1.00
WilStar peer group	International equity	Management expense ratio	1.50

FUND PERFORMANCE

	1 month	1 year	3 years	5 years	10 years	15 years
Returns ending Aug 1998	−11.1%	8.0%	24.0%			
Best historical return	8.3%	52.8%	31.0%			
Average historical return	1.6%	28.0%	28.2%			
Worst historical return	−11.1%	8.0%	24.0%			

RETURNS GREATER THAN

	1 month	1 year	3 years	5 years	10 years	15 years
10 per cent	0%	97%	100%			
Zero	71%	100%	100%			
Percentage of time fund lost $	29%	0%	0%			
Number of periods evaluated	49	38	14			

DOWNSIDE RISK

	Worst setback since start date	In bear 1987	In bear 1990	In bear 1994	In bear 1998
Setback for mutual fund	−12.3%			−3.3%	−12.3%
Setback for peer group	−11.8%			−6.8%	−11.8%
Setback ended in	Aug 1998			Sept 1994	Aug 1998
Months to recover from loss	?			3	?

QUARTILE RANKING OF MUTUAL FUND PERFOMANCE AFTER 12 MONTHS OVER TIME

International equity

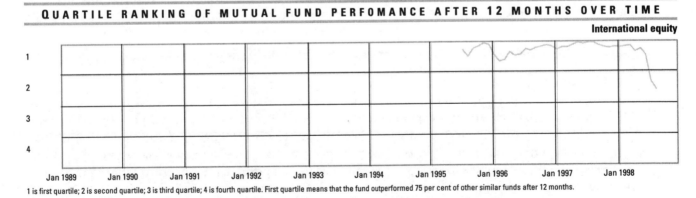

1 is first quartile; 2 is second quartile; 3 is third quartile; 4 is fourth quartile. First quartile means that the fund outperformed 75 per cent of other similar funds after 12 months.

ROLLING 12-MONTH TOTAL RATE OF RETURN FOR THE MUTUAL FUND OVER TIME

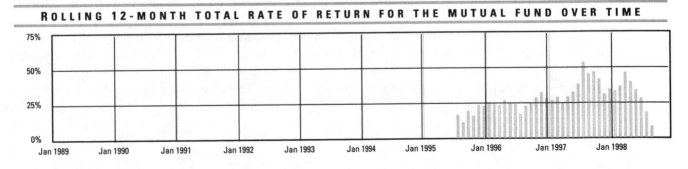

BPI GLOBAL EQUITY VALUE FUND

Vos value rating			WilStar rating		
Reward	**Risk**	**Best balance**	**Reward**	**Risk**	**Best balance**
★★★★★	★★★★★	★★★★★	★★★	★★★★	★★★★

Fund profile

This international equity fund is managed by Daniel Jaworski of BPI Global Asset Management. Driven by the strength of the US and European economies, international equities have done extremely well during the last three years. The investment objective of this fund is to achieve superior long-term growth with global diversification by investing in a portfolio of companies chosen from international markets.

The BPI Global Equity Value Fund invests all over the world. However, the fund has focussed primarily on Europe and North America, which has been a benefit to investors. The fund emphasizes sectors, such as consumer goods and financial services, within countries. It focusses on companies with strong fundamentals, good financial statements, and sustainable competitive and comparative advantages.

The fund has made investments in companies such as America Online Inc., General Electric, the largest publicly traded company in the United States, and banks such as the Bank of Ireland, ING Groep, and Citicorp. These big brand name companies should add some stability to the fund. However, they must all find new sources of growth to generate new shareholder value and sustain such high stock valuations. If this growth does not come to fruition, stock prices may fall.

Fund performance

With a new lead manager, the fund has quickly made a name for itself among international equity funds. Its recent performance is considerably better than its performance in the mid-1990s, going from fourth quartile after 12 months to first quartile after 12 months consistently relative to other international equity funds. This has allowed the fund to earn a triple five-star Vos Value Rating for reward, risk, and best balance between risk and reward. The fund has consistently outperformed other international equity funds after three years within the last five years, outperforming 100 per cent of the time. If this performance continues, the long-term numbers will soon become even more impressive.

Fund risks

Compared with other mutual funds, this one is not very risky. The worst 12-month loss was a mere 3.4 per cent. Although this fund did not experience the stock market crash of 1987, it did perform well during other market downturns. Investors saw their holdings decline by 11.9 per cent during the bear of 1998. During the bear markets of 1990 and 1994 the fund declined by 7.1 per cent and 8.6 per cent respectively and took five and six months to recover. The fund has posted positive rates of return after 12 months 94 per cent of the time since inception.

Future prospects

US and European stock markets have appreciated significantly over the last three years, and stock prices and stock multiples continue to hit new highs. The Asian flu could result in some American companies catching a cold. Therefore, investors should invest for the long term and make regular contributions to reduce the risk. In addition, the value style of this fund should reduce some of the risk.

FUND DETAILS

Fund name	**BPI Global Equity Value**	Start date for data shown	July 1988
Fund family	BPI Capital Management Corporation	Fund size (in $ millions)	$458
Mutual fund classification	International equity	Percentage in foreign holdings	98.47
RRSP eligible	Foreign	Dividend frequency	Annual
		Sales charge	Optional
VVR peer group	International equity	Redemption charge	Optional
Number of mutual funds in VVR category	182	Management fee	2.00
WilStar peer group	International equity	Management expense ratio	2.43

FUND PERFORMANCE

	1 month	1 year	3 years	5 years	10 years	15 years
Returns ending Aug 1998	−11.9%	18.8%	19.0%	14.6%	13.3%	
Best historical return	10.1%	35.8%	22.8%	19.4%	14.4%	
Average historical return	1.1%	14.5%	12.5%	12.9%	14.0%	
Worst historical return	−11.9%	−3.4%	4.9%	8.6%	13.3%	

RETURNS GREATER THAN

	1 month	1 year	3 years	5 years	10 years	15 years
10 per cent	1%	60%	76%	83%	100%	
Zero	66%	94%	100%	100%	100%	
Percentage of time fund lost $	34%	6%	0%	0%	0%	
Number of periods evaluated	122	111	87	63	3	

DOWNSIDE RISK

	Worst setback since start date	In bear 1987	In bear 1990	In bear 1994	In bear 1998
Setback for mutual fund	−11.9%		−7.1%	−8.6%	−11.9%
Setback for peer group	−11.8%		−13.9%	−6.8%	−11.8%
Setback ended in	Aug 1998		Sept 1990	Jan 1995	Aug 1998
Months to recover from loss	?		5	6	?

QUARTILE RANKING OF MUTUAL FUND PERFOMANCE AFTER 12 MONTHS OVER TIME

International equity

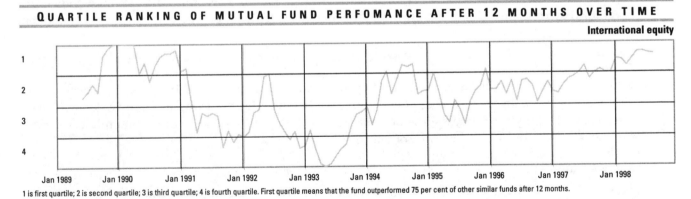

1 is first quartile; 2 is second quartile; 3 is third quartile; 4 is fourth quartile. First quartile means that the fund outperformed 75 per cent of other similar funds after 12 months.

ROLLING 12-MONTH TOTAL RATE OF RETURN FOR THE MUTUAL FUND OVER TIME

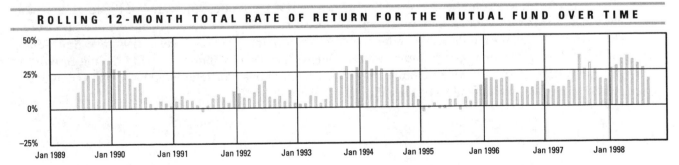

FIDELITY INTERNATIONAL PORTFOLIO FUND

Vos value rating			WilStar rating		
Reward	**Risk**	**Best balance**	**Reward**	**Risk**	**Best balance**
★★★★★	★★★★★	★★★★★	★★★	★★★★	★★★★

Fund profile

The Fidelity International Portfolio Fund is managed by Dick Havermann of Fidelity Management and Research Co. The fund aims for long-term capital appreciation by investing in a large array of companies from a broad range of countries. The manager initially screens geographic regions around the world to find the most promising companies that have earnings momentum and a sustainable growth rate.

Investors who wanted stability, diversification, and long-term growth were not disappointed in the Fidelity International Portfolio Fund. Stock markets in Europe and the United States achieved new record highs, and Fidelity International Portfolio Fund participated. With the ability to invest worldwide and Fidelity's bottom-up investment style, the fund can select the most favourable geographic regions to invest in. This ability to manoeuvre within worldwide stock markets ensures that investors receive a minimum level of diversification with the potential for above-average growth.

The fund invests in such companies as Merck & Co., Safeway, Ford Motor Company, and Dell Computer.

Fund performance

The fund scored a triple five-star Vos Value Rating for reward, risk, and best balance between risk and reward. Such high ratings indicate that the fund was a superior international equity fund relative to other international equity funds during the previous three years. The fund's best 12-month period was a positive rate of return of 41.3 per cent, and the fund's average 12-month rate of return was a positive return of 14.5 per cent since the start date in December 1987. During the early 1990s this fund was frequently third and fourth quartile after 12 months. However, the fund has recently improved performance and has often been first quartile after 12 months.

Fund risks

Recently the fund has experienced some downside risk. During the bear of 1998, the fund declined by 12.3 per cent, more than the average international equity fund. This fund was also more risky than other international equity funds during the bear markets of 1990 and 1994. The worst 12-month loss for the fund was a negative 14.2 per cent rate of return.

Future prospects

This fund reduces the risk of investing internationally by diversifying across several countries. However, a large market correction like the correction in August 1998 will affect the value of the fund. Investors should be prepared for a period of underperformance by the Fidelity International Portfolio Fund, but it should still add value and deliver an adequate rate of return for the given level of risk. Investors seeking the long-term growth of stocks should consider an international equity fund to benefit from the growth and diversification of a worldwide economy. The Fidelity International Portfolio Fund has displayed its ability to add value over the long term historically.

FUND DETAILS

Fund name	**Fidelity International Portfolio**	Start date for data shown	Dec 1987
Fund family	Fidelity Investments Canada Limited	Fund size (in $ millions)	$3,478
Mutual fund classification	International equity	Percentage in foreign holdings	98.81
RRSP eligible	Foreign	Dividend frequency	Annual
		Sales charge	Optional
VVR peer group	International equity	Redemption charge	Optional
Number of mutual funds in VVR category	182	Management fee	2.25
WilStar peer group	International equity	Management expense ratio	2.69

FUND PERFORMANCE

	1 month	1 year	3 years	5 years	10 years	15 years
Returns ending Aug 1998	−12.3%	10.3%	17.1%	13.7%	13.8%	
Best historical return	10.1%	41.3%	23.6%	20.3%	15.3%	
Average historical return	1.0%	14.5%	13.0%	13.7%	13.9%	
Worst historical return	−12.3%	−14.2%	2.5%	6.6%	12.3%	

RETURNS GREATER THAN

	1 month	1 year	3 years	5 years	10 years	15 years
10 per cent	1%	62%	68%	83%	100%	
Zero	67%	88%	100%	100%	100%	
Percentage of time fund lost $	33%	12%	0%	0%	0%	
Number of periods evaluated	129	118	94	70	10	

DOWNSIDE RISK

	Worst setback since start date	In bear 1987	In bear 1990	In bear 1994	In bear 1998
Setback for mutual fund	−19.5%	−5.0%	−19.5%	−9.7%	−12.3%
Setback for peer group	−13.9%	−0.7%	−13.9%	−6.8%	−11.8%
Setback ended in	Sept 1990	Dec 1987	Sept 1990	Feb 1995	Aug 1998
Months to recover from loss	15	13	15	5	?

QUARTILE RANKING OF MUTUAL FUND PERFOMANCE AFTER 12 MONTHS OVER TIME

International equity

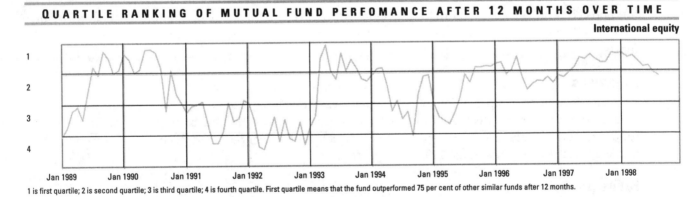

1 is first quartile; 2 is second quartile; 3 is third quartile; 4 is fourth quartile. First quartile means that the fund outperformed 75 per cent of other similar funds after 12 months.

ROLLING 12-MONTH TOTAL RATE OF RETURN FOR THE MUTUAL FUND OVER TIME

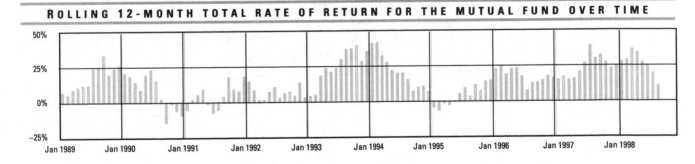

GREYSTONE MANAGED GLOBAL FUND

Vos value rating			WilStar rating		
Reward	**Risk**	**Best balance**	**Reward**	**Risk**	**Best balance**
★★★★★	★★★★★	★★★★★			

Fund profile

The Greystone Managed Global Fund has been managed by the Greystone management team since July 1995. The fund aims for long-term capital growth by investing in a carefully selected diversified portfolio of global companies. International stocks have rewarded investors during the last three to five years, but stock markets took a step back during August 1998 as markets around the world reacted to the Asian flu and Russian meltdown. Investors feared that corporate profits would decline and global growth would slow. In turn, this fund declined by 10.4 per cent in August, but still achieved impressive gains over the year.

Investing in international stocks over the long term will provide the highest rates of return for investors. However, with these higher rates of return investors must incur more risk. Investors may feel uncomfortable investing in stock mutual funds during volatile periods, but this is actually a great time to invest. In addition, international mutual funds offer diversification outside Canada and the potential for higher rates of return.

The fund has invested in McDonalds, Fuji, and Wrigley, the gum company.

Fund performance

This no-load mutual fund has not generated a lot of interest among investors, but its performance has been sensational. The fund has achieved a triple five-star Vos Value Rating for reward, risk, and best balance between risk and return. This indicates the fund has done a superior job of adding value for investors in international equities during the past three years. The best 12-month rate of return for the fund was a gain of 35.3 per cent, and the average 12-month rate of return for the fund was 20 per cent. The fund posted positive rates of return after 12 months 98 per cent of the time since the start of the fund in June 1994. The fund has frequently been first quartile after 12 months relative to other international equity funds.

Fund risks

This fund has done a superior job of preserving investors' money but has not been immune to the bear market of 1998, when it declined in value by 10.4 per cent—less than the average international equity fund. The fund's worst 12-month rate of return was a loss of 1.5 per cent, and the fund's worst one-month loss was 10.4 per cent in August 1998.

Future prospects

Investors benefit from holding international stocks over the long run. Astute investors will invest during bear markets to take advantage of the recovery in stock markets in the future. Conservative investors who want some equity investments will find this mutual fund an ideal choice. It offers the potential for higher rates of return while reducing risk through diversification.

Investors should note that the fund requires a minimum investment of $10,000.

FUND DETAILS

Fund name	**Greystone Managed Global**	Start date for data shown	June 1994
Fund family	Greystone Managed Investments Ltd.	Fund size (in $ millions)	$45
Mutual fund classification	International equity	Percentage in foreign holdings	100.00
RRSP eligible	Foreign	Dividend frequency	Annual
		Sales charge	No
VVR peer group	International equity	Redemption charge	No
Number of mutual funds in VVR category	182	Management fee	2.00
WilStar peer group	International equity	Management expense ratio	2.46

FUND PERFORMANCE

	1 month	1 year	3 years	5 years	10 years	15 years
Returns ending Aug 1998	−10.4%	19.6%	20.5%			
Best historical return	5.6%	35.3%	25.4%			
Average historical return	1.2%	20.0%	20.0%			
Worst historical return	−10.4%	−1.5%	12.4%			

RETURNS GREATER THAN

	1 month	1 year	3 years	5 years	10 years	15 years
10 per cent	0%	88%	100%			
Zero	75%	98%	100%			
Percentage of time fund lost $	25%	3%	0%			
Number of periods evaluated	51	40	16			

DOWNSIDE RISK

	Worst setback since start date	In bear 1987	In bear 1990	In bear 1994	In bear 1998
Setback for mutual fund	−10.4%			−8.9%	−10.4%
Setback for peer group	−11.8%			−6.8%	−11.8%
Setback ended in	Aug 1998			Jan 1995	Aug 1998
Months to recover from loss	?			6	?

QUARTILE RANKING OF MUTUAL FUND PERFOMANCE AFTER 12 MONTHS OVER TIME

International equity

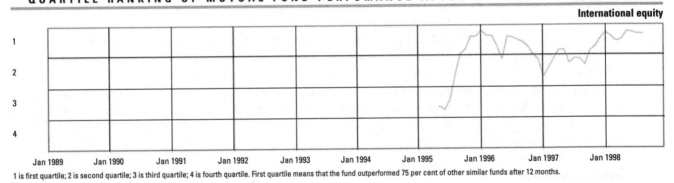

1 is first quartile; 2 is second quartile; 3 is third quartile; 4 is fourth quartile. First quartile means that the fund outperformed 75 per cent of other similar funds after 12 months.

ROLLING 12-MONTH TOTAL RATE OF RETURN FOR THE MUTUAL FUND OVER TIME

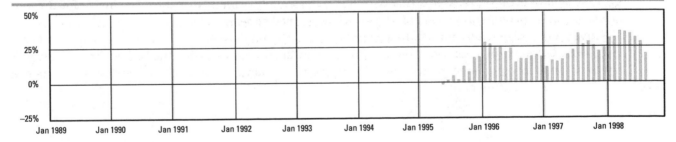

AIC VALUE FUND

Vos value rating			WilStar rating		
Reward	**Risk**	**Best balance**	**Reward**	**Risk**	**Best balance**
★★★★★	★★★★	★★★★★	★★★★★	★★	★★★★

Fund profile

The AIC Value Fund is managed by Neil Murdoch of AIC Limited. The investment objective of the fund is to maximize returns while preserving capital. The fund focusses on a select number of quality businesses with good prospects for the future.

Investors have enjoyed the ride in this fund. Its investments have performed well in aggregate and have produced superior returns for the fund. The fund has participated in the growth of the US economy, and of the US stock market, which has delivered eye-popping returns since the early 1990s. The US stock market is now the largest in the world based on market capitalization, and stock multiplies have achieved new highs. However, US companies must continue to find new sources of growth to sustain these high stock prices.

The AIC Value Fund invests in such brand name companies as American Express, Berkshire Hathaway, Coca Cola Company, Walt Disney, Gillette Company, Johnson & Johnson, and Fairfax Financial Holdings (a Canadian company).

Fund performance

The fund scored a five-star rating based on the Vos Value Rating for reward. In addition, the fund scored a five-star WilStar Rating for reward. The fund has been first quartile after 12 months for the last three years consistently, until the last 12 months, when the fund was second quartile. The fund outperforms other US equity funds during bull markets and tends to underperform during more volatile markets.

Fund risks

The fund is inherently more risky than the average US equity fund, because it owns a smaller number of holdings. The fund has been third or fourth quartile on several occasions after 12 months relative to other US equity funds. The worst 12-month period for the fund was a loss of 7.2 per cent, and the worst one-month decline was 12.4 per cent. The fund tends to go up more than other US equity funds when times are good and down more than others when times are bad. It received a two-star WilStar Rating for risk, indicating that during the last five years the fund has displayed significant risk relative to other international equity mutual funds.

Future prospects

With a smaller number of positions, the fund has the potential to outperform other US equity mutual funds, but the fund also has the potential to underperform over the short term. Which scenario comes to fruition will depend on the performance of the underlying holdings. Investors who invest for the long term in superior companies with brand names have earned superior returns.

Investing in a US equity mutual fund is prudent for all equity investors, and the AIC Value Fund is an excellent US equity fund, and it has some North American exposure outside the United States. However, investors should be prepared to incur periods of underperformance dictated by the underlying investments made by active management.

FUND DETAILS

Fund name	**AIC Value**	Start date for data shown	March 1990
Fund family	AIC Limited	Fund size (in $ millions)	$1,303
Mutual fund classification	US equity	Percentage in foreign holdings	64.10
RRSP eligible	Foreign	Dividend frequency	Annual
		Sales charge	Optional
VVR peer group	US equity	Redemption charge	Optional
Number of mutual funds in VVR category	186	Management fee	2.00
WilStar peer group	International equity	Management expense ratio	2.44

FUND PERFORMANCE

	1 month	1 year	3 years	5 years	10 years	15 years
Returns ending Aug 1998	−15.7%	8.3%	28.8%	20.1%		
Best historical return	16.7%	66.1%	40.2%	29.0%		
Average historical return	1.6%	24.9%	22.9%	22.1%		
Worst historical return	−15.7%	−7.2%	10.5%	12.0%		

RETURNS GREATER THAN

	1 month	1 year	3 years	5 years	10 years	15 years
10 per cent	4%	78%	100%	100%		
Zero	69%	93%	100%	100%		
Percentage of time fund lost $	31%	7%	0%	0%		
Number of periods evaluated	102	91	67	43		

DOWNSIDE RISK

	Worst setback since start date	In bear 1987	In bear 1990	In bear 1994	In bear 1998
Setback for mutual fund	−25.9%		−25.9%	−12.0%	−16.6%
Setback for peer group	−16.5%		−16.5%	−5.6%	−13.5%
Setback ended in	Oct 1990		Oct 1990	June 1994	Aug 1998
Months to recover from loss	4		4	11	?

QUARTILE RANKING OF MUTUAL FUND PERFOMANCE AFTER 12 MONTHS OVER TIME

US equity

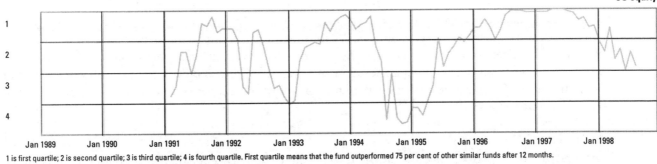

1 is first quartile; 2 is second quartile; 3 is third quartile; 4 is fourth quartile. First quartile means that the fund outperformed 75 per cent of other similar funds after 12 months.

ROLLING 12-MONTH TOTAL RATE OF RETURN FOR THE MUTUAL FUND OVER TIME

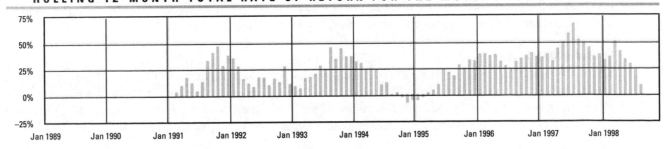

INVESTORS US GROWTH FUND

Vos value rating			WilStar rating		
Reward	Risk	Best balance	Reward	Risk	Best balance
★★★★★	★★★★★	★★★★★	★★★★★	★★★★★	★★★★★

Fund profile

The Investors US Growth Fund has been managed by Terry Wong of Investors Group Inc. since January of 1998. (It was previously managed by Larry Sarbit.) A great fund with a great investment objective usually won't miss a beat with a management change. (When Jerry Javasky took over the management of the Ivy Canadian Fund, the performance did not suffer.) The primary investment objective of the fund is long-term capital appreciation while preserving investor capital. The fund invests in well-researched US companies.

The US stock market has been the place to be for investors. With the bull run into its seventh year, investors are continuing to enjoy all the benefits of equity investing. The stock market continues to hit new highs, and stock multiples are at record highs as well. Many critics argue that the fat lady has arrived and she's just warming up the vocal cords. Regardless, if there's an impending stock market crash, investors—especially young ones—should still establish a systematic investment plan that places a portion of their portfolios in equities.

The Investors US Growth Fund invests in such financial companies as Morgan Stanley and American Express. In addition the fund invests in Warren Buffet's holding company, Berkshire Hathaway, tobacco manufacturer Philip Morris, and oil giant Chevron.

Fund performance

Investors in the US stock market during the last three to five years have enjoyed great returns. In turn, the Investors US Growth fund scored a triple five-star WilStar Rating for reward, risk, and the best balance between risk and reward. This five-star rating is an indication that US stock markets were superior to other international stock markets. The fund also posted a triple five-star Vos Value Rating for reward, risk, and best balance between risk and reward.

This fund is frequently first quartile after 12 months and has been fourth quartile after 12 months only once. This short-term performance translates into superior long-term performance. The fund has outperformed other US equity funds. In addition, this trend has improved during the last 10 years. The best 12-month period for the fund was a positive rate of return of 66.5 per cent, and the average 12-month return was a positive 16 per cent.

Fund risks

The worst 12-month period posted by the fund was a loss of 21.3 per cent, and the fund has posted negative returns after 12 months 18 per cent of the time since inception. During the last five years, investors who invested in the fund did not experience any downside risk During the bear of 1987, the fund declined by 29.3 per cent, and the fund regained its value within 38 months.

Future prospects

There are risks associated with equity investing, which tend to be higher with the stock market at these levels. However, over the long term, investors have earned a reasonable rate of return. The worst 10-year return for the fund was 7.8 per cent. A strategic investment in a US equity fund for a long-term investor is a prudent strategy. Investors who want to invest in this fund will have to deal with an Investors Group representative.

FUND DETAILS

Fund name	**Investors US Growth**	Start date for data shown	July 1980
Fund family	Investors Group Financial Services Inc.	Fund size (in $ millions)	$1,687
Mutual fund classification	US equity	Percentage in foreign holdings	58.96
RRSP eligible	Foreign	Dividend frequency	Annual
		Sales charge	Yes
VVR peer group	US equity	Redemption charge	Deferred
Number of mutual funds in VVR category	186	Management fee	2.00
WilStar peer group	International equity	Management expense ratio	2.41

FUND PERFORMANCE

	1 month	1 year	3 years	5 years	10 years	15 years
Returns ending Aug 1998	−10.7%	25.8%	27.7%	20.2%	18.4%	14.9%
Best historical return	14.1%	66.5%	32.9%	25.2%	19.8%	17.1%
Average historical return	1.3%	16.0%	14.7%	14.1%	13.1%	14.3%
Worst historical return	−23.8%	−21.3%	−4.6%	6.2%	7.8%	11.6%

RETURNS GREATER THAN

	1 month	1 year	3 years	5 years	10 years	15 years
10 per cent	3%	68%	77%	74%	95%	100%
Zero	65%	82%	98%	100%	100%	100%
Percentage of time fund lost $	35%	18%	2%	0%	0%	0%
Number of periods evaluated	218	207	183	159	99	39

DOWNSIDE RISK

	Worst setback since start date	In bear 1987	In bear 1990	In bear 1994	In bear 1998
Setback for mutual fund	−29.3%	−29.3%	−13.7%	−4.9%	−10.7%
Setback for peer group	−29.1%	−29.1%	−17.4%	−5.6%	−13.5%
Setback ended in	Nov 1987	Nov 1987	Oct 1990	Sept 1994	Aug 1998
Months to recover from loss	38	38	3	4	?

QUARTILE RANKING OF MUTUAL FUND PERFOMANCE AFTER 12 MONTHS OVER TIME

US equity

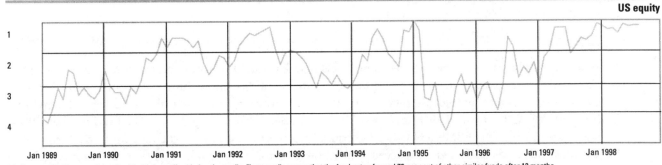

1 is first quartile; 2 is second quartile; 3 is third quartile; 4 is fourth quartile. First quartile means that the fund outperformed 75 per cent of other similar funds after 12 months.

ROLLING 12-MONTH TOTAL RATE OF RETURN FOR THE MUTUAL FUND OVER TIME

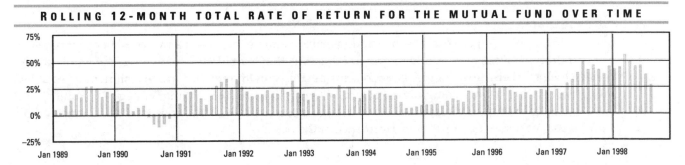

OPTIMA STRATEGY US EQUITY FUND

Vos value rating			WilStar rating		
Reward	Risk	Best balance	Reward	Risk	Best balance
★★★★★	★★★★★	★★★★★			

Fund profile

The Optima Strategy US Equity Fund is managed by David Dreman of Skudder Kemper, formerly Dreman Value Management. The fund's investment objective is to seek long-term capital growth through investment in a diversified portfolio of US companies.

The US markets have achieved phenomenal levels of growth throughout the last seven years. Stock markets continue to set new record highs and, in turn, stocks are trading at very high multiples. Investors seeking exposure to the US market should have realistic expectations about future performance and should not expect the returns of 30 per cent per year that they've become accustomed to. Instead, a realistic expectation of 10 per cent to 15 per cent is more advisable. With increased volatility expected in the stock markets, investors should consider investing periodically to reduce the risk which accompanies equity mutual funds.

To achieve the fund's investment objective, it invests in such companies as Bank America, Ford Motor Company, Philip Morris, Exxon, and Columbia Gas.

Fund performance

The Optima Strategy US Equity Fund's performance has been sensational during the last three years. In turn, the fund scored a triple five-star Vos Value Rating for reward, risk, and best balance between risk and reward. The fund's best 12-month rate of return was 55.8 per cent, and its average 12-month return was 32.9 per cent. The fund posted a positive rate of return after one month 78 per cent of the time and a positive rate of return after 12 months 100 per cent of the time. The fund has outperformed the average US equity fund after 12 months 92 per cent of the time since its start in June 1994. The fund has frequently been first quartile relative to other US equity mutual funds after 12 months.

Fund risks

US equity funds have not displayed the same levels of risk during the last seven years as traditional equity funds should have displayed. Thus, going forward, equity funds could exhibit more downside risk (since August 1998). Investors can reduce their downside risk by investing systematically. Investors who invested in the fund during the bear of 1998 saw their investment decline by 10.7 per cent. The fund has been third quartile after 12 months relative to other US equity mutual funds. The fund could underperform in the future; all good funds underperform occasionally. But investors should not get discouraged unless a long-term trend emerges.

Future prospects

Don't expect 30 per cent per year! US corporations can't continue to grow at a rate of 30 per cent per year. If US corporations were to continue to grow at this rate, they would eventually own the whole world. Nor can stock markets grow forever beyond a sustainable growth rate. In turn, investors must establish realistic expectations about a normal rate of return. Going forward, the Optima Strategy US Equity Fund should continue to outperform similar funds. Investors seeking US equity exposure should consider this fund because of its superior relative performance in the past.

FUND DETAILS

Fund name	**Optima Strategy US Equity**	Start date for data shown	June 1994
Fund family	Loring Ward Investment Counsel Ltd.	Fund size (in $ millions)	$278
Mutual fund classification	US equity	Percentage in foreign holdings	92.78
RRSP eligible	Foreign	Dividend frequency	
		Sales charge	Optional
VVR peer group	US equity	Redemption charge	Optional
Number of mutual funds in VVR category	186	Management fee	2.50
WilStar peer group	International equity	Management expense ratio	0.40

FUND PERFORMANCE

	1 month	1 year	3 years	5 years	10 years	15 years
Returns ending Aug 1998	−10.7%	19.8%	30.7%			
Best historical return	9.0%	55.8%	38.3%			
Average historical return	2.0%	32.9%	33.1%			
Worst historical return	−10.7%	10.9%	25.8%			

RETURNS GREATER THAN

	1 month	1 year	3 years	5 years	10 years	15 years
10 per cent	0%	100%	100%			
Zero	78%	100%	100%			
Percentage of time fund lost $	22%	0%	0%			
Number of periods evaluated	51	40	16			

DOWNSIDE RISK

	Worst setback since start date	In bear 1987	In bear 1990	In bear 1994	In bear 1998
Setback for mutual fund	−10.7%			−7.1%	−10.7%
Setback for peer group	−13.5%			−4.1%	−13.5%
Setback ended in	Aug 1998			Nov 1994	Aug 1998
Months to recover from loss	?			4	?

QUARTILE RANKING OF MUTUAL FUND PERFOMANCE AFTER 12 MONTHS OVER TIME

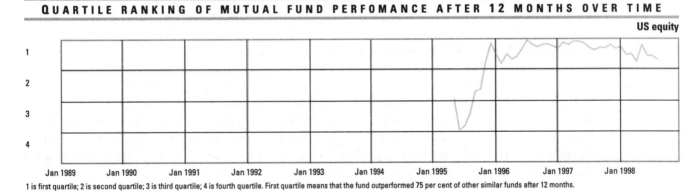

US equity

1 is first quartile; 2 is second quartile; 3 is third quartile; 4 is fourth quartile. First quartile means that the fund outperformed 75 per cent of other similar funds after 12 months.

ROLLING 12-MONTH TOTAL RATE OF RETURN FOR THE MUTUAL FUND OVER TIME

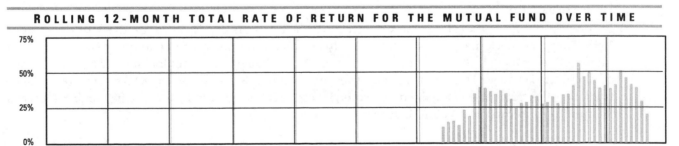

ATLAS EUROPEAN VALUE FUND

Vos value rating			WilStar rating		
Reward	Risk	Best balance	Reward	Risk	Best balance
★★★★	★★★★★	★★★★★			

Fund profile

The Atlas European Value Fund is a conservative European equity mutual fund that has added value through risk reduction. The fund is managed by Stephen Burrows of Pictet International Management. The objective of this fund is to provide long-term capital growth and income by investing in companies in Europe and the United Kingdom and in bonds and cash. The Atlas European Value Fund has made investments in British Petroleum and British Telecom. Outside Britain, the fund has invested in ING Group, an international bank with operations throughout the world, including Canada, and in Telecom Italia.

Europe has provided excellent investment returns for investors during the last several years. However, investors did experience a setback during August 1998 as the Russian economy took a nosedive. In turn, European small cap stocks experienced large setbacks, and large cap funds declined in value on average by 10.8 per cent. However, the Russian economy is a small portion of the overall European economy, and the long-term effects will likely be negligible within a global context.

Fund performance

The Atlas European Value Fund has not won big marks for performance, but it has earned big marks for adding value by reducing risk. The fund scored five-star Vos Value Ratings for risk and for best balance between risk and reward. The fund's best 12-month rate of return was a gain of 41.4 per cent, and the average 12-month rate of return was 20.0 per cent. The fund has posted a positive rate of return after 12 months 100 per cent of the time. It has been second quartile after 12 months frequently, but has also been first or third quartile. The fund has delivered consistent performance, but it has also allowed other European equity mutual funds to outperform. They have done so, however, with considerably more risk, which has not been justified by the additional returns.

Fund risks

Currently, this fund has not displayed any significant downside risk. The fund incurred its worst one-month loss of 9.1 per cent during August 1998, but the fund still posted a gain after 12 months. In turn, its worst 12-month rate of return was a gain of 1.2 per cent. The fund outperforms during bear markets. Thus, its major risk is underperforming similar funds, and it has occasionally posted third quartile performance after 12 months.

Future prospects

Europe is not immune to stock-market corrections, as investors experienced a setback during August 1998. European stock markets have rewarded investors during the last three to five years, but the next three to five years will likely not be as rewarding. Nevertheless, investors looking for equity exposure outside Canada will not be disappointed by investing in Europe. Investors can expect consistent performance from the Atlas European Value Fund. However, investors cannot expect this fund to be number 1, because the fund is concerned with minimizing the downside.

FUND DETAILS

Fund name	**Atlas European Value**	Start date for data shown	Jan 1994
Fund family	Atlas Asset Management Inc.	Fund size (in $ millions)	$67
Mutual fund classification	European equity	Percentage in foreign holdings	94.60
RRSP eligible	Foreign	Dividend frequency	Annual
		Sales charge	Optional
VVR peer group	European equity	Redemption charge	Optional
Number of mutual funds in VVR category	49	Management fee	2.00
WilStar peer group	International equity	Management expense ratio	2.65

FUND PERFORMANCE

	1 month	1 year	3 years	5 years	10 years	15 years
Returns ending Aug 1998	–9.1%	34.2%	25.3%			
Best historical return	8.3%	41.4%	27.8%			
Average historical return	1.5%	20.0%	19.6%			
Worst historical return	–9.1%	1.2%	11.8%			

RETURNS GREATER THAN

	1 month	1 year	3 years	5 years	10 years	15 years
10 per cent	0%	78%	100%			
Zero	73%	100%	100%			
Percentage of time fund lost $	27%	0%	0%			
Number of periods evaluated	56	45	21			

DOWNSIDE RISK

	Worst setback since start date	In bear 1987	In bear 1990	In bear 1994	In bear 1998
Setback for mutual fund	–9.1%			–6.0%	–9.1%
Setback for peer group	–10.8%			–6.0%	–10.8%
Setback ended in	Aug 1998			June 1994	Aug 1998
Months to recover from loss	?			2	?

QUARTILE RANKING OF MUTUAL FUND PERFOMANCE AFTER 12 MONTHS OVER TIME

European equity

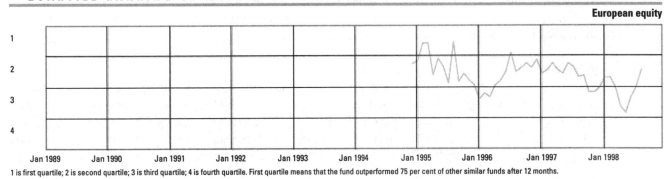

1 is first quartile; 2 is second quartile; 3 is third quartile; 4 is fourth quartile. First quartile means that the fund outperformed 75 per cent of other similar funds after 12 months.

ROLLING 12-MONTH TOTAL RATE OF RETURN FOR THE MUTUAL FUND OVER TIME

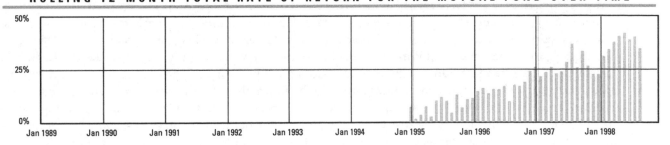

UNIVERSAL EUROPEAN OPPORTUNITIES FUND (MACKENZIE)

Vos value rating			WilStar rating		
Reward	Risk	Best balance	Reward	Risk	Best balance
★★★★★	★★★★	★★★★★			

Fund profile

The Mackenzie Universal European Opportunities Fund is managed by Stephen Peak of Henderson Investors. The investment objective of the fund is to invest in small companies within the emerging markets of Southern European countries, which are modernizing their infrastructures. In addition, the fund will invest in Eastern European countries that are entering privatization and free-trade for the first time in decades.

Investors in small European companies have experienced above-average rates of return for the last three years. Exports in major European countries have increased because of a decline in the exchange rate caused in part by a decrease in interest rates. The prospects for the European Monetary Union (EMU) are looking good. This has improved the confidence of businesses and investors, and in turn has led stock markets higher.

The fund invests in Volkswagen and Telepizza, as well as Ashtead Group, Esat Telecom Group, and Jean Claude Darmon.

Fund performance

During the last three years, small cap European stocks have done well, but they took a pause in 1998. The fund's three-year performance has been excellent, and it scored five-star Vos Value Ratings for reward and for best balance between risk and reward. The fund has frequently been first quartile after 12 months relative to other European equity funds, but has also been fourth quartile after 12 months relative to its peer group. The fund's best 12-month rate of return was 48.2 per cent, and its average has been 32.7 per cent since its start date in October 1994.

Fund risks

Inherently there is more risk in investing in small companies. However, the manager of the fund has done an excellent job of managing this increased risk during the short and long term. Going forward, the fund may underperform and display more downside risk than other European funds that are invested in large cap stocks. During the bear of 1998, the fund declined by 11.8 per cent. The fund has not displayed any significant downside risk recently. The worst 12-month rate of return for the fund was a positive 20 per cent.

Future prospects

European stock markets have forged ahead. This trend cannot last forever (uninterrupted), but investors can still find value and reasonable rates of return. Volatility in these stock markets will increase as the EMU comes on line and economic growth domestically and internationally begins to show signs of slowing. Aggressive investors who want European small cap exposure will benefit from the Mackenzie Universal European Opportunities Fund. However, investors must be aware of the increased risk and reward possibilities associated with small cap investing. In the future the fund's performance will be dictated by Europe's recovery after the Russian capital market meltdown. The fund achieved an above-average score based on the Vos Value Rating because of its strategic investments in small cap stocks, and the performance of small cap stocks versus larger companies will dictate this fund's relative performance in the future.

FUND DETAILS

Fund name	**Universal European Opportunities**	Start date for data shown	Oct 1994
Fund family	Mackenzie Financial Corporation	Fund size (in $ millions)	$873
Mutual fund classification	European equity	Percentage in foreign holdings	98.3
RRSP eligible	Foreign	Dividend frequency	Annual
		Sales charge	Optional
VVR peer group	European equity	Redemption charge	Optional
Number of mutual funds in VVR category	49	Management fee	2.00
WilStar peer group	International equity	Management expense ratio	2.48

FUND PERFORMANCE

	1 month	1 year	3 years	5 years	10 years	15 years
Returns ending Aug 1998	−11.4%	27.9%	30.3%			
Best historical return	8.9%	48.2%	38.3%			
Average historical return	2.1%	32.7%	32.6%			
Worst historical return	−11.4%	20.0%	29.1%			

RETURNS GREATER THAN

	1 month	1 year	3 years	5 years	10 years	15 years
10 per cent	0%	100%	100%			
Zero	83%	100%	100%			
Percentage of time fund lost $	17%	0%	0%			
Number of periods evaluated	47	36	12			

DOWNSIDE RISK

	Worst setback since start date	In bear 1987	In bear 1990	In bear 1994	In bear 1998
Setback for mutual fund	−11.8%			−0.1%	−11.8%
Setback for peer group	−10.8%			−2.6%	−10.8%
Setback ended in	Aug 1998			Oct 1994	Aug 1998
Months to recover from loss	?			1	?

QUARTILE RANKING OF MUTUAL FUND PERFOMANCE AFTER 12 MONTHS OVER TIME

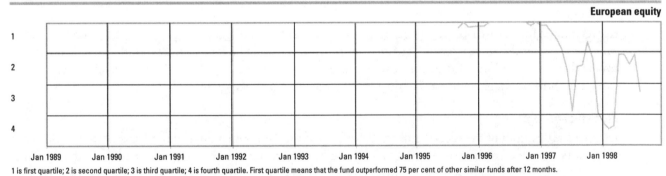

European equity

1 is first quartile; 2 is second quartile; 3 is third quartile; 4 is fourth quartile. First quartile means that the fund outperformed 75 per cent of other similar funds after 12 months.

ROLLING 12-MONTH TOTAL RATE OF RETURN FOR THE MUTUAL FUND OVER TIME

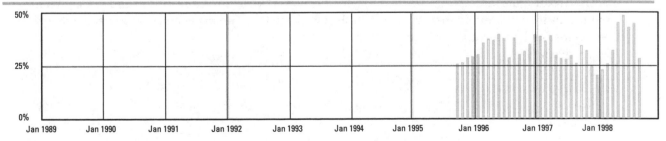

DYNAMIC FAR EAST FUND

Vos value rating			WilStar rating		
Reward	**Risk**	**Best balance**	**Reward**	**Risk**	**Best balance**
★★★★★	★★★★★	★★★★★			

Fund profile

The Dynamic Far East Fund is managed by Jonathan Evershed and Chuk Wong of Goodman and Company Investment Counsel. The investment objective of the fund is to achieve long-term growth through a diversified portfolio of investments in companies based in or with operations primarily in the Far East. Investors have had a difficult and turbulent experience if they have invested in the Far East during the last three to five years. However, investors in the Dynamic Far East Fund have fared better than most.

The Asian flu is far from over, but it cannot and will not continue forever. Companies and countries will have to rejuvenate themselves. As economic conditions improve, investor confidence will increase and stock-market performance should improve.

The Dynamic Far East Fund has made investments in Pentafour Software, Li 7 Fung, and Dsq Software.

Fund performance

The fund scored a triple five-star Vos Value Rating for reward, risk, and the best balance between risk and reward. This indicates that during the previous three years the fund has done an excellent job adding value for investors within a volatile market. Unfortunately, investors did not earn any money, but managers did very well within the Asia and Pacific Rim region. The best 12-month rate of return for the fund was a gain of 23.9 per cent and the average 12-month rate of return of the fund was a gain of 1.7 per cent. The fund has posted positive rates of return after 12 months 70 per cent of the time since its start date of June 1994. The fund has frequently been first quartile after 12 months relative to other Asia and Pacific funds, but it has also been fourth quartile on occasion.

Fund risks

Currently, the fund has displayed larger degrees of downside risk than upside potential. The worst 12-month rate of return for the fund was a loss of 28.9 per cent, and it posted a loss after 12 months 30 per cent of the time. However, the fund did outperform during the bear market of 1998, when it declined by 31.6 per cent, while the average Asia and Pacific fund declined by 47.9 per cent.

Future prospects

Investors are not out of the woods currently. With a meltdown in other emerging countries, there could still be downside pressure on the Asia and Pacific Rim countries. However, having experienced such large setbacks in these companies and countries already, many investors believe that there could be an end in site. This fund is suitable only for more aggressive investors, who should invest in the fund on a regular basis to reduce the underlying risk. In addition, the International Monetary Fund and the US government have intervened in capital markets to establish stability in these unstable markets. Expect higher risks in exchange for the potential for higher returns.

FUND DETAILS

Fund name	**Dynamic Far East**	Start date for data shown	June 1994
Fund family	Goodman and Company Ltd.	Fund size (in $ millions)	$8
Mutual fund classification	Asia and Pacific Rim	Percentage in foreign holdings	88.00
RRSP eligible	Foreign	Dividend frequency	Annual
		Sales charge	Optional
VVR peer group	Asia and Pacific Rim	Redemption charge	Optional
Number of mutual funds in VVR category	59	Management fee	2.00
WilStar peer group	International equity	Management expense ratio	2.78

FUND PERFORMANCE

	1 month	1 year	3 years	5 years	10 years	15 years
Returns ending Aug 1998	−6.3%	−19.3%	−3.5%			
Best historical return	7.4%	23.9%	10.7%			
Average historical return	−0.1%	1.7%	2.7%			
Worst historical return	−14.6%	−28.9%	−3.5%			

RETURNS GREATER THAN

	1 month	1 year	3 years	5 years	10 years	15 years
10 per cent	0%	35%	6%			
Zero	55%	70%	75%			
Percentage of time fund lost $	45%	30%	25%			
Number of periods evaluated	51	40	16			

DOWNSIDE RISK

	Worst setback since start date	In bear 1987	In bear 1990	In bear 1994	In bear 1998
Setback for mutual fund	−31.6%			−3.6%	−31.6%
Setback for peer group	−47.9%			−14.3%	−47.9%
Setback ended in	Aug 1998			Jan 1995	Aug 1998
Months to recover from loss	?			6	?

QUARTILE RANKING OF MUTUAL FUND PERFOMANCE AFTER 12 MONTHS OVER TIME

Asia and Pacific Rim

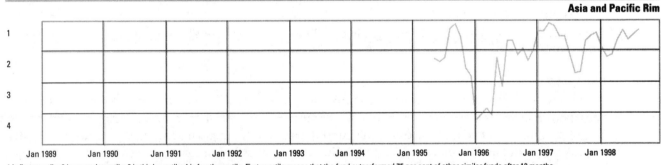

1 is first quartile; 2 is second quartile; 3 is third quartile; 4 is fourth quartile. First quartile means that the fund outperformed 75 per cent of other similar funds after 12 months.

ROLLING 12-MONTH TOTAL RATE OF RETURN FOR THE MUTUAL FUND OVER TIME

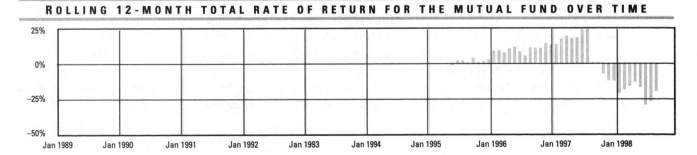

NAVIGATOR ASIA PACIFIC FUND

Vos value rating			WilStar rating		
Reward	**Risk**	**Best balance**	**Reward**	**Risk**	**Best balance**
★★★★★	★★★★	★★★★★			

Fund profile

The Navigator Asia Pacific Fund has been managed by Cheah Cheng and V-Nee Yeh of Value Partners of Hong Kong since January 1997. The investment objective of the fund is to provide long-term growth through investment in a diversified portfolio of companies located in the Asia and Pacific Rim region.

Major problem! The Asia and Pacific Rim markets have been beaten up during the last 18 months. Investors are worried that the currency crisis and instability in Asia would spread to Hong Kong and China. In addition, the collapse of several large financial institutions escalated problems in the region. Investors should expect increased volatility going forward, but over the longer term when Asia resolves its problems the potential for capital appreciation is significant.

The Navigator Asia Pacific Fund is invested in Chinese utilities such as Road King, Shenshen Expressway, and Sichuan Expressway. In addition, the fund invests in companies like Gold Peak, Le Saunda Holdings, and Leefund-Asco Print.

Fund performance

Investors in the Navigator Asia Pacific Fund fared better than most investors in other Asia and Pacific Rim funds. However, over the last year the Navigator Asia Pacific Fund was not immune to the Asian flu, and the fund declined in value and wiped out most of its prior gains. The fund has a great three-year record and has frequently been first quartile after 12 months relative to other Asia and Pacific Rim funds. The fund's best 12-month period was a positive rate of return of 64.2 per cent, and the average 12-month rate of return has been 15.8 per cent since its start date in May 1995. The fund's best three-year rate of return was 12.4 per cent, and its average three-year rate of return was 6.8 per cent. The fund scored five-star Vos Value Ratings for reward and for best balance between risk and reward. This indicates that the fund delivered superior rates of return for the given level of risk incurred by investors during the last three years compared with other Asia and Pacific Rim funds.

Fund risks

There is more downside risk associated with investing in Asia and Pacific Rim funds than in other equity mutual funds. The fund's worst 12-month rate of return was a loss of 41 per cent, and the fund lost money after 12 months 21 per cent of the time. This fund does an excellent job managing downside risk relative to other Asia and Pacific Rim funds, although this may be of little comfort to investors currently!

Future prospects

The Asia and Pacific Rim region has experienced severe difficulty during the last 18 months. A turnaround in the region could lead to potential for capital appreciation. However, this turnaround will not likely occur in the near future. Investors should reduce their risk by investing periodically in the fund to take advantage of any buying opportunities.

An aside: Value Partners were recently named Fund Manager of the Year for Hong Kong equities in the annual South China Morning Post competition, with scoring conducted by Micropal.

FUND DETAILS

Fund name	**Navigator Asia Pacific**	Start date for data shown	May 1995
Fund family	Navigator Fund Company Ltd.	Fund size (in $ millions)	$5
Mutual fund classification	Asia and Pacific Rim	Percentage in foreign holdings	100.00
RRSP eligible	Foreign	Dividend frequency	Annual
		Sales charge	Optional
VVR peer group	Asia and Pacific Rim	Redemption charge	Optional
Number of mutual funds in VVR category	59	Management fee	2.50
WilStar peer group	International equity	Management expense ratio	3.01

FUND PERFORMANCE

	1 month	1 year	3 years	5 years	10 years	15 years
Returns ending Aug 1998	−16.8%	−41.0%	0.1%			
Best historical return	19.5%	64.2%	12.4%			
Average historical return	0.2%	15.8%	6.8%			
Worst historical return	−16.8%	−41.0%	0.1%			

RETURNS GREATER THAN

	1 month	1 year	3 years	5 years	10 years	15 years
10 per cent	5%	55%	20%			
Zero	45%	79%	100%			
Percentage of time fund lost $	55%	21%	0%			
Number of periods evaluated	40	29	5			

DOWNSIDE RISK

	Worst setback since start date	In bear 1987	In bear 1990	In bear 1994	In bear 1998
Setback for mutual fund	−43.4%				−43.4%
Setback for peer group	−47.9%				−47.9%
Setback ended in	Aug 1998				Aug 1998
Months to recover from loss	?				?

QUARTILE RANKING OF MUTUAL FUND PERFOMANCE AFTER 12 MONTHS OVER TIME

Asia and Pacific Rim

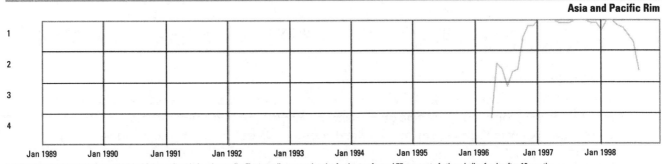

1 is first quartile; 2 is second quartile; 3 is third quartile; 4 is fourth quartile. First quartile means that the fund outperformed 75 per cent of other similar funds after 12 months.

ROLLING 12-MONTH TOTAL RATE OF RETURN FOR THE MUTUAL FUND OVER TIME

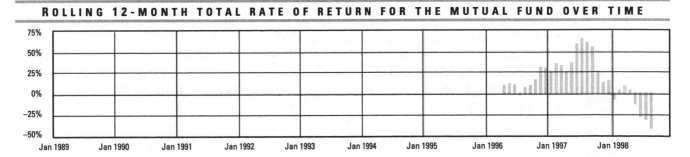

SCOTIA EXCELSIOR PACIFIC RIM FUND

Vos value rating			WilStar rating		
Reward	**Risk**	**Best balance**	**Reward**	**Risk**	**Best balance**
★★★★★	★★★★★	★★★★★			

Fund profile

The Scotia Excelsior Pacific Rim Fund is managed by Scotia Investment Management Ltd. The fund's investment objective is to invest in high-quality companies in the Western portion of the Asia and Pacific Rim region.

Investors in Asia and the Pacific Rim have incurred severe setbacks. In addition, some high-profile financial companies have declared bankruptcy, including Peregrine Group and Capital Asia. Banks have cut financing to small Asian companies, and investors who borrowed money to invest ran for the exits, selling at depressed prices. All these events caused the value of Asia and Pacific Rim stocks to decline significantly during the last 12 months. Within this decline, there were a few rays of hope. February 1998 was a good month, and some Asia and Pacific Rim stocks were up more than 10 per cent. Investors who patiently and strategically invest in the region over time can participate in the recovery of this region. However, no one knows how long the recovery will take or when it will come to fruition.

The fund's investments include Sony Corporation, Mazda, and Singapore Telecomm.

Fund performance

The performance of this fund has been adequate, considering the difficult environment of the Asia and Pacific Rim stock markets. The fund scored a triple five-star Vos Value Rating for reward, risk, and best balance between risk and reward. This indicates that the fund's performance was superior to that of other Asia and Pacific Rim funds. However, on an absolute basis the fund was not spectacular. The best 12-month return was a positive return of 22.1 per cent, while the average 12-month return since the start of the fund in November of 1994 was 0.3 per cent. The fund posted positive rates of return after 12 months 69 per cent of the time. The fund was frequently first quartile after 12 months, but during 1996 it stumbled. Still, the fund has outperformed other Asia and Pacific Rim funds 88 per cent of the time after 12 months since its inception.

Fund risks

This fund has displayed a significant amount of downside risk. During the bear market of 1998, it declined by 39.8 per cent; the average decline by an Asia and Pacfic Rim fund was 47.9 per cent. The fund's worst one-month loss was 11.1 per cent, and its worst 12-month rate of return was a loss of 34.8 per cent.

Future prospects

Inherently there is more risk for investors in a specific geographic region. However, investors also have the opportunity to earn higher rates of return in the future when the Asia and Pacific Rim region recovers. Investors wanting exposure to the region will find that the Scotia Excelsior Pacific Rim fund has delivered superior performance relative to other Asia and Pacific Rim funds. However, with increased levels of volatility in these markets, investors should invest systematically by making regular contributions. In addition, investors should remember that a recovery could take several years to happen.

FUND DETAILS

Fund name	Scotia Excelsior Pacific Rim	Start date for data shown	Nov 1994
Fund family	The Bank of Nova Scotia	Fund size (in $ millions)	$27
Mutual fund classification	Asia and Pacific Rim	Percentage in foreign holdings	92.74
RRSP eligible	Foreign	Dividend frequency	Annual
		Sales charge	No
VVR peer group	Asia and Pacific Rim	Redemption charge	No
Number of mutual funds in VVR category	59	Management fee	2.00
WilStar peer group	International equity	Management expense ratio	2.43

FUND PERFORMANCE

	1 month	1 year	3 years	5 years	10 years	15 years
Returns ending Aug 1998	−7.6%	−34.4%	−8.7%			
Best historical return	8.9%	22.1%	4.2%			
Average historical return	−0.3%	0.3%	−1.4%			
Worst historical return	−11.1%	−34.8%	−8.7%			

RETURNS GREATER THAN

	1 month	1 year	3 years	5 years	10 years	15 years
10 per cent	0%	31%	0%			
Zero	50%	69%	36%			
Percentage of time fund lost $	50%	31%	64%			
Number of periods evaluated	46	35	11			

DOWNSIDE RISK

	Worst setback since start date	In bear 1987	In bear 1990	In bear 1994	In bear 1998
Setback for mutual fund	−39.8%			−3.4%	−39.8%
Setback for peer group	−47.9%			−13.5%	−47.9%
Setback ended in	Aug 1998			Feb 1995	Aug 1998
Months to recover from loss	?			4	?

QUARTILE RANKING OF MUTUAL FUND PERFOMANCE AFTER 12 MONTHS OVER TIME

Asia and Pacific Rim

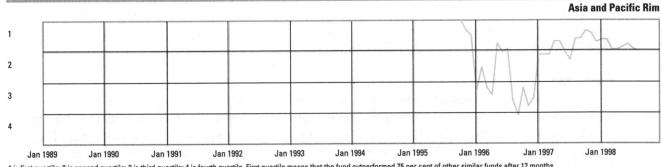

1 is first quartile; 2 is second quartile; 3 is third quartile; 4 is fourth quartile. First quartile means that the fund outperformed 75 per cent of other similar funds after 12 months.

ROLLING 12-MONTH TOTAL RATE OF RETURN FOR THE MUTUAL FUND OVER TIME

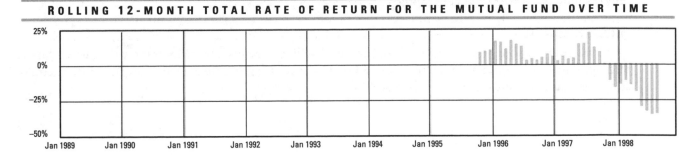

AGF INTERNATIONAL—JAPAN CLASS FUND

Vos value rating			WilStar rating		
Reward	**Risk**	**Best balance**	**Reward**	**Risk**	**Best balance**
★★★★★	★★★★★	★★★★★	★	★★	★

Fund profile

The AGF International Japan Class Fund is managed by Sumio Sakamoto of Nomura Asset Management. Mr. Sakamoto is a senior investment manager with Nomura and has more than 20 years of investment management experience in the Pacific Rim. Nomura Asset Management is currently the largest international investment management company in Japan and has been retained by AGF Group of Funds to advise on the Japan Class Fund. This fund's investment objective is to achieve long-term capital appreciation by investing primarily in Japanese companies that have above-average growth prospects. The fund utilizes a top-down value investment style, selecting stocks in favourable industries that are attractively priced.

However, the Japanese and Asian economies have been faced with numerous uncertainties lately, such as weak domestic demand, increased bankruptcies, and a decline in confidence by both investors and local citizens. The Japanese stock market has experienced severe setbacks because of turmoil in the region and a lack of economic activity. When economic activity in Japan increases, this fund should regain some of its losses.

The fund invests in such companies as Sony Corporation and Honda Motor Company. Both of these companies export a considerable amount of their products.

Fund performance

This fund has not been an enjoyable ride for investors in the short term. The fund has done an excellent job investing in Japan relative to other Japan funds, but it was not immune to the devastating economic conditions that have plagued Japan for the last three years. The fund received a triple five-star Vos Value Rating for reward, risk and the best balance between risk and reward. But many investors will still be disappointed by the returns this fund posted over the last several years. The fund's best 12-month period was a positive rate of return of 102.2 per cent, and the 12-month average for the fund is a positive return of 12.7 per cent since its start date in July 1981.

Fund risks

This fund has above-average risk relative to other international equity investments. The Japanese economy has experienced several large setbacks and, in turn, the value of the fund has declined. Although this fund is an above-average Japanese fund, it is not immune to the economic conditions of Japan. The fund posts a positive rate of return after 12 months only 64 per cent of the time. The fund's worst 12-month period was a decline of 26 per cent. Inherently, the fund is more risky than others, because the fund's investments are concentrated within one geographic region.

Future prospects

The Japanese economy is still in trouble. This fund will experience above-average volatility as Japan attempts an economic recovery. Investors who enjoy investing in mutual funds at the bottom could consider a strategic investment in Japan at this time.

FUND DETAILS

Fund name	**AGF International—Japan Class**	Start date for data shown	July 1981
Fund family	AGF Funds Inc.	Fund size (in $ millions)	$83
Mutual fund classification	Japanese equity	Percentage in foreign holdings	86.90
RRSP eligible	Foreign	Dividend frequency	Annual
		Sales charge	Optional
VVR peer group	Japanese equity	Redemption charge	Optional
Number of mutual funds in VVR category	19	Management fee	2.50
WilStar peer group	International equity	Management expense ratio	3.07

FUND PERFORMANCE

	1 month	1 year	3 years	5 years	10 years	15 years
Returns ending Aug 1998	–6.3%	–12.6%	0.3%	–2.3%	0.3%	8.7%
Best historical return	21.5%	102.2%	47.7%	43.2%	16.4%	13.7%
Average historical return	0.9%	12.7%	11.8%	11.6%	9.1%	10.9%
Worst historical return	–16.7%	–26.4%	–12.2%	–5.8%	–0.5%	8.7%

RETURNS GREATER THAN

	1 month	1 year	3 years	5 years	10 years	15 years
10 per cent	6%	48%	42%	39%	57%	74%
Zero	53%	64%	71%	82%	97%	100%
Percentage of time fund lost $	47%	36%	29%	18%	3%	0%
Number of periods evaluated	206	195	171	147	87	27

DOWNSIDE RISK

	Worst setback since start date	In bear 1987	In bear 1990	In bear 1994	In bear 1998
Setback for mutual fund	–38.9%	–17.4%	–29.6%	–22.1%	–20.5%
Setback for peer group	–39.4%	–14.4%	–33.5%	–20.0%	–42.2%
Setback ended in	July 1992	Oct 1987	Sept 1990	Feb 1995	Aug 1998
Months to recover from loss	19	5	41	?	?

QUARTILE RANKING OF MUTUAL FUND PERFOMANCE AFTER 12 MONTHS OVER TIME

Japanese equity

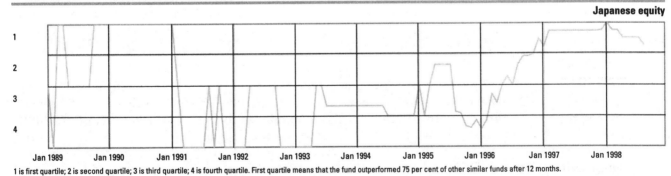

1 is first quartile; 2 is second quartile; 3 is third quartile; 4 is fourth quartile. First quartile means that the fund outperformed 75 per cent of other similar funds after 12 months.

ROLLING 12-MONTH TOTAL RATE OF RETURN FOR THE MUTUAL FUND OVER TIME

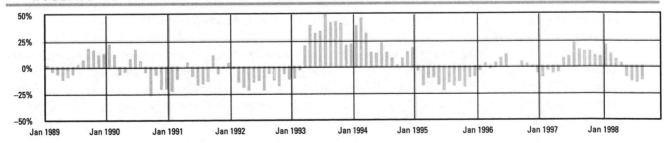

SCOTIA EXCELSIOR LATIN AMERICAN FUND

Vos value rating			WilStar rating		
Reward	Risk	Best balance	Reward	Risk	Best balance
★★★★★	★★★	★★★★			

Fund profile

The Scotia Excelsior Latin American Fund invests in the emerging countries of Latin America. The fund has been managed by the Scotia Investment Management Team since October 1994. It aims to invest in high-quality, publicly traded companies with operations in Latin America, including Mexico, Argentina, Brazil, Venezuela, Peru, and Chile.

Latin America is famous for its raw materials and unique culture. Investors who have invested in Latin American mutual funds recently have experienced a downward spiral in investment performance. Investors who invested in Latin America during the past three years have had a turbulent ride and were lucky to break even. Thus, investors in Latin American mutual funds incur more risk than investors in other mutual funds, but they also have the potential for superior long-term performance. Investors have to diversify their holdings if they own a Latin American mutual fund.

The Scotia Excelsior Latin American Fund has made investments in telecommunications companies including Telecmnicacoes Brasi, Telefonica De Argent, and Compania Telf Chile.

Fund performance

Amidst the turbulent market conditions within Latin America it is difficult for Latin American and emerging market funds to add value. The Scotia Excelsior Latin American fund added enough value to score a five-star Vos Value Rating for reward. However, the fund incurred more risk to generate this return than other Latin American and emerging market funds. The fund has frequently been first or second quartile relative to other Latin American and emerging market funds. Its best 12-month rate of return was a positive return of 43.5 per cent, and its average 12-month rate of return was a gain of 19.3 per cent. The fund has posted positive rates of return after 12 months 83 per cent of the time since the start date in November 1994.

Fund risks

With the above-average downside risk displayed in Latin American and emerging market funds, investors quickly gave back any above-average performance of earlier periods. The fund declined by 40.1 per cent during the bear of 1998. In addition, the worst 12-month period for the fund was a decline of 36.1 per cent.

Future prospects

With Latin American countries moving toward free trade and privatization, the future looks brighter than the recent past. The turmoil may not be over, however, since Latin American countries are starting to feel the side effects of the recent turbulence in Russia. In turn, Latin American countries will have to stabilize their capital markets.

Emerging markets display higher downside risk and volatility than a more conservative equity mutual fund. Therefore, investors should invest for the long term and not maintain an entire portfolio in one Latin American fund. With a successful turnaround, investors can achieve substantial gains in a short time. This fund would be suitable only for speculative investors who can withstand above-average downside risk.

FUND DETAILS

Fund name	**Scotia Excelsior Latin America**	Start date for data shown	Nov 1994
Fund family	The Bank of Nova Scotia	Fund size (in $ millions)	$35
Mutual fund classification	Latin America and Emerging Markets	Percentage in foreign holdings	93.04
RRSP eligible	Foreign	Dividend frequency	Annual
		Sales charge	No
VVR peer group	Latin America and Emerging Markets	Redemption charge	No
Number of mutual funds in VVR category	56	Management fee	2.50
WilStar peer group	International equity	Management expense ratio	2.39

FUND PERFORMANCE

	1 month	1 year	3 years	5 years	10 years	15 years
Returns ending Aug 1998	−27.8%	−36.1%	3.1%			
Best historical return	9.3%	43.5%	23.9%			
Average historical return	0.4%	19.3%	16.8%			
Worst historical return	−27.8%	−36.1%	3.1%			

RETURNS GREATER THAN

	1 month	1 year	3 years	5 years	10 years	15 years
10 per cent	0%	74%	91%			
Zero	59%	83%	100%			
Percentage of time fund lost $	41%	17%	0%			
Number of periods evaluated	46	35	11			

DOWNSIDE RISK

	Worst setback since start date	In bear 1987	In bear 1990	In bear 1994	In bear 1998
Setback for mutual fund	−40.1%			−12.2%	−40.1%
Setback for peer group	−42.0%			−22.6%	−42.0%
Setback ended in	Aug 1998			Feb 1995	Aug 1998
Months to recover from loss	?			5	?

QUARTILE RANKING OF MUTUAL FUND PERFOMANCE AFTER 12 MONTHS OVER TIME

Latin America and Emerging Markets

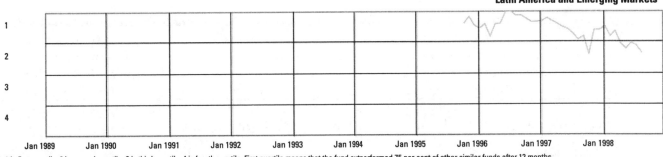

1 is first quartile; 2 is second quartile; 3 is third quartile; 4 is fourth quartile. First quartile means that the fund outperformed 75 per cent of other similar funds after 12 months.

ROLLING 12-MONTH TOTAL RATE OF RETURN FOR THE MUTUAL FUND OVER TIME

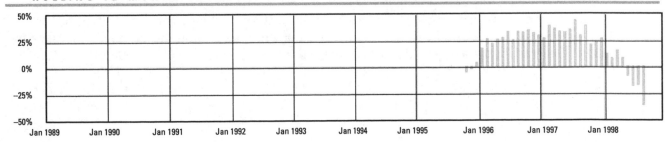

AIM GLOBAL HEALTH SCIENCES FUND

Vos value rating			WilStar rating		
Reward	Risk	Best balance	Reward	Risk	Best balance
★★★★★	★★★★	★★★★★	★★★★★	★★★★	★★★★★

Fund profile

The AIM Global Health Sciences Fund is managed by John Schroer of INVESTCO, the parent company of AIM mutual funds. The fund aims for long-term capital growth by investing primarily in stocks of companies involved in healthcare throughout the world.

With baby boomers reaching their 50s, the healthcare industry is considered one of the hot investment sectors. The AIM Global Health Sciences Fund allows investors to participate in the success of this industry. Specialty funds like this one offer investors the potential for higher returns, but with higher risk. Investors who invest in the right sector at the right time can achieve superior returns. With healthcare companies introducing new products to a captive market, the future looks bright. (Investors could consider sector funds such as healthcare, technology, infrastructure, and telecommunications.) The AIM Global Health Sciences Fund achieves its investment objective by investing in such companies as Merck & Company, Pfizer, Bristol Myers Squibb, and Johnson & Johnson.

Fund performance

Investors have enjoyed the ride in this fund since its start date in November 1992. The fund wasn't number 1 every year, but investors have not been disappointed. Its worst three-year rate of return was 21.7 per cent compounded annually. Relative to other specialty funds, this one scored a five-star Vos Value Rating for reward and a five-star WilStar reward rating. The fund has been first quartile frequently after 12 months relative to other specialty mutual funds, but it has also been third or fourth quartile after 12 months. The fund has posted a positive rate of return after 12 months 97 per cent of the time.

Fund risk

Specialty funds are inherently more risky because they focus on one segment of the economy, and investors will live or die by the performance of that industry. Investors in the AIM Global Health Sciences Fund have currently been rewarded for investing in the healthcare industry. The worst 12-month period for the fund was a loss of 2.5 per cent, but the worst one-month loss was 11.6% in February 1993. In addition, this fund fared better than the average specialty fund during the bear of 1998. The fund scored a four-star WilStar Rating for risk, indicating that this specialty fund did a good job managing risk. Investors can reduce some of the risk by investing monthly, especially during periods of above-average volatility.

Future prospects

Healthcare companies can survive or fail on the success of one drug, so investors must be aware of the inherent increased risk of investing in one specific sector. Factors such as government regulation can significantly alter the landscape of the healthcare industry. Investing in this specialty fund has been beneficial for investors, but the fund is still focussed on one sector within the economy. Investors may not be rewarded for incurring additional risk in the future.

FUND DETAILS

Fund name	**AIM Global Health Sciences**	Start date for data shown	Nov 1992
Fund family	AIM Funds Group Canada Inc.	Fund size (in $ millions)	$307
Mutual fund classification	Specialty	Percentage in foreign holdings	100.00
RRSP eligible	Foreign	Dividend frequency	Annual
		Sales charge	Optional
VVR peer group	Specialty	Redemption charge	Optional
Number of mutual funds in VVR category	62	Management fee	2.25
WilStar peer group	International equity	Management expense ratio	2.94

FUND PERFORMANCE

	1 month	1 year	3 years	5 years	10 years	15 years
Returns ending Aug 1998	−6.7%	23.5%	24.6%	27.9%		
Best historical return	−12.6%	84.5%	40.6%	32.3%		
Average historical return	1.8%	28.6%	31.3%	27.0%		
Worst historical return	−11.6%	−2.5%	21.7%	22.5%		

RETURNS GREATER THAN

	1 month	1 year	3 years	5 years	10 years	15 years
10 per cent	3%	83%	100%	100%		
Zero	67%	97%	100%	100%		
Percentage of time fund lost $	33%	3%	0%	0%		
Number of periods evaluated	70	59	35	11		

DOWNSIDE RISK

	Worst setback since start date	In bear 1987	In bear 1990	In bear 1994	In bear 1998
Setback for mutual fund	−15.4%			−15.4%	−6.7%
Setback for peer group	−5.8%			−2.2%	−11.7%
Setback ended in	July 1996			June 1994	Aug 1998
Months to recover from loss	11			7	?

QUARTILE RANKING OF MUTUAL FUND PERFOMANCE AFTER 12 MONTHS OVER TIME

Specialty

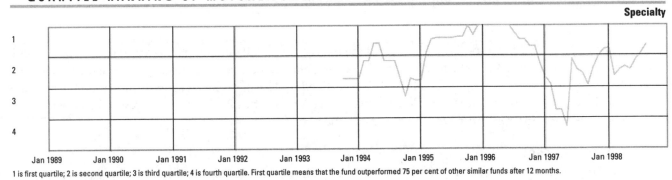

1 is first quartile; 2 is second quartile; 3 is third quartile; 4 is fourth quartile. First quartile means that the fund outperformed 75 per cent of other similar funds after 12 months.

ROLLING 12-MONTH TOTAL RATE OF RETURN FOR THE MUTUAL FUND OVER TIME

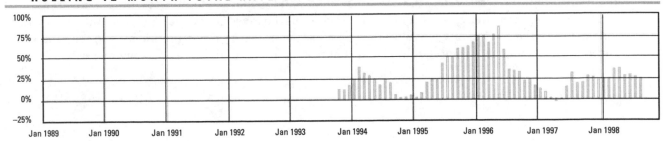

DYNAMIC REAL ESTATE EQUITY FUND

Vos value rating			WilStar rating		
Reward	**Risk**	**Best balance**	**Reward**	**Risk**	**Best balance**
★★★★★	★★★★	★★★★★			

Fund profile

The Dynamic Real Estate Equity Fund is co-managed by Anne Maclean and Michael Cooper of Goodman and Company Investment Counsel. It is a specialty fund that invests only in real estate companies. It maintains a global portfolio of debt and equity securities involved in real estate assets. The fund will invest in publicly traded companies that have the potential to increase in value. The managers look at asset quality, growth prospects, conservative leverage ratios (companies should not carry a lot of debt relative to their equity), and good management ability to select their investments.

Real estate companies are only a portion of the entire economy. Therefore, investors should be aware that Dynamic Real Estate Equity Fund will appreciate in value differently than other mutual fund investments, and that the fund is managed to achieve diversification in the real estate sector.

The fund has made investments in such companies as Brookfield Properties, real estate managers of such office buildings as BCE Place in downtown Toronto.

Fund performance

Investors in this fund have not been disappointed for the last three years. However, the fund had a minor setback during 1998. Relative to other special equity funds, this one has delivered above-average performance. The fund outperformed other special equity funds after 12 months frequently. The best 12-month period was 58.7 per cent, while the best one-month period was 11.6 per cent. The fund received a five-star Vos Value Rating for reward. However, it is important to realize that this fund is unique and should be judged on its own merits. If you see global real estate as a good means of diversification and a hedge against inflation, this fund should meet all your needs.

Fund risks

The biggest risk for this specialty fund is that the bottom might fall out of the real estate market (again) and investors might lose their shirts. The fund has been volatile, but the worst 12-month return was a loss of 4.9 per cent. During the bear market of 1998, it declined by 15.8 per cent, a larger decline than the average special equity fund. Investors should note that going forward this fund's risk and reward characteristics could be very different from what they were in the past.

Future prospects

Real estate had good years in 1996 and 1997, but results will be mixed in 1998. In the long run, investors will be able to participate in the recovery of the real estate market, and real estate offers great benefits for diversification. If interest rates, the Canadian dollar, and global economic growth remain strong, real estate will eventually deliver excellent results. Investors who invest in the fund on a monthly basis will be able to take advantage of any volatility in the real-estate market by buying more units in the fund when fund prices decline. Investors should realize that real estate could display above-average risk.

FUND DETAILS

Fund name	**Dynamic Real Estate Equity**	Start date for data shown	June 1995
Fund family	Goodman and Company Ltd.	Fund size (in $ millions)	$177
Mutual fund classification	Specialty	Percentage in foreign holdings	76.10
RRSP eligible	Foreign	Dividend frequency	Annual
		Sales charge	Optional
VVR peer group	Specialty	Redemption charge	Optional
Number of mutual funds in VVR category	62	Management fee	2.25
WilStar peer group	International equity	Management expense ratio	2.72

FUND PERFORMANCE

	1 month	1 year	3 years	5 years	10 years	15 years
Returns ending Aug 1998	−8.4%	−4.9%	25.0%			
Best historical return	11.6%	58.7%	33.0%			
Average historical return	1.9%	37.0%	29.5%			
Worst historical return	−8.4%	−4.9%	25.0%			

RETURNS GREATER THAN

	1 month	1 year	3 years	5 years	10 years	15 years
10 per cent	3%	93%	100%			
Zero	72%	96%	100%			
Percentage of time fund lost $	28%	4%	0%			
Number of periods evaluated	39	28	4			

DOWNSIDE RISK

	Worst setback since start date	In bear 1987	In bear 1990	In bear 1994	In bear 1998
Setback for mutual fund	−15.8%				−15.8%
Setback for peer group	−11.7%				−11.7%
Setback ended in	Aug 1998				Aug 1998
Months to recover from loss	?				?

QUARTILE RANKING OF MUTUAL FUND PERFOMANCE AFTER 12 MONTHS OVER TIME

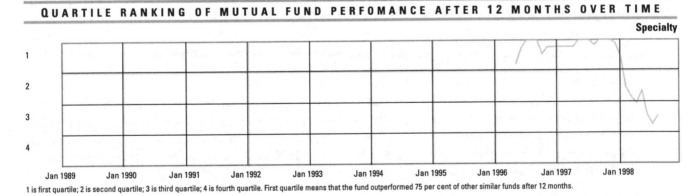

1 is first quartile; 2 is second quartile; 3 is third quartile; 4 is fourth quartile. First quartile means that the fund outperformed 75 per cent of other similar funds after 12 months.

ROLLING 12-MONTH TOTAL RATE OF RETURN FOR THE MUTUAL FUND OVER TIME

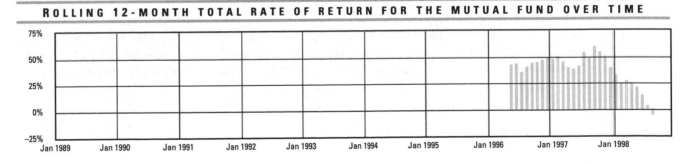

ROYAL PRECIOUS METALS FUND

Vos value rating			WilStar rating		
Reward	**Risk**	**Best balance**	**Reward**	**Risk**	**Best balance**
★★★★★	★★★★★	★★★★★	★★★★	★	★★

Fund profile

The Royal Precious Metals Fund is managed by John Embry of Royal Bank Investment Management Inc. The investment objective of the fund is to provide the potential for capital growth by investing in Canadian and international companies that are involved in exploration for gold, silver, and platinum.

Help! Gold is dying! Somebody help! Once the metal of choice, gold has lost its appeal with many investors. Central banks are selling gold by the tonne, and the price of gold bullion is at its lowest level in over 10 years. However, on the upside, precious metals are cheap compared with historical standards, and pessimism around gold could generate great buying opportunities. Investors must realize that nobody really knows the value of gold. Until a proper valuation can be made, expect above-average volatility going forward. There is potential to earn large profits in an aggressive specialty fund like this.

The fund invests in gold companies such as Euro-Nevada Mining, Newmont Mining Corporation, and Goldcorp, and in resources companies such as Prime Resources and Viceroy Resources.

Fund performance

The absolute performance of this fund recently has been awful. The fund has lost money hand over fist as the price of gold bullion declines further. However, the long-term numbers are more impressive. The worst five-year rate of return posted by the fund was a gain of 1.5 per cent per year compounded annually. On the upside, the best five-year period was a gain of 33.4 per cent per year compounded annually. In addition, the fund has posted tremendous gains in short periods. Its best one-month return was 30.5 per cent, and its best 12-month return was a gain of 163.7 per cent. The fund performed well compared with other precious metals funds, scoring a triple five-star Vos Value Rating for reward, risk, and best balance between risk and reward. However, relative to other domestic equity funds, this fund failed to meet the mark, scoring a two-star WilStar Rating for best balance between risk and reward.

Fund risks

Specialty funds have above-average risk, and this fund is no exception. Its worst 12-month rate of return was a loss of 38.8 per cent. The fund has done a good job of managing the risk relative to other precious metals funds, but relative performance seemed less important to many investors when a fund declined by 64 per cent during the bear of 1998. During the bear of 1990 the fund declined by 17.3 per cent, and it took 26 months to regain its value.

Future prospects

Gold can escalate in price quickly, and investors can regain their losses in the right economic environment. Unfortunately, with central banks selling reserves, the supply of gold is greater than demand, causing downward pressure on the price of gold bullion. Growth-oriented inventors who can withstand the downside risk of investing in gold will find that the Royal Precious Metals Fund is an excellent choice. The fund has a proven track record for a precious metals fund.

FUND DETAILS

Fund name	**Royal Precious Metals**	Start date for data shown	Dec 1988
Fund family	Royal Mutual Funds Inc.	Fund size (in $ millions)	$161
Mutual fund classification	Canadian precious metals	Percentage in foreign holdings	15.66
RRSP eligible	Yes	Dividend frequency	Annual
		Sales charge	No
VVR peer group	Canadian precious metals	Redemption charge	No
Number of mutual funds in VVR category	14	Management fee	1.75
WilStar peer group	Domestic equity	Management expense ratio	2.41

FUND PERFORMANCE

	1 month	1 year	3 years	5 years	10 years	15 years
Returns ending Aug 1998	−19.1%	−45.3%	−10.1%	0.9%		
Best historical return	30.5%	163.7%	47.0%	33.4%		
Average historical return	0.5%	13.4%	15.6%	15.7%		
Worst historical return	−19.1%	−45.3%	−10.1%	0.9%		

RETURNS GREATER THAN

	1 month	1 year	3 years	5 years	10 years	15 years
10 per cent	5%	36%	67%	62%		
Zero	56%	57%	79%	100%		
Percentage of time fund lost $	44%	43%	21%	0%		
Number of periods evaluated	117	106	82	58		

DOWNSIDE RISK

	Worst setback since start date	In bear 1987	In bear 1990	In bear 1994	In bear 1998
Setback for mutual fund	−64.0%		−17.3%	−17.9%	−64.0%
Setback for peer group	−68.5%		−20.7%	−16.8%	−68.5%
Setback ended in	Aug 1998		Feb 1991	Jan 1995	Aug 1998
Months to recover from loss	?		26	3	?

QUARTILE RANKING OF MUTUAL FUND PERFOMANCE AFTER 12 MONTHS OVER TIME

Canadian precious metals

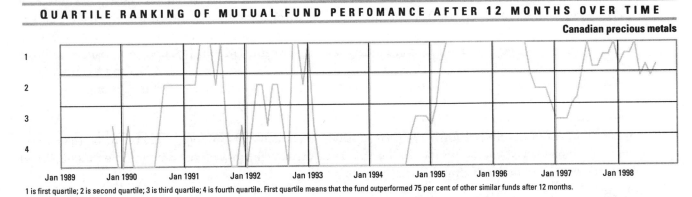

1 is first quartile; 2 is second quartile; 3 is third quartile; 4 is fourth quartile. First quartile means that the fund outperformed 75 per cent of other similar funds after 12 months.

ROLLING 12-MONTH TOTAL RATE OF RETURN FOR THE MUTUAL FUND OVER TIME

ROYAL ENERGY FUND

Vos value rating			WilStar rating		
Reward	**Risk**	**Best balance**	**Reward**	**Risk**	**Best balance**
★★★★★	★★★★★	★★★★★	★★	★	★

Fund profile

The Royal Energy Fund has been managed by Gordon Zive of Royal Bank Investment Management Inc. since 1994. The fund's investment objective is to invest in the shares of Canadian companies that are actively involved directly or indirectly in the exploration, development, production, or distribution of oil and gas products or other energy-related activities. This fund has a more narrow focus than other Canadian resource funds.

This is a sector fund that invests in a small portion of Canada's overall economy. The demand for Canadian resources has declined significantly since Asia and other Far Eastern countries headed into a period of economic turbulence. Until these countries re-establish their economies, demand for natural resources will remain low. When economic activity increases in the Far East, Canadian resource companies will be among the first to benefit. Conditions for commodity prices and resource stocks will remain challenging over the near term. It was a hopeful sign that, in August and September of 1998, gold rallied strongly, but this may not last if the Canadian dollar strengthens.

The fund has made investments in such oil and gas companies as Petro Canada, Suncor, Talisman Energy, and Renaissance Energy.

Fund performance

The fund's WilStar Ratings for reward, risk, and best balance between risk and reward were less than desirable. This indicates that investors did not benefit from investing in Canadian resource companies during the previous five years. The fund scored a triple five-star Vos Value Rating on reward, risk, and best balance between risk and reward. This indicates that the Royal Energy Fund outperformed other Canadian resource funds during the previous three years. The fund's best 12-month period was a gain of 115.6 per cent, and the average 12-month rate of return was 8.9 per cent. The fund has posted positive rates of return after 12 months 57 per cent of the time since the start date of December 1980. The fund has frequently been first quartile after 12 months, but has also frequently been fourth quartile after 12 months.

Fund risks

Ouch! Resource investors have experienced a decline in the value of their investments during the past 12 months. The worst 12-month period for the fund brought a decline of 41.7 per cent and the fund declined in value by 45.7 per cent during the bear of 1998.

Future prospects

This fund should continue to outperform other resource funds because of its bias towards energy stocks. However, resource funds in general are more risky than a well-diversified equity fund, although they offer potential for higher rates of return. If commodity prices increase and investors generate a new love affair with these companies, the fund will have the potential to appreciate in value very quickly. Investors who want exposure to the Canadian energy industry should not be disappointed with this fund. However, the performance of the fund will still be dictated by the resource sector.

FUND DETAILS

Fund name	**Royal Energy**	Start date for data shown	Dec 1980
Fund family	Royal Mutual Funds Inc.	Fund size (in $ millions)	$175
Mutual fund classification	Canadian resource	Percentage in foreign holdings	0.00
RRSP eligible	Yes	Dividend frequency	
		Sales charge	No
VVR peer group	Canadian resource	Redemption charge	No
Number of mutual funds in VVR category	31	Management fee	1.75
WilStar peer group	Domestic equity	Management expense ratio	2.28

FUND PERFORMANCE

	1 month	1 year	3 years	5 years	10 years	15 years
Returns ending Aug 1998	–20.0%	–40.3%	–0.6%	–4.9%	6.9%	4.1%
Best historical return	16.8%	115.6%	28.7%	25.5%	14.0%	10.1%
Average historical return	0.4%	8.9%	7.3%	7.7%	7.5%	7.0%
Worst historical return	–22.8%	–41.7%	–14.9%	–11.5%	–1.3%	3.7%

RETURNS GREATER THAN

	1 month	1 year	3 years	5 years	10 years	15 years
10 per cent	4%	37%	37%	37%	30%	6%
Zero	55%	57%	79%	82%	91%	100%
Percentage of time fund lost $	45%	43%	21%	18%	9%	0%
Number of periods evaluated	213	202	178	154	94	34

DOWNSIDE RISK

	Worst setback since start date	In bear 1987	In bear 1990	In bear 1994	In bear 1998
Setback for mutual fund	–47.9%	–30.8%	–19.2%	–29.3%	–45.7%
Setback for peer group	–21.0%	–28.1%	–33.8%	–22.9%	–50.1%
Setback ended in	July 1986	Nov 1987	Jan 1991	Jan 1995	Aug 1998
Months to recover from loss	49	33	22	20	?

QUARTILE RANKING OF MUTUAL FUND PERFOMANCE AFTER 12 MONTHS OVER TIME

Canadian resource

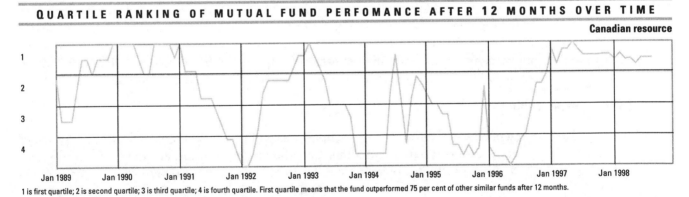

1 is first quartile; 2 is second quartile; 3 is third quartile; 4 is fourth quartile. First quartile means that the fund outperformed 75 per cent of other similar funds after 12 months.

ROLLING 12-MONTH TOTAL RATE OF RETURN FOR THE MUTUAL FUND OVER TIME

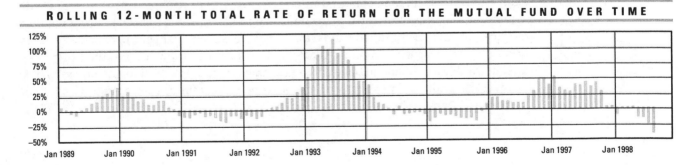

Portfolio Building

Asset allocation has been an intrinsic element in the investing process since the 1950s when Harry Markowitz showed mathematically exactly how diversification reduced volatility without sacrificing return. This process of constructing a portfolio with the highest return for a given level of risk Markowitz called "mean variance optimization" or Modern Portfolio Theory (MPT). This has become the heart of the asset allocation process. Different combinations of assets invested in a portfolio generate different return and risk characteristics.

Investors approach asset allocation in different ways, depending on how they measure return and risk and define different asset classes and securities. But the single most important variable in investing is choosing the right combination of assets. Research shows that applying varying weights to the different asset classes to determine how to divide the money available for investment is responsible for 90 per cent of an investor's returns.

Relative Portfolio Theory introduced

Many investors optimize their portfolios by measuring the risk and reward characteristics of an investment. They measure the risk using a tool called standard deviation; they measure reward using time-weighted rates of return. Relative Portfolio Theory (RPT) takes a different approach. The objective behind RPT is to deliver consistent predictable performance after 12 months relative to other investments. It aims to add value by creating a combination of investments that outperforms the average mutual fund consistently after 12 months. Unlike Modern Portfolio Theory, RPT creates a portfolio of funds that perform individually and follow different trends and influences so that they do not rise or fall in value together. Together, they deliver optimal performance over more than one period. Conversely, MPT defines an optimal portfolio of funds by the upward and downward movements of its individual investments together over one period. Thus, RPT solves some of the deficiencies associated with the measurement of risk and reward in MPT.

Introduction to the portfolios

Each portfolio in the following examples was optimized based on the relative performance of each fund compared with other Canadian balanced mutual funds since November 1992. Each portfolio's objective was to provide the highest rate of return for the given level of risk, and each portfolio aims to achieve top-quartile performance after 12 months relative to other Canadian balanced mutual funds. The portfolios were optimized with a minimum 20 per cent invested in fixed income funds, no more than 20 per cent invested in Canadian dividend mutual funds, and no more than 20 per cent invested in foreign mutual funds in order to remain RRSP-eligible. Each fund included in the portfolio is rated in this book and had to have a five-year track record. In addition, the portfolio may not invest more than 15 per cent of its assets in one mutual fund. Therefore, by default, the portfolio must invest in seven mutual funds.

Even with these restrictions, these portfolios have displayed excellent performance since November 1992. Investors could consider changing some of the underlying mutual-fund mix to suit their own risk and return profiles. In addition, investors should consider any new information that is currently available, and any asset classes that were not included in this optimization, such as international bonds, international money market accounts, or European equity mutual funds.

An investment in a mutual fund that accounts for less than 5 per cent of your total portfolio will not have a significant impact on the overall risk and return profile of your portfolio. Also, an investor can limit his or her selection of mutual funds and still have a well-diversified portfolio; by limiting the number of funds, you can usually meet a fund's minimum investment requirement, if applicable. Remember that some funds are available only through a particular company. For example, if you wish to purchase a mutual fund from Investors Group, you have to contact an Investors Group representative directly.

A word of caution

An investor can construct an infinite number of portfolios depending on his or her risk and reward profile. This summary includes only three sample portfolios to illustrate the objective behind portfolio building. In all three portfolios the investor would have enjoyed superior returns for the given level of risk incurred. Investors have to remember that it is the asset mix that counts; fund selection is just a bonus.

The portfolios have been constructed to achieve superior performance for investors who want to outperform the average Canadian balanced fund. They also demonstrate the benefits of diversification to limit risk without sacrificing reward. These portfolios are all RRSP-eligible. In fact, these portfolios may not be appropriate for investing outside an RRSP.

To develop your own optimal portfolio, you can simply assess the top-performing mutual funds in this book. You do not need the sophisticated computer program that we used to generate these portfolios. Simply keep in mind that the objective is to invest in two (or more) mutual funds that perform very differently from each other during various time periods.

Conservative Portfolio

The Conservative Portfolio is a compilation of 14 different mutual funds listed on the next page. This portfolio focusses heavily on Canadian investments, including bonds and money market mutual funds. Thus, the portfolio is heavily weighted toward interest-rate sensitive securities and income-producing stock investments. Investors who wish to reduce the risk in this portfolio further could consider investing also in an international bond or money market mutual fund. This would reduce the risk of a declining Canadian dollar and achieve a higher level of income. Investors could also consider investing a portion of their portfolios in a top-performing Canadian balanced fund to take advantage of an active manager's skill and his or her daily buying and selling opportunities. These changes would not alter the risk and return profile of the portfolio significantly.

Investors can replace any of the funds listed in the portfolio with another top-performing fund in the proportions indicated. Investors who do not want or need to invest in such a large number of funds might prefer a well-diversified international mutual fund. Conservative investors who require income and who travel outside the country for long periods could consider an international bond or money market mutual fund to reduce the risk of a declining Canadian dollar. When the Canadian dollar declines, their investments increase in value; when the Canadian currency increases, their travel costs decrease (assuming that the currency risk of the mutual fund selected is not hedged).

CONSERVATIVE PORTFOLIO

Fund name	Weight in portfolio Percentage	Value in a $100,000 portfolio Dollars	Peer group
Bissett Money Market	14.8	14,790	Canadian money market
Phillips, Hager & North Dividend Income	13.9	13,930	Canadian dividend
Ethical Growth	11.7	11,710	Canadian equity
Bissett Retirement	11.4	11,440	Canadian balanced
AIC Value	8.6	8,560	US equity
Royal Precious Metals	7.1	7,080	Canadian precious metals
BPI Dividend Income	6.1	6,070	Canadian dividend
Phillips, Hager & North Bond	6.0	5,970	Canadian bond
Standard Life Equity	5.5	5,460	Canadian equity
Investors US Growth	4.1	4,090	US equity
Fidelity International Portfolio	4.0	4,040	International equity
Bissett Small Cap	3.5	3,540	Canadian small cap
BPI Global Equity Value	2.0	2,010	International equity
AGF International—Japan Class	1.3	1,310	Japanese equity
Total	**100.0**	**100,000**	

Portfolio evaluation

Vos value rating			WilStar rating		
Reward	**Risk**	**Best balance**	**Reward**	**Risk**	**Best balance**
★★★★★	★★★★★	★★★★★	★★★★★	★★★★★	★★★★★

Portfolio profile

The Conservative Portfolio is a compilation of 14 different top performing mutual funds. This portfolio has historically achieved top results! The performance of the portfolio can be attributed to the performance of such top-performing mutual funds as Bissett Money Market Fund, Phillips, Hager & North Dividend Income Fund, Ethical Growth Fund, Bissett Retirement Fund, AIC Value Fund, Royal Precious Metals Fund, BPI Dividend Income Fund, and Phillips, Hager & North Bond Fund.

This portfolio has been able to add value consistently for investors. It contains a diverse number of investments and, in turn, has been able to outperform the average Canadian balanced mutual fund after 12 months 100 per cent of the time since the start date in November 1992. Currently, no Canadian balanced mutual fund has been able to outperform consistently to this extent. The average outperformance for this portfolio after 12 months was 4.4 per cent.

This portfolio is less risky than the moderate and aggressive portfolios, but has still displayed upside potential in the past. The portfolio's largest three holdings include one

FUND DETAILS

Fund name	**Conservative Portfolio**	Start date for data shown	Nov 1992
Fund family	*The Best of the Best* Multi-fund family	Fund size (in $ millions)	$—
Mutual fund classification	Canadian balanced	Percentage in foreign holdings	17.27%
RRSP eligible	Yes	Dividend frequency	Monthly
		Sales charge	Optional
VVR peer group	Canadian balanced	Redemption charge	Optional
Number of mutual funds in VVR category	268	Management fee	1.18
WilStar peer group	Balanced	Management expense ratio	1.50

FUND PERFORMANCE

	1 month	1 year	3 years	5 years	10 years	15 years
Returns ending Aug 1998	−11.3%	−2.9%	13.3%	11.1%		
Best historical return	4.9%	31.3%	21.8%	16.9%		
Average historical return	1.1%	16.2%	16.5%	15.8%		
Worst historical return	−11.3%	−4.6%	11.8%	11.1%		

RETURNS GREATER THAN

	1 month	1 year	3 years	5 years	10 years	15 years
10 per cent	0%	76%	100%	100%		
Zero	70%	95%	100%	100%		
Percentage of time fund lost $	30%	5%	0%	0%		
Number of periods evaluated	70	59	35	11		

DOWNSIDE RISK

	Worst setback since start date	In bear 1987	In bear 1990	In bear 1994	In bear 1998
Setback for mutual fund	−13.9%			−6.9%	−13.9%
Setback for peer group	−13.0%			−8.9%	−13.0%
Setback ended in	Aug 1998			June 1994	Aug 1998
Months to recover from loss	?			9	?

QUARTILE BANKING OF MUTUAL FUND PERFOMANCE AFTER 12 MONTHS OVER TIME

Canadian balanced

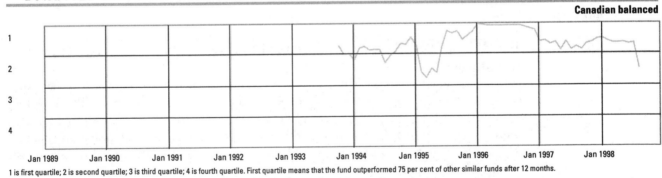

1 is first quartile; 2 is second quartile; 3 is third quartile; 4 is fourth quartile. First quartile means that the fund outperformed 75 per cent of other similar funds after 12 months.

ROLLING 12-MONTH TOTAL RATE OF RETURN FOR THE MUTUAL FUND OVER TIME

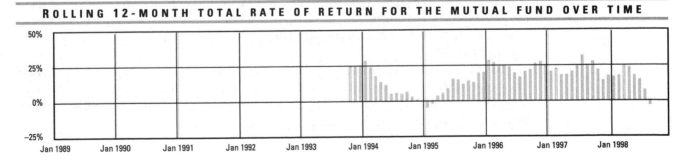

Canadian equity mutual fund, one Canadian dividend fund, and one Canadian money market fund. The portfolio is heavily weighted with funds that invest in large Canadian companies. Investors who want more income potential can reduce their Canadian equity exposure and invest in a Canadian or international bond mutual fund.

Portfolio performance

If this portfolio were a Canadian balanced mutual fund, it would have scored a triple five star Vos Value rating and WilStar rating for reward, risk, and the best balance between risk and reward. This is an indication that the portfolio has been able consistently to add more value than other Canadian balanced and international balanced funds over the previous three and five years respectively. The best 12-month rate of return for the portfolio was a gain of 31.3 per cent, and the average 12-month rate of return for the portfolio was 16.2 per cent. The portfolio posted positive rates of return after 12 months 95 per cent of the time. The portfolio would have been consistently first quartile after 12 months, despite a decline to second quartile on occasion.

Portfolio risks

The worst 12-month rate of return for this portfolio was a decline of 4.6 per cent, and the portfolio posted negative rates of return after 12 months 5 per cent of the time. During the bear market of 1994, the portfolio declined in value by 6.9 per cent, less than the average Canadian balanced fund. After incurring the setback, the portfolio took nine months to recover its loss. In short, the portfolio has done an excellent job of preserving capital.

Future prospects

The theory behind Relative Portfolio Theory assumes that a portfolio of mutual funds that has historically outperformed consistently will continue to outperform in the future. This portfolio of mutual funds has demonstrated its capability of outperforming in the past; therefore, this portfolio would make an excellent investment for the future. *Note on RPT:* Predicting a portfolio's future performance on the basis of its historical performance is reasonable, but this approach does not guarantee future success.

Moderate Portfolio

The Moderate Portfolio is a compilation of 13 different mutual funds, listed opposite. It focusses largely on Canadian and US equities in addition to Canadian dividend-paying stocks and Canadian bonds. The portfolio is heavily weighted toward interest-rate sensitive securities and the North American stock market. Investors who would like to reduce further the risk in this portfolio should consider investing in an international bond or money market mutual fund to reduce the risk of a declining Canadian dollar and achieve a higher level of income. Investors could also invest a portion of their holdings in an Asia and Pacific Rim mutual fund. These funds have recently declined significantly after the currency crisis in Asia, but over the long term could add value. Investors uncomfortable about the outlook for this region could consider a European equity mutual fund. Investors who implement these changes would not alter the risk and return profile of the portfolio significantly.

Investors can replace any of the listed funds with a top-performing fund or a fund of their own choice in the proportions indicated. Investors who do not want or need to invest in such a large number of funds will be best served by investing in a well diversified international mutual fund.

MODERATE PORTFOLIO

Fund name	Weight in portfolio Percentage	Value in a $100,000 portfolio Dollars	Peer group
Standard Life Equity	15.0	15,000	Canadian equity
Investors US Growth	15.0	15,000	US equity
Phillips, Hager & North Dividend Income	13.4	13,440	Canadian dividend
Phillips, Hager & North Bond	13.4	13,370	Canadian bond
Bissett Canadian Equity	8.6	8,600	Canadian equity
Bissett Money Market	6.6	6,630	Canadian money market
Bissett Dividend Income	6.6	6,560	Canadian dividend
Royal Precious Metals	5.3	5,280	Canadian precious metals
Bissett Retirement	3.8	3,790	Canadian balanced
Bissett Small Cap	3.8	3,760	Canadian small cap
AIC Value	3.6	3,580	US equity
Ethical Growth	3.6	3,570	Canadian equity
Fidelity International Portfolio	1.4	1,420	International equity
Total	**100.0**	**100,000**	

Portfolio evaluation

Vos value rating			WilStar rating		
Reward	**Risk**	**Best balance**	**Reward**	**Risk**	**Best balance**
★★★★★	★★★★★	★★★★★	★★★★★	★★★★★	★★★★★

Portfolio profile

The Moderate Portfolio is a compilation of 13 different top-performing mutual funds. This portfolio has historically achieved top results! The performance of the portfolio can be attributed to top-performing mutual funds such as the Standard Life Equity Fund, Investors US Growth Fund, Phillips, Hager & North Dividend Income Fund, Phillips, Hager & North Bond Fund, Bissett Canadian Equity Fund, Bissett Money Market Fund, and Bissett Dividend Income Fund.

This portfolio has been able to add value consistently for investors. It holds a diverse number of investments and has been able to outperform the average Canadian balanced mutual fund after 12 months 100 per cent of the time since the start date in November 1992. Currently, no Canadian balanced mutual fund has been able to outperform consistently to this extent. The average outperformance for this portfolio after 12 months was 6.1 per cent.

This portfolio is more risky than the Conservative Portfolio, but less risky than the Aggressive Portfolio. It has still displayed an excellent risk and return profile in the past. The portfolio's largest three holdings include one Canadian equity mutual fund, one US

FUND DETAILS

Fund name	**Moderate Portfolio**	Start date for data shown	Nov 1992
Fund family	*The Best of the Best* Multi-fund family	Fund size (in $ millions)	$–
Mutual fund classification	Canadian balanced	Percentage in foreign holdings	17.01%
RRSP eligible	Yes	Dividend frequency	Monthly
		Sales charge	Optional
VVR peer group	Canadian balanced	Redemption charge	Optional
Number of mutual funds in VVR category	268	Management fee	1.29
WilStar peer group	Balanced	Management expense ratio	1.54

FUND PERFORMANCE

	1 month	1 year	3 years	5 years	10 years	15 years
Returns ending Aug 1998	−12.0%	−0.8%	15.4%	12.5%		
Best historical return	5.4%	36.0%	24.5%	18.7%		
Average historical return	1.2%	17.9%	17.8%	17.5%		
Worst historical return	−12.0%	−4.2%	12.1%	12.5%		

RETURNS GREATER THAN

	1 month	1 year	3 years	5 years	10 years	15 years
10 per cent	0%	78%	100%	100%		
Zero	70%	95%	100%	100%		
Percentage of time fund lost $	30%	5%	0%	0%		
Number of periods evaluated	70	59	35	11		

DOWNSIDE RISK

	Worst setback since start date	In bear 1987	In bear 1990	In bear 1994	In bear 1998
Setback for mutual fund	−14.6%			−7.2%	−14.6%
Setback for peer group	−13.0%			−8.9%	−13.0%
Setback ended in	Aug 1998			June 1994	Aug 1998
Months to recover from loss	?			9	?

QUARTILE RANKING OF MUTUAL FUND PERFOMANCE AFTER 12 MONTHS OVER TIME

Canadian balanced

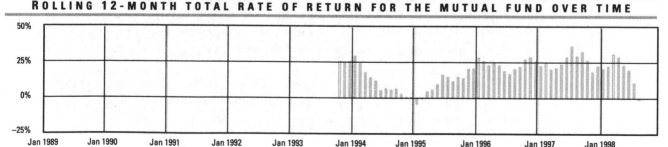

1 is first quartile; 2 is second quartile; 3 is third quartile; 4 is fourth quartile. First quartile means that the fund outperformed 75 per cent of other similar funds after 12 months.

ROLLING 12-MONTH TOTAL RATE OF RETURN FOR THE MUTUAL FUND OVER TIME

equity mutual fund, and one Canadian dividend fund. The portfolio's holdings are heavily invested in large Canadian and US companies. Investors who want equity exposure but prefer a larger investment in small companies can increase their exposure through an international small cap equity fund.

Portfolio performance

If this portfolio were a Canadian balanced mutual fund, the portfolio would have scored a triple five star Vos Value Rating and WilStar Rating for reward, risk, and the best balance between risk and reward. This indicates that the portfolio has been able to add value consistently more than other Canadian balanced and international balanced funds over the previous three and five years respectively. The best 12-month rate of return for the portfolio was a gain of 36 per cent, and the average 12-month rate of return for the portfolio was 17.9 per cent. The portfolio posted positive rates of return after 12 months 95 per cent of the time. The portfolio would have been consistently first quartile after 12 months, despite a decline to second quartile on occasion.

Portfolio risks

The worst 12-month rate of return for this portfolio was a decline of 4.2 per cent, and the portfolio posted negative rates of return after 12 months 5 per cent of the time. During the bear market of 1994 the portfolio declined in value by 7.2 per cent, less than the average Canadian balanced fund declined. After incurring the setback, the portfolio took nine months to recover its loss. In short, the portfolio has done an excellent job of preserving capital.

Future prospects

Relative Portfolio Theory assumes that a portfolio of mutual funds that has historically outperformed consistently will continue to outperform in the future. This portfolio of mutual funds has demonstrated its capability of outperforming in the past. Therefore, it would make an excellent investment for the future if the underlying funds continue to add value.

Aggressive Portfolio

The Aggressive Portfolio is a compilation of 10 different mutual funds, listed on page 136. It focusses on Canadian and US equities in addition to Canadian dividend-paying stocks and, to a smaller extent, Canadian bonds. Thus the portfolio is heavily weighted toward interest-rate-sensitive securities and the North American stock market. In turn, investors who would like to reduce further the risk in this portfolio could consider investing in an international bond or money market mutual fund to reduce the risk of a declining Canadian dollar and achieve a higher level of income. Investors could also invest a portion of their holdings in an Asia and Pacific Rim mutual fund. These funds have recently declined significantly after the currency crisis in Asia, but over the long term could add value.

More aggressive investors who want to achieve higher rates of return with more risk over the long term could consider increasing their equity exposure by investing in international equity funds that are RRSP-eligible or investing in some resource mutual funds. Canadian resource mutual funds have added value over the long term, but have recently experienced new levels of downside risk. Investors uncomfortable about the outlook for this sector could consider an investment in a specialty mutual fund that focusses on real estate, technology, or demographics. Investors who implement these changes would not alter the risk and return profile of the portfolio significantly, but they should be aware of the additional risks associated with investing in specialty funds.

AGGRESSIVE PORTFOLIO

Fund name	Weight in portfolio Percentage	Value in a $100,000 portfolio Dollars	Peer group
Bissett Dividend Income	15.0	15,000	Canadian dividend
Bissett Canadian Equity	15.0	15,000	Canadian equity
Standard Life Equity	15.0	15,000	Canadian equity
Investors US Growth	15.0	15,000	US equity
Altamira Bond	10.9	10,850	Canadian bond
Ivy Canadian	9.3	9,270	Canadian equity
Phillips, Hager & North Bond	9.2	9,150	Canadian bond
AIC Value	5.0	5,000	US equity
Phillips, Hager & North Dividend Income	5.0	5,000	Canadian dividend
Bissett Small Cap	0.7	730	Canadian small cap equity
Total	**100.0**	**100,000**	

Investors can substitute any of the listed funds with a top-performing fund or a fund of their own choice in the proportion indicated. Investors who do not want or need to invest in such a large number of funds will be best served by consolidating some of the smaller investments and investing in a well diversified international equity mutual fund.

Portfolio evaluation

Vos value rating			WilStar rating		
Reward	Risk	Best balance	Reward	Risk	Best balance
★★★★★	★★★★★	★★★★★	★★★★★	★★★★★	★★★★★

Portfolio profile

The Aggressive Portfolio is a compilation of 10 different top-performing mutual funds. This portfolio has historically achieved top results! The success of the portfolio can be attributed to the performance of such top-performing mutual funds as the Bissett Dividend Income Fund, Bissett Canadian Equity Fund, Standard Life Equity Fund, Investors US Growth Fund, and Altamira Bond Fund.

This portfolio has been able to add value consistently for investors. It holds a diverse number of investments (although fewer than the other portfolios) and has been able to outperform the average Canadian balanced mutual fund after 12 months 93 per cent of the time since the start date in November 1992. The average outperformance for this portfolio after 12 months was 6.6 per cent.

This portfolio is more risky than the Conservative and Moderate Portfolios, but has displayed more upside potential in the past. The portfolio's largest three holdings include two Canadian equity mutual funds and one Canadian dividend fund. In turn, the portfolio's holdings focus on large Canadian companies such as chartered banks and Canadian

FUND DETAILS

Fund name	**Aggressive Portfolio**	Start date for data shown	Nov 1992
Fund family	*The Best of the Best* Multi-fund family	Fund size (in $ millions)	$—
Mutual fund classification	Canadian balanced	Percentage in foreign holdings	18.98%
RRSP eligible	Yes	Dividend frequency	Monthly
		Sales charge	Optional
VVR peer group	Canadian balanced	Redemption charge	Optional
Number of mutual funds in VVR category	268	Management fee	1.40
WilStar peer group	Balanced	Management expense ratio	1.65

FUND PERFORMANCE

	1 month	1 year	3 years	5 years	10 years	15 years
Returns ending Aug 1998	–11.3%	3.9%	17.6%	13.6%		
Best historical return	6.1%	40.6%	25.5%	19.0%		
Average historical return	1.2%	18.4%	17.8%	17.9%		
Worst historical return	–11.3%	–4.0%	11.0%	13.6%		

RETURNS GREATER THAN

	1 month	1 year	3 years	5 years	10 years	15 years
10 per cent	0%	80%	100%	100%		
Zero	73%	95%	100%	100%		
Percentage of time fund lost $	27%	5%	0%	0%		
Number of periods evaluated	70	59	35	11		

DOWNSIDE RISK

	Worst setback since start date	In bear 1987	In bear 1990	In bear 1994	In bear 1998
Setback for mutual fund	–13.2%			–8.4%	–13.2%
Setback for peer group	–13.0%			–8.9%	–13.0%
Setback ended in	Aug 1998			June 1994	Aug 1998
Months to recover from loss	?			9	?

QUARTILE RANKING OF MUTUAL FUND PERFOMANCE AFTER 12 MONTHS OVER TIME

Canadian balanced

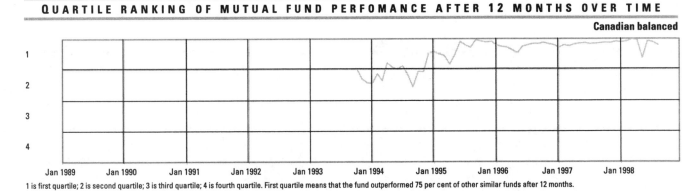

1 is first quartile; 2 is second quartile; 3 is third quartile; 4 is fourth quartile. First quartile means that the fund outperformed 75 per cent of other similar funds after 12 months.

ROLLING 12-MONTH TOTAL RATE OF RETURN FOR THE MUTUAL FUND OVER TIME

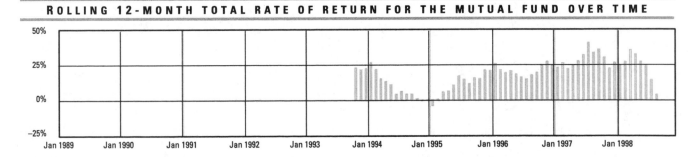

utilities. Investors who want Canadian equity exposure but would rather have a larger investment in small Canadian companies can increase their exposure to a Canadian small cap equity fund and reduce their exposure to a Canadian equity fund.

Portfolio performance

If this portfolio were a Canadian balanced mutual fund, the portfolio would have scored a triple five star Vos Value Rating and WilStar Rating for reward, risk, and the best balance between risk and reward. This indicates that the portfolio has been able to add value consistently more than other Canadian balanced and international balanced funds over the previous three and five years respectively. The best 12-month rate of return for the portfolio was a gain of 40.6 per cent, and the average 12-month rate of return for the portfolio was 18.4 per cent. The portfolio posted positive rates of return after 12 months 95 per cent of the time. The portfolio would have been consistently first quartile after 12 months, although it did decline to second quartile on occasion.

Portfolio risks

The worst 12-month rate of return for this portfolio was a decline of 4.6 per cent, and the portfolio posted negative rates of return after 12 months 5 per cent of the time. During the bear market of 1994 the portfolio declined in value by 8.4 per cent, less than the average Canadian balanced fund. After incurring this setback, the portfolio took nine months to recover its loss. In short, the portfolio has done an excellent job of preserving capital, but underperformed the Conservative and Moderate Portfolios on occasion.

Future prospects

Relative Portfolio Theory assumes that a portfolio of mutual funds that has historically outperformed consistently will continue to outperform in the future if the underlying funds continue to add value. Investors with this aggressive portfolio of mutual funds should realize that this portfolio did not outperform consistently but has added value.

Part B

Stocks

Introduction to Stocks

Investing in stocks

This chapter is an introductory guide for investors interested in investing in stocks. Frequently investors feel confused about investing in stocks, and bewildered by the abundance of advice and apparently rational observations made by professionals, who have spent their careers evaluating the merits of equities as an investment. There are some basic concepts, however, that all investors should understand as they analyze their investment objectives and try to select stocks to further those objectives. This section discusses some of these basic concepts and demonstrates how an investor can use stocks to make money.

Common stock represents ownership in a company. As with ownership of other types of property, stock ownership carries risks and privileges. A shareholder has a right to vote for the company's directors and to participate in the company's annual meeting. A shareholder also shares in the earnings of the corporation. In addition, a shareholder receives a copy of the company's annual report disclosing details of its financial affairs every year. All publicly listed companies that sell shares to investors are required by law to issue an annual report. This document is an excellent source of information for investors.

Along with the rights of ownership, a shareholder also incurs some risk and uncertainty. The returns on the shareholder's investment are based on the success of the firm. The rate of return received by an investor who purchases common stock is equal to the dividends paid by the company plus any capital gain (or capital loss) generated. For example, if Edgar bought stock in *"GOLD 'R' US"* corporation for $10 per share on January 1, 1998, received $1 in dividends on December 1, 1998, and then sold the stock for $12 on December 31, 1998, his rate of return would be:

(Ending price – Beginning price + Dividend) ÷ Beginning price
= (12 – 10 + 1) ÷ 10 = 3/10 (or 30 per cent)

When he first bought his shares in *"GOLD 'R' US,"* Edgar did not know that he would be able to sell the stock at the end of 1998 for $12. He knew that the stock might rise in value. In fact, that's one of the reasons why he bought it. But he also knew that it could lose value. If Edgar had wanted more certainty, he could have invested in a savings account generating a return of 5 per cent. The difference between investing in a savings account and in *"GOLD 'R' US"* is the amount of risk incurred by Edgar. As a stockholder, he could not know with absolute certainty that his shares would generate a predictable rate of return.

Savings accounts are considered risk-free or at least extremely safe investments. Stocks come with higher risk, because the outcome of investing in stocks is never certain. A good return in one year may be followed by a disappointment in the next year.

As we discussed briefly in our introduction to mutual funds, investment risk can be reduced through diversification. Whether you are buying individual stocks or mutual funds, you can reduce risk by combining investments in a way that minimizes risk and maximizes return. For example, Edgar is considering investing in a ski resort in northern British Columbia. He anticipates a 40 per cent return on his investment if British Columbia gets more than four feet of snow this winter. If British Columbia receives less than four feet of snow, the value of his investment will decline by 20 per cent. To hedge his investment, Edgar could invest in a California vacation property, where skiers go from British Columbia if it doesn't snow. If British Columbia receives less than four feet of snow this winter, Edgar's investment in California will increase in value by 40 per cent. However, if British Columbia receives more than four feet of snow, Edgar's investment in California will decline in value by 20 per cent. By investing half his money in each property, Edgar's portfolio will increase in value by 20 per cent regardless of how much snow falls in British Columbia. This is called diversification.

Following a strategy of diversification, investors acquire a number of stocks within their portfolios that come with different risks and rewards. As the number of stocks in a portfolio grows, the overall risk declines. Diversification reduces the risk of loss associated with the performance of one particular stock. This risk is referred to as unsystematic risk.

Unsystematic risk is the risk attributable to a specific company. For example, the risk associated with ski resorts is the risk of unfavourable weather. However, this risk can be diversified away if an investor invests in a company that creates snow-making machines or provides a product or service that will be in demand when there is no snow.

Not all risk can be eliminated through diversification. The risk that remains after diversification is called market or systematic risk. The total risk of investing in stocks consists of unsystematic (or diversifiable) risk plus systematic (or non-diversifiable) risk.

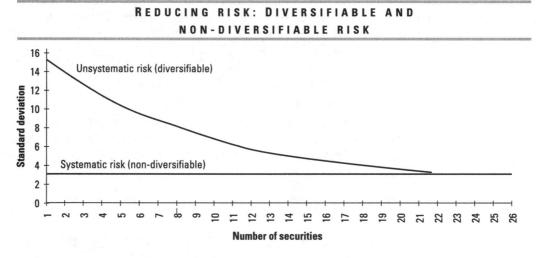

REDUCING RISK: DIVERSIFIABLE AND NON-DIVERSIFIABLE RISK

Why invest in stocks?

As the first part of this book demonstrated, many investors have successfully made money by investing in Canadian equity mutual funds. These mutual funds, in turn, invest in the very same companies as we'll discuss in this section. If these funds earn money by investing in Canadian stocks, why can't you?

This section will show you how to create your own mutual fund by investing in a variety of stocks yourself, or to complement your mutual fund holdings by investing in one or several stocks. Even if you decide not to invest in stocks at all, you will gain a better understanding of common stock investing and the performance of individual stocks.

The likelihood of a significant decline in the value of a mutual fund investment is low; the likelihood of incurring a large loss by investing in a common stock is much higher. Some of the largest Canadian companies have experienced setbacks in the price of their stock of up to 50 per cent, although the value of stock in these same companies may have also doubled or tripled within the same year. In any case, investors who buy common stock encounter much more substantial potential risks and returns than mutual fund investors.

Based on past performance, it has been shown that an investment in stocks will outperform other investments over the long term. For reasons that we discussed earlier, such as management fees and diversification strategies of mutual funds, a direct investment in a single successful company will usually outperform the average mutual fund. However, an investment in an unsuccessful company will compare poorly with the average mutual fund. The critical factor is selecting the right company.

Which company is a good investment?

You have decided to invest in the stock market. You have also decided to invest most of your money in Canadian equity mutual funds while directing a small portion of your money toward the common stock of some Canadian corporations.

Your first step is to identify an industry that you believe will outperform the overall economy in the long term. After all, a company's long-term growth prospects will depend on the growth of the industry in which it operates. A well-run company that manufactures and distributes record players will not grow at the same rate as a company that produces CD players.

Comparing industries

Investing in the right industry is just as important as investing in the right company. The performance of 14 industries in Canada during a period of 10 years has been widely divergent. The table below indicates the historical rates of return for these industries, compared with the TSE 300, the TSE 35, and two BARRA indices. This table illustrates the importance of investing in the right industry. Remember that this ten-year period includes the worst bear markets that investors have experienced.

COMPARING INDUSTRY RETURNS

Index name	3 months %	1 year %	3 years %	5 years %	10 years %
TSE 300	−26.8	−15.0	9.0	8.2	8.3
TSE 35	−27.6	−12.0	10.3	10.4	0.0
TSE Communications and media	−12.7	12.5	20.6	12.4	9.1
TSE Conglomerates	−25.5	−12.9	17.1	12.6	7.9
TSE Consumer products	−20.0	−1.1	7.7	10.2	12.1
TSE Financial services	−32.6	−2.2	29.9	21.0	16.2
TSE Gold and silver	−34.8	−48.0	−25.5	−14.5	−2.8
TSE Industrial products	−24.8	−10.1	15.4	13.2	10.3
TSE Merchandising	−22.8	−14.2	7.1	4.5	5.3
TSE Metals and minerals	−31.6	−48.1	−18.5	−2.6	1.3
TSE Oil and gas products	−28.6	−38.0	0.9	−2.4	3.0
TSE Paper and forest products	−32.9	−36.6	−11.7	−3.5	0.6
TSE Pipelines	−14.5	13.4	21.5	13.1	13.7

continued

Index name	3 months %	1 year %	3 years %	5 years %	10 years %
TSE Real estate	−18.7	15.2	6.9	−3.5	−15.8
TSE Transport and environment	−26.3	−31.0	8.3	8.6	−0.9
TSE Utilities	−23.0	21.5	29.4	19.6	15.3
BARRA Value	−27.0	−18.9	3.7	4.2	10.87
BARRA Growth	−26.1	−8.4	16.1	13.5	5.83

Source: Toronto Stock Exchange and Barra

Industry characteristics

Of all the stocks listed on the TSE, 45 per cent are sensitive to changes in interest rates. These include companies in the following industries:

- banks
- utilities
- insurance companies
- construction companies

When interest rates fall, these interest-sensitive stocks tend to do well.

The other 55 per cent are sensitive to the economy in general. As inflation comes alive, the new market leaders are companies involved in:

- steel
- gold mining
- forestry and lumber

Lower interest rates encourage people to spend money, so when interest rates have been low and are starting to rise, good companies in the following sectors perform well:

- retail stores
- cosmetics
- restaurants
- tobacco

Near the end of a cycle of interest rate levels, when interest rates have peaked and are starting back down, companies perform well in sectors like:

- pharmaceuticals
- chemicals

Promising companies

Once you have identified the right industry, you then have to identify and assess the most promising companies within the industry and evaluate the prices of their common stock.

You can approach this evaluation in the same way as you would evaluate the price of a car. For example, suppose that a new Neon costs $15,000, while a new Sunfire is priced at $10,000. These two cars have similar qualities and, in turn, their prices should be similar. If they are not, purchasers will always buy the cheaper car until demand causes its price to increase to a more realistic level.

When buying stocks, investors can identify ones that are trading below their actual value. When other investors also see this value, the price of the stock will increase as investors acknowledge the actual value of the firm by buying shares in it. The value of the stock is generated by the value of the dividends. Corporations pay dividends to shareholders in order to compensate them for taking the additional risk of investing in the common stock of the company.

Investing in common stocks is more risky than other investments because common stock investors have the least protection in the case of bankruptcy. If a firm goes bankrupt, first the lawyers and accountants appointed to handle the receivership will be paid; then suppliers, employees, banks, and bond holders, in that order. The last individuals that receive payments are the common shareholders. If the firm does not raise enough money through the sale of all its assets, the common shareholders are out of luck and will receive no payment. On the other hand, if the company is prosperous and the firm generates large profits, any additional profits are returned to only the shareholders.

The firm returns money to the shareholders in the form of a dividend. Investors who invest in a savings account at the bank receive interest payments. Investors who invest in common shares receive dividend payments. Thus, a dividend is a payment made to the investors in the common stock of a company from the company's earnings or profits. Some companies pay large dividends; other companies do not pay dividends and instead reinvest the company's profits in the company. This may allow the company to grow faster and pay a larger dividend in the future. Thus, the value of a common stock is derived from the assets the company owns and future dividend payments. The higher those values, the higher the value of the stock.

Investors must realize that there is a difference between investing in the common stock of a great company and investing in a great common stock. Great companies are not always great investments, but not-so-great companies that are attractively priced can be great investments.

Understanding stock tables

Everything you need to know about a company's day-to-day financial performance you can find in the stock tables in newspapers and financial journals, but you have to know how to read these tables. There are minor variations from one newspaper to another, but they are all similar to the following table:

A STOCK TABLE

| 52 weeks | | Stock | Sym | Yld | | Vol | | | Net | Chg |
Hi	Lo			Div	%	100s	Hi	Lo	close	
50-3/8	42	BCE Inc.	B	2.68	5.4	21680	50-3/8	49-1/8	50-1/8	+1-1/8

52 weeks, Hi and Lo: These figures show the highest price and the lowest price (in dollars) that the stock traded at over the previous 52 weeks.

Stock: This is the name of the company whose stock information you are looking at.

Sym: This is the symbol that represents the stock on the ticker. (You can see the ticker in action in brokerage offices.)

Yld, Div: This is the company's estimated annual dividend per share.

Yld, %: This is the stock's dividend yield.

Vol, 100s: This is the number of shares that have been traded throughout the day, in 100s.

Hi and Lo: These figures represent the highest price throughout the day and the lowest price throughout the day.

Net close: This gives the closing price at the end of the day.

Chg: This is the percentage change from the previous day.

To find further information on a particular company, you can look at a series of its annual reports. For instance, if you look at a few consecutive annual reports for BCE or go through back issues of a newspaper's stock pages, you'll see that BCE's current expected dividend of $2.68 is $0.31 more than the $2.37 per share in 1986, and $1.49 more than the $1.19 dividend per share payment in 1976. BCE stockholders have benefitted over the years as earnings more than doubled and the company's directors steadily increased the dividend payment. That helps to explain why BCE's share price has increased from $16.75 in 1982 to over $50 today. Investors can also find useful information on a particular company's financial performance in the next chapter of this book, Selected Stocks.

Value outperforms growth

Companies whose stock price is high relative to the company's underlying assets are considered *growth companies*. Company's with strong financial statements and a reasonable stock price are considered *value companies*. Value companies have low price-to-book (P/B) ratios and low price-to-earnings (P/E) ratios. Growth companies have high price-to-book (P/B) ratios and high price-to-earnings (P/E) ratios.

Value investors look at balance sheets and income statements to find companies that have either fallen out of favour with other investors or are undervalued and whose stock price is low given the company's fundamentals. Value investors are searching for companies that have intrinsic value that other investors are currently overlooking by focussing on companies with high P/B and P/E ratios. Growth investors prefer stocks with earnings that are accelerating faster than the economy. The growth investor is less concerned with the company's intrinsic evaluations as long as earnings continue to grow.

BARRA is a company which collects and analyzes data related to financial markets. BARRA has created indices to measure the performance of companies that exhibited desirable characterisitcs for growth and value investors. BARRA divides the 200 largest companies on the Toronto Stock Exchange (TSE) into two separate groups: value companies and growth companies.

The following graph illustrates the pattern of the BARRA indices since January 1982.

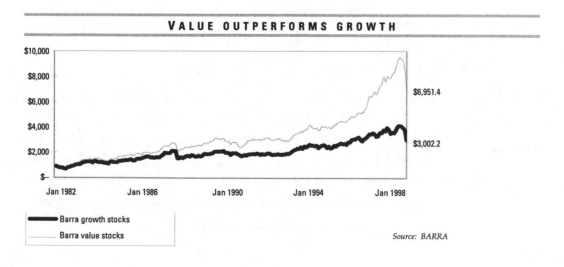

VALUE OUTPERFORMS GROWTH

$6,951.4

$3,002.2

Barra growth stocks
Barra value stocks

Source: BARRA

This graph illustrates that value companies have outperformed during this time. Investors in the TSE 300 would have finished in the middle, but still earned a very respectable rate of return. [The TSE 300 is an index of 300 large companies traded on the Toronto Stock Exchange (TSE). Other indexes are the TSE 100 and the TSE 35.]

Volatility: The bear market of 1998 is normal stock market behaviour.

Investors are cautious about investing in stocks or equity mutual funds during volatile market periods. The most recent volatile period endured by investors was the stock market correction of 1998. The Toronto Stock Exchange 300 Index declined by 29.3 per cent from April 22, 1998, to August 31, 1998. Investors who invested a large portion of their investments in Canadian equities have incurred large setbacks. With such a large setback, many investors were left questioning their future investment strategies. "Should I sell; should I hold; should I buy; what should I do?"

Each investor will have a different answer. However, investors should remember some of the following facts.

- Equities have and will continue to provide a higher rate of return than other investments over the long term, but with more risk.

- Without risk, investors would not earn higher rates of return.

- Long-term investors will incur setbacks, and they should not despair when risk comes to fruition. It is a natural and essential part of investing in equities.

The table below illustrates the risk side of investing in equities. Since January 1960 there have been nine major setbacks affecting the companies included in the TSE 300 index. In each case, investors regained their investment.

DISPERSIONS IN EQUITY MARKET RETURNS

Market correction	Toronto Stock Exchange 300 change	Number of months to recover loss
December 1961 to June 1962	−17.0%	10
January 1966 to September 1966	−15.1%	7
May 1969 to June 1970	−25.4%	33
October 1973 to September 1974	−35.0%	44
February 1980	−17.6%	4
June 1981 to June 1982	−39.0%	10
December 1983 to July 1984	−14.4%	6
July 1987 to September 1987	−25.0%	23
December 1989 to October 1990	−20.1%	27

The time taken to recover the loss varied over different periods. But in each case investors were better off staying invested in equities after a market correction.

Purchasing stocks

Bid and ask

As with most things in life, the people who want to sell stock usually want more than anyone else will pay for it, and the people who want to buy stock usually want to pay less than anyone wants to sell it for!

Buyers bid; sellers ask. A stock may have an ask price of $10 and a bid of $9\frac{3}{4}$. If you wanted to sell the stock right away, you would have to accept the bid price of $9.75. If you wanted to buy the stock right away, you would have to pay the ask price of $10. You can also place an order to buy or sell a stock at a price between the bid and ask, for instance, at $9\frac{7}{8}$, but if you do there's no guarantee that your order will be filled.

Bid and ask prices are constantly changing in relation to supply and demand.

Board lots

When you go to the supermarket to buy eggs, you see a price listed for one dozen. When it comes to eggs, one dozen is the standard unit.

When it comes to stocks, the standard unit is 100 shares. Just as 12 eggs are called a dozen, 100 shares are called a board lot. For stocks trading over $1, the bid and ask prices are quoted per board lot. A purchase of under 100 shares is known as an odd lot.

Placing an order

All investors should know how to place an order properly with a stockbroker to buy or sell stocks. There are three basic types of order:

1. **Market order:** You want to buy a particular stock at the current market price. For example, let's say you want to buy 100 shares of BCE Inc. You would call your stockbroker and ask what BCE is trading at. The broker may say, "50 bid, $50\frac{1}{4}$ ask." If you find this range attractive, you say, "Buy 100 shares of BCE at the market." Your broker will repeat the order to you and then place it. You now own 100 shares of BCE purchased at $50\frac{1}{4}$.

2. **Limit order:** You want to buy or sell a stock only if it trades at a specified price. You also have to set a time limit for your order. You could set the time limit for one day, one month, or any duration in between. Or you could place an order "good until cancelled," in which case the order stays in effect until it is either executed or cancelled by you.

   For example, if BCE is trading at $50, but you don't want to pay more than $48 for it, you would tell your broker to "buy BCE at $48, good for a week." At the end of one week, if the trade has not been executed, it is automatically cancelled.

3. **Stop order:** You want to sell a stock whose price has gone up and is now starting to fall, so you instruct your broker to "place a stop order."

   For example, if you bought a stock at $20, it rose to $40, and it's now starting to head lower, you don't want to lose your profits. So you phone your broker and say, "Place a stop order to sell 100 shares at $35." Now, if the stock drops to $35, your shares will automatically be sold.

HIPs and TIPs

It's sad but true that most mutual funds do not perform as well on a consistent basis as blue-chip stocks. Over any given period, the TSE 35 may increase in value by 20 per cent, outperforming three-quarters of Canadian mutual funds.

As a result, some people have given up trying to beat the market, preferring simply to settle for the same return as the market index itself. To accomplish this, you can invest in an index fund, linked to the return of a particular group of stocks such as the TSE 35, the TSE 100, or some other index.

Alternatively, you can buy index participation units directly from the TSE, saving the administration and management fees charged by most mutual fund operators. TSE 35 Index Participation units (TIPs) allow you to buy a single security, through your broker, that represents the diversified portfolio of Canadian companies comprising the TSE 35

Index. TSE 100 Index Participation units (HIPs) represent Canadian companies comprising the TSE 100 Index. Both vehicles pay dividends, and you can hold them within your RRSP, but investors forego the advantages offered by mutual fund companies that offer index products, such as reporting, consolidation, and access to a larger selection of index products.

Selected Stocks

The TSE 35

The Toronto Stock Exchange has created several indices for use in analyzing various groups of stocks. These indices cover all major sectors of the Canadian economy. The TSE monitors and adjusts these indices to take into consideration current information.

The companies described and analyzed in this chapter are all included in the TSE 35 Index. In fact, there are only 34 stocks in our selection; Nova Corporation was not included because this company recently merged with TransCanada PipeLines. In turn, TransCanada PipeLines converted the chemicals division into a new publicly traded company; this new company is included in the TSE 35, but it has no stock price history. (Nova Corporation information was not included in the historical data for TransCanada PipeLines.) The following is the list of the 34 companies analyzed.

BLUE-CHIP STOCKS FOR THE NEW MILLENIUM

Company name	Ticker symbol	Industry	Page number
Abitibi-Consolidated	A	Paper and forest product	158
Alcan Aluminum Limited	AL	Metals and minerals	160
Bank of Montreal	BMO	Financial services	162
Bank of Nova Scotia	BNS	Financial services	164
Barrick Gold Corporation	ABX	Gold and silver	166
BCE Incorporated	BCE	Utilities	168
Bombardier Incorporated, B	BBD.B	Industrial products	170
Canadian Imperial Bank of Commerce	CM	Financial services	172
Canadian National Railway	CNR	Transportation and environment	174
Canadian Occidental Petrolium	CXY	Oil and gas	176
Canadian Pacific Limited	CP	Conglomerates	178
Canadian Tire Corporated Limited, A	CTR.A	Merchandising	180
Dofasco Incorporated	DFS	Industrial products	182
Imasco Limited	IMS	Consumer products	184
Inco Limited	N	Metals and minerals	186
Laidlaw Incorporated	LDM	Transportation and environment	188
Macmillan Bloedel Limited	MB	Paper and forest products	190
Magna International Limited, A	MG.A	Industrial products	192
Moore Corporation Limited	MCL	Industrial products	194
National Bank of Canada	NA	Financial services	196

continued

Company name	Ticker symbol	Industry	Page number
Noranda Incorporated	NOR	Metals and minerals	198
Nortel Networks (Northern Telecom)	NTL	Industrial products	200
Petro Canada	PCA	Oil and gas	202
Placer Dome Incorporated	PDG	Gold and silver	204
Renaissance Energy	RES	Oil and gas	206
Royal Bank of Canada	RY	Financial services	208
Seagram Company Limited	VO	Consumer products	210
Suncor Energy Incorporated	SU	Oil and gas	212
Talisman Energy Incorporated	TLM	Oil and gas	214
Teck Corporation, B	TEK.B	Gold and silver	216
Thomson Corporation	TOC	Communications and media	218
Toronto-Dominion Bank	TD	Financial services	220
TransAlta Corporation	TA	Utilities	222
TransCanada Pipelines	TRP	Pipelines	224

How to read the stock charts in this book

In this chapter, there is a description of each company in the above list; this descripton is accompanied by a one-page stock chart. The stock chart is a combination of six tables that illustrate the historical performance of a stock. An explanation of how to read a stock chart follows.

COMPANY DETAILS

Company name	Canadian Tire Corporation Limited, A	Industry classification	Merchandising
Recent price	$32.00	Market capitalization (in $ millions)	$2,521
Phone number for annual report	416-480-3660	Stock analysis start date	July 1980
Ticker symbol	CTR.A	Weight in TSE 35	3.7%
Number of mutual funds that hold this stock as a top 15 holding	38		

Company name: This gives the name of the company that is being analyzed.

Recent price: This discloses the price per share for the stock that is being analyzed. The price given is the price of the stock at the end of August 1998.

Phone number for annual report: An annual report is published by the company for investors or other individuals. The annual report describes the company's business and its current and future activities, and highlights its financial performance. Investors who want to order an annual report can call this number and request a copy. Investors can also contact *The Globe and Mail Report on Business* Annual Reports Club by telephone (1-800-965-6199) or fax (1-800-617-7678).

Ticker symbol: The Toronto Stock Exchange provides information on the performance of a company based on its ticker symbol.

The number of mutual funds that hold this stock in their top-15 holdings: Canadian equity, dividend, and balanced funds all invest in a variety of Canadian companies. For example, Canadian Tire Corporation is owned by 38 funds in Canada among their top 15 holdings, that is, among the 15 stocks that have the highest proportions in the fund. (This information was provided by Paltrak, a software company which provides information on mutual funds—1-800-531-4725 or 416-489-7074.)

Industry classification: This indicates the industry in which the company operates.

Market capitalization (in $ millions): The market capitalization is the total value of the company's stock. An investor who wanted to buy all the shares of Canadian Tire based on a price of $32 would have to pay $2.46 billion for the entire firm.

Stock analysis start date: This is the date of the earliest data on the company's historical performance analyzed for its stock chart. Many companies in this book have a history longer than the start date, but using more recent data (the last 20 years or so) provides a better assessment of the company's performance.

Weight in TSE 35: Each stock within the TSE 35 Index is included in this book, and each stock makes a different contribution to the overall movement of the TSE 35 Index. This contribution is based on the stock's performance and weight in the index. Larger companies have a larger weight, and smaller companies have a smaller weight. The sum of all the weights of each company in the TSE 35 index is 100. Canadian Tire has a weight of 3.7 in the index. Thus, 3.7 per cent of the movement in the TSE 35 Index can be attributed to the movement of Canadian Tire stock.

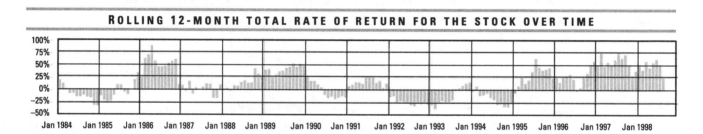

ROLLING 12-MONTH TOTAL RATE OF RETURN FOR THE STOCK OVER TIME

The first bar in this graph indicates the stock's performance for the period February 1, 1983, to January 31, 1984. The next bar illustrates the performance for the period March 1, 1983, to February 28, 1984. As we move to the right, the bars illustrate the performance of the stock closer to the current date. Thus, the return for the Canadian Tire Stock for the one-year period ending August 31, 1998, is 24.3 per cent, as indicated by the last bar at the right. Investors should note that some investments have large swings in performance from one period to the next.

STOCK PERFORMANCE

	1 month	1 year	3 years	5 years	10 years	15 years
Returns ending Aug 1998	−21.1%	24.3%	27.7%	16.3%	8.9%	9.0%
Best historical return	25.0%	97.7%	45.3%	28.9%	18.2%	12.7%
Average historical return	1.3%	17.2%	11.7%	9.1%	8.6%	10.2%
Worst historical return	−23.7%	−37.2%	−22.7%	−13.4%	1.5%	8.4%

Returns ending August 1998: These are the returns earned by the stock for the various periods (that is, one month, one year, and so on) ending August 1998. For example, the one-month rate of return for Canadian Tire stock was a decline of 21.1 per cent. The one-year rate of return from September 1, 1997, to August 31, 1998, was 24.3 per cent; the three-year rate of return from September 1, 1995, to August 31, 1998, was 27.7 per cent annualized; and the five-year rate of return from September 1, 1993, to August 31, 1998, was 16.3 per cent annualized. The 10-year rate of return for the stock from September 1, 1988, to August 31, 1998, was 8.9 per cent annualized.

Best historical return: This figure summarizes the stock's historical range of rates of return. The best historical return discloses the very best performance the stock has achieved since the start date of our analysis. The best one-month return for Canadian Tire stock was a gain of 25 per cent. Thus, an investor who had invested in Canadian Tire prior to its best one-month rate of return would have gained 25 per cent in that month. The best one-year rate of return was a gain of 97.7 per cent; an investor who held Canadian Tire stock throughout this stock's best one-year period would have gained 97.7 per cent, and so on. With this information, investors can compare the performance of the stock ending August 1998 with the stock's best performance. *Note:* All numbers are calculated using average annual compounded rates of return.

Average historical return: The average historical rate of return shows how the stock has performed historically on average. Investors in Canadian Tire stock on average earned 1.3 per cent per month. After one year, investors on average earned 17.2 per cent; the average three-year rate of return for the stock was 11.7 per cent; the average five-year rate of return for the stock was 9.1 per cent; and the average 10-year rate of return was 8.6 per cent.

Worst historical return: The worst historical return gives investors an indication of the downside risk associated with a particular stock. Investors in Canadian Tire stock prior to the stock's worst one-month loss would have seen their investment decline in value by 23.7 per cent. The worst one-year loss posted by the stock was a decline of 37.2 per cent. The worst rate of return posted by the stock during a period of three years was an annualized loss of 22.7 per cent. Thus, investors who invested in this stock for a minimum of three years could still have lost money historically. The worst five-year rate of return for the stock was a loss of 13.4 per cent, and the worst 10-year rate of return was a gain of 1.5 per cent.

RETURNS GREATER THAN						
	1 month	**1 year**	**3 years**	**5 years**	**10 years**	**15 years**
10 per cent	11%	57%	61%	50%	37%	56%
Zero	55%	70%	78%	75%	100%	100%
Percentage of time stock lost $	45%	30%	22%	25%	0%	0%
Number of periods evaluated	218	207	183	159	99	39

This table illustrates the frequency with which a particular stock achieves or fails to meet an investor's goals. The table is divided into three achievement levels:

1. The frequency with which the stock achieved a return greater than 10 per cent over different periods

2. The frequency with which the stock achieved a return greater than zero

3. The frequency with which the stock achieved a return less than zero (or lost money) over different periods

In this example, Canadian Tire stock achieved a return greater than zero after one month 55 per cent of the time and a return greater than zero after one year 70 per cent of the time. After three and five years, the stock still posted losses 22 per cent and 25 per cent of the time. However, after 10 years the stock has always posted a return greater than zero.

The last line in the table entitled "Number of periods evaluated" indicates the number of periods included in this analysis.

DOWNSIDE RISK

	Worst setback since start date	In bear 1987	In bear 1990	In bear 1994	In bear 1998
Setback for stock	−55.2%	−24.6%	−19.1%	−55.2%	−24.8%
Setback for TSE 35	−5.2%	−26.5%	−16.8%	−9.0%	−27.6%
Setback ended in	July 1994	Oct 1987	Sept 1990	July 1994	Aug 1998
Months to recover from loss	28	7	6	28	?

The downside risk table evaluates the performance of the stock during different periods when capital markets have displayed significant declines in value, referred to as bear markets. It is useful for investors to evaluate the performance of their investments during more difficult economic environments. Some investments will decline significantly during bear markets; some will not decline in value. In addition, companies that operate in different industries will have very different performances. Investors can read the downside risk table and get a good approximation of how different investments react during these difficult times.

The table is divided into five setback periods, the worst setback since the stock analysis date and the four recent bear periods (in the 1980s and 1990s).

The worst setback since start date measures the worst decline an investor could have experienced with this stock in the period analyzed. Many stocks fluctuate over time; this figure discloses the largest drop from high to low that the stock has ever posted. Canadian Tire stock declined in value by 55.2 per cent, and the setback ended in July 1994. During the same period, the TSE 35 index declined in value by 5.2 per cent. However, after incurring this loss, Canadian Tire Stock regained its former value within 28 months. Investors should note that this column discloses the worst setback for the stock since the start date. The columns that disclose the stock's performance during the four bear markets evaluate the performance of the stock only during those periods.

STOCK FINANCIAL FUNDAMENTAL INFORMATION

	1988	1989	1990	1991	1992	1993	1994	1995	1996	1997	Change
Average share price	$15.93	$22.11	$21.29	$23.60	$18.02	$14.94	$11.94	$14.44	$17.63	$26.61	5.3%
Earnings per share	$1.38	$1.65	$1.60	$1.41	$0.80	$0.90	$0.06	$1.38	$1.51	$1.79	2.6%
Book value per share	$9.11	$10.15	$11.39	$12.36	$12.83	$13.36	$12.59	$14.05	$14.88	$15.65	5.6%
Price-to-earnings ratio	11.5	13.4	13.3	16.7	22.5	16.6	199.0	10.5	11.7	14.9	2.6%
Price-to-book ratio	1.7	2.2	1.9	1.9	1.4	1.1	0.9	1.0	1.2	1.7	−0.3%
Profit margin	4.7%	5.0%	4.7%	4.2%	2.3%	2.4%	0.2%	3.2%	3.4%	3.7%	−2.5%
Asset turnover	1.73	1.72	1.56	1.35	1.36	1.43	1.35	1.41	1.50	1.41	−2.0%
Leverage	1.9	1.9	1.9	2.0	2.0	2.0	2.3	2.2	2.0	2.2	1.8%
Return on equity	15.1%	16.3%	14.1%	11.4%	6.2%	6.7%	0.5%	9.8%	10.2%	11.4%	−2.8%
Dividend per share	$0.24	$0.30	$0.38	$0.40	$0.40	$0.40	$0.40	$0.40	$0.40	$0.40	5.2%
Dividend yield	1.5%	1.4%	1.8%	1.7%	2.2%	2.7%	3.4%	2.8%	2.3%	1.5%	0.0%

This table provides investors with a summary of some key financial information reported by the company during the previous 10 years. The rows in the table indicate the different variables used in our analysis. The columns provide data based on the company's annual or fiscal period (the period over which they report their financial information) ending in the stated year. The first data column provides financial information for 1988, and the second-last column, at the right, provides information for the company in 1997. The last column at the right side of the table, headed "Change," provides the annualized change that the company reported for the 10-year period ending in 1997. The change is reported only if the company provided complete information for our analysis and did not post negative variables. All stock financial fundamental information was provided by the underlying companies' annual reports.

Average share price: The average share price is the average price for the year, adjusted for stock splits.

Earnings per share: A company that generates larger profits is more valuable than a company that generates smaller profits. The value of a stock includes the current value of all the dividend payments. Dividend payments are made to investors by the company from profits to compensate investors for holding the stock. The larger the profits, the better the probability that companies will pay higher dividends. A company's earnings per share equals the company's total earnings divided by the number of shares outstanding. In 1988, earnings per share for Canadian Tire was $1.38. Therefore, each share of the company generated $1.38 of earnings. The calculation for Canadian Tire is equal to (approximately) 91,112,318 shares outstanding; each share generated $1.38 per share in earnings. Multiply the two figures together and you can see that Canadian Tire posted a profit of $124 million (with some rounding). Investors like to see an upward trend in profits, but the most important factor is that investors pay a reasonable price for each share of common stock.

Book value per share: The book value per share is equal to the value of the company's assets after paying all creditors. The creditors are the banks and the company's suppliers in addition to the company's bond holders. Therefore, the book value is the value of the company if the company sold all its assets for a price equal to the price reported in the financial statements and paid off all its debts. What is left over is the book value of the firm. Dividing the book value of the firm by the number of shares outstanding gives the book value per share. In 1988, the book value per share for Canadian Tire was $9.11, which is less than the average price for the stock of $15.93 per share. Here the company's stock was trading at more than book value per share. So, if you had bought all the shares in the company at the current (1988) price and sold all the assets for a price equal to their book value, you would have suffered a loss. Many companies trade at a price higher than their book value per share, but some mismanaged companies trade at less than book value per share. Book value per share is not always the best estimate of the actual value of the stock. Investors like companies whose book value per share increases over time, but the stock price is still a reasonable proxy for the book value per share.

Price-to-earnings ratio: The price-to-earnings ratio is equal to the company's stock price divided by the company's earnings per share. The price-to-earnings ratio or P/E ratio gives investors a good indication of how much they are paying for the company's historical earnings. The P/E ratio for Canadian Tire in 1988 was 11.5, which is the company's stock price of $15.93 divided by earnings per share $1.38. Therefore, investors paid $11.50 for every $1 in historical earnings. If the company's earnings did not grow, and the company paid all its earnings in the form of a dividend, investors would receive their money back in 11.5 years. It is important for investors that companies grow. If companies grow, earnings increase, and investors get their money back faster. Earnings growth can also be accomplished through cost reductions and other means. In general, lower P/E multiples with strong earnings growth is better than higher P/E multiples with low earnings growth.

Price-to-book ratio: The price-to-book ratio is equal to the company's average share price divided by its book value per share. In 1988, Canadian Tire's price-to-book ratio or P/B ratio was equal to 1.7. The company's average stock price was $15.93 divided by $9.11, which is equal to 1.7 or the P/B ratio. Thus, investors are paying $1.70 for every $1 of assets the company reported. Lower P/B ratios with high earnings growth are better than higher P/B ratios with low earnings growth.

Profit margin: The profit margin is equal to the company's net income divided by its sales. Higher profit margins are better than lower profit margins. Higher profit margins will increase the company's net income faster with each $1 increase in its sales. A profit margin of 4.7 per cent indicates that the company would earn $.047 more for every $1 increase in sales. Thus, companies with high profit margins can increase net income faster than companies with lower profit margins, because companies with lower profit margins have to sell more.

Asset turnover: Asset turnover measures how efficiently the senior management of the company manages the company's assets. The asset turnover ratio is equal to the company's sales divided by the assets the company utilizes. If a company has assets of $5 and sales of $10, its asset turnover ratio would equal $10 divided by $5 or 2. This means the company can generate $2 worth of sales for every $1 of assets employed. Therefore, higher asset turnover ratios are better. Investors like companies that have an increasing asset turnover ratio, because senior management is utilizing the assets of the company more efficiently and effectively to generate additional sales.

Leverage: When a company borrows money to invest, it is leveraging. Therefore, when a company borrows more money to invest in buildings or equipment it is increasing its leverage. Leverage is equal to the assets of the firm divided by the value of the firm owned by the shareholders. For example, a firm has assets worth $10. It borrows $5 from the bank and receives $5 from the owners. The leverage ratio would equal $10 (assets) divided by $5 (shareholders) or 2. The higher the leverage the better for investors, if the company is making money. But the reverse is true if the company is losing money. Leverage increases net income when the company is making money and increases losses if the company is losing money.

Return on equity: Return on equity is one of the key ratios that investors use to gauge the financial health of a company. The higher the return on equity is, the better. The return on equity measures how fast the company's earnings will grow. Investors like fast earnings growth because it leads to higher dividends, which generate a larger return. The return on equity is equal to the firm's net income divided by shareholder equity (the value of the firm to investors). A good approximation of the shareholders' equity is the book value of the firm (although this is not true in all cases). Canadian Tire's 1988 earnings per share was $1.38, and divided by the book value per share of $9.11 this gives a 15.15 per cent return on equity.

However, there is a second method for calculating earnings per share. Multiplying the profit margin (4.7 per cent), asset turnover (1.73), and leverage (1.9) ratios for Canadian Tire together will also generate a return on equity of 15.45 per cent (the difference is due to rounding). Thus, it is essential for investors to monitor the trend of earnings. The earnings trend can be explained by the firm's trend in profit margin, asset turnover, and leverage.

Dividend per share: The dividend per share is equal to the amount of income that the investor receives from holding a share of the company's stock. Companies pay dividends from earnings. Thus, higher earnings can sustain higher dividends. Higher dividends provide investors with more income.

Dividend yield: The dividend yield is equal to the dividend per share divided by the stock price for the company. In 1988 Canadian Tire paid a dividend of $.24. Dividing this dividend by the share price of $15.93 generates a dividend yield of 1.5 per cent. A higher yield is better for investors, but higher dividend payments will also deplete the company's cash, which it could reinvest in the company and ensure future sustained growth.

ABITIBI-CONSOLIDATED

Company profile

Abitibi-Consolidated was formed in 1997 by the amalgamation of Abitibi-Price and Stone-Consolidated. Abitibi-Consolidated is the world's second largest manufacturer of communications paper (including newsprint) in the world. In addition, Abitibi-Consolidated manufactures and markets value-added uncoated groundwood specialties. However, newsprint represents the bulk of their business.

Senior management is committed to the company's core values to ensure that the company grows the right way and maintains a competitive edge. These core values include being committed to results, customers, integrity, continuous improvement, and prudent spending to ensure value-added performance for shareholders.

The company operates 19 mills throughout North America and the United Kingdom. In 1997 it achieved net sales of $3.7 billion, but had a net operating loss of $121 million caused by the amalgamation. Without these costs, the company would have earned $57 million. The company's history can be traced back to the Great Depression. Throughout this history, Abitibi has experienced extreme highs and lows because of the cyclical nature of the pulp-and-paper business.

Stock performance

The common stock of Abitibi-Consolidated has been volatile. The best 12-month rate of return for the stock was a positive gain of 146.8 per cent, but the 12-month average return was 14.4 per cent. The common stock posted positive rates of return after 12 months 57 per cent of the time. Historically, this stock has had its moments but has also drastically underperformed because of the cyclical nature of the pulp-and-paper industry. Thus, investors can make significant money when and if the company makes a profitable turnaround.

Stock risks

Abitibi-Consolidated has experienced above-average downside risk. The common stock has been extremely volatile, and investors would have lost money after 12 months 44 per cent of the time since the start date in July 1980. Thus, investors will experience more risk in this common stock than in a well diversified Canadian equity mutual fund, but there is more upward potential with a stock. The worst 12-month period for the stock was a loss of 42.9 per cent and the stock underperforms during bear markets. In 1990, 1994, and 1998 the stock declined by more than 40 per cent.

Stock financial fundamentals

Theoretically the financial statements should improve going forward as the new company completes its amalgamation. In 1997 the company lost money, but Abitibi-Consolidated has had years with positive earnings. The book value per share in 1997 was $16.34, and the price-to-book (P/B) ratio was 1.4. This means that investors are paying $1.40 for every $1 of assets that belong to the shareholders. The profit margin has declined over the last 10 years as a result of a decline in the forestry industry.

Future prospects

This company has had prosperous times and difficult times. Currently it is experiencing some difficult times. However, with amalgamation and improved newsprint prices, the company's future prospects are good. The cyclical nature of the industry will lead to both buying and selling opportunities for the astute investor. This stock should be considered only by more speculative investors because of its historical downside risk.

COMPANY DETAILS

Company name	Abitibi-Consolidated	Industry classification	Paper and forest products
Recent price	$12.25	Market capitalization (in $ millions)	$2,377
Phone number for annual report	514-394-3254	Stock analysis start date	July 1980
Ticker symbol	A	Weight in TSE 35	1.4%
Number of mutual funds that hold this stock as a top 15 holding	13		

ROLLING 12-MONTH TOTAL RATE OF RETURN FOR THE STOCK OVER TIME*

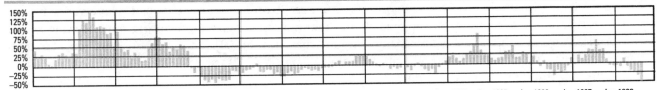

STOCK PERFORMANCE*

	1 month	1 year	3 years	5 years	10 years	15 years
Returns ending Aug 1998	−33.5%	−48.4%	−16.8%	0.3%	−3.1%	5.3%
Best historical return	46.3%	146.8%	71.8%	53.8%	16.0%	14.4%
Average historical return	1.0%	13.5%	12.6%	11.1%	6.6%	10.6%
Worst historical return	−33.5%	−48.4%	−24.2%	−13.9%	−4.6%	5.3%

RETURNS GREATER THAN*

	1 month	1 year	3 year	5 year	10 year	15 year
10 per cent	13%	45%	40%	41%	34%	64%
Zero	50%	56%	72%	70%	78%	100%
Percentage of time stock lost $	50%	44%	28%	30%	22%	0%
Number of periods evaluated	218	207	183	159	99	39

DOWNSIDE RISK*

	Worst setback since start date	In bear 1987	In bear 1990	In bear 1994	In bear 1998
Setback for stock	−66.0%	−41.0%	−64.9%	−49.9%	−60.4%
Setback for TSE 35	−3.7%	−26.5%	−16.8%	−9.0%	−27.6%
Setback ended in	Sept 1993	Nov 1987	Dec 1990	April 1994	Aug 1998
Months to recover from loss	?	?	?	?	?

STOCK FINANCIAL FUNDAMENTAL INFORMATION

	1988	1989	1990	1991	1992	1993	1994	1995	1996	1997	Change
Average share price	$21.76	$18.07	$14.66	$15.05	$14.87	$13.81	$17.66	$21.47	$19.36	$22.90	0.5%
Earnings per share	$2.64	$0.70	$(0.76)	$(1.12)	$(3.19)	$(1.58)	$(0.43)	$2.92	$1.39	$(0.62)	n/a
Book value per share	$17.48	$17.50	$16.27	$14.37	$10.75	$14.01	$13.78	$16.38	$17.63	$16.34	−0.7%
Price-to-earnings ratio	8.2	25.8	n/a	n/a	n/a	n/a	n/a	7.4	13.9	n/a	n/a
Price-to-book ratio	1.2	1.0	0.9	1.0	1.4	1.0	1.3	1.3	1.1	1.4	1.2%
Profit margin	10.9%	3.2%	−3.7%	−6.0%	−16.9%	−7.8%	−2.1%	11.8%	6.6%	−3.2%	n/a
Asset turnover	0.63	0.55	0.51	0.53	0.64	0.37	0.62	0.65	0.64	0.60	−0.6%
Leverage	2.2	2.3	2.5	2.5	2.7	3.9	2.4	2.3	1.9	2.0	−1.0%
Return on equity	15.1%	4.0%	−4.7%	−7.8%	−29.7%	−11.3%	−3.1%	17.8%	7.9%	−3.8%	n/a
Dividend per share	$1.00	$1.00	$0.50	$0.50	$0.50	$0.25		$0.20	$0.40	$0.40	−8.8%
Dividend yield	4.6%	5.5%	3.4%	3.3%	3.4%	1.8%	0.0%	0.9%	2.1%	1.7%	−9.2%

•Source: The raw data used in developing this table was provided by Datastream.

ALCAN ALUMINUM LIMITED

Company profile

Alcan Aluminum is one of the world's leading integrated aluminum companies. It is a fabricator and marketer of aluminum products with operations in over 30 countries. In addition, it is involved in bauxite mining, aluminum refining, power generation, aluminum smelting, manufacturing, and recycling as well as research and technology. The company's origins began close to 100 years ago as the Northern Aluminum Company. Currently, the company employs approximately 33,000 people directly and thousands more indirectly through related companies.

Alcan is a well positioned global player in its industry. The company has its own hydro electricity facilities in Canada, and has developed proprietary process technology. The company's strategic priorities include strengthening the position of aluminum as the material of choice in the marketplace, while aggressively seeking opportunities to maximize shareholder value.

Alcan Aluminum generated $7.7 billion in sales during 1997 while posting a net income of $485 million. Going forward, Alcan is committed to growth. To this end, the company is building a smelting operation in Alma, Quebec.

Stock performance

The best 12-month rate of return for Alcan Aluminum common stock was 95.2 per cent, and the average rate of return after 12 months was 11.3 per cent. The common stock posted positive rates of return after 12 months 65 per cent of the time. Recently, the stock has fallen out of favour with investors as demand from Asia is expected to decline and hurt Alcan's profits adversely.

Stock risks

The historical downside risk of Alcan Aluminum has been above average. During bear markets the stock has underperformed significantly. The worst 12-month rate of return for the common stock was a loss of 47.1 per cent. During the bear market of 1994, this stock declined by 25.8 per cent but regained its losses within four months. Historically, the stock has displayed significant downside risk but has also recovered quickly on many occasions during difficult market conditions.

Stock financial fundamentals

The book value per share of Alcan Aluminum has increased during the last 10 years from $21.42 to $30.22, and the price-to-book (P/B) ratio has increased to 1.5 from 1.1. Return on equity has declined over the last 10 years because of lower profit margins, lower asset turnover, and less leverage. In turn, the performance of the stock has been below average. Relative to other stocks, the company's stock multiples are lower. Lower stock multiples are usually associated with companies that are growing at a slower rate. However, value investors could consider Alcan Aluminum as an excellent investment if top management can ensure continuing growth.

Future prospects

Alcan Aluminum is not immune to a global recession or the Asian flu. Uncertainty around the Asian crisis can continue to put downward pressure on the common stock. Alcan Aluminum is a world leader in a commodity product. If Alcan Aluminum becomes the cost leader in the industry, investors will be rewarded. This stock is suitable only for speculative investors who are aware of the above-average risks associated with investing in this industry.

COMPANY DETAILS

Company name	Alcan Aluminum Limited	Industry classification	Metals and minerals
Recent price	$29.55	Market capitalization (in $ millions)	$6,718
Phone number for annual report	514-848-8368	Stock analysis start date	July 1980
Ticker symbol	AL	Weight in TSE 35	2.6%
Number of mutual funds that hold this stock as a top 15 holding	75		

ROLLING 12-MONTH TOTAL RATE OF RETURN FOR THE STOCK OVER TIME*

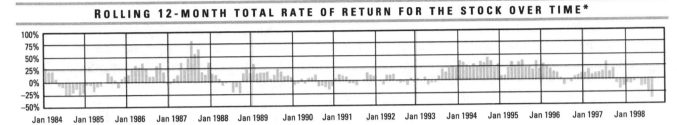

STOCK PERFORMANCE*

	1 month	1 year	3 years	5 years	10 years	15 years
Returns ending Aug 1998	−23.5%	−37.8%	−10.7%	3.3%	4.2%	4.7%
Best historical return	20.5%	95.2%	33.3%	28.8%	14.4%	14.6%
Average historical return	0.9%	10.7%	11.0%	10.5%	9.6%	10.6%
Worst historical return	−29.0%	−47.1%	−10.7%	−3.7%	3.9%	4.7%

RETURNS GREATER THAN*

	1 month	1 year	3 years	5 years	10 years	15 years
10 per cent	12%	49%	53%	52%	44%	51%
Zero	52%	64%	92%	96%	100%	100%
Percentage of time stock lost $	48%	36%	8%	4%	0%	0%
Number of periods evaluated	218	207	183	159	99	39

DOWNSIDE RISK*

	Worst setback since start date	In bear 1987	In bear 1990	In bear 1994	In bear 1998
Setback for stock	−47.7%	−34.2%	−25.8%	−10.1%	−43.9%
Setback for TSE 35	−32.4%	−26.5%	−16.8%	−9.0%	−27.6%
Setback ended in	Mar 1982	Nov 1987	Nov 1990	Apr 1994	Aug 1998
Months to recover from loss	14	69	33	3	?

STOCK FINANCIAL FUNDAMENTAL INFORMATION

	1988	1989	1990	1991	1992	1993	1994	1995	1996	1997	Change
Average share price	$24.2	$26.4	$24.4	$23.7	$23.3	$25.0	$32.8	$40.9	$43.5	$46.7	6.8%
Earnings per share	$4.81	$4.26	$2.73	$(0.29)	$(0.71)	$(0.70)	$0.46	$1.46	$2.38	$2.86	−5.1%
Book value per share	$21.42	$23.72	$25.86	$23.65	$23.51	$23.93	$26.36	$26.64	$27.58	$30.22	3.5%
Price-to-earnings ratio	5.0	6.2	9.0	n/a	n/a	n/a	70.9	28.0	18.3	16.3	12.5%
Price-to-book ratio	1.1	1.1	0.9	1.0	1.0	1.0	1.2	1.5	1.6	1.5	3.2%
Profit margin	10.4%	9.0%	5.8%	−0.7%	−1.8%	−1.7%	0.9%	2.5%	5.1%	6.0%	−5.3%
Asset turnover	1.0	1.0	0.8	0.7	0.7	0.7	0.8	1.0	0.8	0.8	−2.4%
Leverage	2.1	2.1	2.2	2.3	2.4	2.4	2.3	2.2	2.0	1.9	−0.8%
Return on equity	22.5%	18.0%	10.5%	−1.2%	−3.0%	−2.9%	1.8%	5.5%	8.6%	9.5%	−8.3%
Dividend per share	$0.72	$1.31	$1.31	$0.96	$0.56	$0.40	$0.41	$0.60	$0.80	$0.85	1.6%
Dividend yield	2.98%	4.96%	5.37%	4.07%	2.40%	1.58%	1.23%	1.47%	1.85%	1.81%	−4.9%

•Source: The raw data used in developing this table was provided by Datastream.

BANK OF MONTREAL

Company profile

The Bank of Montreal is a major Canadian chartered bank that operates 1,246 branches in all the provinces and territories of Canada and around the world. The bank offers a full range of commercial, corporate, government, international, investment, and retail banking products and services, in addition to brokerage, underwriting, and investment management services provided by wholly owned subsidiary Nesbitt Burns. The Bank of Montreal also offers financial services across the US through wholly owned Harris Bankcorp, and has interests in other financial services companies.

The bank's history can be traced back to the early 1800s, when it opened its first branch in the heart of the business district of Montreal. From the early days of lending to fur traders, the bank has established a dynamic global network that includes 2,035 automatic banking machines. In addition, the Bank of Montreal introduced mbanx, a direct banking division that provides clients with full-service banking via the Internet.

In 1997 the bank generated sales of over $15 billion with net income of more than $1.3 billion. In addition, the Bank of Montreal has stated intentions of merging with the Royal Bank of Canada pending regulatory approval.

Stock performance

During 1997, the common stock of the Bank of Montreal significantly increased in value. The best 12-month rate of return posted by the common stock was 83.0 per cent, and the average 12-month rate of return was 18.5 per cent. The stock appreciated significantly in 1992 and in 1997.

Stock risks

The worst 12-month period for the common stock of the Bank of Montreal was a decline of 31.4 per cent. The stock posted a positive rate of return 74 per cent of the time after 12 months. The stock has also underperformed during bear markets. Investors prior to the bear market in 1987 saw their investment decline by 30.2 per cent, but the stock regained its loss within 17 months. The stock's worst decline was a loss of 43.2 per cent. The stock regained that loss within eight months.

Stock financial fundamentals

The earnings per share for the Bank of Montreal have increased during the previous 10 years. Over the same period, the common stock value has increased significantly. With this increased growth, the stock multiples have increased. The price-to-earnings (P/E) ratio rose from 6.3 in 1988 to 11.1 in 1997. In turn, investors have to pay a larger premium for $1 in historical earnings today than in 1988. In 1989 the company had some difficulties, losing $0.39 per share. The results in 1989 were uncharacteristic of bank stocks, since their earnings have been less cyclical than other companies. In fact their earnings record has been sensational.

Future prospects

The bank's profits are closely tied with the direction and level of interest rates as well as to stock market activity. With a little bad news, bank stocks could decline significantly. However, banks have historically added a lot of value for shareholders over the long term. The worst 15-year rate of return posted by Bank of Montreal common stock was 10.7 per cent compounded annually. Investors looking for enhanced Canadian equity exposure should carefully evaluate the prospects of bank stocks in the future. Investors should be aware that bank earnings will be more volatile during periods of volatile capital markets.

COMPANY DETAILS

Company name	**Bank of Montreal**	Industry classification	Financial services
Recent price	$55.15	Market capitalization (in $ millions)	$14,418
Phone number for annual report	514-877-2500	Stock analysis start date	July 1980
Ticker symbol	BMO	Weight in TSE 35	4.5%
Number of mutual funds that hold this stock as a top 15 holding	256		

ROLLING 12-MONTH TOTAL RATE OF RETURN FOR THE STOCK OVER TIME*

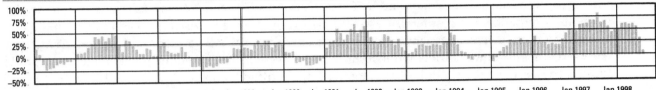

STOCK PERFORMANCE*

	1 month	1 year	3 years	5 years	10 years	15 years
Returns ending Aug 1998	−25.1%	6.0%	27.1%	20.0%	20.7%	15.9%
Best historical return	15.9%	83.0%	47.3%	33.4%	26.5%	19.8%
Average historical return	1.3%	18.5%	16.1%	15.3%	14.6%	15.4%
Worst historical return	−25.1%	−31.4%	−3.4%	1.7%	5.1%	10.7%

RETURNS GREATER THAN*

	1 month	1 year	3 years	5 years	10 years	15 years
10 per cent	6%	62%	68%	71%	87%	100%
Zero	60%	74%	95%	100%	100%	100%
Percentage of time stock lost $	40%	26%	5%	0%	0%	0%
Number of periods evaluated	218	207	183	159	99	39

DOWNSIDE RISK*

	Worst setback since start date	In bear 1987	In bear 1990	In bear 1994	In bear 1998
Setback for stock	−43.2%	−30.2%	−23.7%	−20.9%	−32.6%
Setback for TSE 35	−41.0%	−26.5%	−16.8%	−9.0%	−27.6%
Setback ended in	June 1982	Nov 1987	Apr 1990	June 1994	Aug 1998
Months to recover from loss	9	20	9	11	?

STOCK FINANCIAL FUNDAMENTAL INFORMATION

	1988	1989	1990	1991	1992	1993	1994	1995	1996	1997	Change
Average share price	$13.60	$15.70	$13.89	$18.18	$22.50	$25.20	$25.73	$28.58	$35.02	$54.77	14.9%
Earnings per share	$2.16	$(0.39)	$2.10	$2.31	$2.36	$2.55	$2.97	$3.38	$4.13	$4.62	7.9%
Book value per share	$14.40	$30.97	$13.88	$14.88	$15.97	$17.39	$20.44	$21.16	$23.79	$27.01	6.5%
Price-to-earnings ratio	6.3	n/a	6.6	7.9	9.5	9.9	8.7	8.5	8.5	11.9	6.5%
Price-to-book ratio	0.9	0.5	1.0	1.2	1.4	1.4	1.3	1.4	1.5	2.0	7.9%
Profit margin	6.3%	−0.4%	5.5%	6.9%	8.5%	9.8%	11.0%	9.5%	10.9%	11.0%	5.7%
Asset turnover	0.10	0.12	0.11	0.09	0.07	0.06	0.05	0.07	0.06	0.06	−5.3%
Leverage	24.0	25.5	25.3	25.8	25.2	24.2	24.3	24.6	25.2	27.2	1.3%
Return on equity	15.0%	−1.3%	15.1%	15.5%	14.8%	14.7%	14.5%	16.0%	17.4%	17.1%	1.3%
Dividend per share	$1.00	$1.05	$1.06	$1.06	$1.06	$1.11	$1.18	$1.29	$1.41	$1.60	4.8%
Dividend yield	7.4%	6.7%	7.6%	5.8%	4.7%	4.4%	4.6%	4.5%	4.0%	2.9%	−8.8%

•Source: The raw data used in developing this table was provided by Datastream.

BANK OF NOVA SCOTIA

Company profile

The Bank of Nova Scotia is a major Canadian chartered bank that operates 1,658 branches in all the provinces and territories of Canada and in 50 other countries. The bank offers a full range of commercial, corporate, international, investment, and retail banking products and services, in addition to brokerage, underwriting, and investment management services provided by wholly owned subsidiary Scotia McLeod. Trust services including pension and investment management are offered by wholly owned subsidiary Montreal Trustco. The Bank of Nova Scotia recently acquired National Trust, and also offers life and property insurance products.

The company's history dates back to 1832 in the city of Halifax, where the bank was established to handle banking for the economic activity developing in the area, such as lumbering, farming, and fishing, and for international trade.

In 1997 the Bank of Nova Scotia generated sales of more than $10 billion and had profits above $1 billion. The company employs over 38,000 people, and has over 1,600 bank machines in Canada.

Stock performance

The Bank has its own line of Scotia Excelsior mutual funds, but its common stock proved to the better investment (not adjusting for risk). The best 12-month rate of return was a gain of 123.2 per cent, and the average 12-month rate of return was 21.3 per cent. The common stock posted a positive rate of return after 12 months 75 per cent of the time, and increased significantly in both 1991 and 1997.

Stock risks

This stock has experienced above-average downside risk. During the bear markets, Bank of Nova Scotia stock has underperformed. Investors during 1994 saw their investment decline by 21.8 per cent, although the stock regained its loss within 11 months. During the bear of 1998, the stock declined by 33.9 per cent.

Stock financial fundamentals

Because of the increased growth in the Bank of Nova Scotia's earnings, the stock multiples have expanded during the last 10 years. These stock levels can be justified if the bank continues to increase earnings and grow. However, a small decline in earnings could have a significant impact on the price of the underlying stock. The profit margin for the bank has increased since 1988, but return on equity still decreased because the bank had lower asset turnover and leverage.

Future prospects

The bank's profits are closely tied to the direction and level of interest rates and to stock-market activity. Going forward, a little bad news could send the bank's stock into a decline. However, banks have historically added a lot of value for shareholders over the long term. The worst 15-year rate of return posted by Bank of Nova Scotia stock was 11.8 per cent compounded annually. Investors who want a Canadian stock in their portfolio could consider a bank stock at a reasonable price. Considering the large setback many bank stocks incurred during the bear of 1998, astute investors could consider this an excellent opportunity to buy stocks at a lower price. Over the long term, these shares will increase in value. However, in the interim anything can happen.

COMPANY DETAILS

Company name	**Bank of Nova Scotia**	Industry classification	Financial services
Recent price	$25.80	Market capitalization (in $ millions)	$12,637
Phone number for annual report	416-866-3750	Stock analysis start date	July 1980
Ticker symbol	BNS	Weight in TSE 35	3.0%
Number of mutual funds that hold this stock as a top 15 holding	203		

ROLLING 12-MONTH TOTAL RATE OF RETURN FOR THE STOCK OVER TIME*

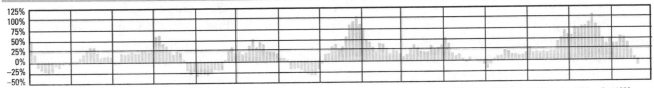

Jan 1984 Jan 1985 Jan 1986 Jan 1987 Jan 1988 Jan 1989 Jan 1990 Jan 1991 Jan 1992 Jan 1993 Jan 1994 Jan 1995 Jan 1996 Jan 1997 Jan 1998

STOCK PERFORMANCE*

	1 month	1 year	3 years	5 years	10 years	15 years
Returns ending Aug 1998	–24.0%	–12.0%	24.6%	18.2%	19.4%	14.6%
Best historical return	17.4%	123.2%	47.1%	30.3%	25.9%	21.6%
Average historical return	1.4%	21.1%	17.3%	16.0%	14.9%	16.5%
Worst historical return	–24.0%	–32.5%	–7.1%	–0.6%	4.4%	11.8%

RETURNS GREATER THAN*

	1 month	1 year	3 years	5 years	10 years	15 years
10 per cent	9%	65%	77%	71%	92%	100%
Zero	54%	74%	95%	99%	100%	100%
Percentage of time stock lost $	46%	26%	5%	1%	0%	0%
Number of periods evaluated	218	207	183	159	99	39

DOWNSIDE RISK*

	Worst setback since start date	In bear 1987	In bear 1990	In bear 1994	In bear 1998
Setback for stock	–39.3%	–39.3%	–38.9%	–21.8%	–33.9%
Setback for TSE 35	–26.5%	–26.5%	–16.8%	–9.0%	–27.6%
Setback ended in	Nov 1987	Nov 1987	Nov 1990	July 1994	Aug 1998
Months to recover from loss	18	18	6	18	?

STOCK FINANCIAL FUNDAMENTAL INFORMATION

	1988	1989	1990	1991	1992	1993	1994	1995	1996	1997	Change
Average share price	$6.80	$8.31	$6.72	$8.65	$11.08	$13.10	$13.74	$14.14	$17.57	$29.32	15.7%
Earnings per share	$1.37	$0.51	$1.17	$1.41	$1.47	$1.49	$0.88	$1.69	$2.04	$2.96	8.0%
Book value per share	$8.31	$7.61	$8.82	$10.07	$11.04	$12.32	$11.39	$14.12	$14.79	$18.34	8.2%
Price-to-earnings ratio	5.0	16.5	5.8	6.2	7.5	8.8	15.6	8.4	8.6	9.9	7.2%
Price-to-book ratio	0.8	1.1	0.8	0.9	1.0	1.1	1.2	1.0	1.2	1.6	6.9%
Profit margin	8.0%	2.8%	6.0%	7.5%	9.3%	10.3%	6.2%	8.3%	10.3%	14.4%	6.1%
Asset turnover	0.09	0.10	0.15	0.10	0.07	0.07	0.06	0.07	0.06	0.05	–4.5%
Leverage	24.3	24.2	14.7	19.4	19.2	18.0	21.3	20.1	21.3	20.8	–1.5%
Return on equity	16.5%	6.6%	13.2%	14.0%	13.3%	12.1%	7.7%	12.0%	13.8%	16.1%	–0.2%
Dividend per share	$0.38	$0.44	$0.50	$0.50	$0.52	$0.56	$0.58	$0.62	$0.65	$0.74	6.9%
Dividend yield	5.6%	5.3%	7.4%	5.8%	4.7%	4.3%	4.2%	4.4%	3.7%	2.5%	–7.6%

•Source: The raw data used in developing this table was provided by Datastream.

BARRICK GOLD CORPORATION

Company profile

Barrick Gold Corporation is a major gold producer with extensive interests in North and South America, including the Betze-Post and Meikle mines in Nevada, the Holt-McDermott mine in Canada, and the El Indio mine in Chile. Barrick Gold was formed by a merger of CamFlo Mines Ltd., Bob-Claire Investments, and the former Barrick Resources.

Barrick is a different gold company! The company has more than 50 million ounces of reserves and a major hedging advantage, with the ability to sell gold at $400 per ounce for the next two to three years. In addition, the company is a low-cost producer, has strong cash flows, a commitment to technology, and solid financial flexibility.

The company earned over $1.2 billion from the sale of more than three million ounces of gold. It employs 5,700 people throughout the world.

Stock performance

Ouch! This stock has travelled a difficult road with many peaks and valleys. During the early 1990s, the stock significantly outperformed other Canadian common stocks, but recently it has had a difficult time posting positive rates of return. This underperformance arises from a decline in the average selling price of gold, caused by oversupply. And the Bre-X fraud hasn't helped investor sentiment toward gold stocks in general.

The best 12-month period for Barrick Gold Corporation was a positive rate of return of 326.2 per cent, and the average 12-month return was 37.4 per cent. The stock has posted a positive rate of return after 12 months 69 per cent of the time.

Stock risk

The worst 12-month period for this stock was a loss of 45.3 per cent. The stock has posted positive rates of return after 12 months 31 per cent of the time since the start date in June 1993. The stock underperforms during bear markets. During the bear of 1987, it declined by 38.9 per cent and took 25 months to regain its loss. Currently, the stock has declined by 52.3 per cent during 1998. In general, gold stocks have displayed a lot of downside risk, but significant upside potential as well.

Stock financial fundamentals

The company has had a volatile period during the past 10 years. Investor enthusiasm for this growth stock and a decline in earnings have increased the stock's multiples to higher levels. The stock price has declined recently as investors react to a decline in earnings and a less than favourable outlook for the price of gold.

Future prospects

To properly evaluate the company, investors must take into consideration the impact of changes in the price of gold. Inherently, this gold company is less risky than other gold companies because it has a large reserve base and is financially sound. In addition, the company has an extensive hedging program in place to ensure that it receives the most favourable price possible for its gold. The major risk to gold companies in the future is oversupply in world markets as central banks continue to sell. This oversupply depresses the price of gold and, in turn, investors' appetite for gold stocks. Speculative investors with a long-term horizon and the ability to withstand above-average volatility may find an investment in a gold stock a profitable acquisition.

COMPANY DETAILS

Company name	**Barrick Gold Corporation**	Industry classification	Gold and silver
Recent price	$20.35	Market capitalization (in $ millions)	$7,591
Phone number for annual report	1-800-720-7415	Stock analysis start date	June 1983
Ticker symbol	ABX	Weight in TSE 35	2.4%
Number of mutual funds that hold this stock as a top 15 holding	57		

ROLLING 12-MONTH TOTAL RATE OF RETURN FOR THE STOCK OVER TIME*

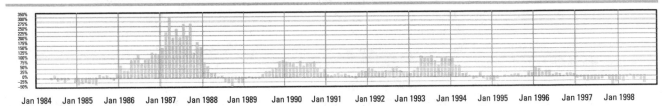

Jan 1984   Jan 1985   Jan 1986   Jan 1987   Jan 1988   Jan 1989   Jan 1990   Jan 1991   Jan 1992   Jan 1993   Jan 1994   Jan 1995   Jan 1996   Jan 1997   Jan 1998

STOCK PERFORMANCE*

	1 month	1 year	3 years	5 years	10 years	15 years
Returns ending Aug 1998	−17.6%	−34.6%	−15.1%	−9.3%	14.5%	21.3%
Best historical return	35.0%	326.2%	104.9%	69.1%	45.7%	24.5%
Average historical return	2.1%	36.7%	34.5%	33.3%	32.9%	23.1%
Worst historical return	−38.9%	−45.3%	−15.1%	−9.3%	13.2%	21.3%

RETURNS GREATER THAN*

	1 month	1 year	3 years	5 years	10 years	15 years
10 per cent	21%	57%	82%	91%	100%	100%
Zero	52%	69%	89%	97%	100%	100%
Percentage of time stock lost $	48%	31%	11%	3%	0%	0%
Number of periods evaluated	183	172	148	124	64	4

DOWNSIDE RISK*

	Worst setback since start date	In bear 1987	In bear 1990	In bear 1994	In bear 1998
Setback for stock	−52.3%	−38.9%	−15.3%	−25.2%	−52.3%
Setback for TSE 35	−27.6%	−26.5%	−16.8%	−9.0%	−27.6%
Setback ended in	Aug 1998	Oct 1987	Apr 1990	Jan 1995	Aug 1998
Months to recover from loss	?	27	2	12	?

STOCK FINANCIAL FUNDAMENTAL INFORMATION

	1988	1989	1990	1991	1992	1993	1994	1995	1996	1997	Change
Average share price	$5.86	$7.09	$11.19	$12.64	$16.79	$28.78	$32.86	$33.70	$39.11	$31.92	18.5%
Earnings per share	$0.15	$0.17	$0.27	$0.39	$0.73	$0.95	$1.09	$1.13	$0.82	$(0.45)	n/a
Book value per share	$1.84	$2.33	$2.95	$3.44	$4.25	$5.46	$11.26	$11.09	$12.91	$12.57	21.2%
Price-to-earnings ratio	39.1	42.6	41.6	32.3	23.1	30.1	30.2	29.8	47.6	n/a	n/a
Price-to-book ratio	3.2	3.0	3.8	3.7	3.9	5.3	2.9	3.0	3.0	2.5	−2.2%
Profit margin	17.2%	14.9%	20.5%	24.9%	31.6%	31.3%	26.3%	22.3%	16.5%	−9.5	n/a
Asset turnover	0.25	0.23	0.25	0.29	0.35	0.41	0.28	0.38	0.30	0.29	1.6%
Leverage	1.9	2.1	1.8	1.6	1.5	1.4	1.3	1.2	1.3	1.3	−3.7%
Return on equity	8.2%	7.1%	9.1%	11.4%	17.1%	17.5%	9.7%	10.2%	6.4%	−3.6%	n/a
Dividend per share	$0.02	$0.04	$0.05	$0.06	$0.08	$0.09	$0.11	$0.13	$0.16	$0.20	23.3%
Dividend yield	0.4%	0.5%	0.4%	0.5%	0.5%	0.3%	0.3%	0.4%	0.4%	0.6%	4.0%

•Source: The raw data used in developing this table was provided by Datastream.

BCE INCORPORATED

Company profile

BCE Inc. is currently Canada's largest telecommunications company and is the parent company of Bell Canada, Bell Canada International, Northern Telecom (now called Nortel Networks), and other subsidiaries. Through its subsidiaries, BCE Inc. designs, manufactures, and markets telecommunications equipment, including cellular phones and paging equipment, and provides telecommunications and directory (telephone book) services.

Northern Telecom, one of the largest designers and manufacturers of telecommunications equipment in North America, became Nortel Networks after merging recently with Bay Networks, a leader in the worldwide data networking market.

The saga of BCE can be traced back to Alexander Graham Bell, whose initial experiments led to the formation of Bell Telephone in 1880. The company diversified and grew into one of Canada's largest and most successful companies. BCE Inc. has grown over the last 100 years from its modest beginnings to employing 70,000 Canadians in 1997 and generating over $13.8 billion in sales. BCE Inc. is surely one of Canada's great success stories. The company is fueling its growth by becoming a global communications power. With increased investments in telephone services, satellite television, and internet services, BCE is determined to meet its growth objectives.

Stock performance

The common stock of BCE Inc. has been on a tear. The best 12-month rate of return for the stock was a gain of 92.9 per cent, and the average 12-month rate of return for the stock was 18.4 per cent. BCE Inc. common stock has posted positive rates of return after 12 months 82 per cent of the time. Historically, this stock has been a leader, not a follower, posting above-average gains.

Stock risks

BCE Inc.'s worst 12-month rate of return was a loss of 10.8 per cent, and the stock posted losses after 12 months 18 per cent of the time since the start date in July 1980. However, the stock has always posted a positive rate of return after three years. During the bear of 1990, the stock declined in value by 18.7 per cent and took five months to regain its value. Thus, BCE Inc. has experienced less downside risk than the average stock, and historically has taken less time to recover from a setback.

Stock financial fundamentals

BCE Inc.'s common stock multiples have expanded over the last several years. The price-to-earnings (P/E) ratio has increased to 18.2 in 1997 from 12.7 in 1988. Thus, investors are paying $18.20 for every $1 of earnings currently instead of $12.70 for every $1 of earnings. This is still significantly less that the average common stock's P/E ratio but is still high by historical standards for BCE Inc. In addition, BCE Inc. has increased its profit margin, asset turnover, and leverage to improve return on equity for shareholders. Investors have begun to pay a premium for future growth, but the growth is coming to fruition as BCE Inc. continues to increase sales.

Future prospects

Investors haven't been disappointed as Ma Bell continues to deliver. BCE Inc. is not immune to a Canadian or global recession, but top management has proven its ability to add value for shareholders in both the short and long term. BCE Inc. common stock is expensive currently by historical standards, but this premium could be justified by BCE Inc.'s global growth potential. Astute investors can utilize the bear of 1998 to acquire stock in this company at lower prices. Over the long term, BCE Inc. has added value for investors.

COMPANY DETAILS

Company name	**BCE Incorporated**	Industry classification	Utilities
Recent price	$50.60	Market capitalization (in $ millions)	$32,182
Phone number for annual report	514 397-7056	Stock analysis start date	July 1980
Ticker symbol	BCE	Weight in TSE 35	11.8%
Number of mutual funds that hold this stock as a top 15 holding	289		

ROLLING 12-MONTH TOTAL RATE OF RETURN FOR THE STOCK OVER TIME*

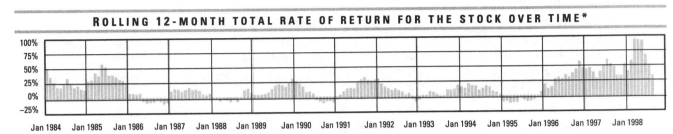

Jan 1984　Jan 1985　Jan 1986　Jan 1987　Jan 1988　Jan 1989　Jan 1990　Jan 1991　Jan 1992　Jan 1993　Jan 1994　Jan 1995　Jan 1996　Jan 1997　Jan 1998

STOCK PERFORMANCE*

	1 month	1 year	3 years	5 years	10 years	15 years
Returns ending Aug 1998	−16.9%	32.1%	37.7%	22.9%	16.1%	14.6%
Best historical return	18.6%	92.9%	51.5%	29.7%	19.2%	17.6%
Average historical return	1.3%	18.8%	15.9%	13.7%	12.5%	15.0%
Worst historical return	−16.9%	−10.8%	0.4%	3.0%	5.6%	12.3%

RETURNS GREATER THAN*

	1 month	1 year	3 years	5 years	10 years	15 years
10 per cent	5%	59%	61%	59%	73%	100%
Zero	60%	82%	100%	100%	100%	100%
Percentage of time stock lost $	40%	18%	0%	0%	0%	0%
Number of periods evaluated	218	207	183	159	99	39

DOWNSIDE RISK*

	Worst setback since start date	In bear 1987	In bear 1990	In bear 1994	In bear 1998
Setback for stock	−24.5%	−12.9%	−18.7%	−12.6%	−24.5%
Setback for TSE 35	−27.6%	−26.5%	−16.8%	−9.0%	−27.6%
Setback ended in	Aug 1998	Nov 1987	Sept 1990	Jan 1995	Aug 1998
Months to recover from loss	?	18	8	12	?

STOCK FINANCIAL FUNDAMENTAL INFORMATION

	1988	1989	1990	1991	1992	1993	1994	1995	1996	1997	Change
Average share price	$18.82	$19.99	$19.86	$21.64	$22.60	$22.32	$23.75	$21.88	$27.50	$38.44	7.4%
Earnings per share	$1.48	$1.22	$1.75	$2.00	$2.11	$(1.22)	$1.76	$1.12	$1.70	$2.11	3.6%
Book value per share	$16.21	$16.09	$16.63	$17.37	$18.05	$15.77	$16.41	$16.18	$16.62	$12.10	−2.9%
Price-to-earnings ratio	12.7	16.4	11.3	10.8	10.7	n/a	13.5	19.5	16.2	18.2	3.7%
Price-to-book ratio	1.2	1.2	1.2	1.2	1.3	1.4	1.4	1.4	1.7	3.2	10.6%
Profit margin	5.7%	4.6%	6.3%	6.7%	6.6%	−3.8%	5.0%	2.8%	3.8%	4.3%	−2.9%
Asset turnover	0.56	0.55	0.56	0.55	0.53	0.54	0.57	0.63	0.68	0.82	3.9%
Leverage	2.8	3.0	3.0	3.1	3.3	3.8	3.8	3.9	3.9	5.0	5.8%
Return on equity	9.1%	7.6%	10.5%	11.5%	11.7%	−7.7%	10.7%	6.9%	10.2%	17.4%	6.7%
Dividend per share	$1.22	$1.25	$1.26	$1.28	$1.30	$1.33	$1.34	$1.36	$1.36	$1.36	1.1%
Dividend yield	6.5%	6.3%	6.3%	5.9%	5.8%	6.0%	5.6%	6.2%	4.9%	3.5%	−5.9%

•Source: The raw data used in developing this table was provided by Datastream.

BOMBARDIER INCORPORATED, B

Company profile

Bombardier is one of Canada's biggest success stories. The saga of Bombardier began near an eastern Quebec village named Valcourt in 1937. Joseph-Armand Bombardier, an inventor and entrepreneur, devised a solution to the difficulty of travelling during the harsh Quebec winters by producing the first prototypes of the snowmobile, the B-7. In 1942, Mr. Bombardier founded L'Auto-Neige Bombardier to manufacture tracked vehicles.

Currently the company has five main manufacturing groups. *Transportation Equipment* manufactures and markets rail transit vehicles and diesel engine components. Customers include GO Transit and the Toronto Transit Commission. *Aerospace* manufactures and markets various surveillance systems and aircraft. *Motorized Consumer Products* manufactures and markets snowmobiles, recreational watercraft, and small gasoline engines. *Bombardier Services* provides technical and support services for aviation customers and for snow-grooming equipment. *Bombardier Capital* provides financial and real estate services.

In 1997 Bombardier had over 47,000 employees. The company generated close to $8 billion in sales by marketing its products and services on five continents. Bombardier had a high concentration of sales in North America and Europe, and approximately 90 per cent of sales were generated outside Canada.

Stock performance

The common stock of Bombardier has appreciated to the extent that there are currently more millionaire employees working at Bombardier than at any other company in Canada. In short, investors or employees who invested in the common stock of Bombardier have been richly rewarded.

The best 12-month return for the common stock was a positive return of 177.5 per cent, and the average 12-month return for the common stock was 38.3 per cent. The common stock posted positive rates of return after 12 months 82 per cent of the time. During the past 10 years the stock has appreciated by an average of 30 per cent per year. Historically, Bombardier has set the standards to which its competitors aspire.

Stock risks

The road to success for Bombardier has included several setbacks. The worst 12-month period for the common stock was a loss of 44.4 per cent. Bombardier has also experienced periods of underperformance, which may occur again in the future. During the bear of 1998, the stock declined in value by 19.7 per cent, less than the industry average. During the bear of 1994, the stock declined by 8.3 per cent but recovered its loss within one month.

Stock financial fundamentals

Bombardier has had a phenomenal 10-year run. However, with this success the common stock has become increasingly more expensive. Earnings in 1988 were $0.13 per share and have increased on average by 16.3 per cent per year to $0.59 per share. This growth has increased the price-to-earnings (P/E) ratio for the company from 10.9 in 1988 to 24 in 1997. Thus investors are currently paying $24 for every $1 of historical earnings. This growth can be attributed to Bombardier's high return on equity, its large increase in sales, and a decline in interest rates.

Future prospects

Investors haven't been disappointed as Bombardier continued to deliver throughout the last five years. However, going forward Bombardier will have to find significant avenues of growth to continue its upward momentum. If this growth does not come to fruition, investors may experience new levels of downside risk.

COMPANY DETAILS

Company name	**Bombardier Incorporated, B**	Industry classification	Industrial products
Recent price	$16.70	Market capitalization (in $ millions)	$11,894
Phone number for annual report	514-861-9481 ext. 390	Stock analysis start date	March 1981
Ticker symbol	BBD.B	Weight in TSE 35	3.9%
Number of mutual funds that hold this stock as a top 15 holding	95		

ROLLING 12-MONTH TOTAL RATE OF RETURN FOR THE STOCK OVER TIME*

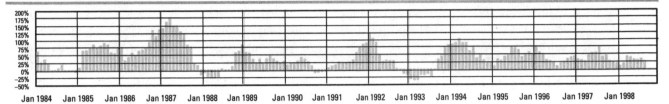

STOCK PERFORMANCE*

	1 month	1 year	3 years	5 years	10 years	15 years
Returns ending Aug 1998	−19.7%	25.2%	28.1%	36.6%	30.0%	35.8%
Best historical return	37.8%	177.5%	90.2%	69.3%	43.9%	39.4%
Average historical return	2.6%	38.2%	36.1%	36.1%	34.0%	34.8%
Worst historical return	−25.9%	−44.4%	−0.1%	17.2%	24.5%	30.0%

RETURNS GREATER THAN*

	1 month	1 year	3 years	5 years	10 years	15 years
10 per cent	20%	77%	94%	100%	100%	100%
Zero	59%	82%	99%	100%	100%	100%
Percentage of time stock lost $	41%	18%	1%	0%	0%	0%
Number of periods evaluated	210	199	175	151	91	31

DOWNSIDE RISK*

	Worst setback since start date	In bear 1987	In bear 1990	In bear 1994	In bear 1998
Setback for stock	−47.5%	−45.5%	−28.0%	−8.3%	−19.7%
Setback for TSE 35	−32.4%	−26.5%	−16.8%	−9.0%	−27.6%
Setback ended in	Mar 1982	Dec 1987	Nov 1990	Jan 1995	Aug 1998
Months to recover from loss	14	10	6	1	?

STOCK FINANCIAL FUNDAMENTAL INFORMATION

	1988	1989	1990	1991	1992	1993	1994	1995	1996	1997	Change
Average share price	$1.34	$1.80	$2.04	$2.66	$3.53	$3.41	$5.29	$7.65	$10.12	$14.13	26.6%
Earnings per share	$0.13	$0.17	$0.18	$0.18	$0.22	$0.28	$0.37	$0.23	$0.59	$0.59	16.3%
Book value per share	$0.70	$0.86	$1.14	$1.43	$1.51	$2.11	$2.37	$2.35	$2.95	$3.40	17.2%
Price-to-earnings ratio	10.3	10.6	11.7	14.8	16.4	12.2	14.5	34.0	17.2	23.9	8.8%
Price-to-book ratio	1.9	2.1	1.8	1.9	2.3	1.6	2.2	3.3	3.4	4.2	8.0%
Profit margin	4.8%	4.3%	3.5%	3.5%	3.0%	3.7%	4.2%	2.2%	5.1%	4.9%	0.3%
Asset turnover	1.24	1.11	1.13	1.00	1.05	10.49	1.09	1.11	1.00	0.80	−4.2%
Leverage	3.1	4.2	3.9	3.6	4.5	0.3	3.4	3.9	3.9	4.4	3.4%
Return on equity	18.6%	19.8%	15.4%	12.6%	14.3%	13.3%	15.4%	9.6%	20.0%	17.3%	−0.7%
Dividend per share	$0.31	$0.31	$0.04	$0.04	$0.05	$0.05	$0.08	$0.10	$0.10	$0.15	−6.7%
Dividend yield	22.9%	17.0%	2.1%	1.6%	1.5%	1.6%	1.5%	1.3%	1.0%	1.1%	−26.3%

•Source: The raw data used in developing this table was provided by Datastream.

CANADIAN IMPERIAL BANK OF COMMERCE

Company profile

The Canadian Imperial Bank of Commerce is a major Canadian chartered bank that operates 1,386 branches in all the provinces and territories of Canada. The bank also has operations outside Canada to service international clients and has recently acquired Oppenheimer and Company, a major US equity underwriting, trading, and distribution company. The bank offers a full range of commercial, corporate, international, investment, and retail banking products and services in addition to brokerage, underwriting, and investment management services provided by wholly owned subsidiary Wood Gundy in Canada and Oppenheimer in the US. Insurance and trust products and services are offered through CIBC Insurance and CIBC Trust.

The company's history can be traced back to 1867, when William McMaster acquired a charter to open the Canadian Bank of Commerce. The bank grew quickly and opened offices in Montreal and New York.

In 1997, CIBC generated sales of over $15 billion and had profits over $1.5 billion. The company employed in excess of 42,000 people and has more than 3,100 bank machines in Canada and around the world.

Stock performance

The bank has its own line of CIBC mutual funds, but its common stock proved to be the better investment for investors (not taking risk into account). The best 12-month rate of return was a gain of 100.6 per cent, and the average 12-month rate of return was 20.1 per cent. The common stock posted a positive rate of return after 12 months 75 per cent of the time. The common stock has increased significantly during the last several years because of favourable economic conditions, good capital markets, and declines in interest rates.

Stock risks

The stock has experienced above-average downside risk. During bear markets, this stock has underperformed other blue-chip stocks. During the market correction of 1990, this stock declined by 16.3 per cent, more than the decline of the average stock. It regained its loss within eight months.

Stock financial fundamentals

CIBC has posted profits in nine out of the last ten fiscal years. In 1992, the company reported a small loss of $0.30 per share. CIBC has increased its return on equity to 17.77 per cent, with increases in profit margins and leverage during the last 10 years. The stock multiples have increased during these 10 years as the price-to-earnings (P/E) ratio increased from 6.6 in 1988 to 9.7 in 1997. This increase in the P/E ratio is attributable to a decline in interest rates and increased growth rates.

Future prospects

The bank's profits are closely tied to the direction and level of interest rates and to stock and capital-market activity. With a little bad news, bank stocks could decline significantly. However, banks have historically added a lot of value for shareholders over the long term and have recovered from major setbacks before. Investors looking for enhanced Canadian equity exposure should carefully evaluate the prospects of bank stocks when these stocks are reasonably priced. During the bear of 1998, CIBC stock declined by 41.7 per cent. Such a decline could be considered a buying opportunity, but investors should realize that bank stocks could decline further if a bear market continues. Over the long term, CIBC shares have added value.

COMPANY DETAILS

Company name	**Canadian Imperial Bank of Commerce**	Industry classification	Financial services
Recent price	$29.45	Market capitalization (in $ millions)	$12,201
Phone number for annual report	416-980-6657	Stock analysis start date	July 1980
Ticker symbol	CM	Weight in TSE 35	4.3%
Number of mutual funds that hold this stock as a top 15 holding	292		

ROLLING 12-MONTH TOTAL RATE OF RETURN FOR THE STOCK OVER TIME*

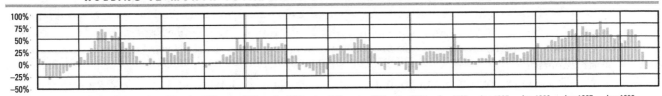

STOCK PERFORMANCE*

	1 month	1 year	3 years	5 years	10 years	15 years
Returns ending Aug 1998	−34.9%	−16.0%	25.1%	16.6%	13.9%	14.1%
Best historical return	23.1%	100.6%	49.0%	34.9%	22.2%	21.5%
Average historical return	1.4%	19.9%	16.7%	15.6%	14.9%	15.9%
Worst historical return	−34.9%	−30.6%	−2.6%	3.3%	9.7%	11.9%

RETURNS GREATER THAN*

	1 month	1 year	3 years	5 years	10 years	15 years
10 per cent	8%	62%	72%	82%	98%	100%
Zero	59%	75%	99%	100%	100%	100%
Percentage of time stock lost $	41%	25%	1%	0%	0%	0%
Number of periods evaluated	218	207	183	159	99	39

DOWNSIDE RISK*

	Worst setback since start date	In bear 1987	In bear 1990	In bear 1994	In bear 1998
Setback for stock	−41.7%	−20.0%	−30.2%	−16.3%	−41.7%
Setback for TSE 35	−27.6%	−26.5%	−16.8%	−9.0%	−27.6%
Setback ended in	Aug 1998	Oct 1987	Sept 1990	Apr 1994	Aug 1998
Months to recover from loss	?	8	6	17	?

STOCK FINANCIAL FUNDAMENTAL INFORMATION

	1988	1989	1990	1991	1992	1993	1994	1995	1996	1997	Change
Average share price	$11.25	$14.64	$13.13	$15.50	$14.53	$14.96	$15.99	$17.27	$23.52	$36.48	12.5%
Earnings per share	$1.66	$1.14	$2.02	$1.97	$(0.30)	$1.50	$1.76	$20.90	$3.02	$3.50	7.7%
Book value per share	$12.16	$12.25	$13.73	$14.99	$14.38	$15.22	$15.85	$169.33	$18.47	$21.03	5.6%
Price-to-earnings ratio	6.8	12.8	6.5	7.9	n/a	10.0	9.1	0.8	7.8	10.4	4.4%
Price-to-book ratio	0.9	1.2	1.0	1.0	1.0	1.0	1.0	0.1	1.3	1.7	6.5%
Profit margin	5.9%	3.5%	5.4%	5.5%	−0.9%	5.5%	6.6%	6.6%	8.1%	8.5%	3.7%
Asset turnover	0.10	0.11	0.11	0.11	0.09	0.07	0.07	0.07	0.07	0.07	−3.1%
Leverage	23.6	23.6	23.7	22.4	25.5	24.4	23.3	25.5	27.4	27.3	1.4%
Return on equity	13.6%	9.3%	14.7%	13.1%	−2.1%	9.9%	11.1%	12.3%	16.3%	16.6%	2.0%
Dividend per share	$0.57	$0.62	$0.66	$0.66	$0.66	$0.66	$0.66	$0.74	$0.85	$1.05	6.3%
Dividend yield	5.1%	4.2%	5.0%	4.3%	4.5%	4.4%	4.1%	4.3%	3.6%	2.9%	−5.5%

•Source: The raw data used in developing this table was provided by Datastream.

CANADIAN NATIONAL RAILWAY

Company profile

Canadian National Railway operates Canada's largest railway system with more than 23,200 route kilometres of track in Canada and 1,200 route kilometres of track in the United States. CN's rail network serves all five of Canada's major ports: Halifax, Montreal, Thunder Bay, Prince Rupert, and Vancouver. CN moves forest products, grain and grain products, coal, sulphur, and fertilizers for over 4,900 customers across North America.

CN's business is consolidated into three groups: Merchandise, Bulk, and Intermodal & Automotive. The company was incorporated in 1919, but its history goes back to the first railways in Canada. Formerly a Crown corporation, CN became a public company through an initial public offering that generated proceeds of over $2.2 billion for the Canadian government.

In 1997, CN generated revenue in excess of $4.3 billion and posted a profit of $403 million. The company employs 22,800 people. Company equipment consumed 272 million gallons of diesel fuel in 1997, an increase of 16 million gallons from 1996.

Stock performance

Since the company went public, investors have increased their love affair with CN. The best 12-month rate of return for the common stock was a gain of 88.4 per cent, and the average 12-month rate of return was 45.1 per cent. However, the common stock has not been tested over a long period, and investors should not regard increases of 40 per cent per year as the norm.

Stock risks

Currently, the worst 12-month rate of return for the stock was a positive rate of return of 4.5 per cent. During the stock market correction in 1998, the stock declined by 23.7 per cent, less than the average stock decline. The stock's worst one-month decline was a loss of 11.2 per cent during August 1998.

Stock financial fundamentals

CN had difficult financial times while the firm was owned by the Canadian government. However, during the last three years the company has made impressive strides to become a viable and sustainable public company. Its earnings per share have improved to $4.95 per share in 1997, an impressive gain from 1993 when the firm lost $0.13 per share. The improvement in earnings can be attributed to an increase in return on equity.

Future prospects

Going forward, CN will face new challenges. With mergers in US railroads, CN will have to create and sustain new strategic initiatives and relationships to compete effectively in the US market. The company has fuelled its growth by acquiring, in July 1998, Illinois Central Corporation (IC) (pending regulatory approval). In addition, CN has established a marketing alliance with Kansas City Southern Railway to operate an efficient Chicago–Kansas City service that was made possible by the IC acquisition. CN will also have to compete against and work with the trucking industry to become a carrier of choice within their customers' transportation networks.

CN has currently delivered impressive results. It will experience some growing pains, but they should not be severe if the company increases its operating efficiency. Investors who acquire stock in CN at a reasonable price should earn above-average returns. In addition, CN should continue to provide stable earnings as clients rely more on CN to provide specialized transportation services.

COMPANY DETAILS

Company name	**Canadian National Railway**	Industry classification	Transportation and environment
Recent price	$70.80	Market capitalization (in $ millions)	$6,025
Phone number for annual report	514-399-0039	Stock analysis start date	Dec 1996
Ticker symbol	CNR	Weight in TSE 35	0.4%
Number of mutual funds that hold this stock as a top 15 holding	65		

ROLLING 12-MONTH TOTAL RATE OF RETURN FOR THE STOCK OVER TIME*

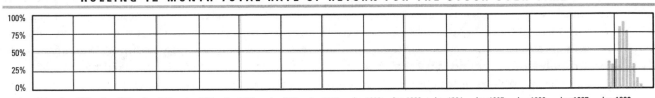

Jan 1984 Jan 1985 Jan 1986 Jan 1987 Jan 1988 Jan 1989 Jan 1990 Jan 1991 Jan 1992 Jan 1993 Jan 1994 Jan 1995 Jan 1996 Jan 1997 Jan 1998

STOCK PERFORMANCE*

	1 month	1 year	3 years	5 years	10 years	15 years
Returns ending Aug 1998	−11.2%	4.5%				
Best historical return	21.6%	88.4%				
Average historical return	1.7%	45.1%				
Worst historical return	−11.2%	4.5%				

RETURNS GREATER THAN*

	1 month	1 year	3 years	5 years	10 years	15 years
10 per cent	10%	90%				
Zero	57%	100%				
Percentage of time stock lost $	43%	0%				
Number of periods evaluated	21	10				

DOWNSIDE RISK*

	Worst setback since start date	In bear 1987	In bear 1990	In bear 1994	In bear 1998
Setback for stock	−23.7%				−23.7%
Setback for TSE 35	−27.6%				−27.6%
Setback ended in	Aug 1998				Aug 1998
Months to recover from loss	?				?

STOCK FINANCIAL FUNDAMENTAL INFORMATION

	1988	1989	1990	1991	1992	1993	1994	1995	1996	1997	Change
Average share price									$51.79	$62.18	n/a
Earnings per share	$3.51	$2.56	$0.10	$(0.18)	$(13.50)	$(0.13)	$3.36	$4.49	$12.39	$4.95	3.5%
Book value per share	$41.90	$44.01	$44.10	$43.46	$33.46	$31.36	$33.19	$28.68	$31.44	$40.18	−0.4%
Price-to-earnings ratio									4.2	12.6	n/a
Price-to-book ratio									1.6	1.5	n/a
Profit margin	6.0%	4.9%	0.2%	−0.4%	−24.8%	−0.3%	6.5%	9.1%	30.5%	9.7%	4.8%
Asset turnover	0.68	0.59	0.58	0.58	0.57	0.54	0.53	0.64	0.58	0.62	−0.9%
Leverage	2.0	2.0	2.0	2.0	2.8	2.9	2.9	2.7	2.2	2.1	0.1%
Return on equity	8.4%	5.8%	0.2%	−0.4%	−40.4%	−0.4%	10.1%	15.7%	39.4%	12.3%	3.9%
Dividend per share									$0.80	$0.92	n/a
Dividend yield									1.5%	1.5%	n/a

•Source: The raw data used in developing this table was provided by Datastream.

CANADIAN OCCIDENTAL PETROLEUM

Company profile

Canadian Occidental Petroleum business activities include exploration for and development, production, and marketing of crude oil and natural gas in Canada, Yemen, the Gulf of Mexico, the North Sea, and Ecuador. CanOxy's oil and gas business is complemented by a chemicals operation, as one of the top sodium chlorate producers in North America. In 1997, CanOxy successfully acquired Wascana Energy for $1.7 billion. The combined company has become a major player in the oil and gas industry. CanOxy's worldwide oil and gas production in 1997 reached 234,000 barrels of oil per day. In turn, the company generated $1.6 billion in sales and posted a profit of $139 million.

Stock performance

Canadian Occidental Petroleum's common stock's best 12-month rate of return was a positive 162.2 per cent, and the average 12-month rate of return for the common stock was a gain of 20.3 per cent. This has been exceptional performance for a global energy and chemical company. The common stock outperformed significantly in 1992, 1995, and 1997. CanOxy's common stock posted positive rates of return after 12 months 69 per cent of the time.

Stock risks

CanOxy's common stock has displayed less downside risk than other resource companies. The worst 12-month rate of return for the common stock was a loss of 44.8 per cent, and the common stock posted negative rates of return after 12 months 31 per cent of the time since the start date in July 1980. During bear markets, the stock has declined more than the average stock. In 1987 it declined by 28.5 per cent but regained its loss within 15 months. During the bears of 1990 and 1994, the stock declined in value by 33.4 per cent and 26.6 per cent respectively and took eight and nine months to recover its losses.

Stock financial fundamentals

The company has improved its financial data during the last 10 years and, in turn, the common stock has appreciated in value. Earnings per share have increased on average by 10.2 per cent from $0.39 per share in 1988 to $1.02 per share in 1997. CanOxy increased its return on equity by an average of 3.9 per cent per year to 11.12 per cent, because of an increase in profit margins and leverage ratios. The company maintained a small dividend payment, but reinvested most of its earnings back into the company.

Future prospects

Oil prices are forecast to remain soft in the near future. Lower oil prices will make it increasingly difficult for CanOxy to continue improving profits and cash flow. Oil prices have declined because of excess supply from a reduction in demand from Asia. However, the company will continue to increase its drilling operations to replace the crude that it sells. If the company's exploration and drilling are successful, the future looks bright, especially once oil prices recover. Senior management has done a good job of adding value within a difficult environment, but investors should expect some volatility in the future. Investors who try to acquire shares in companies once they have declined will find CanOxy attractively priced, since its stock has declined by 48.9 per cent during the bear of 1998. Investors have earned money in this stock over the long term, but performance seems to be unpredictable and erratic. Thus, this stock is most suitable for speculative investors who believe a turnaround is inevitable.

COMPANY DETAILS

Company name	**Canadian Occidental Petroleum**	Industry classification	Oil and gas
Recent price	$18.75	Market capitalization (in $ millions)	$2,561
Phone number for annual report	416-643-5500	Stock analysis start date	July 1980
Ticker symbol	CYX	Weight in TSE 35	1.5%
Number of mutual funds that hold this stock as a top 15 holding	40		

ROLLING 12-MONTH TOTAL RATE OF RETURN FOR THE STOCK OVER TIME*

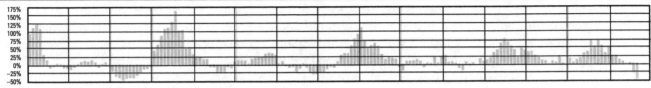

Jan 1984 Jan 1985 Jan 1986 Jan 1987 Jan 1988 Jan 1989 Jan 1990 Jan 1991 Jan 1992 Jan 1993 Jan 1994 Jan 1995 Jan 1996 Jan 1997 Jan 1998

STOCK PERFORMANCE*

	1 month	1 year	3 years	5 years	10 years	15 years
Returns ending Aug 1998	−29.8%	−44.8%	−2.7%	6.8%	10.6%	8.3%
Best historical return	51.5%	162.2%	48.5%	33.0%	20.8%	20.1%
Average historical return	1.3%	20.3%	16.8%	14.7%	14.1%	16.0%
Worst historical return	−29.8%	−44.8%	−13.3%	1.7%	7.8%	8.3%

RETURNS GREATER THAN*

	1 month	1 year	3 years	5 years	10 years	15 years
10 per cent	14%	52%	75%	70%	79%	97%
Zero	54%	69%	91%	100%	100%	100%
Percentage of time stock lost $	46%	31%	9%	0%	0%	0%
Number of periods evaluated	218	207	183	159	99	39

DOWNSIDE RISK*

	Worst setback since start date	In bear 1987	In bear 1990	In bear 1994	In bear 1998
Setback for stock	−48.9%	−28.5%	−33.4%	−26.6%	−48.9%
Setback for TSE 35	−27.6%	−26.5%	−16.8%	−9.0%	−27.6%
Setback ended in	Aug 1998	Dec 1987	Nov 1990	June 1994	Aug 1998
Months to recover from loss	?	18	8	9	?

STOCK FINANCIAL FUNDAMENTAL INFORMATION

	1988	1989	1990	1991	1992	1993	1994	1995	1996	1997	Change
Average share price	$8.44	$9.86	$8.86	$9.68	$13.42	$14.00	$14.26	$20.06	$23.01	$31.01	13.9%
Earnings per share	$0.39	$0.29	$0.24	$0.18	$0.13	$0.05	$0.72	$1.05	$1.40	$1.02	10.2%
Book value per share	$5.08	$5.13	$5.23	$5.27	$5.27	$5.15	$6.19	$6.93	$8.27	$9.17	6.1%
Price-to-earnings ratio	21.9	34.0	37.7	55.3	103.2	280.0	19.8	19.1	16.4	30.4	3.3%
Price-to-book ratio	1.7	1.9	1.7	1.8	2.5	2.7	2.3	2.9	2.8	3.4	7.4%
Profit margin	7.0%	6.6%	4.8%	3.9%	3.1%	1.1%	9.1%	11.5%	13.6%	7.9%	1.3%
Asset turnover	0.55	0.42	0.45	0.39	0.28	0.28	0.47	0.55	0.58	0.39	−3.3%
Leverage	2.0	2.0	2.1	2.2	2.9	3.1	2.8	2.4	2.1	3.6	6.2%
Return on equity	7.6%	5.7%	4.5%	3.3%	2.5%	1.0%	11.6%	15.2%	16.9%	11.1%	3.9%
Dividend per share	$0.20	$0.20	$0.20	$0.20	$0.20	$0.20	$0.20	$0.23	$0.30	$0.30	4.1%
Dividend yield	2.4%	2.0%	2.3%	2.1%	1.5%	1.4%	1.4%	1.1%	1.3%	1.0%	−8.6%

•Source: The raw data used in developing this table was provided by Datastream.

CANADIAN PACIFIC LIMITED

Company profile

Canadian Pacific Railway Company was incorporated on February 16, 1881, pursuant to an act of the Government of Canada. The company was given a mandate to construct and operate a national railway. Currently, the company is directly involved in rail and ship transportation, energy development and exploration, and hotel operations in North America and various locations throughout the world. The company owns the Canadian Pacific Railway, Soo Line Railroad, and the Delaware and Hudson Railway Company. CP is involved in the energy business through various holdings including PanCanadian Petroleum. Through its affiliated companies, CP explores for, develops, and markets hydrocarbons, coal, and other metallurgical resources. CP Ships owns or leases and operates ships to provide container and bulk services between the United States, Montreal, Northern Europe, and various Mediterranean and African countries. Canadian Pacific Hotels and Resorts is CP's most famous asset, well-known around the world with both business and recreational travellers, and Canada's largest operator of full-service hotels, with more than 11,000 rooms in 26 different hotels or resorts, including the Banff Springs Hotel in Alberta and Le Chateau Frontenac in Quebec City.

Stock performance

Canadian Pacific has been plagued by the poor performance of its railway division, which has translated into periods of underperformance for Canadian Pacific common stock. However, during the last five years Canadian Pacific investors have kept up with other blue-chip companies since the railway division has started to make some significant contributions to the company.

The best 12-month rate of return for Canadian Pacific common stock was a positive return of 103.1 per cent, and the average 12-month rate of return was 11.6 per cent. The common stock of Canadian Pacific posted positive rates of return 61 per cent of the time since the start date in July 1980.

Stock risks

The common stock of Canadian Pacific has displayed some severe downside risk, posting a worst 12-month loss of 45.3 per cent. In addition, the common stock posted a negative rate of return after 12 months 39 per cent of the time. Investors during the bear market of 1987 had their investment decline by 32.8 per cent, and the stock regained its loss within 14 months. During the bear of 1990, investors were not so fortunate. The stock declined by 32.5 per cent and took 37 months to recover its loss. Thus, Canadian Pacific stock has underperformed during bear markets.

Stock financial fundamentals

Canadian Pacific has delivered variable results during the last 10 years. In turn, the balance sheet information of the company has undergone several changes, including the sale and acquisition of different assets. The earnings of the company have improved during the past 10 years. Earnings per share increased from $2.77 per share in 1997 to $3.64 per share in 1998, attributable to the company's ability to better utilize its assets. Asset turnover ratio increased by an average of 7.3 per cent per year for the past 10 years.

Future prospects

Going forward, the fortunes of Canadian Pacific investors will lie with the ability of senior management to extract value for shareholders from the railway assets. CP has other great assets, such as the hotel business, but utilizing railway assets prudently is essential to remaining competitive in the future. This stock has displayed a lot of upside potential, but CP has been unable to deliver value consistently over the long term.

COMPANY DETAILS

Company name	Canadian Pacific Limited	Industry classification	Conglomerates
Recent price	$29.75	Market capitalization (in $ millions)	$10,136
Phone number for annual report	1-800-332-0095	Stock analysis start date	July 1980
Ticker symbol	CP	Weight in TSE 35	5.2%
Number of mutual funds that hold this stock as a top 15 holding	85		

ROLLING 12-MONTH TOTAL RATE OF RETURN FOR THE STOCK OVER TIME*

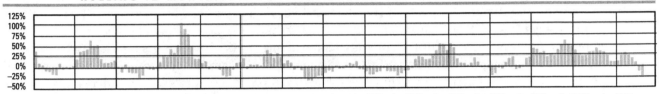

Jan 1984 Jan 1985 Jan 1986 Jan 1987 Jan 1988 Jan 1989 Jan 1990 Jan 1991 Jan 1992 Jan 1993 Jan 1994 Jan 1995 Jan 1996 Jan 1997 Jan 1998

STOCK PERFORMANCE*

	1 month	1 year	3 years	5 years	10 years	15 years
Returns ending Aug 1998	–17.6%	–25.6%	10.7%	8.1%	5.6%	6.9%
Best historical return	22.2%	103.1%	38.4%	30.7%	11.5%	13.7%
Average historical return	0.8%	11.6%	9.7%	8.4%	6.8%	9.0%
Worst historical return	–17.6%	–45.3%	–13.7%	–7.5%	2.4%	5.0%

RETURNS GREATER THAN*

	1 month	1 year	3 years	5 years	10 years	15 years
10 per cent	11%	44%	46%	38%	9%	31%
Zero	50%	61%	84%	86%	100%	100%
Percentage of time stock lost $	50%	39%	16%	14%	0%	0%
Number of periods evaluated	218	207	183	159	99	39

DOWNSIDE RISK*

	Worst setback since start date	In bear 1987	In bear 1990	In bear 1994	In bear 1998
Setback for stock	–47.0%	–32.8%	–32.5%	–20.9%	–29.3%
Setback for TSE 35	–34.6%	–26.5%	–16.8%	–9.0%	–27.6%
Setback ended in	April 1982	Nov 1987	Sept 1990	Jan 1995	Aug 1998
Months to recover from loss	12	20	58	6	?

STOCK FINANCIAL FUNDAMENTAL INFORMATION

	1988	1989	1990	1991	1992	1993	1994	1995	1996	1997	Change
Average share price	$22.05	$24.18	$21.33	$19.51	$16.89	$19.95	$21.98	$22.23	$29.90	$38.23	5.7%
Earnings per share	$2.77	$2.46	$1.23	$(2.76)	$(1.39)	$(0.49)	$1.27	$(2.30)	$2.52	$3.64	2.8%
Book value per share	$23.87	$24.90	$25.09	$21.62	$20.36	$19.67	$20.97	$17.92	$19.51	$21.95	–0.8%
Price-to-earnings ratio	8.0	9.8	17.3	n/a	n/a	n/a	17.3	n/a	11.9	10.5	2.8%
Price-to-book ratio	0.9	1.0	0.9	0.9	0.8	1.0	1.0	1.2	1.5	1.7	6.5%
Profit margin	17.6%	16.7%	7.7%	–17.5%	–9.0%	–2.8%	6.7%	–10.7%	10.3%	13.1%	–2.9%
Asset turnover	0.27	0.24	0.25	0.24	0.24	0.32	0.37	0.44	0.54	0.55	7.3%
Leverage	2.4	2.4	2.6	3.0	3.2	2.8	2.5	2.7	2.3	2.3	–0.5%
Return on equity	11.6%	9.9%	4.9%	–12.8%	–6.8%	–2.5%	6.1%	–12.8%	12.9%	16.6%	3.6%
Dividend per share	$0.68	$0.84	$0.92	$0.63	$0.32	$0.32	$0.32	$0.36	$0.48	$0.48	–3.4%
Dividend yield	3.1%	3.5%	4.3%	3.2%	1.9%	1.6%	1.5%	1.6%	1.6%	1.3%	–8.6%

*Source: The raw data used in developing this table was provided by Datastream.

CANADIAN TIRE CORPORATION LIMITED, A

Company profile

Canadian Tire is a Canadian success story. Started in 1922 by brothers John and Alfred Billes, who opened a service garage and auto parts depot in Toronto, Canadian Tire has expanded to more than 420 stores across Canada, using marketing tactics like Canadian Tire money and catalogue promotions. The retail stores offer customers the convenience of three specialty stores in one: automotive, sports and leisure, and home products. In addition, the company offers financing and credit cards to customers through a financial services division. Canadian Tire also has a petroleum division, the country's largest independent retailer of gasoline. The petroleum division offers great opportunities to cross sell to Canadian Tire customers.

Currently, Canadian Tire and its associate dealers employ over 34,000 people. In 1997, the company generated more than $4 billion in revenue and earned more than $148 million in net income.

Stock performance

Investors who strategically invested in the common stock of Canadian Tire during the last five years have earned above-average profits. The best 12-month period for the common stock was a positive gain of 97.7 per cent, and the average 12-month gain was 17.2 per cent. Astute investors who bought low and sold high stood the most to gain by avoiding losses, but buy-and-hold investors still earned above-average returns with above-average risk.

Stock risks

Inherently, the Canadian retail market is very competitive, and increased competition can threaten Canadian Tire's future success. However, with a strong brand name and excellent distribution system, Canadian Tire will continue to be a dominant player in the industry.

The worst 12-month return for the stock was a loss of 37.2 per cent, and the common stock posted negative rates of return 30 per cent of the time after 12 months. Investors during the bear of 1987 saw their investment decline in value by 24.6 per cent, but the stock regained its loss within five months. During the bear of 1994, the stock declined in value by 55.2 per cent, attributable to the entry of Wal-Mart into Canada. The risk did not come to fruition, and the stock regained its loss within 28 months.

Stock financial fundamentals

The company's growth prospects have turned around since 1992 as earnings improved. Currently the company's price-to-earnings (P/E) ratio is 14.9. Thus, investors are paying $14.90 for every $1 of historical earnings. The company's return on equity has decreased, and it has increased its debt in an attempt to reverse this trend.

Future prospects

Canadian Tire common stock experienced a severe setback in 1992 and 1993 because of the threat of Wal-Mart. In turn, Canadian Tire combatted that threat by effectively creating its own strategy to be the best at what their customers value most. Customers, employees, and shareholders all reacted favourably, and Canadian Tire has regained and enhanced its former glory. If consumer confidence continues to improve in Canada, Canadian Tire should continue to enhance shareholder value, but investors should be aware that the retail industry can be extremely unpredictable.

COMPANY DETAILS

Company name	**Canadian Tire Corporation Limited, A**	Industry classification	Merchandising
Recent price	$32.00	Market capitalization (in $ millions)	$2,521
Phone number for annual report	416 480 3660	Stock analysis start date	July 1980
Ticker symbol	CTR.A	Weight in TSE 35	3.7%
Number of mutual funds that hold this stock as a top 15 holding	38		

ROLLING 12-MONTH TOTAL RATE OF RETURN FOR THE STOCK OVER TIME*

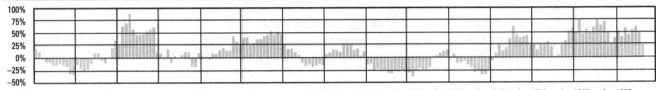

STOCK PERFORMANCE*

	1 month	1 year	3 years	5 years	10 years	15 years
Returns ending Aug 1998	−21.1%	24.3%	27.7%	16.3%	8.9%	9.0%
Best historical return	25.0%	97.7%	45.3%	28.9%	18.2%	12.7%
Average historical return	1.3%	17.2%	11.7%	9.1%	8.6%	10.2%
Worst historical return	−23.7%	−37.2%	−22.7%	−13.4%	1.5%	8.4%

RETURNS GREATER THAN*

	1 month	1 year	3 years	5 years	10 years	15 years
10 per cent	11%	57%	61%	50%	37%	56%
Zero	55%	70%	78%	75%	100%	100%
Percentage of time stock lost $	45%	30%	22%	25%	0%	0%
Number of periods evaluated	218	207	183	159	99	39

DOWNSIDE RISK*

	Worst setback since start date	In bear 1987	In bear 1990	In bear 1994	In bear 1998
Setback for stock	−55.2%	−24.6%	−19.1%	−55.2%	−24.8%
Setback for TSE 35	−5.2%	−26.5%	−16.8%	−9.0%	−27.6%
Setback ended in	July 1994	Oct 1987	Sept 1990	July 1994	Aug 1998
Months to recover from loss	28	7	6	28	?

STOCK FINANCIAL FUNDAMENTAL INFORMATION

	1988	1989	1990	1991	1992	1993	1994	1995	1996	1997	Change
Average share price	$15.93	$22.11	$21.29	$23.60	$18.02	$14.94	$11.94	$14.44	$17.63	$26.61	5.3%
Earnings per share	$1.38	$1.65	$1.60	$1.41	$0.80	$0.90	$0.06	$1.38	$1.51	$1.79	2.6%
Book value per share	$9.11	$10.15	$11.39	$12.36	$12.83	$13.36	$12.59	$14.05	$14.88	$15.65	5.6%
Price-to-earnings ratio	11.5	13.4	13.3	16.7	22.5	16.6	199.0	10.5	11.7	14.9	2.6%
Price-to-book ratio	1.7	2.2	1.9	1.9	1.4	1.1	0.9	1.0	1.2	1.7	−0.3%
Profit margin	4.7%	5.0%	4.7%	4.2%	2.3%	2.4%	0.2%	3.2%	3.4%	3.7%	−2.5%
Asset turnover	1.73	1.72	1.56	1.35	1.36	1.43	1.35	1.41	1.50	1.41	−2.0%
Leverage	1.9	1.9	1.9	2.0	2.0	2.0	2.3	2.2	2.0	2.2	1.8%
Return on equity	15.1%	16.3%	14.1%	11.4%	6.2%	6.7%	0.5%	9.8%	10.2%	11.4%	−2.8%
Dividend per share	$0.24	$0.30	$0.38	$0.40	$0.40	$0.40	$0.40	$0.40	$0.40	$0.40	5.2%
Dividend yield	1.5%	1.34%	1.8%	1.7%	2.2%	2.7%	3.4%	2.8%	2.3%	1.5%	0.0%

*Source: The raw data used in developing this table was provided by Datastream.

DOFASCO INCORPORATED

Company profile

Dofasco is a fully integrated steel producer located in Hamilton, Ontario. It manufactures a range of specialized flat-rolled and tubular steel products and castings for customers throughout North America. The company also has interests in other companies involved in iron-ore mining and processing. The company utilizes both oxygen steel-making and scrap-based electric-arc furnace technology. Dofasco's steel products are sold to a variety of customers including companies in the automotive, construction, appliance, and energy industries.

Dofasco's history can be traced back to Clifton Sherman, who built a foundry in Hamilton in 1912. The company became an industry leader through the growth of this small foundry. A series of name changes—through Dominion Steel Foundry and Dominion Foundries and Steel Company Limited—led to the name Dofasco. The company grew quickly through the years of World War II as demand for steel products increased. During periods of falling demand, Dofasco has had to contend with overcapacity. In general, companies dislike operating at undercapacity, because they cannot fully utilize their assets, a major problem for cyclical industries.

In 1997, Dofasco generated over $3 billion worth of sales and earned a profit of more than $190 million. The company increased shipments from and reduced the costs of the Gallatin Steel Mill, a minimill in Kentucky, through a joint venture with BIEC International.

Stock performance

Historically this stock has tended to go up or down, but neither consistently. The common stock's best 12-month rate of return was 129.2 per cent, but the average 12-month return was 5.2 per cent. The common stock posted positive rates of return after 12 months 50 per cent of the time. In turn, investors who could successfully buy low and sell high were able to earn above-average rates of return; buy-and-hold investors did not fare so well.

Stock risks

Inherently, the company is susceptible to broad economic conditions and fluctuations that could lead to a decline in corporate profits. If net income declines, the company could suspend dividend payments, as it did in 1993. However, in 1997 the company paid a $1 dividend, an attractive dividend yield. Such a dividend yield can offset a capital loss, but Dofasco's common stock's worst 12-month loss was 48.3 per cent. Investors during the bear of 1990 saw their investment decline by 41.4 per cent, and the stock took 36 months to recover its loss.

Stock financial fundamentals

The company's income statement and balance sheet have experienced wide fluctuations. During the past 10 years the company's net income declined, but earnings have recently recovered. In addition, book value per share has declined as the firm continues to restructure its assets.

Future prospects

Going forward, Dofasco may tell a different story. Investors should not overlook this stock because of its historical risk-and-return profile. Bargain-hunters who patiently acquire stock over the long term could be rewarded when other investors see the hidden value in undervalued stocks. If senior management can repeat the financial results of 1997 and increase profit margins, investors should be rewarded, although repeating the results of 1997 in the highly cyclical steel industry will not be an easy task, and investors should be aware of the extreme volatility in earnings Dofasco has reported in the past 10 years. In addition, the industry is susceptible to technological changes that could make certain operations at Dofasco obsolete.

COMPANY DETAILS

Company name	**Dofasco Incorporated**	Industry classification	Industrial products
Recent price	$15.50	Market capitalization (in $ millions)	$1,332
Phone number for annual report	905-544-3761	Stock analysis start date	June 1985
Ticker symbol	DFS	Weight in TSE 35	0.9%
Number of mutual funds that hold this stock as a top 15 holding	21		

ROLLING 12-MONTH TOTAL RATE OF RETURN FOR THE STOCK OVER TIME*

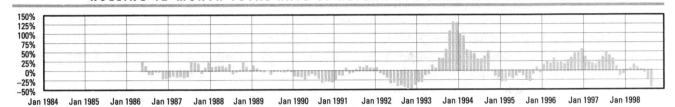

STOCK PERFORMANCE*

	1 month	1 year	3 years	5 years	10 years	15 years
Returns ending Aug 1998	−28.6%	−43.0%	0.6%	1.6%	−2.7%	
Best historical return	25.6%	129.2%	28.6%	24.8%	4.5%	
Average historical return	0.2%	5.2%	1.8%	0.6%	0.9%	
Worst historical return	−28.6%	−48.3%	−26.2%	−15.5%	−2.7%	

RETURNS GREATER THAN*

	1 month	1 year	3 years	5 years	10 years	15 years
10 per cent	11%	35%	26%	18%	0%	
Zero	46%	50%	58%	41%	63%	
Percentage of time stock lost $	54%	50%	42%	59%	38%	
Number of periods evaluated	159	148	124	100	40	

DOWNSIDE RISK*

	Worst setback since start date	In bear 1987	In bear 1990	In bear 1994	In bear 1998
Setback for stock	−65.9%	−29.2%	−41.4%	−33.6%	−44.9%
Setback for TSE 35	−6.7%	−26.5%	−16.8%	−9.0%	−27.6%
Setback ended in	Nov 1992	Oct 1987	Dec 1990	Feb 1995	Aug 1998
Months to recover from loss	48	109	71	21	?

STOCK FINANCIAL FUNDAMENTAL INFORMATION

	1988	1989	1990	1991	1992	1993	1994	1995	1996	1997	Change
Average share price	$27.71	$27.03	$21.01	$19.15	$13.33	$15.86	$21.83	$17.86	$21.56	$25.76	−0.7%
Earnings per share	$3.37	$2.95	$(10.64)	$(0.73)	$(2.96)	$1.41	$2.33	$1.98	$2.12	$2.12	−4.5%
Book value per share	$36.60	$34.85	$22.65	$22.69	$17.33	$18.68	$21.17	$21.91	$23.05	$20.48	−5.6%
Price-to-earnings ratio	8.2	9.2	n/a	n/a	n/a	11.2	9.4	9.0	10.2	12.2	4.0%
Price-to-book ratio	0.8	0.8	0.9	0.8	0.8	0.8	1.0	0.8	0.9	1.3	5.2%
Profit margin	7.9%	7.5%	−30.0%	−2.5%	−12.0%	5.3%	8.0%	6.4%	6.2%	5.9%	−2.8%
Asset turnover	0.98	0.94	1.04	0.87	0.91	1.03	1.11	1.20	1.30	1.46	4.1%
Leverage	1.2	1.2	1.5	1.5	1.6	1.4	1.2	1.2	1.1	1.2	0.0%
Return on equity	9.2%	8.5%	−47.0%	−3.2%	−17.1%	7.5%	11.0%	9.0%	9.2%	10.4%	1.2%
Dividend per share	$1.07	$1.28	$1.28	$0.80	$0.15	$–	$0.30	$0.80	$0.85	$1.00	−0.7%
Dividend yield	3.9%	4.7%	6.1%	4.2%	1.1%	0.00%	1.4%	4.5%	3.9%	3.9%	0.1%

*Source: The raw data used in developing this table was provided by Datastream.

IMASCO LIMITED

Company profile

Imasco is a holding company for a variety of different companies, including:

- Imperial Tobacco, a manufacturer and marketer of tobacco products and an industry leader in Canada, with 68 per cent market share, producing Canada's two largest-selling brands, du Maurier and Player's
- Canada Trust, provider of a range of personal banking and wealth-management services, including mutual funds, through 422 full-service branches and 927 automated bank machines
- Shoppers Drug Mart/Pharmaprix, Canada's largest drugstore chain with 815 locations nationwide
- Genstar Development Company, developer of planned residential communities and serviced lots sold to home builders in Canada and the United States

In 1997, Imasco generated revenue in excess of $10 billion and posted a profit, before special items, of $668 million.

Stock performance

Investors in Imasco common stock have not been disappointed, as the company continues to grow. The best 12-month period for the common stock was a positive gain of 103.3 per cent, and the average 12-month rate of return was 22.9 per cent. The company has frequently outperformed other blue-chip stocks.

Stock risks

The worst 12-month rate of return for Imasco common stock was a loss of 26.7 per cent. During bear markets, the stock has underperformed the average stock. During the market correction of 1987, the stock declined in value by 33.8 per cent and took 20 months to recover its loss. The stock fared better during the market corrections of 1990, 1994, and 1998. It declined more than the average during 1990 and 1994, but took only eight and six months respectively to recover its losses. During the bear of 1998 the stock outperformed, declining by 11.6 per cent versus the TSE 35 Index, which declined 27.6 per cent.

Stock financial fundamentals

Imasco has improved its balance sheet situation during the past 10 years and, in turn, the stock has appreciated in value. Earnings per share have increased by an average of 2.5 per cent per year from $0.63 per share in 1988 to $1.44 per share in 1997. Return on equity has increased by an average of 0.9 per cent per year to 18.8 per cent in 1997. The increase in return on equity can be attributed to Imasco's increase in profit margin and asset turnover ratios. The firm has reduced its leverage during the last 10 years.

Future prospects

The company still generates 53 per cent of its earnings (from operations) from Imperial Tobacco. With increased regulation and a decline in demand in the tobacco industry, Imasco will have to continue to gain market share. During the last 25 years, Imperial Tobacco has been able to gain market share consistently—1.4 per cent in 1997 alone—but this trend cannot last forever. Historically, senior management has proven they can add value. Investors who acquire the stock at a reasonable price should not be disappointed. This firm has become one of Canada's largest corporations, but its future success will depend on how well it manages the tobacco operations—a task that could become increasingly difficult as Canadians become more health-conscious, although Imasco's holdings in the healthcare industry could offset any decline in the tobacco industry.

COMPANY DETAILS

Company name	**Imasco Limited**	Industry classification	Consumer products
Recent price	$25.20	Market capitalization (in $ millions)	$11,501
Phone number for annual report	514-982-9111	Stock analysis start date	July 1980
Ticker symbol	IMS	Weight in TSE 35	4.1%
Number of mutual funds that hold this stock as a top 15 holding	88		

ROLLING 12-MONTH TOTAL RATE OF RETURN FOR THE STOCK OVER TIME*

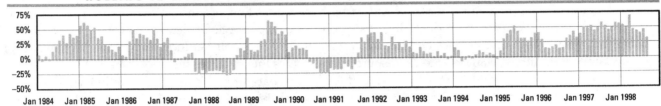

STOCK PERFORMANCE*

	1 month	1 year	3 years	5 years	10 years	15 years
Returns ending Aug 1998	−11.6%	31.0%	31.3%	26.6%	19.1%	17.1%
Best historical return	26.4%	103.3%	50.0%	38.2%	23.6%	19.6%
Average historical return	1.8%	22.9%	18.6%	16.2%	13.9%	17.6%
Worst historical return	−19.8%	−26.7%	−4.1%	−3.6%	6.9%	15.6%

RETURNS GREATER THAN*

	1 month	1 year	3 years	5 years	10 years	15 years
10 per cent	11%	69%	63%	71%	85%	100%
Zero	61%	83%	99%	98%	100%	100%
Percentage of time stock lost $	39%	17%	1%	2%	0%	0%
Number of periods evaluated	218	207	183	159	99	39

DOWNSIDE RISK*

	Worst setback since start date	In bear 1987	In bear 1990	In bear 1994	In bear 1998
Setback for stock	−33.8%	−33.8%	−27.8%	−20.5%	−11.6%
Setback for TSE 35	−26.5%	−26.5%	−16.8%	−9.0%	−27.6%
Setback ended in	Nov 1987	Nov 1987	Feb 1991	June 1994	Aug 1998
Months to recover from loss	20	20	10	8	?

STOCK FINANCIAL FUNDAMENTAL INFORMATION

	1988	1989	1990	1991	1992	1993	1994	1995	1996	1997	Change
Average share price	$6.65	$8.68	$8.43	$7.59	$9.27	$9.49	$9.42	$11.74	$14.14	$20.43	11.9%
Earnings per share	$0.63	$0.72	$0.56	$0.64	$0.74	$0.82	$1.05	$1.15	$1.28	$1.44	2.5%
Book value per share	$3.90	$4.32	$4.41	$4.74	$5.26	$5.87	$6.61	$6.44	$7.17	$8.03	7.5%
Price-to-earnings ratio	16.8	12.1	15.1	11.9	12.5	11.6	9.0	25.8	11.1	12.0	−3.3%
Price-to-book ratio	1.7	2.0	1.9	1.6	1.8	1.6	1.4	1.8	2.0	2.5	4.1%
Profit margin	4.5%	4.5%	3.1%	3.5%	3.9%	4.3%	5.5%	5.5%	5.6%	6.0%	0.9%
Asset turnover	0.21	0.22	0.24	0.21	0.20	0.19	0.17	0.18	0.18	0.23	0.9%
Leverage	17.0	17.0	17.1	18.9	18.0	17.1	16.7	17.9	17.7	13.5	−2.3%
Return on equity	16.0%	16.5%	12.7%	13.5%	14.1%	13.9%	15.8%	19.5%	17.8%	18.8%	0.9%
Dividend per share	$0.26	$0.28	$0.32	$0.32	$0.34	$0.37	$0.39	$0.49	$0.54	$0.60	8.7%
Dividend yield	3.9%	3.2%	3.8%	4.2%	3.7%	3.9%	4.1%	4.2%	3.8%	2.9%	−2.8%

*Source: The raw data used in developing this table was provided by Datastream.

INCO LIMITED

Company profile

Inco is the world's leading low-cost producer of nickel, supplying a significant portion of the world's demand. With its corrosion-resistance and strength at extreme temperatures, nickel is found in thousands of business and consumer products. Inco also produces copper, precious metals, and cobalt. The company has operations in 22 countries and has interests in International Nickel Indonesia, Voisey's Bay Nickel Company Limited, Diamond Fields Resources, and Alloys International Inc.

Inco was founded in 1902, when demand for nickel soared for manufacturing military equipment. With access to the Sudbury, Ontario, nickel belt, Inco was the premier provider to the world.

In 1997, Inco generated over $US 2.3 billion in sales and earned a profit of $US 75 million. In this competitive environment, it is essential that Inco remain the low-cost producer of nickel. The company continues to reinvest in technology and equipment to reduce costs and increase cash flow and profitability.

Stock performance

Inco was not immune to the adverse economic and business conditions that have plagued resource stocks during the last half of the 1990s. With weak Asian demand and lower commodity prices, many resource stocks have declined in value. On the upside, Inco has demonstrated its ability to add value for shareholders. The best 12-month return for Inco stock was 83.1 per cent, but the average 12-month return was 4.1 per cent. These results demonstrate the cyclical nature of the industry and the importance of favourable commodity prices to add shareholder value.

Stock risks

The worst 12-month rate of return for investors in Inco common stock was a loss of 64.4 per cent. The stock posted negative rates of return after 12 months 47 per cent of the time. Investors in Inco during the bear of 1994 saw their investment decline by 22.7 per cent, but the stock regained its value within eight months. More recent investors have not been so fortunate. The stock declined by 72.1 per cent during the bear of 1998 and will take some time to recover.

Inherently, resource stocks are more risky because of the cyclical nature of the industry. However, investors must be aware that an environment with favourable commodity prices can also lead to periods of substantial profits. In short, investing in resource stocks involves above-average risk.

Stock financial fundamentals

Historically, Inco has demonstrated large variances in its income and balance sheet statements. During the last 10 years the company has had a severe reversal in its fortunes, reporting a decline in net income. In turn, return on equity has decreased with a decline in the profit margin, asset turnover, and leverage ratios.

Future prospects

Inco is still a world leader in nickel. If nickel prices rebound, the outlook for investors will become more favourable, since profit margins and cash flow should increase. Investors who have an above-average risk tolerance and who buy stocks after they have declined in value significantly should carefully monitor Inco. With favourable market conditions, Inco should quickly rebound to its former glory. Regardless of the outlook for this stock, it should be considered only by the speculative investor within a diversified portfolio.

COMPANY DETAILS

Company name	Inco Limited	Industry classification	Metals and minerals
Recent price	$13.25	Market capitalization (in $ millions)	$2,200
Phone number for annual report	416-643-5500	Stock analysis start date	July 1980
Ticker symbol	N	Weight in TSE 35	0.8%
Number of mutual funds that hold this stock as a top 15 holding	15		

ROLLING 12-MONTH TOTAL RATE OF RETURN FOR THE STOCK OVER TIME*

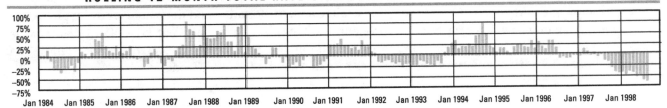

STOCK PERFORMANCE*

	1 month	1 year	3 years	5 years	10 years	15 years
Returns ending Aug 1998	−18.8%	−64.4%	−33.7%	−12.5%	−8.9%	−2.3%
Best historical return	29.6%	83.1%	37.9%	23.5%	12.8%	10.2%
Average historical return	0.2%	4.6%	5.8%	6.3%	6.5%	5.2%
Worst historical return	−30.8%	−64.4%	−33.7%	−12.5%	−8.9%	−2.3%

RETURNS GREATER THAN*

	1 month	1 year	3 years	5 years	10 years	15 years
10 per cent	16%	43%	37%	36%	20%	3%
Zero	49%	53%	68%	74%	92%	95%
Percentage of time stock lost $	51%	47%	32%	26%	8%	5%
Number of periods evaluated	218	207	183	159	99	39

DOWNSIDE RISK*

	Worst setback since start date	In bear 1987	In bear 1990	In bear 1994	In bear 1998
Setback for stock	−72.1%	−41.7%	−38.4%	−22.7%	−72.1%
Setback for TSE 35	−27.6%	−26.5%	−16.8%	−9.0%	−27.6%
Setback ended in	Aug 1998	Jan 1987	Jan 1990	Feb 1994	Aug 1998
Months to recover from loss	?	14	66	17	?

STOCK FINANCIAL FUNDAMENTAL INFORMATION

	1988	1989	1990	1991	1992	1993	1994	1995	1996	1997	Change
Average share price	$33.86	$35.95	$30.74	$37.06	$33.10	$28.91	$36.63	$41.95	$44.24	$39.58	1.6%
Earnings per share	$8.65	$8.46	$4.89	$0.85	$(0.25)	$0.10	$0.04	$2.51	$1.60	$0.34	−27.6%
Book value per share	$7.97	$14.34	$18.49	$17.72	$19.03	$15.30	$19.58	$18.16	$32.63	$27.73	13.3%
Price-to-earnings ratio	3.9	4.2	6.3	43.5	n/a	280.1	897.8	16.7	27.6	115.6	40.3%
Price-to-book ratio	4.2	2.5	1.7	2.1	1.7	1.9	1.9	2.3	1.4	1.4	−10.3%
Profit margin	26.9%	23.0%	18.0%	3.3%	−1.1%	0.6%	0.2%	7.8%	6.4%	1.7%	−24.0%
Asset turnover	0.68	0.90	0.59	0.54	0.46	0.41	0.48	0.61	0.33	0.30	−8.0%
Leverage	5.9	2.8	2.5	2.7	2.6	3.0	2.8	2.9	2.3	2.4	−8.6%
Return on equity	108.6%	59.0%	26.5%	4.8%	−1.3%	0.7%	0.2%	13.8%	4.9%	1.2%	−36.1%
Dividend per share	$0.85	$0.99	$1.17	$1.12	$1.05	$0.53	$0.54	$0.54	$0.54	$0.56	−4.1%
Dividend yield	2.5%	2.8%	3.8%	3.0%	3.2%	1.8%	1.5%	1.3%	1.2%	1.4%	−5.5%

*Source: The raw data used in developing this table was provided by Datastream.

LAIDLAW INCORPORATED

Company profile

Laidlaw is a leading North American service company. It provides school bussing and public transit in addition to emergency and non-emergency healthcare transportation and the management of physicians' practices within hospital emergency departments. Laidlaw also owns 35 per cent of Laidlaw Environmental Services Inc., a public company that removes and manages the waste of North American industrial companies. Laidlaw Environmental Services recently acquired Safety Kleen.

The company was founded by Robert Laidlaw in 1924 as a truck transportation company. In 1959, Michael DeGroote bought the business and subsequently began expanding it into a school bus, inter-city bus, and waste management services business. The last-mentioned division has been sold, and Laidlaw is currently focussing on increasing their ambulance service, school bus service, contracted municipal transit service, and emergency department management service throughout North America.

In 1997, Laidlaw Inc. employed 79,500 people in 900 locations around North America. Laidlaw generated over \$US 3 billion in revenue and earned over \$US 199 million in profits. The company has aggressively acquired several companies since 1997, including American Medical Response Inc., a US ambulance service, Vancom Inc., the largest privately owned school bus company in the US, and EmCare Holdings Inc., a manager of emergency physicians' practices and hospital emergency departments.

Stock performance

The stock performance of Laidlaw Inc. was phenomenal in the 1970s, but more recently investors have been disappointed. The best 12-month rate of return for the stock was a positive 59.1 per cent, and the average 12-month rate of return was 5.2 per cent. The common stock of Laidlaw Inc. posted positive rates of return after 12 months 66 per cent of the time.

Stock risks

Laidlaw Inc. has experienced some growing pains during the last 10 years, and the stock experienced severe underperformance during the early 1990s. The worst 12-month rate of return for the stock was a loss of 51.1 per cent, and it posted negative rates of return after 12 months 33 per cent of the time. The stock experienced a decline of 57.1 per cent in 1993 and still has not recovered from the loss. Going forward, performance will be different, but the company will have to complete a turnaround first. This stock outperformed during the bear of 1998, but has declined significantly during the early 1990s. Value investors who prefer to invest in companies that have declined in value significantly and are currently reorganizing their businesses could investigate Laidlaw further.

Stock financial fundamentals

During the past 10 years, Laidlaw has increased its assets by acquiring companies and financing a portion of its investments with long-term debt. The company's return on equity has declined, but the firm has been able to increase its asset turnover and leverage ratios.

Future prospects

If senior management increases the company's profit margin and asset turnover, earnings per share could increase substantially. Government cutbacks for school budgets are favourable for Laidlaw's school bus division, as school boards download transportation services to subcontractors. Increased environmental regulations and concerns should ensure a viable market for Laidlaw Environmental Services. Investors who believe senior management can build value from Laidlaw's assets will enjoy above-average profits as profit margins and corporate profits increase. Although management has not proven their ability to add value currently, investors who anticipate that management will be able to do so in the future could earn above average returns.

COMPANY DETAILS

Company name	**Laidlaw Incorporated**	Industry classification	Transportation and environment
Recent price	$13.60	Market capitalization (in $ millions)	$4.416
Phone number for annual report	416-813-4600	Stock analysis start date	March 1987
Ticker symbol	LDM	Weight in TSE 35	1.8%
Number of mutual funds that hold this stock as a top 15 holding	25		

ROLLING 12-MONTH TOTAL RATE OF RETURN FOR THE STOCK OVER TIME*

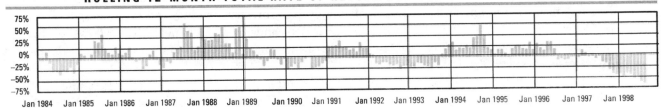

STOCK PERFORMANCE*

	1 month	1 year	3 years	5 years	10 years	15 years
Returns ending Aug 1998	–3.6%	7.2%	14.9%	12.6%	4.1%	
Best historical return	19.2%	59.1%	20.5%	15.2%	4.9%	
Average historical return	0.5%	5.2%	2.2%	–0.3%	2.8%	
Worst historical return	–22.8%	–51.1%	–24.2%	–12.1%	0.6%	

RETURNS GREATER THAN*

	1 month	1 year	3 years	5 years	10 years	15 years
10 per cent	7%	49%	35%	15%	0%	
Zero	53%	67%	53%	39%	100%	
Percentage of time stock lost $	47%	33%	47%	61%	0%	
Number of periods evaluated	138	127	103	79	19	

DOWNSIDE RISK*

	Worst setback since start date	In bear 1987	In bear 1990	In bear 1994	In bear 1998
Setback for stock	–57.1%	–28.0%	–31.0%	–53.5%	–17.4%
Setback for TSE 35	0.0%	–26.5%	–16.8%	–9.0%	–27.6%
Setback ended in	May 1993	Oct 1987	Feb 1991	July 1994	Nov 1997
Months to recover from loss	?	23	?	?	?

STOCK FINANCIAL FUNDAMENTAL INFORMATION

	1988	1989	1990	1991	1992	1993	1994	1995	1996	1997	Change
Average share price	$23.62	$26.36	$30.85	$19.42	$17.21	$13.64	$13.88	$14.33	$16.72	$18.56	–2.4%
Earnings per share	$0.53	$0.64	$0.91	$0.38	$0.46	$0.45	$0.33	$0.37	$0.55	$0.86	5.1%
Book value per share	$5.21	$7.88	$9.83	$7.23	$9.12	$7.30	$7.84	$8.20	$9.77	$12.42	9.1%
Price-to-earnings ratio	45.0	41.0	33.8	51.2	37.1	30.2	42.5	38.5	30.5	21.5	–7.1%
Price-to-book ratio	4.5	3.3	3.1	2.7	1.9	1.9	1.8	1.7	1.7	1.5	–10.5%
Profit margin	15.0%	15.7%	18.4%	7.8%	9.3%	7.9%	4.8%	4.3%	5.1%	6.6%	–7.9%
Asset turnover	0.38	0.29	0.27	0.32	0.30	0.36	0.40	0.43	0.48	0.48	2.4%
Leverage	1.8	1.8	1.9	2.1	1.8	2.2	2.2	2.4	2.3	2.2	2.2%
Return on equity	10.1%	8.2%	9.3%	5.2%	5.1%	6.2%	4.2%	4.5%	5.6%	7.0%	–3.6%
Dividend per share	$0.19	$0.23	$0.27	$0.31	$0.16	$0.16	$0.16	$0.16	$0.19	$0.20	0.8%
Dividend yield	0.8%	0.9%	0.9%	1.6%	0.9%	1.2%	1.1%	1.1%	1.1%	1.1%	3.2%

*Source: The raw data used in developing this table was provided by Datastream.

MACMILLAN BLOEDEL LIMITED

Company profile

MacMillan Bloedel is one of Canada's largest forest products companies with integrated operations in North America and Mexico. The company is involved in forestry, logging, and sawmill operations and produces lumber, container board, corrugated containers, and structural panel boards. MacMillan Bloedel has a partnership with Trus Joist MacMillan to supply and manufacture engineering wood products such as TJI joists.

In 1997, the company utilized its 46 distribution centres across North America to generate over $4.5 billion in sales, but posted a loss of more than $350 million. The company has more than 10,000 employees and manages in excess of two million hectares of productive timberlands, approximately half in British Columbia.

Stock performance

Investors in the common stock of MacMillan Bloedel during the past 10 years have been disappointed. However, the company has displayed upside potential, posting a best 12-month rate of return of 173.0 per cent and an average 12-month rate of return of 9.1 per cent. Unfortunately, the company has also displayed periods of significant underperformance because of the unfavourable and cyclical nature of the forestry business.

Stock risks

The common stock of Macmillan Bloedel during the last 10 years has had above-average downside risk. The worst 12-month rate of return was a loss of 59 per cent, and the common stock posted negative returns after 12 months 48 per cent of the time. Investors during the stock market correction of 1987 saw their investment decline in value by 36.2 per cent, and the stock took 43 months to recover. Investors in the stock during the bear of 1994 were not so fortunate. They saw their investment decline in value by 31.8 per cent, and the stock still has not recovered; a decline of 47.1 per cent during the bear of 1998 did not help the situation.

Stock financial fundamentals

The company's sales have increased during the past 10 years, but profit margins have decreased, and the company lost money in 1997. During this time, the company has increased its debt, which in turn increases earnings variability and risk for investors.

Future prospects

With the economic volatility in Asia, MacMillan Bloedel could continue to experience difficulties going forward. However, within a cyclical industry the opportunity to profit from the timely acquisition of stock can lead to above-average profits. MacMillan Bloedel has recently sold off some unprofitable divisions and acquired a new chief executive officer. These are all positive moves. Investors who can withstand above-average volatility could consider an investment in a resource stock. A small change in operating performance can lead to big profits, but resource stocks have been out of favour and could remain out of favour for several years. Investors should realize that financial results should improve for MacMillan Bloedel in the short term, but rebuilding the company to its former glory will take several years and success will depend on outside factors such as the situation in Japan.

COMPANY DETAILS

Company name	**Macmillan Bloedel Limited**	Industry classification	Paper and forest products
Recent price	$12.00	Market capitalization (in $ millions)	$1,493
Phone number for annual report	604-661-8671	Stock analysis start date	July 1980
Ticker symbol	MB	Weight in TSE 35	1.3%
Number of mutual funds that hold this stock as a top 15 holding	8		

ROLLING 12-MONTH TOTAL RATE OF RETURN FOR THE STOCK OVER TIME*

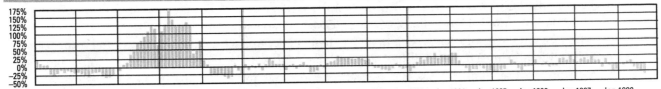

STOCK PERFORMANCE*

	1 month	1 year	3 years	5 years	10 years	15 years
Returns ending Aug 1998	−19.2%	−30.2%	−10.6%	−11.2%	−2.2%	3.7%
Best historical return	30.7%	173.0%	52.5%	38.2%	15.2%	10.6%
Average historical return	0.6%	9.1%	7.1%	7.8%	7.7%	6.2%
Worst historical return	−29.5%	−59.0%	−14.8%	−13.2%	−2.7%	2.3%

RETURNS GREATER THAN*

	1 month	1 year	3 years	5 years	10 years	15 years
10 per cent	11%	35%	26%	40%	41%	5%
Zero	50%	52%	63%	77%	89%	100%
Percentage of time stock lost $	50%	48%	37%	23%	11%	0%
Number of periods evaluated	218	207	183	159	99	39

DOWNSIDE RISK*

	Worst setback since start date	In bear 1987	In bear 1990	In bear 1994	In bear 1998
Setback for stock	−64.9%	−36.2%	−39.6%	−31.8%	−47.1%
Setback for TSE 35	−41.0%	−26.5%	−16.8%	−9.0%	−27.6%
Setback ended in	June 1982	Oct 1987	Oct 1990	Jan 1995	Aug 1998
Months to recover from loss	55	?	?	?	?

STOCK FINANCIAL FUNDAMENTAL INFORMATION

	1988	1989	1990	1991	1992	1993	1994	1995	1996	1997	Change
Average share price	$19.96	$18.55	$17.18	$19.05	$17.96	$20.53	$19.67	$17.81	$18.17	$18.54	−0.2%
Earnings per share	$2.97	$2.21	$0.37	$(0.98)	$(0.52)	$0.42	$1.36	$2.08	$0.36	$(2.99)	n/a
Book value per share	$14.84	$16.15	$16.32	$15.86	$13.86	$14.82	$14.51	$16.01	$15.98	$12.83	−1.4%
Price-to-earnings ratio	6.4	8.4	46.4	n/a	n/a	48.9	14.5	8.6	50.5	n/a	n/a
Price-to-book ratio	1.3	1.1	1.1	1.2	1.3	1.4	1.4	1.1	1.1	1.4	1.2%
Profit margin	10.4%	8.0%	1.3%	−3.9%	−1.9%	1.6%	4.7%	6.3%	1.1%	−8.2%	n/a
Asset turnover	1.08	0.88	0.77	0.67	0.78	0.72	0.81	0..82	0.88	0.99	−0.8%
Leverage	1.8	2.0	2.2	2.3	2.6	2.5	2.5	2.5	2.4	2.9	4.8%
Return on equity	20.0%	13.7%	2.3%	−6.2%	−3.8%	2.8%	9.4%	13.0%	2.3%	−23.3%	n/a
Dividend per share	$0.90	$0.80	$0.80	$0.60	$0.60	$0.60	$0.60	$0.60	$0.60	$0.30	−10.4%
Dividend yield	4.7%	4.3%	4.7%	3.1%	3.3%	2.9%	3.1%	3.4%	3.3%	1.6%	−10.2%

*Source: The raw data used in developing this table was provided by Datastream.

MAGNA INTERNATIONAL LIMITED, A

Company profile

Magna International Limited is a leading global supplier of technologically advanced automotive systems. The company designs, develops, and manufactures a range of automotive supplies and systems for cars and trucks. Customers include Ford, Chrysler, GM, and Volkswagen.

The company's history dates back to 1957, when Frank Stronach set up his own tool-and-die company called Multimatic Investments Limited. Stronach has built Magna into a multi-million-dollar automotive parts supplier. The company has experienced phenomenal growth during its 40-year history, although it has also incurred severe setbacks occasionally.

In 1997 the company employed more than 36,000 people in 128 manufacturing divisions and 26 product-development and engineering centres throughout the world. In 1997, Magna generated sales in excess of $7.6 billion and posted a profit of $603 million. During that year, Magna made acquisitions to expand its global seat systems capabilities. The company acquired Douglas and Lomason and Tricom Group Holdings Ltd., which allowed Magna to increase its customer base to include Toyota and Mitsubishi.

Stock performance

Wow! Investors could have made or lost a bundle in this stock as they experienced above-average upside potential and downside risk. The best 12-month rate of return for Magna International common stock was a positive 817.1 per cent, and the average 12-month rate of return was 43.6 per cent. The common stock posted a positive rate of return after 12 months 67 per cent of the time. The company has made considerable advancements in its operations and can provide value-added services to all major car manufactures. In turn, investors have been handsomely rewarded.

Stock risks

Ouch! Investors who invested in Magna International common stock have experienced above-average risk. The worst 12-month rate of return for the common stock was a decline of 75.5 per cent. The stock's worst setback since the start date in July 1980 was a decline of 93 per cent. Amazingly, the stock recovered this loss in 18 months. During the stock market correction of 1987, the stock declined in value by 71.8 per cent and took 54 months to recover its loss. In short, when companies report losses and the future looks bleak investors lose money.

Stock financial fundamentals

During the past 10 years, earnings per share grew as Magna recovered in the 1990s from a financial nightmare to become one of Canada's largest companies. In turn, the price-to-earnings (P/E) ratio has declined. The key to Magna's success was its ability to increase profit margins and asset turnover ratios to improve financial performance.

Future prospects

The common stock of Magna International has appreciated quickly during the mid 1990s and continues to outperform. Investors must be aware that growth of 800 per cent is not going to continue. Magna International has become a large company, and improving operations will become increasingly difficult. However, investors who want exposure to a growing company in the automotive industry could consider Magna International. The stock declined in price by 15.1 per cent during the bear of 1998, thus significantly outperforming. This may indicate that the company's troubles are all in the past.

COMPANY DETAILS

Company name	**Magna International Limited, A**	Industry classification	Industrial products
Recent price	$93.80	Market capitalization (in $ millions)	$7,237
Phone number for annual report	1-800-558-9071	Stock analysis start date	July 1980
Ticker symbol	MG.A	Weight in TSE 35	2.7%
Number of mutual funds that hold this stock as a top 15 holding	73		

ROLLING 12-MONTH TOTAL RATE OF RETURN FOR THE STOCK OVER TIME*

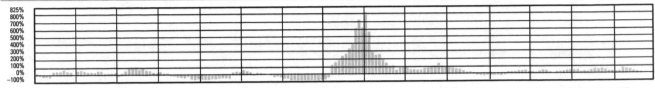

Jan 1984   Jan 1985   Jan 1986   Jan 1987   Jan 1988   Jan 1989   Jan 1990   Jan 1991   Jan 1992   Jan 1993   Jan 1994   Jan 1995   Jan 1996   Jan 1997   Jan 1998

STOCK PERFORMANCE*

	1 month	1 year	3 years	5 years	10 years	15 years
Returns ending Aug 1998	−8.5%	3.3%	17.9%	13.9%	24.0%	17.1%
Best historical return	80.5%	817.1%	203.6%	94.5%	27.3%	20.4%
Average historical return	2.1%	43.6%	23.6%	19.2%	12.1%	16.3%
Worst historical return	−48.2%	−75.5%	−50.2%	−34.4%	−13.7%	12.8%

RETURNS GREATER THAN*

	1 month	1 year	3 years	5 years	10 years	15 years
10 per cent	21%	62%	64%	62%	76%	100%
Zero	51%	67%	74%	74%	89%	100%
Percentage of time stock lost $	49%	33%	26%	26%	11%	0%
Number of periods evaluated	218	207	183	159	99	39

DOWNSIDE RISK*

	Worst setback since start date	In bear 1987	In bear 1990	In bear 1994	In bear 1998
Setback for stock	−93.0%	−71.8%	−93.0%	−29.9%	−15.1%
Setback for TSE 35	−14.4%	−26.5%	−16.8%	−9.0%	−27.6%
Setback ended in	Nov 1990	Nov 1987	Nov 1990	Nov 1994	Aug 1998
Months to recover from loss	18	54	18	18	?

STOCK FINANCIAL FUNDAMENTAL INFORMATION

	1988	1989	1990	1991	1992	1993	1994	1995	1996	1997	Change
Average share price	$12.21	$12.34	$3.95	$11.32	$29.02	$48.69	$57.31	$56.46	$64.13	$83.32	21.2%
Earnings per share	$0.35	$0.60	$(4.03)	$0.29	$2.08	$2.55	$3.87	$5.16	$4.71	$7.74	36.3%
Book value per share	$8.01	$8.22	$4.15	$4.71	$12.53	$15.34	$21.79	$27.17	$40.68	$41.89	18.0%
Price-to-earnings ratio	34.9	20.7	n/a	39.0	14.0	19.1	14.8	10.9	13.6	10.8	−11.1%
Price-to-book ratio	1.5	1.5	1.0	2.4	2.3	3.2	2.6	2.1	1.6	2.0	2.7%
Profit margin	1.3%	1.6%	−10.6%	0.7%	3.8%	4.9%	6.0%	6.6%	5.5^	7.8%	20.0%
Asset turnover	0.87	1.07	1.13	1.40	1.68	1.72	1.59	1.54	1.34	1.44	5.2%
Leverage	4.0	4.2	8.1	5.9	2.6	2.0	1.9	1.9	1.6	1.6	−8.5%
Return on equity	4.4%	7.2%	−97.0%	6.2%	16.6%	16.6%	17.8%	19.0%	11.6%	18.5%	15.5%
Dividend per share	$0.48	$0.48	$0.24	$—	$0.20	$0.55	$0.81	$1.08	$1.08	$1.14	9.0%
Dividend yield	3.9%	3.9%	6.1%	0.0%	0.7%	1.1%	1.4%	1.9%	1.7%	1.4%	−10.0%

*Source: The raw data used in developing this table was provided by Datastream.

MOORE CORPORATION LIMITED

Company profile

Moore Corporation provides print and digital technologies for companies. It designs, manufactures, and delivers end-to-end business communications solutions such as label systems, direct marketing, database management, information printing, and distribution.

The company's history goes back to 1882, when Samuel Moore began to print sales books that contained a carbon copy to standardize sales slips and provide a duplicate copy. The original concept was generated by John Carter, who became Moore's first sales representative. The company quickly grew and expanded into the United States under the name Carter & Company. However, the Carter & Company name was used for only 11 years.

In 1997, the company generated sales in excess of $2.6 billion and reported net income of $55 million, it was still a difficult year for Moore Corporation as financial results failed to meet expectations. In addition, the company has to combat the effects of laser printing and other technological advances in desktop publishing and printing systems.

Stock performance

The best 12-month rate of return of the common stock of Moore Corporation was a positive rate of return of 80.1 per cent, and the average 12-month rate of return was 9.5 per cent. The common stock posted positive rates of return after 12 months 57 per cent of the time. During the past 10 years, Moore has not delivered eye-popping results, but it enjoyed periods of excellent performance in the 1980s.

Stock risks

The common stock of Moore Corporation has displayed periods of above-average downside risk. Investors in Moore during the bear of 1994 saw their investment decline in value by 26.6 per cent. The stock regained its loss within 29 months after the decline. The worst 12-month rate of return for the common stock was a decline of 44.1 per cent. The stock has underperformed during bear markets, and the bear of 1998 was no exception, as the stock declined by 48.2 per cent.

Stock financial fundamentals

The return on equity of Moore Corporation has declined significantly, from 20.1 per cent in 1988 to 4.05 per cent in 1997, attributable to lower profit margins and lower asset turnover. As a result, the company's earnings have significantly decreased from $2.51 per share in 1988 to $0.81 per share in 1997. The company has a policy of paying a high portion of earnings as a dividend and, in turn, the stock does provide an attractive dividend yield, although investors should expect a decline in the dividend if financial performance does not rebound in the near future.

Future prospects

Going forward, if profit margins improve for Moore Corporation, net income should appreciate quickly. In turn, investors will benefit as the stock price appreciates. Moore is the world's largest manufacturer of business forms and related products, but the company's future business may be threatened by technological advances in personal computing, although that can be said of any company. Those that adapt and persevere can make great investments. Speculative investors should acquire this stock only if it is attractively priced versus the company's value.

COMPANY DETAILS

Company name	**Moore Corporation Limited**	Industry classification	Industrial products
Recent price	$15.10	Market capitalization (in $ millions)	$1,336
Phone number for annual report	416-643-5500	Stock analysis start date	July 1980
Ticker symbol	MCL	Weight in TSE 35	0.9%
Number of mutual funds that hold this stock as a top 15 holding	4		

ROLLING 12-MONTH TOTAL RATE OF RETURN FOR THE STOCK OVER TIME*

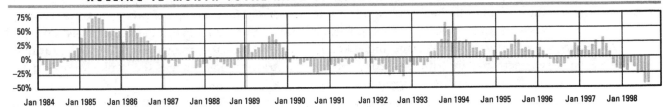

STOCK PERFORMANCE*

	1 month	1 year	3 years	5 years	10 years	15 years
Returns ending Aug 1998	−5.9%	−43.4%	−15.2%	−5.6%	−1.8%	2.6%
Best historical return	20.2%	80.1%	39.0%	29.4%	15.2%	10.7%
Average historical return	0.7%	9.5%	8.8%	8.2%	6.1%	8.1%
Worst historical return	−21.5%	−44.1%	−16.1%	−7.0%	−1.8%	2.6%

RETURNS GREATER THAN*

	1 month	1 year	3 years	5 years	10 years	15 years
10 per cent	7%	43%	40%	38%	23%	18%
Zero	51%	57%	81%	74%	95%	100%
Percentage of time stock lost $	49%	43%	19%	26%	5%	0%
Number of periods evaluated	218	207	183	159	99	39

DOWNSIDE RISK*

	Worst setback since start date	In bear 1987	In bear 1990	In bear 1994	In bear 1998
Setback for stock	−48.2%	−31.0%	−31.2%	−26.6%	−48.2%
Setback for TSE 35	−27.6%	−26.5%	−16.8%	−9.0%	−27.6%
Setback ended in	Aug 1998	Nov 1987	Nov 1990	June 1994	Aug 1998
Months to recover from loss	?	17	72	29	?

STOCK FINANCIAL FUNDAMENTAL INFORMATION

	1988	1989	1990	1991	1992	1993	1994	1995	1996	1997	Change
Average share price	$29.18	$35.15	$30.52	$27.77	$22.33	$22.98	$25.36	$27.29	$25.98	$27.30	−0.7%
Earnings per share	$2.51	$2.56	$1.49	$1.05	$(0.02)	$(1.01)	$1.66	$3.70	$2.06	$0.81	−10.7%
$12.50	$12.50	$12.85	$12.70	$14.44	$(1.51)	$13.90	$16.62	$47.04	$21.84	$19.96	4.8%
Price-to-earnings ratio	11.6	13.7	20.5	26.5	n/a	n/a	15.3	7.4	12.6	33.8	11.3%
Price-to-book ratio	2.3	2.7	2.4	1.9	(14.8)	1.7	1.5	0.6	1.2	1.4	−5.2%
Profit margin	10.0%	10.4%	6.5%	4.5%	1.0%	−4.2%	5.6%	0.0%	5.7%	1.9%	−15.4%
Asset turnover	1.41	1.37	1.26	1.20	1.16	1.15	1.19	8.7	1.16	1.18	−1.8%
Leverage	1.4	1.4	1.4	1.3	1.4	1.5	1.5	1.5	1.4	1.8	2.5%
Return on equity	20.1%	19.9%	11.7%	7.2%	1.6%	−7.2%	10.0%	7.9%	9.4%	4.0%	−14.8%
Dividend per share	$0.95	$1.03	$1.10	$1.05	$1.17	$1.24	$1.27	$1.26	$1.26	$1.33	3.4%
Dividend yield	3.3%	2.9%	3.6%	3.8%	5.2%	5.4%	5.0%	4.6%	4.8%	4.9%	4.1%

*Source: The raw data used in developing this table was provided by Datastream.

NATIONAL BANK OF CANADA

Company profile

The National Bank of Canada, Canada's sixth-largest chartered bank, focusses on Quebec but operates throughout Canada and in other countries. The National Bank offers a range of products and services to individual, business, and government clients. The bank has a controlling interest in Levesque Beaublen and Company, which offers full brokerage, underwriting, and investment-management services. In addition, National Bank Securities Inc. offers discount brokerage services and manages the bank's InvesNat and Natcan mutual funds and pension operations.

The National Bank of Canada was established on October 25, 1979, through the amalgamation of the Provincial Bank of Canada and Banque Nationale. The new bank began operations on November 1, 1979. In 1997 the company had 637 branches and 738 automated banking machines, with access to 300,000 more through the Cirrus, Interac, and MasterCard ATM networks. It is a market leader among Canadian banks of similar size in providing financing to independent business, with a 14 per cent market share for bank loans of under $500,000, approximately double the share it controls in other segments of the banking industry. In 1997, the bank earned more than $1.3 billion in net interest income and reported a profit of $342 million.

Stock performance

The common stock of the National Bank of Canada has delivered value for shareholders over the long term. In the short term, the best 12-month period for the common stock of the National Bank of Canada was a positive rate of return of 170.2 per cent, and the average 12-month return was 21.1 per cent. The common stock posted a positive rate of return after 12 months 68 per cent of the time.

Stock risks

The worst 12-month rate of return for the stock was a decline of 61.5 per cent, and the common stock posted negative rates of return after 12 months 32 per cent of the time. This bank stock tends to underperform during bear markets. During the bear of 1987, it declined by 39.8 per cent and took 20 months to recover from its loss.

Stock financial fundamentals

Earnings per share have remained flat for the National Bank of Canada from 1988 to 1997. However, its price-to-earnings (P/E) ratio has increased by an average of 4.2 per cent per year because of a decline in interest rates. The company's return on equity declined over the past 10 years because of a decline in asset turnover that could not be offset by the increase in profit margin or leverage ratio.

Future prospects

The National Bank of Canada is not immune to a global or domestic recession. Also, a large portion of the bank's assets and operations are located in Quebec, with all the uncertainty that that entails. Bank stocks have historically added value over the long term, but have also under-performed during bear markets. The level and direction of interest rates will affect the performance of these stocks.

COMPANY DETAILS

Company name	**National Bank of Canada**	Industry classification	Financial services
Recent price	$20.30	Market capitalization (in $ millions)	$3,460
Phone number for annual report	514-871-7171	Stock analysis start date	July 1980
Ticker symbol	NA	Weight in TSE 35	1.2%
Number of mutual funds that hold this stock as a top 15 holding	46		

ROLLING 12-MONTH TOTAL RATE OF RETURN FOR THE STOCK OVER TIME*

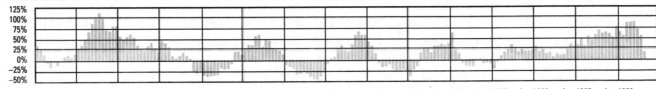

STOCK PERFORMANCE*

	1 month	1 year	3 years	5 years	10 years	15 years
Returns ending Aug 1998	−25.1%	16.5%	26.5%	19.0%	12.1%	13.7%
Best historical return	28.0%	170.2%	69.6%	51.0%	23.2%	20.3%
Average historical return	1.2%	21.1%	15.5%	13.5%	10.5%	14.0%
Worst historical return	−25.1%	−61.5%	−12.3%	−5.0%	3.1%	8.3%

RETURNS GREATER THAN*

	1 month	1 year	3 years	5 years	10 years	15 years
10 per cent	11%	61%	47%	51%	52%	67%
Zero	53%	68%	83%	87%	100%	100%
Percentage of time stock lost $	47%	32%	17%	13%	0%	0%
Number of periods evaluated	218	207	183	159	99	39

DOWNSIDE RISK*

	Worst setback since start date	In bear 1987	In bear 1990	In bear 1994	In bear 1998
Setback for stock	−64.3%	−39.8%	−47.3%	−24.5%	−31.2%
Setback for TSE 35	−34.8%	−26.5%	−16.8%	−9.0%	−27.6%
Setback ended in	July 1982	Nov 1987	Oct 1990	July 1994	Aug 1998
Months to recover from loss	10	20	39	11	?

STOCK FINANCIAL FUNDAMENTAL INFORMATION

	1988	1989	1990	1991	1992	1993	1994	1995	1996	1997	Change
Average share price	$10.73	$13.51	$9.26	$10.51	$9.35	$9.72	$9.56	$10.49	$12.01	$17.72	5.1%
Earnings per share	$1.81	$0.01	$1.09	$1.19	$(0.29)	$1.01	$1.12	$1.26	$1.76	$1.86	-0.3%
Book value per share	$10.57	$0.48	$8.70	$8.97	$10.08	$8.92	$9.21	$9.95	$11.75	$12.97	2.1%
Price-to-earnings ratio	5.9	1,351.0	8.5	8.8	n/a	9.6	8.5	8.3	6.8	9.5	4.9%
Price-to-book ratio	1.0	28.4	1.1	1.2	0.9	1.1	1.0	1.1	1.0	1.4	3.0%
Profit margin	7.7%	0.7%	4.1%	5.0%	−1.2%	5.9%	7.5%	6.8%	9.8%	11.0%	3.6%
Asset turnover	0.09	0.11	0.11	0.10	0.08	0.07	0.06	0.07	0.06	0.05	−6.6%
Leverage	23.9	27.4	26.6	26.0	31.1	27.7	25.1	25.3	25.0	27.8	1.5%
Return on equity	17.1%	2.1%	12.5%	13.3%	−2.9%	11.3%	12.2%	12.7%	15.0%	14.3%	−1.8%
Dividend per share	$0.64	$0.72	$0.80	$0.80	$0.70	$0.40	$0.40	$0.40	$0.49	$0.58	−1.1%
Dividend yield	6.0%	5.3%	8.6%	7.6%	7.5%	4.1%	4.2%	3.8%	4.1%	3.2%	−5.9%

*Source: The raw data used in developing this table was provided by Datastream.

NORANDA INCORPORATED

Company profile

Noranda Inc. is a diversified natural resource company with operations throughout Canada and the world. It mines, smelts, refines, and markets copper, nickel, zinc, lead, gold, and silver. In addition, the company is a significant producer of primary and fabricated aluminum. The company sells over 80 per cent of its products outside Canada and has begun to sell off its oil and gas and forest-products assets to focus on and reinvest in its metals business.

In the early 1920s, a prospector named Edmund Horne led a team of prospectors to the Rouyn district in northeastern Quebec. The prospectors entered new territory and soon found sulphur, iron, copper, and gold. Noranda Mines Limited was incorporated in 1922 and, with government assistance and private capital, began operations.

In 1997, Noranda Inc. employed more than 21,500 people worldwide and generated revenue of more than $6.4 billion, with a profit of $261 million. The company had more than $16 billion in assets in 1997, but this will decline to $10 billion after the sale of the company's oil and gas and forest products assets.

Stock performance

This company has been plagued by a decline in metal prices caused by fears associated with Asia and overcapacity in the industry. Thus, Noranda was unable to add significant value for shareholders during the last 10 years. However, the best 12-month rate of return for the common stock of Noranda was a gain of 133.6 per cent, and the average 12-month rate of return was 7.1 per cent. The common stock posted positive rates of return after 12 months 60 per cent of the time.

Stock risks

Noranda Inc. has not been immune to setbacks incurred by most Canadian resource stocks. The worst 12-month period for the common stock was a loss of 63.2 per cent, and the common stock lost money after 12 months 40 per cent of the time. Investors who invested during the bear of 1987 saw their investment decline by 39.6 per cent, and the stock took 75 months to regain its loss.

Stock financial fundamentals

The company's earnings per share have declined over the past 10 years. In 1988, earnings per share were $3.14, declining by an average of 10.8 per cent to $1 per share in 1997. However, the company has increased its dividend per share throughout this period from $0.90 to $1. In turn, investors should expect a dividend decline unless Noranda significantly increases its cash flow and earnings in the near future.

Future prospects

Senior management have a policy of paying a high dividend. In turn, they are sending a strong signal to investors that they believe in the company's future prospects. Noranda Inc.'s fortunes will be dictated by the selling price of metal products. High metal prices will increase Noranda's fortunes, but these high metal prices may not appear in the near future because of overcapacity and the Asian turmoil. This turmoil caused stock markets to decline in August 1998, when Noranda declined 24.9 per cent. Astute investors who believe that equities add value over the long term will benefit from buying low, but defining low is a difficult proposition when investing in resource stocks.

COMPANY DETAILS

Company name	**Noranda Incorporated**	Industry classification	Metals and minerals
Recent price	$17.25	Market capitalization (in $ millions)	$4,095
Phone number for annual report	416-982-7337	Stock analysis start date	July 1980
Ticker symbol	NOR	Weight in TSE 35	1.0%
Number of mutual funds that hold this stock as a top 15 holding	29		

ROLLING 12-MONTH TOTAL RATE OF RETURN FOR THE STOCK OVER TIME*

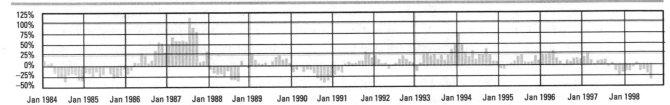

STOCK PERFORMANCE*

	1 month	1 year	3 years	5 years	10 years	15 years
Returns ending Aug 1998	−24.9%	−33.7%	−10.9%	−1.6%	1.7%	0.9%
Best historical return	27.9%	133.6%	30.1%	24.2%	11.9%	10.4%
Average historical return	0.5%	7.1%	5.8%	5.7%	4.7%	5.2%
Worst historical return	−38.1%	−63.2%	−19.0%	−11.6%	−3.6%	0.9%

RETURNS GREATER THAN*

	1 month	1 year	3 years	5 years	10 years	15 years
10 per cent	11%	41%	42%	28%	6%	3%
Zero	50%	60%	63%	79%	87%	100%
Percentage of time stock lost $	50%	40%	37%	21%	13%	0%
Number of periods evaluated	218	207	183	159	99	39

DOWNSIDE RISK*

	Worst setback since start date	In bear 1987	In bear 1990	In bear 1994	In bear 1998
Setback for stock	−63.2%	−39.6%	−54.1%	−13.9%	−44.4%
Setback for TSE 35	−41.0%	−26.5%	−16.8%	−9.0%	−27.6%
Setback ended in	June 1982	Oct 1987	Oct 1990	Feb 1995	Aug 1998
Months to recover from loss	57	75	39	3	?

STOCK FINANCIAL FUNDAMENTAL INFORMATION

	1988	1989	1990	1991	1992	1993	1994	1995	1996	1997	Change
Average share price	$22.83	$24.30	$19.09	$18.13	$18.64	$21.05	$25.43	$26.26	$28.72	$29.00	2.4$
Earnings per share	$3.14	$2.19	$0.36	$(1.04)	$0.10	$(0.41)	$1.45	$2.26	$1.02	$1.00	−10.8%
Book value per share	$21.49	$22.28	$13.99	$34.44	$5.18	$48.49	$18.14	$20.28	$20.24	$19.34	−1.0%
Price-to-earnings ratio	7.3	11.1	53.0	n/a	186.4	n/a	17.5	11.6	28.2	29.0	14.8%
Price-to-book ratio	1.1	1.1	1.4	0.5	3.6	0.4	1.4	1.3	1.4	1.5	3.5%
Profit margin	6.8%	4.8%	1.3%	−1.5%	0.9%	−0.6%	4.4%	5.2%	3.8%	4.1%	−5.0%
Asset turnover	0.95	0.78	0.75	0.69	0.70	0.63	0.78	0.90	0.52	0.45	−7.2%
Leverage	2.3	2.6	2.7	2.8	3.0	2.1	2.3	2.3	2.6	2.8	2.2%
Return on equity	14.6%	9.8%	2.6%	−3.0%	1.9%	−0.8%	8.0%	11.1%	5.0%	5.2%	−9.9%
Dividend per share	$0.90	$1.00	$1.00	$1.00	$1.00	$1.00	$1.00	$1.00	$1.00	$1.00	1.1%
Dividend yield	3.9%	4.1%	5.2%	5.5%	5.4%	4.8%	3.9%	3.8%	3.5%	3.4%	−1.3%

*Source: The raw data used in developing this table was provided by Datastream.

NORTEL NETWORKS

Company profile

Nortel Networks is the new name for Northern Telecom. Northern Telecom was recently able to merge with Bay Networks by exchanging shares of Northern Telecom worth $US 7.2 billion (approximately $10.8 billion Canadian) for shares in Bay Networks, a leader in the worldwide data networking market. The Bay Networks shares were retired, and the number of shares outstanding of the newly named Nortel Networks (Nortel) was increased. Bay Networks is now a subsidiary of Nortel. Thus, because of its origins in Northern Telecom, Nortel is a major designer, developer, manufacturer, marketer, and installer of, and service provider for fully digital telecommunications systems, and provides support and financing for all its products. Through the merger with Bay Networks, the company has become a major player also in the global telecommunications industry, second only to AT&T in the United States.

Northern Telecom began as a department within Bell Canada to allow Bell to develop and manufacture adequate telephone equipment. The department grew, and in 1985 became a separate company. BCE Inc. still owns a significant stake in Nortel, although this stake has been reduced somewhat by the issuance of new shares to exchange for Bay Networks.

In 1997 the company generated more than $15 billion in sales and posted a profit of $828 million. Nortel employed more than 68,000 worldwide in 1997 and reported assets of $12.5 billion.

Stock performance

Nortel has rewarded investors for accepting above-average risk. The best 12-month period for the common stock of Nortel was a gain of 231.4 per cent, and the average 12-month return was 27.3 per cent. Nortel common stock has posted positive rates of return after 12 months 71 per cent of the time. Thus, the common stock has displayed significant periods of upside potential.

Stock risks

With above-average performance, investors incur above-average risk. Nortel has displayed above-average downside risk. The worst 12-month period for the stock was a decline of 29.5 per cent. In addition, the stock has underperformed during bear markets, but during the bear of 1998 it declined by 19.2 per cent, less than the average. During other bear markets, the stock has declined further—by 31 per cent in 1994, for example, after which it took 20 months to recover its loss.

Stock financial fundamentals

Nortel grew quickly during the past 10 years, and the company's stock multiples have increased, assisted by a decline in interest rates and investor anticipation of continued growth. Nortel maintained its profit margin while increasing its asset turnover and leverage ratios. In turn, these actions have led to a higher return on equity, which has increased earnings per share.

Future prospects

This company has grown rapidly during the past 10 years and its common stock has appreciated in value. The telecommunications industry is a dynamic and fast-paced industry, and the potential for continued growth is very realistic. However, the company's stock has become expensive based on historical standards, and Nortel will have to find new sources of growth other than Bay Networks. Investors who can acquire stock in Northern Telecom at a realistic price should benefit over the long term. Considering how well the stock has performed during the market correction of 1998, it is clear that investors are having a love affair with this company. Going forward, astute investors will have to invest at a reasonable price to ensure continued success.

COMPANY DETAILS

Company name	**Nortel Networks**	Industry classification	Industrial products
Recent price	$75.25	Market capitalization (in $ millions)	$39,543
Phone number for annual report	1-800-663-9097	Stock analysis start date	July 1980
Ticker symbol	NTL	Weight in TSE 35	8.8%
Number of mutual funds that hold this stock as a top 15 holding	131		

ROLLING 12-MONTH TOTAL RATE OF RETURN FOR THE STOCK OVER TIME*

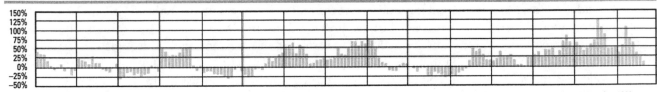

Jan 1984 Jan 1985 Jan 1986 Jan 1987 Jan 1988 Jan 1989 Jan 1990 Jan 1991 Jan 1992 Jan 1993 Jan 1994 Jan 1995 Jan 1996 Jan 1997 Jan 1998

STOCK PERFORMANCE*

	1 month	1 year	3 years	5 years	10 years	15 years
Returns ending Aug 1998	–15.2%	9.9%	46.3%	34.9%	22.7%	13.8%
Best historical return	30.8%	231.4%	74.2%	43.6%	25.3%	23.1%
Average historical return	1.9%	27.3%	20.0%	15.2%	14.7%	17.7%
Worst historical return	–25.5%	–29.5%	–10.1%	–6.3%	2.9%	13.8%

RETURNS GREATER THAN*

	1 month	1 year	3 years	5 years	10 years	15 years
10 per cent	17%	60%	52%	72%	70%	100%
Zero	55%	71%	85%	94%	100%	100%
Percentage of time stock lost $	45%	29%	15%	6%	0%	0%
Number of periods evaluated	218	207	183	159	99	39

DOWNSIDE RISK*

	Worst setback since start date	In bear 1987	In bear 1990	In bear 1994	In bear 1998
Setback for stock	–45.8%	–34.4%	–16.5%	–31.0%	–19.2%
Setback for TSE 35	0.0%	–26.5%	–16.8%	–9.0%	–27.6%
Setback ended in	July 1993	Nov 1987	Sept 1990	Mar 1994	Aug 1998
Months to recover from loss	28	30	3	20	?

STOCK FINANCIAL FUNDAMENTAL INFORMATION

	1988	1989	1990	1991	1992	1993	1994	1995	1996	1997	Change
Average share price	$11.04	$11.15	$14.83	$20.95	$24.33	$21.04	$21.82	$25.25	$36.33	$59.80	18.4%
Earnings per share	$0.44	$0.87	$1.05	$1.17	$1.29	$(2.28)	$1.09	$1.27	$1.64	$2.14	17.2%
Book value per share	$6.25	$6.55	$7.79	$8.41	$9.69	$8.02	$8.88	$9.90	$11.64	$12.74	7.4%
Price-to-earnings ratio	25.2	12.7	14.1	17.9	18.9	n/a	20.1	19.9	22.1	28.0	1.0%
Price-to-book ratio	1.8	1.7	1.9	2.5	2.5	2.6	2.5	2.6	3.1	4.7	10.3%
Profit margin	3.1%	5.8%	6.4%	6.1%	6.5%	–10.8%	4.6%	4.4%	4.8%	5.4%	5.7%
Asset turnover	0.96	0.98	0.99	0.88	0.86	0.84	1.02	1.16	1.20	1.20	2.3%
Leverage	2.4	2.3	2.1	2.6	2.4	3.1	2.6	2.5	2.4	2.6	0.9%
Return on equity	7.0%	13.4%	13.5%	13.9%	13.3%	–28.5%	12.3%	12.8%	14.1%	16.8%	9.1%
Dividend per share	$0.16	$0.16	$0.18	$0.18	$0.21	$0.24	$0.24	$0.28	$0.34	$0.41	9.9%
Dividend yield	1.4%	1.5%	1.2%	0.9%	0.9%	1.1%	1.1%	1.1%	0.9%	0.7%	–7.2%

*Source: The raw data used in developing this table was provided by Datastream.

PETRO CANADA

Company profile

Petro Canada is the largest Canadian-owned integrated oil and gas company. In the upstream, Petro Canada explores and develops for, and produces and markets crude oil, natural gas, and natural gas liquids, including ethane, propane, butane, and condensate. Petro Canada has three main business segments: exploration for and production of natural gas and conventional oil in Western Canada and throughout the world; exploration and development for and production of oil reserves off Canada's east coast; and refining and marketing petroleum products, including lubricants. In the downstream, Petro Canada transports, refines, distributes, and markets a full range of petroleum products and services.

Petro Canada was formed in 1975, when the Government of Canada transferred many of its energy assets to a newly formed Crown corporation, Petro Canada. Petro Canada bought Atlantic Richfield Canada, Pacific Petroleum, Petrofina Canada, and refining and marketing assets of BP Canada. In 1985, the company bought Gulf Canada's downstream assets west of Quebec, and in 1986 bought Gulf's Edmonton refinery.

With the privatization of government assets in the early 1990s, Petro Canada became a publicly traded company. Its initial public offering was in July 1991. Subsequently, Petro Canada restructured to improve profitability and earn investor confidence. Currently, the company is working with Chevron Canada and Mobil Oil Canada in the construction of an oil trans-shipment terminal to accommodate transportation of crude oil from Hibernia, an offshore oil well near Newfoundland. The Hibernia oil platform weighs as much as six aircraft carriers and is as tall as a 75-storey building. In 1997, Petro Canada generated sales of more than $6 billion and posted a profit of $306 million.

Stock performance

Since the company's initial public offering, investors have been rewarded for investing in Petro Canada. The best 12-month rate of return was a gain of 84.4 per cent, and the average 12-month rate of return was 19.1 per cent. The common stock has frequently outperformed after 12 months and performed very well in 1994.

Stock risks

Petero Canada stock recently incurred a major setback during the bear of 1998, declining by 47.8 per cent. The worst 12-month rate of return for the common stock was a loss of 36.9 per cent, and the stock has posted negative rates of return after 12 months 31 per cent of the time. During the bear of 1994, the stock declined in value by 16.5 per cent and took six months to recover the loss.

Stock financial fundamentals

Since 1993, Petro Canada's earnings per share have increased from $0.71 per share to $1.13 per share in 1997. The book value per share in 1997 was $13.41, up from $11.04 in 1993. Price-to-book (P/B) ratio increased from 0.96 in 1993 to 1.8 in 1997. The company's return on equity has increased, but asset turnover and leverage ratios declined.

Future prospects

Petro Canada's continued profitability in the future will be determined by senior management's ability to maintain or increase profit margin while improving operating efficiency (by increasing the asset turnover ratio). The company will be affected by a lower price for oil, but has a strong retail presence with 1,780 retail outlets, which sold more than 6 billion litres of gasoline in 1997. Petro Canada common stock investors will benefit from an increase in the price of oil, although it could remain low during the near future as supply exceeds demand. Investors may find this stock more attractive currently, considering the large setback during the market correction in August 1998.

COMPANY DETAILS

Company name	**Petro Canada**	Industry classification	Oil and gas
Recent price	$15.00	Market capitalization (in $ millions)	$4,065
Phone number for annual report	416-643-5500	Stock analysis start date	July 1991
Ticker symbol	PCA	Weight in TSE 35	1.9%
Number of mutual funds that hold this stock as a top 15 holding	56		

ROLLING 12-MONTH TOTAL RATE OF RETURN FOR THE STOCK OVER TIME*

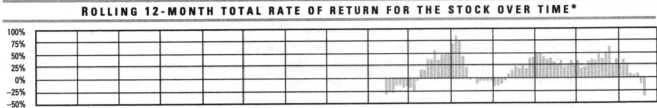

STOCK PERFORMANCE*

	1 month	1 year	3 years	5 years	10 years	15 years
Returns ending Aug 1998	–30.7%	–36.9%	5.0%	4.0%		
22.2%	22.2%	84.5%	33.7%	30.1%		
Average historical return	0.6%	19.1%	18.7%	19.3%		
Worst historical return	–30.7%	–36.9%	–2.8%	4.0%		

RETURNS GREATER THAN*

	1 month	1 year	3 years	5 years	10 years	15 years
10 per cent	12%	64%	80%	85%		
Zero	51%	69%	96%	100%		
Percentage of time stock lost $	49%	31%	4%	0%		
Number of periods evaluated	86	75	51	27		

DOWNSIDE RISK*

	Worst setback since start date	In bear 1987	In bear 1990	In bear 1994	In bear 1998
Setback for stock	–47.8%			–16.5%	–47.8%
Setback for TSE 35	–27.6%			–9.0%	–27.6%
Setback ended in	Aug 1998			Jan 1995	Aug 1998
Months to recover from loss	?			6	?

STOCK FINANCIAL FUNDAMENTAL INFORMATION

	1988	1989	1990	1991	1992	1993	1994	1995	1996	1997	Change
Average share price				$11.10	$8.93	$10.64	$12.43	$13.24	$17.65	$23.65	n/a
Earnings per share	$(0.42)	$0.08	$0.91	$(2.77)	$0.02	$0.71	$1.06	$0.71	$0.92	$1.13	n/a
Book value per share	$11.89	$11.81	$13.30	$11.55	$12.06	$11.04	$13.90	$12.53	$13.64	$13.41	1.2%
Price-to-earnings ratio				n/a	384.0	15.1	11.7	18.8	19.2	20.9	n/a
Price-to-book ratio				1.0	0.7	1.0	0.9	1.1	1.3	1.8	n/a
Profit margin	–1.7%	0.3%	3.0%	–12.1%	0.1%	3.8%	4.7%	3.6%	4.4%	5.4%	n/a
Asset turnover	0.72	0.75	0.81	0.82	0.86	0.81	0.78	0.74	0.72	0.73	0.1%
Leverage	2.9	2.9	2.8	2.4	2.1	2.1	2.1	2.1	2.1	2.1	–2.9%
Return on equity	–3.5%	0.7%	6.8%	–24.0%	0.2%	6.4%	7.6%	5.6%	6.7%	8.4%	n/a
Dividend per share											n/a
Dividend yield											n/a

*Source: The raw data used in developing this table was provided by Datastream.

PLACER DOME INCORPORATED

Company profile

Placer Dome Inc. is one of the world's largest gold mining companies. It also mines silver and copper in Canada, the United States, Australia, Latin America, and New Guinea. In 1997, the company had reserves of 31 million ounces of gold and produced 2.6 million ounces of gold. Currently, the company operates 14 mines, but this number will change as Placer Dome closes high-cost mines to reduce expenses and combat the weak price of gold.

In 1987, the amalgamation of Placer Development, Dome Mines, amd Campbell Red Lake Mines created Placer Dome. Dome Mines history can be traced back to 1910, when Dome Mines gained recognition for the discovery and development of Canada's first large gold mine. The company was established when a prospector "accidentally" stumbled on some gold at Porcupine Lake in Ontario. Placer Development was established in the 1930s when it began operations in New Guinea.

In 1997, the company earned revenues in excess of $US 1.2 billion and posted a net loss of $US 249 million while employing more than 8,400 people throughout the world. The company has introduced a hedging policy to support the selling price of gold, hedging one-third of its production until the year 2002 to provide upward potential and limit downside risk.

Stock performance

With a decline in the price of gold, Placer Dome common stock has fallen on hard times. Buy-and-hold investors are fortunate if they have made money on a gold stock in the past 10 years.

Placer Dome has displayed upside potential, however, with a positive 12-month rate of return of 129.9 per cent and an average 12-month rate of return of 10.4 per cent. Unfortunately, stock performance tends to be erratic and inconsistent. The stock posted positive rates of return after 12 months 53 per cent of the time.

Stock risks

Ouch! Inherently, gold and resource stocks are more risky because of the cyclical nature of the industry and the volatility of commodity prices. Placer Dome common stock has also displayed above-average downside risk. Investors in Placer Dome before the stock market correction of 1998 saw their investment decline in value by 68.1 per cent. Investors during the bear of 1994 were more fortunate; the stock declined by 24.8 per cent but regained its loss within six months.

Stock financial fundamentals

Senior management at Placer Dome have done a good job managing the company's assets given economic conditions within the gold industry, but investors haven't benefitted. With lower gold prices, the company's profit margins decreased, causing the company to lose money.

Future prospects

With bleak prospects for the price of gold, Placer Dome stock will not recover in the short term. However, commodity prices cannot remain at this level forever, and investors who can withstand above-average volatility could patiently invest in gold companies at historically low prices. In short, gold prices will remain unpredictable, but with gold at these prices it could be an attractive investment. However, investors could have made this argument in 1997 and then would have lost money in 1998.

COMPANY DETAILS

Company name	**Placer Dome Incorporated**	Industry classification	Gold and silver
Recent price	$12.45	Market capitalization (in $ millions)	$3,113
Phone number for annual report	416-813-4600	Stock analysis start date	July 1980
Ticker symbol	PDG	Weight in TSE 35	1.5%
Number of mutual funds that hold this stock as a top 15 holding	24		

ROLLING 12-MONTH TOTAL RATE OF RETURN FOR THE STOCK OVER TIME*

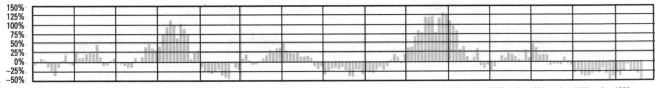

STOCK PERFORMANCE*

	1 month	1 year	3 years	5 years	10 years	15 years
Returns ending Aug 1998	−20.6%	−45.5%	−28.2%	−14.5%	−1.3%	0.5%
Best historical return	27.7%	129.9%	44.0%	35.0%	14.8%	12.0%
Average historical return	0.7%	10.4%	9.1%	9.4%	7.6%	8.1%
Worst historical return	−36.5%	−52.1%	−28.2%	−14.5%	−1.3%	0.5%

RETURNS GREATER THAN*

	1 month	1 year	3 years	5 years	10 years	15 years
10 per cent	17%	41%	44%	53%	32%	31%
Zero	51%	53%	64%	83%	97%	100%
Percentage of time stock lost $	49%	47%	36%	17%	3%	0%
Number of periods evaluated	218	207	183	159	99	39

DOWNSIDE RISK*

	Worst setback since start date	In bear 1987	In bear 1990	In bear 1994	In bear 1998
Setback for stock	−68.1%	−43.9%	−37.8%	−24.8%	−68.1%
Setback for TSE 35	−27.6%	−26.5%	−16.8%	−9.0%	−27.6%
Setback ended in	Aug 1998	Feb 1988	Jan 1991	Nov 1994	Aug 1998
Months to recover from loss	?	64	29	6	?

STOCK FINANCIAL FUNDAMENTAL INFORMATION

	1988	1989	1990	1991	1992	1993	1994	1995	1996	1997	Change
Average share price	$16.10	$17.63	$19.59	$14.84	$12.91	$24.10	$30.65	$33.05	$35.23	$23.83	4.0%
Earnings per share	$1.25	$0.55	$0.82	$(1.15)	$0.56	$0.58	$0.60	$0.43	$(0.37)	$(1.45)	n/a
Book value per share	$8.83	$8.23	$8.75	$7.03	$7.66	$8.40	$8.65	$8.65	$9.65	$9.79	1.0%
Price-to-earnings ratio	12.9	32.2	23.9	n/a	23.1	41.5	51.2	77.3	n/a	n/a	n/a
Price-to-book ratio	1.8	2.1	2.2	2.1	1.7	2.9	3.5	3.8	3.7	2.4	2.9%
Profit margin	28.5%	12.4%	16.3%	−23.1%	10.2%	10.7%	10.9%	6.9%	−5.3%	−19.7%	n/a
Asset turnover	0.35	0.36	0.38	0.46	0.50	0.44	0.43	0.43	0.42	0.47	2.8%
Leverage	1.4	1.5	1.5	1.5	1.4	1.5	1.5	1.7	1.7	1.6	1.3%
Return on equity	14.2%	6.7%	9.4%	−16.4%	7.3%	6.9%	6.9%	4.9%	−3.8%	−14.8%	n/a
Dividend per share	$0.24	$0.30	$0.30	$0.29	$0.32	$0.34	$0.36	$0.40	$0.40	$0.42	6.0%
Dividend yield	1.5%	1.7%	1.6%	2.0%	2.5%	1.4%	1.2%	1.2%	1.1%	1.8%	1.9%

*Source: The raw data used in developing this table was provided by Datastream.

RENAISSANCE ENERGY

Company profile

Renaissance Energy Ltd. is an oil and gas company with operations located primarily in Western Canada. The company is involved in the exploration for, and the development, production, and distribution of petroleum and natural gas in Western Canada. The company has been aggressively expanding operations in the 1990s and recently acquired Pinnacle Resources. Renaissance actively seeks potential acquisitions while exploring for oil and drilling new wells to expand its long-term prospects.

Unfortunately for Renaissance, the price of oil has been at a 10-year low, and a recovery will not likely occur soon. Fluctuations in the price of oil reflect the imbalance in supply and demand for oil in North America. However, the prospects for natural gas prices are better. With the expansion of pipelines, natural gas will be available to more consumers, and demand should increase.

In 1997, Renaissance Energy Ltd. drilled 1,645 wells in search of oil and gas. In turn, the company generated $948 million in sales and reported net income of $115 million. The company employed over 700 employees and has over $3.5 billion in assets.

Stock performance

Investors in Renaissance Energy Ltd. after December 1996 have not experienced the upside potential that Renaissance common stock displayed in the early to mid-1990s. The best 12-month return posted by the common stock was 234.2 per cent, and the average 12-month return was 32.0 per cent. The common stock posted positive rates of return after 12 months 72 per cent of the time.

Stock risks

The worst 12-month rate of return for the common stock was a loss of 52.2 per cent, and the common stock posted negative rates of return after 12 months 28 per cent of the time. Renaissance Energy Ltd. common stock has underperformed during the last 18 months. Investors prior to the stock-market correction of 1998 saw their investment decline in value by 64.3 per cent. During the bear market of 1994, the stock declined by 26.8 per cent and took 11 months to recover.

Stock financial fundamentals

The company's earnings per share have increased by an average of 21.5 per cent per year for the past 10 years, from $0.14 per share in 1988 to $0.98 per share in 1997. However, earnings per share have declined from a high in 1996 of $1.61 per share. The company's growth can be attributed to the growth in sales and assets. The company continues to reinvest all earnings while increasing long-term debt to finance this growth. The company has increased return on equity during the previous 10 years by increasing profit margins. The benefits of high profit margins were offset by the company's lower asset-turnover ratio, which declined during the past 10 years.

Future prospects

The company should continue to earn profits, but declines in the price of oil are putting downward pressure on its profit potential. Investors looking for a pure Western Canadian oil and gas asset could consider Renaissance Energy Ltd. However, without a rally in the price of oil, investors may have to wait for a turnaround in the industry. Considering the loss posted by the stock during 1998, the stock has to generate a big turnaround. If this turnaround comes to fruition in the near term, investors willl earn above average rates of return.

COMPANY DETAILS

Company name	**Renaissance Energy**	Industry classification	Oil and gas
Recent price	$17.10	Market capitalization (in $ millions)	$1,987
Phone number for annual report	800-558-0046	Stock analysis start date	Nov 1983
Ticker symbol	RES	Weight in TSE 35	1.5%
Number of mutual funds that hold this stock as a top 15 holding	17		

ROLLING 12-MONTH TOTAL RATE OF RETURN FOR THE STOCK OVER TIME*

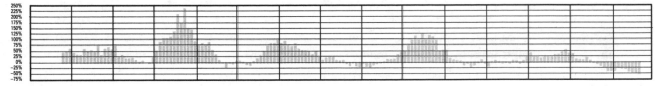

Jan 1984 Jan 1985 Jan 1986 Jan 1987 Jan 1988 Jan 1989 Jan 1990 Jan 1991 Jan 1992 Jan 1993 Jan 1994 Jan 1995 Jan 1996 Jan 1997 Jan 1998

STOCK PERFORMANCE*

	1 month	1 year	3 years	5 years	10 years	15 years
Returns ending Aug 1998	−11.4%	−52.2%	−16.5%	−12.8%	9.9%	
Best historical return	27.2%	234.2%	70.2%	55.6%	40.5%	
Average historical return	1.9%	32.0%	29.3%	28.5%	27.8%	
Worst historical return	−21.3%	−52.2%	−16.5%	−12.8%	9.9%	

RETURNS GREATER THAN*

	1 month	1 year	3 years	5 years	10 years	15 years
10 per cent	17%	59%	84%	92%	98%	
Zero	53%	72%	96%	96%	100%	
Percentage of time stock lost $	47%	28%	4%	4%	0%	
Number of periods evaluated	178	167	143	119	59	

DOWNSIDE RISK*

	Worst setback since start date	In bear 1987	In bear 1990	In bear 1994	In bear 1998
Setback for stock	−64.3%	−22.8%	−14.6%	−26.8%	−64.3%
Setback for TSE 35	−27.6%	−26.5%	−16.8%	−9.0%	−27.6%
Setback ended in	Aug 1998	Nov 1987	Jan 1991	Jan 1995	Aug 1998
Months to recover from loss	?	4	21	11	?

STOCK FINANCIAL FUNDAMENTAL INFORMATION

	1988	1989	1990	1991	1992	1993	1994	1995	1996	1997	Change
Average share price	$6.96	$9.05	$14.29	$14.90	$15.08	$28.22	$29.22	$29.18	$38.43	$37.90	18.5%
Earnings per share	$0.14	$0.31	$0.38	$0.32	$0.35	$0.60	$0.70	$0.66	$1.61	$0.98	21.5%
Book value per share	$3.60	$3.48	$3.83	$4.74	$6.31	$8.74	$11.66	$15.18	$17.61	$17.90	17.4%
Price-to-earnings ratio	49.7	29.2	37.6	46.6	43.1	47.0	41.7	44.2	23.9	38.7	−2.5%
Price-to-book ratio	1.9	2.6	3.7	3.1	2.4	3.2	2.5	1.9	2.2	2.1	0.9%
Profit margin	8.1%	13.7%	12.8%	10.2%	9.4%	12.8%	12.1%	10.4%	18.9%	12.1%	4.1%
Asset turnover	0.30	0.40	0.44	0.37	0.35	0.36	0.32	0.27	0.34	0.28	−0.8%
Leverage	1.6	1.6	1.8	1.8	1.7	1.5	1.6	1.5	1.4	1.6	0.2%
Return on equity	3.9%	8.9%	9.9%	6.8%	5.5%	6.9%	6.0%	4.3%	9.1%	5.5%	3.5%
Dividend per share	$—	$—	$—	$—	$—	$—	$—	$—	$—	$—	n/a
Dividend yield	0.0%	0.0%	0.0%	0.0%	0.0%	0.0%	0.0%	0.0%	0.0%	0.0%	n/a

*Source: The raw data used in developing this table was provided by Datastream.

ROYAL BANK OF CANADA

Company profile

The Royal Bank of Canada is a major Canadian chartered bank that operates 1,400 branches in all provinces and territories of Canada and through 105 offices in 36 other countries. The company was founded in 1864 in Halifax to handle trade and commerce in the area. Today, the bank offers a full range of commercial, corporate, international, investment, and retail banking products and services and provides brokerage, underwriting, and investment management services through wholly owned subsidiary RBC Dominion Securities and Canada's second-largest discount brokerage, Royal Bank Action Direct. Trust services including pension and investment management are offered by wholly owned subsidiary Royal Trust. The Royal Bank of Canada also offers creditor life and disability insurance and individual life and travel insurance. The Royal Bank of Canada recently agreed to merge with the Bank of Montreal to increase their global presence in the industry.

In 1997 the Royal Bank of Canada generated gross revenues of $9.3 billion and had profits over $1.6 billion. The company employed over 58,000 people and has over 4,200 bank machines in Canada.

Stock performance

The Royal Bank has its own line of Royal Bank mutual funds, but the common stock proved to be a better investment (not adjusted for risk). The best 12-month rate of return was a gain of 104.6 per cent, and the average 12-month rate of return was 19.1 per cent. The common stock posted a positive rate of return after 12 months 75 per cent of the time. The value of the common stock increased significantly in 1997.

Stock risks

This stock has experienced above-average downside risk. Investors in Royal Bank prior to the market correction in 1998 saw their investment decline by 33.2 per cent. This stock has tended to underperform during bear markets. In 1990 the stock declined 17.1 per cent, but took only four months to recover its loss.

Stock financial fundamentals

With the increased growth in Royal Bank of Canada's earnings, the stock multiples have expanded during the last 10 years. The price-to-earnings (P/E) ratio has increased by 6.8 per cent annually from 6.0 to 11.6, which means that, in 1988, investors paid $6 for $1 of historical earnings while, in 1997, investors paid $11.40 for every $1 of historical earnings. These stock levels can be justified if the bank continues to increase earnings and growth. However, a small decline in earnings could have a significant impact on the price of the underlying stock.

Future prospects

If the Royal Bank succeeds in merging with the Bank of Montreal, they will become Canada's largest bank by far. Largest bank or not, the bank's profits are closely tied with the direction and level of interest rates in addition to capital market activity. In the future, bank stocks could decline significantly with a little bad news. However, banks have historically added a lot of value for shareholders over the long term. The worst 15-year rate of return posted by the Royal Bank of Canada stock was 10.9 per cent compounded annually. Considering that the stock has declined during 1998, investors who patiently acquire stock at attractive prices will benefit over the long term.

COMPANY DETAILS

Company name	**Royal Bank of Canada**	Industry classification	Financial services
Recent price	$59.15	Market capitalization (in $ millions)	$18,238
Phone number for annual report	514-982-7555	Stock analysis start date	July 1980
Ticker symbol	RY	Weight in TSE 35	5.2%
Number of mutual funds that hold this stock as a top 15 holding	280		

ROLLING 12-MONTH TOTAL RATE OF RETURN FOR THE STOCK OVER TIME*

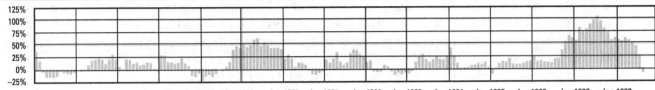

STOCK PERFORMANCE*

	1 month	1 year	3 years	5 years	10 years	15 years
Returns ending Aug 1998	−27.9%	−7.3%	29.4%	20.1%	18.4%	15.0%
Best historical return	17.8%	104.6%	47.8%	31.9%	25.2%	19.6%
Average historical return	1.3%	19.1%	15.7%	14.5%	14.7%	15.1%
Worst historical return	−27.9%	−26.1%	1.9%	1.7%	10.7%	10.9%

RETURNS GREATER THAN*

	1 month	1 year	3 years	5 years	10 years	15 years
10 per cent	8%	60%	68%	74%	100%	100%
Zero	58%	75%	100%	100%	100%	100%
Percentage of time stock lost $	42%	25%	0%	0%	0%	0%
Number of periods evaluated	218	207	183	159	99	39

DOWNSIDE RISK*

	Worst setback since start date	In bear 1987	In bear 1990	In bear 1994	In bear 1998
Setback for stock	−33.7%	−23.9%	−17.1%	−14.1%	−33.2%
Setback for TSE 35	−41.0%	−26.5%	−16.8%	−9.0%	−27.6%
Setback ended in	June 1982	Nov 1987	Sept 1990	June 1994	Aug 1998
Months to recover from loss	6	10	4	11	?

STOCK FINANCIAL FUNDAMENTAL INFORMATION

	1988	1989	1990	1991	1992	1993	1994	1995	1996	1997	Change
Average share price	$15.72	$21.96	$22.48	$25.75	$24.56	$26.75	$28.30	$29.70	$36.25	$63.20	14.9%
Earnings per share	$2.52	$1.64	$3.00	$2.92	$(0.05)	$0.46	$3.19	$3.49	$4.09	$5.01	7.1%
Book value per share	$16.48	$16.37	$18.32	$20.24	$18.48	$18.63	$20.15	$22.38	$24.37	$27.85	5.4%
Price-to-earnings ratio	6.2	13.4	7.5	8.8	n/a	58.2	8.9	8.5	8.9	12.6	7.3%
Price-to-book ratio	1.0	1.3	1.2	1.3	1.3	1.4	1.4	1.3	1.5	2.3	9.1%
Profit margin	6.0%	3.5%	6.2%	6.2%	−0.1%	1.2%	7.2%	7.0%	7.8%	8.8%	4.0%
Asset turnover	0.10	0.12	0.11	0.11	0.09	0.07	0.08	0.08	0.07	0.07	−2.9%
Leverage	26.6	24.8	23.7	21.7	23.4	27.9	27.4	27.8	30.2	28.4	0.7%
Return on equity	15.3%	10.0%	16.4%	14.4%	−0.3%	2.5%	15.8%	15.6%	16.8%	18.0%	1.6%
Dividend per share	$1.04	$1.10	$1.16	$1.16	$1.16	$1.16	$1.16	$1.18	$1.33	$1.52	3.9%
Dividend yield	6.6%	5.0%	5.2%	4.5%	4.7%	4.3%	4.1%	4.0%	3.7%	2.4%	−9.6%

*Source: The raw data used in developing this table was provided by Datastream.

SEAGRAM COMPANY LIMITED

Company profile

The Seagram Company Ltd. has a very colourful history in Canada. It is a world leader in the production and marketing of whiskeys, rums, gins, brandies, vodkas, liqueurs, wines, beers, wine and spirit coolers, and mixers. Its brands include Crown Royal, Seagram's VO, Chivas Regal, Captain Morgan, and Barton and Guestier. Seagram has operations in over 40 countries and sells its products in more than 150 countries. The Seagram distillery was founded by Sam Bronfman, who took advantage of prohibition in the US by selling Canadian whiskey to distributors, who shipped it over the border.

Seagram has an 80 per cent interest in Universal Studios Inc., which produces and distributes entertainment products and operates retail stores and theme parks. Universal recently acquired PolyGram, a music company which produces such shows as *Hercules*, *Xena*, and Jim Carey's *Liar Liar*. Seagram still has a small interest in the du Pont Company, a chemical producer, and Time Warner, a large US entertainment and media company, and a 40 per cent interest in Cineplex Odeon Corporation, a chain of movie theatres.

In 1997, the company reported sales of over $US 12.5 billion and reported a profit of $US 502 million. It employs more than 31,000 people worldwide. Seagram recently sold Tropicana Beverage Group to Pepsi Co.

Stock performance

Over the past 10 years, this company's stock has appreciated but has delivered mixed results during the last five years. The best 12-month rate of return for the common stock was a positive gain of 102.0 per cent, and the average 12-month rate of return was 18.5 per cent. The common stock posted positive rates of return 82 per cent of the time.

Stock risks

The worst 12-month rate of return for the common stock was a loss of 34.5 per cent. The stock has displayed downside risk but less than other blue-chip companies. The stock declined by 22.7 per cent during the bear of 1998, less than the average stock.

Stock financial fundamentals

The company's earnings have remained unchanged during the past 10 years. Earnings per share declined 0.9 per cent per year from $1.70 in 1988 to $1.86 per share in 1997. The company's return on equity has declined during the past 10 years from 11.98 per cent to 5.18 per cent because of a major decline in profit margins, which could not be offset by an increase in leverage and asset turnover ratios.

Future prospects

During a recession, consumers still drink alcohol. Thus a portion of Seagram's business is more recession-proof than other cyclical businesses. Senior management of Seagram has acquired and sold several businesses throughout the company's history in an attempt to diversify the company. Future growth will depend on the performance of Seagram's new business, and the distilling business will continue to provide cash flow. Currently, many investors are taking a wait-and-see approach to Seagram. If Seagram proves that it can successfully integrate Universal Studios into the Seagram family, the stock price will likely appreciate. Conservative investors who want to invest in a stock directly could consider this one.

COMPANY DETAILS

Company name	**Seagram Company Limited**	Industry classification	Consumer products
Recent price	$49.00	Market capitalization (in $ millions)	$17,899
Phone number for annual report	416-643-5500	Stock analysis start date	July 1980
Ticker symbol	VO	Weight in TSE 35	4.3%
Number of mutual funds that hold this stock as a top 15 holding	53		

ROLLING 12-MONTH TOTAL RATE OF RETURN FOR THE STOCK OVER TIME*

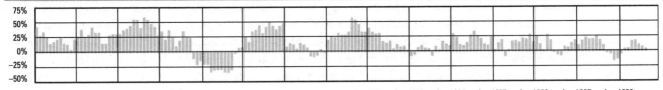

Jan 1984   Jan 1985   Jan 1986   Jan 1987   Jan 1988   Jan 1989   Jan 1990   Jan 1991   Jan 1992   Jan 1993   Jan 1994   Jan 1995   Jan 1996   Jan 1997   Jan 1998

STOCK PERFORMANCE*

	1 month	1 year	3 years	5 years	10 years	15 years
Returns ending Aug 1998	−10.5%	2.9%	1.5%	8.5%	13.6%	13.1%
Best historical return	19.1%	102.0%	47.4%	43.0%	24.7%	19.7%
Average historical return	1.4%	18.5%	17.8%	16.9%	15.8%	17.3%
Worst historical return	−22.9%	−34.5%	−3.4%	7.7%	8.6%	13.1%

RETURNS GREATER THAN*

	1 month	1 year	3 years	5 years	10 years	15 years
10 per cent	10%	63%	73%	87%	94%	100%
Zero	58%	82%	97%	100%	100%	100%
Percentage of time stock lost $	42%	18%	3%	0%	0%	0%
Number of periods evaluated	218	207	183	159	99	39

DOWNSIDE RISK*

	Worst setback since start date	In bear 1987	In bear 1990	In bear 1994	In bear 1998
Setback for stock	−37.9%	−34.1%	−18.2%	−9.7%	−22.7%
Setback for TSE 35	−15.2%	−26.5%	−16.8%	−9.0%	−27.6%
Setback ended in	Mar 1988	Nov 1987	Sept 1990	Nov 1994	Aug 1998
Months to recover from loss	21	25	5	4	?

STOCK FINANCIAL FUNDAMENTAL INFORMATION

	1988	1989	1990	1991	1992	1993	1994	1995	1996	1997	Change
Average share price	$17.06	$22.53	$23.47	$29.58	$34.28	$34.81	$40.57	$45.01	$48.08	$51.60	11.7%
Earnings per share	$1.70	$1.82	$2.15	$2.31	$2.28	$(3.07)	$1.39	$2.73	$0.63	$1.86	0.9%
Book value per share	$14.19	$15.12	$16.22	$17.72	$21.23	$17.21	$18.17	$19.86	$33.04	$35.99	9.8%
Price-to-earnings ratio	10.0	12.4	10.9	12.8	15.0	n/a	29.2	16.5	76.3	27.7	10.7%
Price-to-book ratio	1.2	1.5	1.4	1.7	1.6	2.0	2.2	2.3	1.5	1.4	1.8%
Profit margin	13.7%	11.6%	12.7%	12.3%	11.5%	−14.8%	6.3%	11.5%	1.8%	4.0%	−11.6%
Asset turnover	0.52	0.53	0.55	0.55	0.51	0.59	0.52	0.51	0.47	0.58	1.2%
Leverage	1.7	1.9	1.9	1.9	1.8	2.0	2.3	2.4	2.3	2.2	2.8%
Return on equity	12.0%	12.0%	13.3%	13.0%	10.8%	−17.8%	7.6%	13.8%	1.9%	5.2%	−8.0%
Dividend per share	$0.32	$0.34	$0.41	$0.52	$0.62	$0.72	$0.76	$0.78	$0.80	$0.91	11.0%
Dividend yield	1.9%	1.5%	1.7%	1.8%	1.8%	2.1%	1.9%	1.7%	1.7%	1.8%	−0.6%

*Source: The raw data used in developing this table was provided by Datastream.

SUNCOR ENERGY INCORPORATED

Company profile

Suncor is a world leader in drilling for and extracting crude oil from the oil sands deposits of northern Canada. The company also explores for, develops, and markets conventional crude oil and natural gas in Western Canada and markets its products under the Sunoco brand name in Central Canada. Sunoco refines crude oil and manufactures, distributes, and markets transportation fuels, petrochemicals, and heating oils. In 1997, Sunoco began marketing natural gas directly to Ontario home owners. In Queensland, Australia, Suncor and partners are on schedule to begin commissioning a demonstration shale-oil production plant early in 1999.

The company, which began operations by selling lubricating oils, kerosene, and spirits to Canadian war plants in 1917, has grown into a major Canadian energy company. It has assets of $3.5 billion and produces 119,700 barrels of oil equivalent per day

In 1997 Suncor generated sales of more than $2.1 billion and posted net earnings of $223 million. The company operates the Sunoco network of more than 500 retail gasoline outlets throughout Ontario, and received a pollution-prevention award from the Ontario Ministry of Environment and Energy for eliminating leaks from underground storage tanks.

Stock performance

The best 12-month rate of return for Suncor common stock was a positive 111.2 per cent, and the average 12-month rate of return was 37.2 per cent. The stock has performed extremely well considering the economic conditions affecting resource stocks, such as low oil prices. The common stock performed well in 1996 and 1997.

Stock risks

The worst 12-month rate of return for the stock was a loss of 4.5 per cent. During the market correction of 1994, the stock declined in value by 8.1 per cent and took seven months to recover. During the market correction of 1998, the stock declined in value by 15.5 per cent, outperforming the average stock.

Stock financial fundamentals

This company has made big improvements over the past six years. Earnings per share increased to $2.04 in 1997 from a loss in 1992 of $2.10. In 1997 Suncor Energy's return on equity was 15.92 per cent. This increase can be attributed to an increase in profit margins and in the company's debt.

Future prospects

Investors will not be disappointed if Suncor Energy continues to increase its profit margins and sales. If this scenario comes to fruition, the company's profitability will increase and its share price should appreciate as well. However, competing in the oil and gas business is not an easy task, and Suncor has already accomplished impressive gains. Investors who acquire Suncor Energy common stock at a reasonable price should not be disappointed. Investors who are looking for a conservative investment in the oil and gas industry could consider Suncor Energy. Although the company is not immune to conditions that plague the industry historically, its stock has fared better than the stock of other resource companies.

COMPANY DETAILS

Company name	**Suncor Energy Incorporated**	Industry classification	Oil and gas
Recent price	$43.85	Market capitalization (in $ millions)	$4,819
Phone number for annual report	1-800-558-9071	Stock analysis start date	April 1993
Ticker symbol	SU	Weight in TSE 35	0.3%
Number of mutual funds that hold this stock as a top 15 holding	83		

ROLLING 12-MONTH TOTAL RATE OF RETURN FOR THE STOCK OVER TIME*

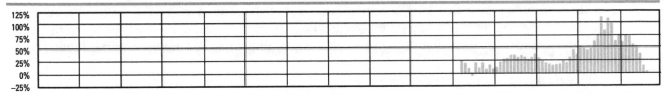

Jan 1984	Jan 1985	Jan 1986	Jan 1987	Jan 1988	Jan 1989	Jan 1990	Jan 1991	Jan 1992	Jan 1993	Jan 1994	Jan 1995	Jan 1996	Jan 1997	Jan 1998

STOCK PERFORMANCE*

	1 month	1 year	3 years	5 years	10 years	15 years
Returns ending Aug 1998	−14.1%	2.1%	32.6%	27.8%		
Best historical return	23.4%	111.2%	48.8%	36.2%		
Average historical return	2.3%	37.2%	34.6%	32.2%		
Worst historical return	−15.4%	−4.5%	14.3%	27.8%		

RETURNS GREATER THAN*

	1 month	1 year	3 years	5 years	10 years	15 years
10 per cent	8%	89%	100%	100%		
Zero	66%	98%	100%	100%		
Percentage of time stock lost $	34%	2%	0%	0%		
Number of periods evaluated	65	54	30	6		

DOWNSIDE RISK*

	Worst setback since start date	In bear 1987	In bear 1990	In bear 1994	In bear 1998
Setback for stock	−15.5%			−8.1%	−15.5%
Setback for TSE 35	−27.6%			−9.0%	−27.6%
Setback ended in	Aug 1998			Feb 1994	Aug 1998
Months to recover from loss	?			7	?

STOCK FINANCIAL FUNDAMENTAL INFORMATION

	1988	1989	1990	1991	1992	1993	1994	1995	1996	1997	Change
Average share price						$14.43	$15.48	$19.20	$23.18	$39.33	n/a
Earnings per share					$(2.10)	$0.69	$1.11	$1.38	$1.71	$2.04	n/a
Book value per share					$8.75	$8.92	$9.49	$10.30	$11.40	$12.82	n/a
Price-to-earnings ratio						20.9	13.9	13.9	13.6	19.3	n/a
Price-to-book ratio						1.6	1.6	1.9	2.0	3.1	n/a
Profit margin					−14.6%	4.8%	7.4%	7.9%	8.9%	10.4%	n/a
Asset turnover					0.79	0.77	0.74	0.78	0.74	0.62	n/a
Leverage					2.1	2.1	2.1	2.2	2.3	2.5	n/a
Return on equity					−23.9%	7.7%	11.7%	13.4%	15.0%	15.9%	n/a
Dividend per share					$0.52	$0.52	$0.53	$0.57	$0.64	$0.68	n/a
Dividend yield						3.6%	3.4%	3.0%	2.8%	1.7%	n/a

*Source: The raw data used in developing this table was provided by Datastream.

TALISMAN ENERGY INCORPORATED

Company profile

Talisman Energy Inc. is a Canadian energy company whose core business is oil and gas. Talisman business operations include exploration for and development, production, and marketing of crude oil, natural gas, and natural gas liquids. Talisman has production operations in Canada, the North Sea, and Indonesia and active interests in a number of high-potential exploration areas, including Algeria, Trinidad, and Peru.

In 1997, the company generated revenue in excess of $1.4 billion and a profit of $77 million. The company has its head office in Calgary, Alberta, and employs 1,000 people worldwide. Talisman has more than $5 billion in assets. In 1997, Talisman acquired Pembina Resources Limited for a cost of $605 million.

Stock performance

The stock has been either up or down but neither consistently, although the common stock's performance is above-average for a resource stock, and long-term investors have made money. The best 12-month rate of return for the stock was a positive gain of 170.0 per cent, and the average 12-month rate of return was 14.5 per cent. The stock outperformed significantly in 1993 and in 1997.

Stock risks

The stock underperforms during bear markets. The worst 12-month rate of return posted by the stock was a decline of 49.2 per cent, and the stock posted negative rates of return after 12 months 42 per cent of the time. Investors in Talisman Energy prior to the market correction in 1987 saw their investment decline in value by 34.9 per cent, and the stock took 68 months to recover. Investors prior to the stock market corrections of 1990 and 1994 fared better. Their investments declined by 41.9 per cent and 34.5 per cent respectively, and the stock recovered within 28 months and 20 months respectively.

Stock financial fundaments

During the past several years, there have been improvements in Talisman's financial statements. Earnings per share increased from $0.43 per share in 1993 to $0.70 per share in 1997. However, the company's profit margin has declined from 7.8 per cent in 1993 to 5.4 per cent in 1997. The company also increased its leverage by increasing long-term debt. It stopped paying a dividend in 1992, and investors should not expect a dividend in the near term as Talisman weathers this difficult environment.

Future prospects

Talisman has continued to generate cash flow to sustain operations while increasing oil and gas reserves to maintain and expand the business. However, if future growth in earnings and cash flow does not occur, investors could experience new levels of downside risk. With a soft oil price and weak demand for crude, Talisman will have a difficult time continuing to improve performance. However, with recent acquisitions and improved profit margins investors who acquire Talisman common stock at a reasonable price could earn above-average returns if and when oil prices recover. An investment in Talisman Energy should be made only in the context of a well-diversified portfolio, and investors should expect above-average volatility in the future. On the other hand, with above-average risk there is potential for above-average returns, although these have not come to fruition for several years.

COMPANY DETAILS

Company name	**Talisman Energy Incorporated**	Industry classification	Oil and gas
Recent price	$23.10	Market capitalization (in $ millions)	$2,532
Phone number for annual report	1-800-564-6253	Stock analysis start date	April 1983
Ticker symbol	TLM	Weight in TSE 35	2.4%
Number of mutual funds that hold this stock as a top 15 holding	56		

ROLLING 12-MONTH TOTAL RATE OF RETURN FOR THE STOCK OVER TIME*

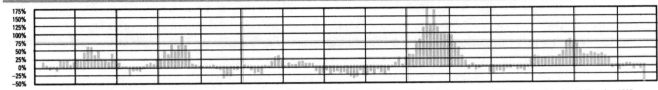

Jan 1984 Jan 1985 Jan 1986 Jan 1987 Jan 1988 Jan 1989 Jan 1990 Jan 1991 Jan 1992 Jan 1993 Jan 1994 Jan 1995 Jan 1996 Jan 1997 Jan 1998

STOCK PERFORMANCE*

	1 month	1 year	3 years	5 years	10 years	15 years
Returns ending Aug 1998	−39.6%	−49.2%	−4.2%	−7.6%	2.8%	5.5%
Best historical return	28.6%	170.0%	34.8%	32.7%	12.7%	10.9%
Average historical return	0.9%	14.5%	10.2%	9.0%	8.5%	8.9%
Worst historical return	−39.6%	−49.2%	−13.8%	−14.0%	2.8%	5.5%

RETURNS GREATER THAN*

	1 month	1 year	3 years	5 years	10 years	15 years
10 per cent	13%	44%	54%	44%	27%	33%
Zero	55%	58%	75%	83%	100%	100%
Percentage of time stock lost $	45%	42%	25%	17%	0%	0%
Number of periods evaluated	185	174	150	126	66	6

DOWNSIDE RISK*

	Worst setback since start date	In bear 1987	In bear 1990	In bear 1994	In bear 1998
Setback for stock	−57.3%	−34.9%	−41.9%	−34.5%	−54.4%
Setback for TSE 35	−4.4%	−26.5%	−16.8%	−9.0%	−27.6%
Setback ended in	June 1992	Oct 1987	Feb 1991	Jan 1995	Aug 1998
Months to recover from loss	12	68	28	20	?

STOCK FINANCIAL FUNDAMENTAL INFORMATION

	1988	1989	1990	1991	1992	1993	1994	1995	1996	1997	Change
Average share price	$18.55	$18.40	$18.80	$14.46	$13.06	$25.38	$29.05	$25.72	$34.86	$45.05	9.3%
Earnings per share						$0.43	$0.82	$0.42	$0.91	$0.70	n/a
Book value per share						$10.24	$20.25	$16.87	$20.08	$19.85	n/a
Price-to-earnings ratio						59.0	35.4	61.2	38.3	64.4	n/a
Price-to-book ratio						2.5	1.4	1.5	1.7	2.3	n/a
Profit margin						7.8%	10.4%	4.5%	7.8%	5.4%	n/a
Asset turnover						0.31	0.19	0.29	0.32	0.28	n/a
Leverage						1.8	2.1	1.9	1.8	2.3	n/a
Return on equity						4.2%	4.0%	2.5%	4.5%	3.5%	n/a
Dividend per share						$—	$—	$—	$—	$—	n/a
Dividend yield						0.0%	0.0%	0.0%	0.0%	0.0%	n/a

*Source: The raw data used in developing this table was provided by Datastream.

TECK CORPORATION, B

Company profile

Teck Corporation is a mine development and mine operating company based in Vancouver, British Columbia. Teck produces metallurgical coal, silver, gold, copper, zinc, lead, molybdenum, and niobium. The company operates eleven mines, nine in Canada, one in Chile and one in Australia. Teck's exploration interests include projects in such countries as Indonesia, Peru, and Bolivia, among others. It has interests in other companies including Cominco Ltd., a world leader in zinc and lead and a producer of copper.

In 1997, Teck was plagued by a decline in the price of gold, which affected its financial performance. However, the company did participate in two mineral discoveries: the Pogo gold deposit in Alaska and the San Icolar copper, zinc, and silver deposit in Mexico. The company has joined forces with Sumitomo Group to develop the Pogo gold deposit. In 1997, Teck generated $720 million in revenue, but posted a loss of $176 million because of writedowns on assets that have depreciated in value after a decline in the price of gold.

Stock performance

Investors in Teck have been lucky to break even. However, there have been periods of upside potential, which could occur again. The best 12-month rate of return for the common stock was 142.1 per cent, and the average 12-month rate of return was 11.5 per cent. Thus, really long-term investors have made money, but they have not been compensated for the above-average risk.

Stock risks

Inherently, gold and other resource stocks have been risky. These stocks have tended to underperform consistently, although occasionally they make exceptional gains. Investors who participate in these gains will benefit financially. Playing the gold game can lead to a windfall; it can also lead to a downfall. In short, investing in gold is highly speculative and risky. The worst 12-month rate of return for Teck Corporation was a loss of 69.3 per cent. Investors prior to the bear of 1998 saw their investment decline in value by 71.9 per cent. The stock has had a similar setback in the past, including a decline of 73.9 per cent in June 1982, and it took 45 months to recover from the loss by posting a cumulative gain of 200 per cent. Investors should note that the stock-specific risk associated with investing in gold stocks can be diversified away.

Stock financial fundamentals

This company has had a difficult journey during the past 10 years, and the balance sheet and income statement reflect this fact. Earnings per share have declined from $1.40 in 1988 to a loss of $1.81 in 1997. In turn, the leverage of the company has increased, and the firm's profit margin and asset turnover ratio have all decreased. This financial situation has come to fruition because the selling price for gold has fallen to a 15-year low.

Future prospects

Buy-and-hold investors who invested in gold during the past 10 years have been disappointed. Speculative investors who believe a recovery in the price of gold is inevitable will benefit in buying low and selling high. Based on historical financial statements, senior management at Teck Corporation have the ability to do good things. In the past, the stock price has appreciated quickly—the best one-month rate of return was a gain of 40.6 per cent—but, as many investors are aware, these potential gains come with above-average risk.

COMPANY DETAILS

Company name	**Teck Corporation, B**	Industry classification	Gold and silver
Recent price	$9.25	Market capitalization (in $ millions)	$853
Phone number for annual report	1-800-387-0825	Stock analysis start date	July 1980
Ticker symbol	TEK.B	Weight in TSE 35	0.5%
Number of mutual funds that hold this stock as a top 15 holding	12		

ROLLING 12-MONTH TOTAL RATE OF RETURN FOR THE STOCK OVER TIME*

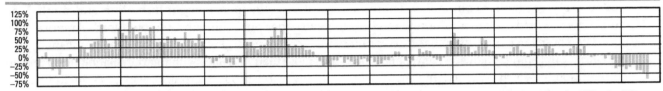

STOCK PERFORMANCE*

	1 month	1 year	3 years	5 years	10 years	15 years
Returns ending Aug 1998	−33.9%	−64.0%	−28.8%	−13.2%	−4.0%	2.9%
Best historical return	40.6%	142.1%	69.9%	43.3%	23.0%	17.9%
Average historical return	0.7%	11.5%	12.2%	13.2%	12.3%	11.0%
Worst historical return	−33.9%	−69.3%	−28.8%	−13.2%	−4.0%	2.9%

RETURNS GREATER THAN*

	1 month	1 year	3 years	5 years	10 years	15 years
10 per cent	15%	49%	55%	45%	72%	51%
Zero	50%	59%	72%	91%	98%	100%
Percentage of time stock lost $	50%	41%	28%	9%	2%	0%
Number of periods evaluated	218	207	183	159	99	39

DOWNSIDE RISK*

	Worst setback since start date	In bear 1987	In bear 1990	In bear 1994	In bear 1998
Setback for stock	−73.9%	−25.1%	−29.1%	−14.8%	−71.9%
Setback for TSE 35	−41.0%	−26.5%	−16.8%	−9.0%	−27.6%
Setback ended in	June 1982	Jan 1988	Jan 1991	July 1994	Aug 1998
Months to recover from loss	45	12	52	10	?

STOCK FINANCIAL FUNDAMENTAL INFORMATION

	1988	1989	1990	1991	1992	1993	1994	1995	1996	1997	Change
Average share price	$15.48	$21.67	$24.00	$20.84	$19.05	$19.33	$24.32	$25.56	$28.90	$27.72	6.0%
Earnings per share	$1.40	$1.39	$1.10	$0.45	$0.30	$0.35	$0.77	$0.97	$2.65	$(1.81)	n/a
Book value per share	$7.41	$8.39	$8.60	$10.07	$9.88	$11.71	$11.51	$13.95	$15.91	$13.85	6.5%
Price-to-earnings ratio	11.1	15.6	21.8	46.3	63.5	55.2	31.6	26.4	10.9	n/a	n/a
Price-to-book ratio	2.1	2.6	2.8	2.1	1.9	1.7	2.1	1.8	1.8	2.0	−0.4%
Profit margin	31.8%	27.3%	19.1%	9.3%	6.8%	5.9%	12.5%	12.5%	34.8%	−24.4%	n/a
Asset turnover	0.34	0.41	0.41	0.34	0.27	0.33	0.31	0.36	0.28	0.31	−1.1%
Leverage	1.7	1.5	1.6	1.4	1.6	1.5	1.7	1.5	1.7	1.8	0.1%
Return on equity	18.9%	16.6%	12.8%	4.5%	3.0%	3.0%	6.7%	7.0%	16.7%	−13.1%	n/a
Dividend per share	$0.14	$0.18	$0.20	$0.20	$0.20	$0.20	$0.20	$0.20	$0.20	$0.20	3.6%
Dividend yield	0.9%	0.8%	0.8%	1.0%	1.0%	1.0%	0.8%	0.8%	0.7%	0.7%	−2.2%

*Source: The raw data used in developing this table was provided by Datastream.

THOMSON CORPORATION

Company profile

The Thomson Corporation, one of the world's largest information and publishing businesses, is made up of an array of smaller companies. Thomson has interests in specialized information and publishing businesses worldwide in addition to interests in newspaper publishing throughout North America.

The Thomson Corporation has three primary lines of business: newspapers, corporate publishing, and financial publishing. Thomson Newspapers publishes more than 70 dailies with total circulation of more than 1.8 million in North America. In Canada, the company publishes numerous newspapers, including *The Globe and Mail*, with an average circulation of 325,000. Thomson Corporation Publishing International publishes information targeted at major sectors such as professional and business education. The Thomson Financial and Professional Publishing Group provides information products and services to the financial community. In 1996, Thomson acquired West Publishing Company for $3.4 billion and integrated it with Thomson's existing US legal information companies. In addition, the company sold the Thomson Travel Group.

In 1997, the company generated sales of more than $8.7 billion and posted a profit of $550 million. The Thomson Corporation employs more than 48,000 employees, and 73 per cent of the company is still owned by the Thomson family.

Stock performance

The best 12-month rate of return for the common stock of the Thomson Corporation was a positive rate of return of 91.5 per cent, and the average 12-month rate of return for the common stock was 19.8 per cent. The stock has done well over the longer term, posting positive rates of return after 10 years 100 per cent of the time. 1997 was a particularly good year for the company and its investors.

Stock risks

The worst 12-month return posted by the common stock of the Thomson Corporation was a loss of 52.7 per cent. The stock has displayed periods of significant downside risk, but the stock has generally outperformed during stock-market corrections. During the bear of 1994, the stock declined in value by 13.3 per cent and recovered its loss within six months. During the bear of 1987, the stock declined by 37.3 per cent and took 15 months to recover.

Stock financial fundamentals

The company's financial statements have improved during the past 10 years, and the appreciation of the company's stock has reflected this information. The return on equity for the company has decreased during the past 10 years, attributable to a decline in profit margins.

Future prospects

The Thomson Corporation will have to continue finding and generating new sources of growth to maintain and increase the current stock price. The acquisition of West Publishing and the divestiture of the Thomson Travel Group should fuel growth, but this information is already embedded in the price of the stock. The stock has not fallen to the same extent as other stocks during the market correction of 1998. If Thomson repeats the success it has displayed during the past 15 years for the next 15 years, investors should not be disappointed.

COMPANY DETAILS

Company name	**Thomson Corporation**	Industry classification	Communications and media
Recent price	$33.05	Market capitalization (in $ millions)	$20,168
Phone number for annual report	1-800-663-9097	Stock analysis start date	July 1980
Ticker symbol	TOC	Weight in TSE 35	3.9%
Number of mutual funds that hold this stock as a top 15 holding	39		

ROLLING 12-MONTH TOTAL RATE OF RETURN FOR THE STOCK OVER TIME*

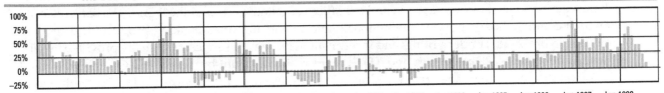

STOCK PERFORMANCE*

	1 month	1 year	3 years	5 years	10 years	15 years
Returns ending Aug 1998	−17.5%	6.9%	26.2%	20.5%	13.0%	15.1%
Best historical return	20.2%	91.5%	59.3%	44.7%	23.9%	20.8%
Average historical return	1.4%	19.8%	18.0%	15.9%	14.0%	17.0%
Worst historical return	−29.0%	−52.7%	−7.5%	−0.8%	8.6%	11.8%

RETURNS GREATER THAN*

	1 month	1 year	3 years	5 years	10 years	15 years
10 per cent	11%	66%	68%	64%	93%	100%
Zero	57%	78%	93%	98%	100%	100%
Percentage of time stock lost $	43%	22%	7%	2%	0%	0%
Number of periods evaluated	218	207	183	159	99	39

DOWNSIDE RISK*

	Worst setback since start date	In bear 1987	In bear 1990	In bear 1994	In bear 1998
Setback for stock	−56.3%	−37.3%	−29.3%	−13.3%	−24.9%
Setback for TSE 35	−21.6%	−26.5%	−16.8%	−9.0%	−27.6%
Setback ended in	Sept 1981	Nov 1987	Apr 1990	June 1994	Aug 1998
Months to recover from loss	19	15	45	6	?

STOCK FINANCIAL FUNDAMENTAL INFORMATION

	1988	1989	1990	1991	1992	1993	1994	1995	1996	1997	Change
Average share price	$13.77	$17.30	$14.92	$15.81	$15.01	$15.44	$16.56	$18.15	$23.13	$32.11	8.8%
Earnings per share	$0.88	$0.93	$0.82	$0.61	$0.36	$0.62	$1.01	$1.85	$1.30	$1.25	3.6%
Book value per share	$5.23	$6.45	$6.95	$6.55	$6.74	$6.84	$7.61	$8.95	$10.40	$11.54	8.2%
Price-to-earnings ratio	15.7	18.6	18.2	25.9	42.0	24.9	16.5	9.8	17.8	25.8	5.0%
Price-to-book ratio	2.6	2.7	2.1	2.4	2.2	2.3	2.2	2.0	2.2	2.8	0.6%
Profit margin	8.0%	8.2%	7.2%	5.2%	2.8%	4.7%	6.6%	10.9%	7.4%	6.3%	−2.5%
Asset turnover	0.91	0.75	0.68	0.70	0.73	0.71	0.69	0.75	0.60	0.64	−3.5%
Leverage	2.3	2.3	2.4	2.5	2.6	2.7	2.9	2.5	2.8	2.7	1.7%
Return on equity	16.7%	14.4%	11.8%	9.3%	5.3%	9.0%	13.2%	20.7%	12.5%	10.8%	−4.3%
Dividend per share	$–	$0.24	$0.52	$0.51	$0.56	$0.60	$0.63	$0.69	$0.75	$0.83	n/a
Dividend yield	0.0%	1.4%	3.5%	3.2%	3.7%	3.9%	3.8%	3.8%	3.2%	2.6%	n/a

*Source: The raw data used in developing this table was provided by Datastream.

TORONTO-DOMINION BANK

Company profile

The Toronto-Dominion Bank is a major Canadian chartered bank that operates more than 900 branches in all provinces and territories of Canada and has offices in countries around the world. The bank offers a full range of commercial, corporate, international, investment, and retail banking products and services in addition to brokerage, underwriting, and investment management services, which are provided by wholly owned subsidiaries TD Securities and TD Evergreen and discount brokerage TD Greenline. In the US, TD offers discount brokerage services through Waterhouse Investor Services, and has recently acquired similar companies in Australia and other parts of the world. TD recently agreed to merge with CIBC to increase the global presence of both banks in the industry and remain competitive with the Royal Bank and the Bank of Montreal after their propsed merger.

TD was formed in 1955 through the amalgamation of the Bank of Toronto and the Dominion Bank.

In 1997, TD generated total net revenues of $5.6 billion and had profits over $1.08 billion. The company employed over 32,000 people and has over 2,000 bank machines called Green Machines.

Stock performance

The Bank administers its own line of Green Line mutual funds, but its common stock proved to be a better investment (not adjusted for risk). The best 12-month rate of return was a gain of 139.5 per cent, and the average 12-month rate of return was 22.2 per cent. The common stock posted a positive rate of return after 12 months 75 per cent of the time. The common stock value has increased significantly in 1997.

Stock risks

The stock has experienced above-average downside risk. During the bear markets, TD common stock has underperformed. During the market correction of 1998, the stock declined in value by 39.8 per cent. During the market correction of 1990, the stock declined in value by 21.9 per cent, and it took the stock eight months to recover its loss.

Stock financial fundamentals

Because of the increased growth in TD's earnings, the stock multiples have increased during the past 10 years. The price-to-earnings (P/E) ratio has increased by 4.7 per cent annually from 7.2 to 11.4. This means that in 1988 investors paid $7.20 for $1 of historical earnings, while in 1997 investors paid $11.40 for every $1 of historical earnings. These stock levels can be justified if the bank continues to increase earnings and grow. However, a small decline in earnings could have a significant impact on the price of the underlying stock. The bank's merger plans with CIBC may bring some of this growth to fruition.

Future prospects

The bank's profits are closely tied to the direction and level of interest rates in addition to capital-market activity. Going forward, a little bad news could cause bank stocks to decline. However, banks have historically added a lot of value for shareholders over the long term. The worst 15-year rate of return posted by TD common stock was 10.1 per cent compounded annually. Investors who patiently acquire stock at attractive prices will benefit over the long term.

COMPANY DETAILS

Company name	**Toronto-Dominion Bank**	Industry classification	Financial services
Recent price	$40.05	Market capitalization (in $ millions)	$11,893
Phone number for annual report	416-643-5500	Stock analysis start date	July 1980
Ticker symbol	TD	Weight in TSE 35	4.2%
Number of mutual funds that hold this stock as a top 15 holding	285		

ROLLING 12-MONTH TOTAL RATE OF RETURN FOR THE STOCK OVER TIME*

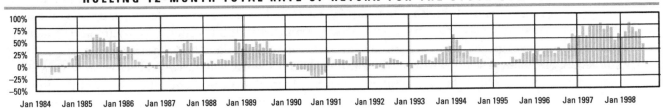

STOCK PERFORMANCE*

	1 month	1 year	3 years	5 years	10 years	15 years
Returns ending Aug 1998	−32.9%	−3.0%	26.5%	18.9%	13.0%	15.1%
Best historical return	20.8%	139.5%	53.3%	37.3%	21.8%	22.0%
Average historical return	1.5%	22.2%	18.7%	16.9%	15.3%	17.7%
Worst historical return	−32.9%	−25.9%	−3.3%	1.9%	10.1%	14.1%

RETURNS GREATER THAN*

	1 month	1 year	3 years	5 years	10 years	15 years
10 per cent	9%	60%	78%	69%	100%	100%
Zero	62%	75%	94%	100%	100%	100%
Percentage of time stock lost $	38%	25%	6%	0%	0%	0%
Number of periods evaluated	218	207	183	159	99	39

DOWNSIDE RISK*

	Worst setback since start date	In bear 1987	In bear 1990	In bear 1994	In bear 1998
Setback for stock	−39.8%	−21.9%	−31.0%	−13.4%	−39.8%
Setback for TSE 35	−27.6%	−26.5%	−16.8%	−9.0%	−27.6%
Setback ended in	Aug 1998	Oct 1987	Sept 1990	June 1994	Aug 1998
Months to recover from loss	?	8	35	15	?

STOCK FINANCIAL FUNDAMENTAL INFORMATION

	1988	1989	1990	1991	1992	1993	1994	1995	1996	1997	Change
Average share price	$15.84	$20.35	$17.50	$18.20	$17.50	$18.54	$21.07	$21.69	$26.91	$43.32	10.6%
Earnings per share	$2.14	$2.20	$1.80	$1.51	$1.25	$0.82	$2.14	$2.51	$2.95	$3.54	5.2%
Book value per share	$11.38	$12.79	$13.80	$14.61	$15.16	$15.36	$16.78	$18.32	$20.55	$22.63	7.1%
Price-to-earnings ratio	7.4	9.3	9.7	12.1	14.0	22.6	9.8	8.6	9.1	12.2	5.2%
Price-to-book ratio	1.4	1.6	1.3	1.2	1.2	1.2	1.3	1.2	1.3	1.9	3.2%
Profit margin	10.9%	9.1%	7.0%	6.3%	6.2%	3.9%	9.2%	8.7%	9.7%	10.1%	−0.8%
Asset turnover	0.10	0.01	0.12	0.10	0.08	0.07	0.07	0.08	0.07	0.06	−4.3%
Leverage	17.4	156.2	16.1	15.7	16.3	18.4	19.8	20.9	21.2	24.2	3.4%
Return on equity	18.8%	17.2%	13.0%	10.3%	8.2%	5.2%	12.8%	13.7%	14.4%	15.6%	−1.8%
Dividend per share	$0.51	$0.71	$0.76	$0.76	$0.76	$0.76	$0.79	$0.88	$1.00	$1.12	8.2%
Dividend yield	3.2%	3.5%	4.3%	4.2%	4.3%	4.1%	3.7%	4.1%	3.7%	2.6%	−2.2%

*Source: The raw data used in developing this table was provided by Datastream.

TransAlta Corporation

Company profile

From its head office in Calgary, Alberta, TransAlta Corporation operates two energy-related lines of business in Canada and throughout the world. TransAlta Energy provides electric and thermal energy in Canada, Australia, New Zealand, and Argentina. TransAlta Utilities operates a hydroelectric facility.

TransAlta Energy also provides gas and electricity in New Zealand and wholesale energy marketing and energy services in selected regions of North America. TransAlta Utilities operates electricity generation and transmission and distribution facilities that supply more than 66 per cent of the power to the province of Alberta. The utility company operates more than 100,000 kilometres of transmission and distribution lines. TransAlta Utilities has served the citizens of Alberta since 1911. The utility rates that TransAlta charges are subject to regulatory approval under the terms of Alberta's Electric Utilities Act, although it claims to offer one of the lowest electricity rates in the world. In 1997, the company earned revenue of over $1.6 billion and posted a profit of $182.6 million.

Stock performance

TransAlta Corporation's common stock's best 12-month rate of return was a gain of 53.3 per cent, and the average 12-month rate of return for the common stock was 9.6 per cent. The common stock posted positive 12-month rates of return 71 per cent of the time. The stock's performance over the long term has been in line with the market as a whole.

Stock risks

The common stock of TransAlta corporation has displayed periods of above-average downside risk. The worst 12-month return for the stock was a loss of 35.5 per cent. The stock has underperformed during bear markets. During the market correction of 1994, the stock declined in value by 22.9 per cent and took 25 months to recover its losses.

Stock financial fundamentals

During the past 10 years, the stock price has appreciated, and the company still provides an attractive dividend yield at 5.6 per cent on the average stock price of 1997. The earnings per share and book value per share for the company have been stable. By 1997, the company's return on equity had increased during the previous 10 years to 11.45 per cent, because the company increased its leverage and asset turnover ratios, but the profit margin for the company declined. *Note:* 1990 financial results were adjusted for discontinued operations, and 1996 and 1997 financial results were adjusted for the Electric Utilities Board (EUB) rate adjustment.

Future prospects

Conservative investors looking for an attractive dividend yield may find this stock suitable for their financial needs. However, going forward, growth in TransAlta Energy may require the company to reduce its dividend to finance further growth. In addition, the company will have to ensure that its profit margin does not erode further, because achieving additional productivity gains in the future will be difficult.

Investors must realize that TransAlta's utility company will incur additional pressure from regulations and, in turn, profits will likely decline. However, TransAlta's senior management is committed to increasing the size of TransAlta Energy, which should offset any decline in the utility company.

COMPANY DETAILS

Company name	TransAlta Corporation	Industry classification	Utilities
Recent price	$19.00	Market capitalization (in $ millions)	$3,040
Phone number for annual report	1-800-387-0825	Stock analysis start date	July 1985
Ticker symbol	TA	Weight in TSE 35	2.2%
Number of mutual funds that hold this stock as a top 15 holding	21		

ROLLING 12-MONTH TOTAL RATE OF RETURN FOR THE STOCK OVER TIME*

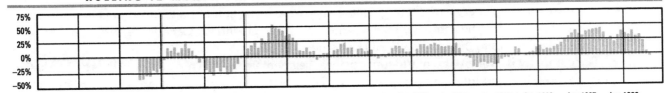

STOCK PERFORMANCE*

	1 month	1 year	3 years	5 years	10 years	15 years
Returns ending Aug 1998	–11.1%	–1.8%	14.6%	5.8%	11.7%	
Best historical return	15.7%	53.3%	28.2%	18.0%	14.7%	
Average historical return	0.5%	9.6%	8.4%	8.2%	8.3%	
Worst historical return	–15.4%	–35.5%	–15.7%	–2.2%	1.3%	

RETURNS GREATER THAN*

	1 month	1 year	3 years	5 years	10 years	15 years
10 per cent	2%	51%	39%	31%	28%	
Zero	59%	71%	93%	96%	100%	
Percentage of time stock lost $	41%	29%	7%	4%	0%	
Number of periods evaluated	158	147	123	99	39	

DOWNSIDE RISK*

	Worst setback since start date	In bear 1987	In bear 1990	In bear 1994	In bear 1998
Setback for stock	–42.9%	–42.1%	–17.3%	–22.9%	–26.7%
Setback for TSE 35	–13.8%	–26.5%	–16.8%	–9.0%	–27.6%
Setback ended in	Aug 1988	Feb 1988	Apr 1990	June 1994	Aug 1998
Months to recover from loss	31	37	11	25	?

STOCK FINANCIAL FUNDAMENTAL INFORMATION

	1988	1989	1990	1991	1992	1993	1994	1995	1996	1997	Change
Average share price	$10.42	$13.11	$14.18	$14.87	$15.14	$16.80	$15.69	$15.72	$18.16	$23.29	4.2%
Earnings per share	$0.86	$1.01	$1.07	$1.12	$1.18	$1.16	$1.18	$1.14	$1.18	$1.30	2.9%
Book value per share	$9.05	$9.08	$8.51	$8.87	$9.35	$9.33	$9.57	$9.68	$9.97	$9.95	1.0%
Price-to-earnings ratio	12.1	13.0	13.3	13.3	12.8	14.5	13.3	13.8	15.4	17.9	4.0%
Price-to-book ratio	1.2	1.4	1.7	1.7	1.6	1.8	1.6	1.6	1.8	2.3	7.3%
Profit margin	12.8%	14.3%	13.7%	13.6%	14.2%	13.2%	12.3%	9.9%	9.4%	10.6%	–1.8%
Asset turnover	0.26	0.26	0.29	0.31	0.33	0.33	0.36	0.42	0.40	0.35	3.3%
Leverage	2.9	3.0	3.2	3.0	2.7	2.8	2.8	2.8	3.0	3.1	0.5%
Return on equity	9.5%	11.1%	12.6%	12.6%	12.6%	12.4%	12.3%	11.8%	11.4%	11.5%	1.9%
Dividend per share	$0.93	$0.97	$0.98	$0.98	$0.98	$0.98	$0.98	$0.98	$0.98	$0.98	0.5%
Dividend yield	8.9%	7.4%	6.9%	6.6%	6.5%	5.8%	6.2%	6.2%	5.4%	4.2%	–7.2%

*Source: The raw data used in developing this table was provided by Datastream.

TRANSCANADA PIPELINES

Company profile

TransCanada PipeLines Limited is a leading North American energy service company. It provides integrated energy transmission, energy marketing, and energy processing solutions to customers in Canada and throughout the world. The company operates the largest gas pipeline in Canada, 14,492 kilometres from the Canadian Rockies to the Quebec-Vermont border.

The company is broken down into four business segments: Energy Transmission, Energy Marketing, Energy Processing, and International. The Energy Transmission business transports energy from Western Canada to markets in Eastern Canada and the United States. Energy Marketing sells energy products and services throughout North America. Energy Processing uses TransCanada PipeLines assets to produce energy and specialty chemical products. The International segment focusses on international sales. TransCanada PipeLines Limited recently acquired Nova Corporation and will spin off Nova's chemical division into a newly minted Nova Corporation.

Stock performance

TransCanada PipeLines Limited common stock's best 12-month rate of return was a positive gain of 59.8 per cent, and the average 12-month return for the common stock was 12.7 per cent. The common stock has performed consistently with the overall economy until recently, when it outperformed.

Stock risks

TransCanada PipeLines Limited common stock has displayed less risk than other blue-chip stocks. The worst 12-month rate of return for the common stock was a loss of 16.8 per cent, and the common stock posted negative rates of return after 12 months 13 per cent of the time. The common stock outperformed during bear markets. During the stock market correction of 1994, the stock declined by 9.7 per cent and took nine months to recover its losses.

Stock financial fundamentals

TransCanada PipeLines Limited has cleaned up its income statement and balance sheet during the last eight years. In turn, the common stock has appreciated in value, and stock multiples have increased as a result of improved financial results. In addition, investors are more optimistic about future prospects. The company's earnings per share have increased during the past eight years from $1.23 in 1990 to $1.85 in 1997. The company has maintained a policy of paying out a large portion of its earnings in the form of a dividend.

Future prospects

TransCanada is laying pipe aggressively to expand its operations, and the merger with Nova will likely fuel growth into the future. This merger will allow TransCanada to build a regulated business on a larger scale while focussing other efforts on expanding the company's non-regulated business. Investors who have a desire for a high dividend yield and who patiently acquire stock at a reasonable price should achieve above-average returns in the future. Investors should note that high-dividend-paying stocks experience less downside risk, but that risk is still present. The stock declined by 19.5 per cent during the market correction of 1998. However, the stock has added value over the long term. Investors who patiently acquire stock in excellent companies will earn above average returns over the long term and achieve their own financial objectives.

COMPANY DETAILS

Company name	**TransCanada PipeLines**	Industry classification	Pipelines
Recent price	$21.30	Market capitalization (in $ millions)	$9,835
Phone number for annual report	1-800-558-0046	Stock analysis start date	July 1980
Ticker symbol	TRP	Weight in TSE 35	3.1%
Number of mutual funds that hold this stock as a top 15 holding	105		

ROLLING 12-MONTH TOTAL RATE OF RETURN FOR THE STOCK OVER TIME*

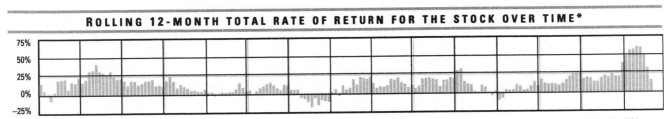

Jan 1984 Jan 1985 Jan 1986 Jan 1987 Jan 1988 Jan 1989 Jan 1990 Jan 1991 Jan 1992 Jan 1993 Jan 1994 Jan 1995 Jan 1996 Jan 1997 Jan 1998

STOCK PERFORMANCE*

	1 month	1 year	3 years	5 years	10 years	15 years
Returns ending Aug 1998	−10.6%	14.9%	16.8%	12.3%	10.6%	11.6%
Best historical return	15.8%	59.8%	27.9%	21.4%	13.2%	13.3%
Average historical return	0.9%	12.7%	11.5%	10.9%	9.8%	11.2%
Worst historical return	−13.0%	−16.8%	−0.8%	2.7%	7.2%	9.4%

RETURNS GREATER THAN*

	1 month	1 year	3 years	5 years	10 years	15 years
10 per cent	2%	56%	53%	60%	44%	85%
Zero	57%	87%	99%	100%	100%	100%
Percentage of time stock lost $	43%	13%	1%	0%	0%	0%
Number of periods evaluated	218	207	183	159	99	39

DOWNSIDE RISK*

	Worst setback since start date	In bear 1987	In bear 1990	In bear 1994	In bear 1998
Setback for stock	−23.6%	−9.3%	−17.8%	−9.7%	−19.5%
Setback for TSE 35	−21.6%	−26.5%	−16.8%	−9.0%	−27.6%
Setback ended in	Sept 1981	Oct 1987	Sept 1990	Jan 1995	Aug 1998
Months to recover from loss	13	4	11	9	?

STOCK FINANCIAL FUNDAMENTAL INFORMATION

	1988	1989	1990	1991	1992	1993	1994	1995	1996	1997	Change
Average share price	$14.03	$14.18	$12.64	$12.79	$13.38	$14.39	$14.65	$14.23	$15.42	$17.52	2.2%
Earnings per share			$1.23	$1.34	$1.56	$1.62	$1.60	$1.75	$1.85	$1.85	n/a
Book value per share			$7.33	$8.85	$9.96	$10.54	$11.32	$12.18	$14.02	$14.10	n/a
Price-to-earnings ratio			10.3	9.5	8.6	8.9	9.2	8.1	8.3	9.5	n/a
Price-to-book ratio			1.7	1.4	1.3	1.4	1.3	1.2	1.1	1.2	n/a
Profit margin			6.9%	7.8%	8.3%	7.8%	6.9%	5.7%	3.9%	3.2%	n/a
Asset turnover			0.52	0.42	0.42	0.49	0.53	0.67	0.85	0.98	n/a
Leverage			4.7	4.6	4.5	4.0	3.9	3.8	3.9	4.2	n/a
Return on equity			16.8%	15.1%	15.7%	15.4%	14.1%	14.4%	13.2%	13.1%	n/a
Dividend per share			$0.69	$0.73	$0.78	$0.86	$0.94	$1.02	$1.10	$1.18	n/a
Dividend yield			5.5%	5.7%	5.8%	6.0%	6.4%	7.2%	7.1%	6.7%	n/a

*Source: The raw data used in developing this table was provided by Datastream.

Glossary of Terms

Accrued interest: Interest accumulated on a bond since the last interest payment

Affiliated company: A company that has less than 50 per cent of its shares owned by another company (See **Subsidiary**.)

Annual report: The formal financial statements issued by a company to its shareholders after the company's year end

Arrears: Dividends which were not paid when due and are still owed to shareholders. This is a common feature for preferred shares.

Ask: The lowest price a seller is willing to accept for the security

Assets: All the valuables of a corporation or an individual

Averaging down: Investing in additional securities of a particular investment to reduce your average cost

Average cost: The average cost of acquiring an investment. For example, if an investor bought 100 shares at $50 each and 100 shares at $100 each, the average cost would be 100 x $50 plus 100 x $100 divided by 200 which is equal to $75 per share. The taxable capital gain for an investment is the selling price minus the average cost.

Balance sheet: A financial statement disclosing a company's assets, liabilities, and owners' equity as of a particular date

Bankrupt: The legal status of a corporation (or an individual) which has not been able to pay its debts in an orderly fashion

Basis point: A financial industry term. 1/100th of 1 per cent is 1 basis point.

Bear: An investor who expects the market will decline

Bear market: A capital market displaying significant declines in value

Bid: The highest price a buyer is willing to pay for a security

Bid and ask: See **Bid** and **Ask**.

Blue chip: A "brand name" leading company with an established record of earnings and dividend payments. The term *blue chip* is generated from the card game, poker, in which the blue chips are the most valuable. In turn, blue-chip companies have been the most valuable for investors.

Board lot: A regular trading unit (number of shares) which has been established uniformly by stock exchanges.

Bond: A certificate proving a debt on which the issuer promises to pay the debt holder an interest payment and repay the loan at maturity

Book value: The value of the assets belonging to the shareholders of a company after the creditors have been paid

Broker: An individual who acts as an agent to facilitate the trade of securities for buyers and sellers. Brokers charge a fee for their services.

Bull: An investor who expects an increase in capital markets

Bull market: An increasing capital market

Canadian Investor Protection Fund: A protection fund established by the stock exchanges and the Investment Dealers Association (IDA) to protect investors from losses resulting from the failure of a member firm

Capital gain or loss: The profit or loss generated from the sale of an investment

Capital stock: All shares that represent ownership of a corporation, including preferred and common stock

Closed-end mutual fund: A mutual fund with a limited number of shares issued. When these shares have been sold, the fund is closed.

Commission: The fee charged by a individual who sells investments for buying or selling these investments

Common stock: A security that represents ownership in a company

Compounded rate of return: Interest and capital gains accumulated over a period of time which are added to the original investment, as a percentage of the original investment

Conglomerate: A corporation that operates in a variety of different industries

Coupon: A certificate entitling the owner to an interest payment from the bond issuer

Currency risk: The risk that a loss may be incurred because of currency exchange rates when buying foreign bonds

Current yield: The annual income (interest and dividends) received from a security throughout the year, divided by the current market value of the security

Cyclical stock: A stock that is very sensitive to changes in economic conditions

Day order: An order to buy or sell a stock that is valid only for the trading day the order is given

Debenture: Similar to a bond, but the collateral behind the debenture is only the general earning power of the company

Default: A bond is considered in default when the issuer is no longer able to make regular interest payments. Bankruptcy may result from a company's defaulting on its bond obligations.

Defensive stock: The stock of a corporation with a excellent record of stable profits and dividend payments. In addition, defensive stocks tend to outperform during "bear markets."

Diversifiable risk: See **Unsystematic risk.**

Diversification: Investing in more than one security or asset class in order to reduce the overall risk

Dividend: A payment made by a corporation to shareholders from the company's profits. There is no legal obligation to pay a dividend on common shares.

Dollar cost averaging: Investing a fixed dollar amount in an investment on a regular basis to take advantage of volatility

Dominion Bond Rating Service: A Canadian bond rating service which evaluates the credit quality of a short-term bond. R1 is the highest rating. Each rating—R1, R2, and R3—is subdivided into high, middle, and low levels.

Earnings per share: The portion of the company's profits that can be attributed to one common share. If the company earned $1,000 and had 1,000 shares outstanding, the earnings per share would be $1.

Fiscal year or period: A corporation's accounting year. A corporation's tax year can end in any month; an individual's tax year ends on December 31.

Fixed income securities: Investments that generate a predicable and consistent flow of income or returns for investors. Fixed income investments include money market mutual funds, Canadian bond funds, and international bond funds.

Foreign-pay bond: A bond which pays interest in a currency other than the Canadian dollar

Fundamental analysis: The evaluation of a common stock based on the attractiveness of the company's financial statements (See **Technical analysis.**)

Growth company: A company with stock prices which are high relative to the company's underlying assets

Guaranteed investment certificate (GIC): A deposit investment available at all major banks and trust companies. GICs are non-redeemable until maturity and offer a predetermined rate of interest.

Income statement: A financial statement that discloses the corporation's sales revenue, expenditures, and profits during the fiscal period

Index: A measure which indicates the status of a group of companies or investments. For example, the TSE 300 measures the performance of 300 of Canada's largest publicly traded companies.

Interest: Fee (or rent) charged by a lender to a borrower for the use of the lender's money

Investment: The use of money to generate more money, to receive income, dividends, or capital gains

Investment counsellor: An individual who is qualified to give investment advice for a fee

Leverage: A strategy which uses borrowing to invest with the objective of increasing returns

Liabilities: The debts of a company

Limit order: An order to buy or sell a security at a particular price or better. If a limit order cannot be executed at that price or better, the order will not be executed. A specific time limit may be applied to the order.

Load: The portion of the investment that is used to pay selling expenses. Loads are common in front-end load mutual funds.

Long bond: A bond which does not have to pay back its principal for 30 years or more

Management expenses ratio (MER): The ratio of total management costs (including management, administration, accounting, and marketing) to the total value of the mutual fund

Marginal utility: The incremental amount of utility (value added) provided by an additional unit of rate of return, for instance an increase of 1 per cent in rate of return

Market correction: A period when there is a significant decline in capital markets

Market order: An order to buy shares at the current market price

Market risk: See **Systematic risk**.

Multiple: See **Stock multiple**.

Mutual fund family: The complete set of mutual funds offered by a mutual fund company

Net asset value (NAV): The actual true value of each share in a mutual fund. The NAV is calculated by dividing the total value of the fund by the number of shares outstanding.

No-load fund: A mutual fund that can be purchased, sold, and owned without any commission charges. The only charges involved are management fees. Shares are sold at the net asset value price, and no salesperson is paid to sell the shares.

Non-diversifiable risk: See **Systematic risk**.

No transaction fee (NTF) program: A program which allows investors to buy hundreds of different no-load funds within the same account without paying any transaction fees. The program is so popular that even full-service brokerage firms are beginning to follow this practice.

Odd lot: An order for a number of shares below the board lot number (i.e., under 100 shares)

Open-end mutual fund: A mutual fund which imposes no limit on the number of shares which can be issued, and thus will issue and redeem shares at an investor's request

P/E ratio: The price of a stock divided by the yearly earnings per share. It compares the price of a stock relative to its earnings, which is important to know when you compare one stock with another. It is also important in determining whether a stock is under- or over-priced relative to other stocks.

Privately held company: A company whose shares are not publicly traded. Privately held stock is issued to a small number of shareholders, and the value or price of the stock is usually determined by comparisons with other similar companies, using factors such as earnings and gross income.

Pro-forma financial statements: Financial statements which are used to project the estimated financial results of a new company. They consist of an income statement, balance sheet, and cash flow statement.

Qualified plans: A plan which allows an individual to make a pre-tax deposit and have income tax deferred. A registered company pension plan allows employees to deposit part of their incomes in the plan with the tax-deferral privilege. A registered retirement savings plan (RRSP) is the only other type of plan qualified. An individual can select from a large number of different RRSP investment choices.

Quantitative analysis: The study and analysis of numerical financial information for the basis of decision making. The principle of quantitative theory is that everything is expressed in measurable form and therefore is also predictable. Investors who use this theory believe that by studying specific market data they can accurately predict the market's movements.

Return on investment (ROI): A company's return on investment calculated by dividing the net income by the amount of capital invested in the company. There are two ways to increase ROI: (1) reduce expenses, and (2) increase sales.

No load fund: A mutual fund that does not charge a sales fee for buying and selling an investor's shares

Secondary market: Any market where previously issued securities are traded. The Toronto Stock Exchange (TSE) is the best known example in Canada. Here investors can buy and sell stocks from each other through the Exchange.

Shareholders' equity: The ownership interest in the firm held by common shareholders. The shareholders' or owners' equity in the firm is equal to the firm's assets minus the firm's liabilities.

Stock: See **Common stock**.

Stock multiple: The price of a stock divided by a factor such as earnings per share, book value per share, or cash flow per share. For instance, if a stock trading at $10 per share posts earnings per share of $1, it will trade at an earnings-per-share multiple of 10. If the stock price increases faster than earnings per share, the multiple will increase, and if the earnings per share grow faster than the stock price, the multiple will decline.

Stop order: An order to sell a stock which is declining in value, with a lower limit set on the price at which it is to be sold. In other words, when the price drops to the stop-order price, the stock will be sold.

Subsidiary: A company that is owned by another company through the ownership of 50 per cent or more of the common shares outstanding.

Systematic risk: Risk which cannot be eliminated or reduced through diversification. This is also called non-diversifiable or market risk.

Target savings goal (TSG): The amount of money required each year to build a portfolio large enough to support an investor's preferred standard of living at retirement

Technical analysis: Using charts to read the price history and other statistical patterns of stocks or mutual funds. Many investors and most professionals use these charts to make investment decisions. A technical analyst is also known as a *chartist*.

Ticker: A device which transfers information on purchases and sales of publicly traded stocks

Total return: The percentage return of a portfolio, which includes dividends, interest, and capital gains. Total return is also known as portfolio performance.

Underwriter: A brokerage firm that handles the process of offering a company's stock to the public through an initial public offering.

Unsystematic risk: Risk which can be eliminated or reduced by diversification. Unsystematic risk is also called diversifiable risk.

Value manager: A manager who searches for undervalued stocks that are priced below what the manager actually thinks they're worth. The goal of the value-oriented manager is to sell at a profit once the market realizes the stock's true value.

Value company: A company with strong financial statements and a reasonable stock price

Variable annuity: An annuity whose value and paid-out amount vary according to the performance of a portfolio of mutual funds from which the contract holder can select. Typically, these policies offer a stock fund, a bond fund, and a money market fund.

Index